Paul Merkley

P9-DDA-074

1991.

Clink this to section on Shimon Peres in christian
(ref to)   Attitudes
— the construction of identity
        = the literature & the concept XII
            = invention
    — the

— population —

— exp p. 143 f
        172,
            174–175
            177 f 18

— administrative boundaries 151

— refugees
        265

PALESTINIAN IDENTITY

PALESTINIAN IDENTITY

The Construction

of Modern

National Consciousness

RASHID KHALIDI

Columbia University Press   *New York*

Columbia University Press
Publishers Since 1893
New York   Chichester, West Sussex
Copyright © 1997 Columbia University Press
All rights reserved

Library of Congress Cataloging-in-Publication Data
Khalidi, Rashid.
    Palestinian Identity : the construction of modern national consciousness /
Rashid Khalidi.
        p.   cm.
    ISBN 0–231–10514–2 (CL : alk. paper)
    1. Palestinian Arabs—Israel—Ethnic identity.   2. Jewish–Arab
relations—1917–   3. Palestinian Arabs—Jerusalem.   I. Title.
DS113.7.K53   1997
305.892'740569442—dc20   96–45757
                                                              CIP

Casebound editions of Columbia University Press books are printed on permanent and
durable acid-free paper.
Printed in the United States of America
c 10 9 8 7 6 5 4 3 2

Acknowledgments

An earlier version of chapter 2 appeared in *The Geography of Identity*, edited by
Patricia Yeager, published by the University of Michigan Press in 1996. Chapter 3
derives in part from an earlier version commissioned for *Ottoman Jerusalem* edited by
Robert Hillenbrand and Sylvia Auld, to be published by the World of Islam Festival
Trust in 1997. Parts of chapter 4 were published in a different form in Vol. 84, no. 1–2
of the *Muslim World*. Chapter 7 is based on an earlier version, published by Columbia
University Press in 1997, in *Rethinking Nationalism in the Arab World*, edited by James
Jankowski and Israel Gershoni.

CONTENTS

Contents

PREFACE

I

Like most projects of this size, this book has gone through several metamorphoses. The initial idea, which I developed about eight years ago, was for a text that would reinterpret and rework the received versions of the history of Palestine over perhaps the past two centuries. But for several reasons I eventually saw that such a project was unfeasible: it would have involved a huge amount of research over many years and would have culminated in a massive volume (or volumes)—an unappealing prospect. I felt that there was a need for a book that would be accessible to a broad circle of readers beyond a specialist audience, and would be available soon, in order to meet the widespread current interest in the subject of the Palestinians. In addition, I found that the existing specialized works on Palestinian history covered some topics well, and that I had nothing original to say regarding certain other aspects of Palestinian history. The idea of writing a comprehensive history of Palestine thus made increasingly little sense to me.

In the next phase, my involvement in the restoration of the Khalidi family library in Jerusalem gradually led me to the idea of an intellectual history of Jerusalem over the past century or so. This project was the focus of a twelve-month serial Fulbright grant to do research in Jerusalem over three years, from 1991 until 1993. While in Jerusalem over these three extended summers, I did much of the research for this book, and once again modified this project. In the end, I broadened its scope from Jerusalem to the entirety of Palestine, and shifted its focus from general intellectual history to a study of the emergence of Palestinian identity. I narrowed the focus because I felt that the issue of identity was perhaps the most important problem of Palestinian history which needed to be explained to both a general and an academic audience. If one takes identity as the answer to the question, "Who are you?" it is clear that the response of the inhabitants of Palestine has changed considerably over time. I sought to explain the reasons for that change.

When I first conceived of this project in its present form, it involved studying Palestinian national identity in some detail from its beginnings in the late nineteenth century until the present day. But as my research progressed, the conclusions which emerged from it, as well as my circumstances from 1991 until 1993, brought me to limit its scope even further. During this three-year period, in addition to extensive summer research and work on the restoration of the family library in Jerusalem, I continued with my teaching and other full-time duties at the University of Chicago. But beyond that, in a moment of incaution during my first stay in Jerusalem during the summer of 1991, I had agreed to the request of Faisal al-Husayni that, if the Palestinians became involved in negotiations with Israel (negotiations whose format and participants were at that time being determined in intensive shuttle diplomacy with all the parties concerned by U.S. Secretary of State James Baker) I would serve as an adviser to the Palestinian delegation.

At the time, I had no reason to assume that Baker would have any more success than his many predecessors, all of whom had failed to get the Palestinians and Israelis to sit around the same negotiating table. I felt especially secure in this assumption since the Israeli government then headed by Yitzhaq Shamir was deeply opposed to such a prospect. I thus did not give much thought to my agreement to Faysal al-Husayni's proposition, until late one night on the eve of the sudden convocation of the Madrid conference, I received a call from PLO officials in Tunis asking me to confirm that I was indeed going to Madrid, since the names of the delegation and its advisers had to be presented to Secretary Baker's assistants that very night.

I thereafter served as one of several advisers to the Palestinian delegation at the Madrid conference in October–November 1991, and participated in part of each of the ten Palestinian-Israeli bilateral negotiating sessions in Washington which continued until June 1993. These negotiations generally went on for a few intense weeks of nonstop work, followed by many weeks or months of recess. I did not participate in the entirety of every round of negotiations, and obtained welcome respite during the often lengthy breaks between them. Nevertheless, my colleagues and I on the Palestinian delegation worked extremely hard while the talks were in session, and the overlap between these negotiations and my research, teaching, and other duties was naturally stressful and often frustrating. It undoubtedly limited the amount of research and writing on this project that I was able to undertake.

However, my involvement in the negotiations did have some positive results for my research. Being in Madrid, Washington, and Jerusalem over these three years watching Palestinian national identity slowly but inexorably become embodied in concrete form—however unsatisfactory this form may have seemed to some at the time or later—convinced me of the centrality of the topic of the book I was working on. It also convinced me that I should not try to bring my narrative down to the present day, since it would be difficult to obtain the perspective necessary for writing history, given the speed with which the circumstances affecting Palestinian national identity were evolving.

At the same time, being in the midst of such momentous events made it clearer to me than ever before how rapidly views of self and other, of history, and of time and space, could shift in situations of extreme political stress, which could be seen as watersheds in terms of identity. I had already witnessed such swift changes in similar situations while living in Lebanon from the early 1970s until 1983, and had observed that constructs of identity and of political preference, and understandings of history, which appeared long-lasting and persistent in certain circumstances, could crumble or evolve almost overnight.

My earliest research, started in 1970, explored the first stirrings of Arab nationalism in Syria, Lebanon, and Palestine in the years before World War I.[1] This work brought to my attention examples of rapid changes in political attitudes in these areas, specifically during the Balkan wars of 1912–1913, when it seemed that the Ottoman Empire was on the brink of collapse. Suddenly, the population of the Arab provinces of the Empire was faced with the possible dissolution of the Ottoman political framework within which their region had operated for four centuries. The consequences of this realization—and of the shock when the Empire actually did collapse a few years later—for this population's sense of identity were momentous. Insofar as they relate to Palestine, they will be touched on in chapter 7.

My next major research project, on the decisions made by the PLO during the 1982 war, dealt with very different examples of rapid changes in political attitudes, changes I had witnessed in Beirut.[2] Notable among them were the reversal in Lebanese attitudes toward the Palestinians from the late 1960s to the early 1980s, and how the PLO and their supporters in Lebanon came to be reconciled to the idea of a negotiated evacuation from Beirut during the seventy days of Israel's bombardment and siege of the city. In relatively short order, a Lebanese population, large parts of which had been supportive of Palestinian political and military activities, came to oppose them, alienated by the behavior of the PLO, and under intense pressure from the Israel and its allies. In another such rapid shift, during the watershed of the 1982 war, the Palestinians accepted under extreme duress both the evacuation of the PLO from Beirut, and fundamental changes in their political strategy.

As my research in Jerusalem broadened my understanding of the issue of Palestinian identity, it became clear to me that there had been a similar watershed with respect to the Palestinian self-view in the first decades of this century. I realized that it was sufficient to explain the circumstances of this shift, and unnecessary to continue my narrative with a detailed examination of Palestinian identity from the time of its emergence to the present. The final chapter of this book nevertheless briefly recapitulates the story of the evolution of Palestinian national identity from the early 1920s to the mid-1990s.

This end point is necessarily an arbitrary one—for Palestinian national identity has of course not stopped evolving, and it is still too early to tell whether it has reached a watershed comparable to that of the early years of the century. In any case, tempting though the examination of such a question might have been, I had to send this book to press (a point my editor, Kate Wittenberg, kindly but forcefully kept impressing upon me). As I write these words, Palestinian national identity continues to unfold and reconfigure itself under the impact of a cascade of startling events and powerful historical forces which have changed the Middle East almost beyond recognition.

II

The treatment of Palestinian identity in this book should have resonance for readers interested in the Palestinians and their role in the Arab-Israeli conflict; for those concerned with post-colonial nationalisms in the Arab world and elsewhere; and for anyone studying nationalism who wishes to understand an instance of national consciousness emerging in the absence of a nation-state. It can also serve as a test-case for theories about nationalism, identity, and the role of the state in forming both. The case of Palestinian identity also seems particularly relevant for consideration by those in the growing fields studying diasporas and transnational and global phenomena.

The scholarly attention currently devoted to the topic of national identity guarantees a wealth of theoretical material on which to draw, and many possible comparisons with the evolution of other national identities.[3] There also exists a considerable literature on nationalism, including both classics and more recent works, as well as case studies of specific national movements. At the same time, dealing with Palestinian history in terms of national identity also poses problems, because the literature on identity, nationalism, and the nation, while voluminous, is of varied quality; in many instances it is not applicable to the Palestinian case.

It is worth stating at the outset that this treatment of identity starts from the firmly held premise that national identity is constructed; it is not an essential, transcendent given, as the apostles of nationalism, and some students of culture, politics and history claim.[4] While this can easily be shown to be the case as far as the Palestinians are concerned, their example also has a certain universal applicability for issues of national identity generally. Although it may be argued that the specificity of the circumstances affecting the Palestinians is so extreme that one cannot generalize from their example, the case of the Palestinians is not unique. This is true as regards a number of ways in which the Palestinians mirror other national groups, including the manner in which preexisting elements of identity are reconfigured and history is used to give shape to a certain vision, the impact of powerful shocks and extreme stress on the framing of questions of identity, and the role of contingent external factors in shaping national identity.

Whereas, to use Ernest Gellner's terminology, the Palestinian cultural and political communities have not yet coincided in time and space[5]—

that is to say, a Palestinian national state encompassing all or most of the world's Palestinians has not yet been established—in no way does this condition diminish the relevance of the Palestinian case for understanding national identity in general, or for substantiating the argument that this identity is constructed. A close examination of the way in which the Palestinian national narrative has been created shows myriad features similar to those of other national movements, albeit exhibiting a specificity peculiar to the circumstances that have affected the Palestinians in recent decades.

Several of the most respected writers on nationalism and identity have put forward arguments on which this approach, which sees national identity as constructed, can be solidly based. In one of his more recent writings on this subject, Eric Hobsbawm agrees with Gellner in stressing "the element of artifact, invention and social engineering which enters into the making of nations."[6] Gellner is even blunter: "Nations as a natural, God-given way of classifying men, as an inherent . . . political destiny, are a myth; nationalism, which sometimes takes preexisting cultures and turns them into nations, sometimes invents them, and often obliterates preexisting cultures: *that* is a reality."[7] In short, nations and the identity linked to them are a construct for Gellner; the nationalism that does this work of construction is a real political force.

Hobsbawm stresses another element in this process of construction of identity, pointing in the introduction to the influential volume he edited with Terence Ranger, *The Invention of Tradition,* to "the use of ancient material to construct invented traditions of a novel type for quite novel purposes," referring specifically to cases related to the building of national feeling.[8] Benedict Anderson goes perhaps the farthest in this regard, with his argument for the nation as an "imagined political community," which is "imagined as both limited and sovereign" and which essentially constitutes a shared consciousness of a certain set of elements of identity made possible by a conjunction of factors, including what he describes as "print-capitalism."[9] Although Anthony Smith appears less sympathetic to this approach in some of his writings,[10] given his concern with the ethnic origins of nations, he nevertheless admits in a recent article that "the nation that emerges in the modern era must be regarded as both construct and process."[11]

It may be argued (and is, incessantly, in the Palestinian case), that certain identities are recent, flimsy, and artificial, whereas by contrast others are long-standing, deep-rooted and natural. (A specific identity, the Israeli-Jewish one, is usually mentioned in this context, although similar arguments can be made in favor of Arab or Islamic identities.) This is not the place to dispute these sorts of arguments, which are often not amenable to rational dispute in any case (as Hobsbawm puts it: "no serious historian of nations and nationalism can be a committed political nationalist. . . . Nationalism requires too much belief in what is patently not true.")[12] But it will become clear whether Palestinian identity is as insubstantial as it is made out to be by the skeptics, while some of the fundamental similarities between it and other national identities will be brought out.

One further aspect of the emergence of Palestinian identity deserves mention here: the role played by those whose voices we often do not hear in the historical record. Such concerns have been brought out both theoretically and as they apply to South Asian historiography in the work of the Subaltern Studies school,[13] and are only beginning to be applied to the study of the Middle East. In much of what follows the elite voices, engaged in the construction of a nationalism that often served as the vehicle of elite interests, will predominate. But as is clear from the events examined in chapter 5, non-elite subaltern elements of Palestinian society played an important, and perhaps central, role in the crucial early years of the emergence of a separate Palestinian identity, and thereafter. Much more remains to be done to determine the place of such actors, whose words often do not reach us, even at so short a remove as four or five generations. This chapter makes a start at doing so, and contains a welcome corrective to the impression that may be derived from the emphasis on elite-generated discourse in much of the literature, and much of the rest of this book. Throughout this book, the question will remain not only regarding the agency of individuals and groups of the subaltern classes, but also how they responded to the writings and words of the elite which feature so prominently in the historical record. For the time being these remain questions without answers.

III

My work on this project has gone on for so long, and has involved so many people, that it will be impossible to thank them all adequately. Among those who helped me in Jerusalem, many individuals deserve my special thanks: without the access to sources they provided, their help and advice in interpreting them, and the warmth and hospitality they extended to me and to my family, this book could never have been written. Among them, Khadr Salama, the Director of the al-Aqsa Library and the Islamic Museum, and Sa'id al-Husayni and Musa al-Budayri, who generously provided me with access to invaluable primary source materials, deserve my warm thanks. So do Nazmi al-Ju'ba, 'Adnan al-Husayni, Yusuf al-Natshe, Faysal al-Husayni, Fu'ad al-Budayri, Butros Abu-Manneh, 'Adil Manna', Amnon Cohen, Danny Bahat, Su'ad al-'Amiry, Salim Tamari, Albert Aghazarian and George Hintlian for their assistance in various ways. Without Michael Metrinko's intervention I might never have made it to Jerusalem in May 1991 to begin the research on this book.

Haifa al-Khalidi, her mother Raqiyya (Um Kamil), and her late father, Haydar al-Khalidi, did more than extend to us the warmth of their home. In addition, each one contributed in different concrete ways to the process of research on this book: Haydar al-Khalidi by encouraging my interest in this project and by preserving the Khalidi Library and a trove of family documents almost single-handed until outside support became available; Haifa by continuing her father's work against difficult odds and giving me invaluable guidance in my research (and much-appreciated sustenance and support throughout); and Raqiyya by offering me her recollections of the first decades of this century. In doing this, she added further invaluable personal details to a picture of that era that I had originally obtained from my late aunts, 'Anbara, Wahidi, and Fatima al-Khalidi. Kamil al-Khalidi, *mutawalli* of the Khalidi Library *waqf*, was helpful and supportive in many ways, not least of which was his discovery of a number of useful documents. Walid Khalidi, who encouraged me to go to Jerusalem to examine the Khalidi Library in the first place, has since then been the mainstay of the Library restoration effort, and has throughout been supportive of my work, deserves my special thanks.

Many others in various places contributed to this book by reading parts of it, by their comments on versions of chapters presented at conferences, or by sharpening my thinking on this subject in discussions with them. Those who did so are too numerous to recall or to mention, but I owe special thanks in this regard to Edward Said, Nubar Hovsepian, Anton Shammas, Nadia Abu al-Hajj, Çaglar Keyder, Sükrü Hanioglu, Patricia Yaeger, 'Azmi Bishara, Jim Jankowski, Israel Gershoni, Joel Beinin, Philip Khoury, Gabby Piterberg, David Laitin, Ron Suny, Norma Field, Jim Chandler, and Michael Geyer, as well as Muhammad Ali Khalidi, Ariela Finkelstein, Julie Peteet, Uday Mehta, May Seikaly, and Lisa Wedeen. David Peters and Michael Raley deserve my thanks for assistance with my research in ways above and beyond the call of duty.

Many of my students contributed to this book by their comments and questions about early drafts of various chapters.

One other group deserves my special gratitude: these are my friends and colleagues who held the fort at the Center for Middle Eastern Studies at the University of Chicago during my lengthy absences over the summers and at other times when I was working on this book. Notable among them are John Woods, Richard Chambers, Vera Beard, Ralph Austen, Cornell Fleischer, Karen Shrode, Susan Hubbard, and Michael Christiana. My fellow residents at the Villa Serbelloni in Bellagio during the summer of 1995 helped me complete this book by their companionship and their suggestions, especially John Kleiner for help with the idea of failure, Bill Beardslee for help with the idea of identity, and both of them, as well as Don Campbell and Jerry Kelly, for less serious but more strenuous kinds of inspiration. To Dorothy and Rudy Pozzati go my special thanks for their friendship and companionship throughout my stay there.

I benefited from much institutional support in the writing of this book. The Council for the International Exchange of Scholars and the J. William Fulbright Foreign Scholarship Board, the Rockefeller Foundation, the Humanities Institute at the University of Michigan, Cornell University, the State University of New York at Binghamton, the University of Colorado at Boulder, the Van Leer Jerusalem Institute, the Center for Behavioral Research of the American University of Beirut, and the Divisions of Social Sciences and Humanities at the University of Chicago all provided me with support that made it possible to do the research and writing for this project, or with venues at which I was enabled to present parts of it. In this regard, I am particularly grateful to Gary Garrison of the CIES, to the late Gil Sherman of the U.S. Information Agency in Jerusalem, to Gianna Celli, Pasquale Pesce, and Susan Garfield of the Rockefeller Foundation, to Shibli Telhami at Cornell, to Samir Khalaf at the American University of Beirut, and to Bruce Craig, Fayez Masad, and the skilled staff of the Middle East section of the Regenstein Library at the University of Chicago.

My wife Mona, who put up with my seemingly unending absences, both physical and psychological, while I was working on this book, deserves thanks beyond measure. She and my three children spent three summers in Jerusalem, during most of which time I was totally wrapped up in the cocoon of my research and writing, and they showed great forbearance then and at many other times. All of them, but especially Mona, have contributed to this volume in ways they know, and others they cannot know.

In a sense, a work of history is written as much by the individuals about whom it is written as by the historian, who can be thought of as no more than their interpreter, giving voice once again to their forgotten words, and illustrating and explaining their actions and the forces that affected them so that another generation can understand them. I dedicate this book to members of another generation than my own, to Lamya, Dima, and Ismail, in the hope that it will speak to them and many others of an important time in the past, and help them to carry some understanding of these ideas, actions, and forces with them into a better future.

Rashid Khalidi
Chicago, August 1996

PALESTINIAN IDENTITY

CHAPTER 1

Introduction

I

        The quintessential Palestinian experience, which illustrates some of the most basic issues raised by Palestinian identity, takes place at a border, an airport, a checkpoint: in short, at any one of those many modern barriers where identities are checked and verified. What happens to Palestinians at these crossing points brings home to them how much they share in common as a people. For it is at these borders and barriers that the six million Palestinians are singled out for "special treatment," and are forcefully reminded of their identity: of who they are, and of why they are different from others.

    Such borders and barriers are rarely more than a source of passing inconvenience for most of those citizens of the world who are fortunate enough to possess an American, European, or other first world passport, along with a sense of belonging so secure that it renders them blandly oblivious to the problems identity can pose for others. But for Palestinians, arrival at such barriers generates shared sources of profound anxiety. This is true whether this is a formal frontier between states, or a military checkpoint like those erected by Israel a few years ago between

Arab East Jerusalem and its suburbs and immediate hinterland in the West Bank,[1] or those currently maintained by Israeli and Palestinian security forces through the West Bank and Gaza Strip.

Borders are a problem for Palestinians since their identity—which is constantly reinforced in myriad positive and negative ways—not only is subject to question by the powers that be; but also is in many contexts suspect almost by definition. As a result, at each of these barriers which most others take for granted, every Palestinian is exposed to the possibility of harassment, exclusion, and sometimes worse, simply because of his or her identity.[2] The dread with which Palestinians regard such boundaries, and the potent—albeit negative—reinforcement of their identity this fear engenders, can be understood only in light of the many anecdotal examples of incidents at crossing points.

Countless stories bear out the reasons for this dread, such as that of the Palestinian who was shuttled back and forth on airliners between an Arab Gulf state and Lebanon for three weeks in 1991 because his identity documents were not satisfactory to the authorities at either end of his trajectory. In September 1991, Gaza Strip Palestinians carrying Egyptian travel papers who were expelled from Kuwait spent twelve days sleeping in Cairo Airport because they did not have the proper documents to enter Egypt or the Israeli-occupied Gaza Strip, to go back to Kuwait, or to go anywhere else. Similarly, in July 1993, numerous Palestinians expelled by Libya were stranded for weeks on the Libyan-Egyptian border. Entire refugee camps sprang up in the same no-man's-land the following year, after the Libyan authorities expelled thousands more Palestinians, whose travel papers were not acceptable to any country. In August 1995, Palestinians with valid refugee travel documents issued by Lebanon were suddenly denied re-entry into that country because they did not have a visa—a requirement that had been imposed during their absence. Among them were members of the Palestinian delegation returning from the international women's conference in Beijing, who were shunted from airport to airport for ten days before being readmitted into Lebanon—where most of them had been born. Such stories of exclusion and denial, which are common knowledge to Palestinians, and have long been a feature of their literature,[3] are but the grotesque tip of an iceberg. Such problems touch every Palestinian in some way, although there are important gradations.

Most unfortunate of all Palestinians are the carriers of travel documents—which are not technically passports—issued by Egypt or Israel for residents of the Gaza Strip (those issued by Israel list "undefined" under the category of "Nationality"), or by Lebanon for Palestinian refugees residing there. Because their travel documents list them as stateless Palestinians (and there are more than one million people among this category in the Gaza Strip and Lebanon), they are more subject than any of their compatriots to anxiety, humiliation, and frustration at barriers or border crossings. It remains to be seen what protection from such concerns will be provided by the Palestinian passports the Palestinian Authority began to issue in Gaza and the West Bank in 1995, but whose validity is still not recognized by some states. They will not in any case help Palestinians in Lebanon, who are not entitled to carry them.

Beyond all this, inhabitants of the Gaza Strip must have at least three different identity documents to get out of the Strip and into Israel, or anywhere else, since all access to and from the Gaza Strip is via Israel. Most of them are originally from regions of Palestine incorporated into Israel during the 1948 war, at which time the indigenous population was driven into the Gaza Strip, in an early example of what is now fashionably called "ethnic cleansing." Only a lucky few, currently under 5 percent of the Gaza Strip's population of 800,000, possess all three of these identity documents. For the rest of this population, even today, after the signing of the Palestinian-Israeli accords of September 1993 and September 1995, the 323 sq. km. of the Strip are their prison, surrounded on all sides by closely guarded barbed wire fences with only one exit, which most of them are not allowed to use, and beyond which lie their former lands, now part of Israel.

In an intermediate category are Palestinians residing in Jordan and Syria; the former carry Jordanian passports, and the latter Syrian passports marked as Palestinian travel documents. Travelers from among these two groups are often singled out for adverse treatment, since it is well known to international security authorities that a large proportion of Jordanian passport holders are Palestinians, while the Syrian travel document clearly identifies them as such. Since 1988, West Bank residents have carried Jordanian passports which, unlike those held by other Jordanians, are valid only for two years.[4] West Bankers, who used to be able to obtain Israeli travel documents before the 1995 Palestinian-Israeli accords, are no longer eligible for these, but can now obtain only the new passports issued by the Palestinian Authority.

Even those few Palestinians who by the chance of birth, marriage, or emigration have managed to acquire United States, European, or other first world passports, find that barriers and borders remind them inexorably of who they are. This is especially true if they return to their homeland, which they have to do via points of entry controlled exclusively by Israel; or if they travel to virtually any Arab country. The border guard's ominous words "Step out of line and follow me" are depressingly familiar to Palestinians waiting their turn at these crossing points. They all know well that notwithstanding their first world passports, their troubles—and the special interrogations they are subjected to just because they are Palestinians—have only just begun.

This condition of suspense in which Palestinians find themselves at borders means that as far as the world, or at least a large part of it, is concerned, the Palestinian's identity remains in question. This identity is therefore a source of anxiety to governments and their security authorities, which like things to be unambiguous and explicitly designated.[5] This is particularly true of the governments of Israel, Jordan, Lebanon, Syria, and Egypt, under whose jurisdiction the majority of Palestinians have lived since 1948.

The anxiety of these governments is displayed notably at the frontiers Palestinians are obliged to cross most often. Thus at the Allenby Bridge between Jordan and the West Bank, the main avenue of entry and egress for the Palestinians of the West Bank, the hundreds of thousands of Palestinians who travel back and forth annually have for three decades been routinely subject to a border crossing ordeal imposed by Israel. This has not improved much since the Palestinian-Israeli self-rule accords. In summertime, when most families travel, these formalities can more than triple the length of the journey from Amman to Jerusalem, which took under three hours before 1967. In one of the hottest places on the face of the earth, located 1,200 feet below sea level in the Jordan River Valley, Palestinian travelers have to stand in the blazing sun, waiting to be subjected to a minute and humiliating search process during which electrical devices, cosmetics, and any tubes or containers are confiscated (foreigners are not subject to this ordeal, although the process can be lengthy for them as well).

With entry from the Gaza Strip into Israel being restricted only to the lucky few possessing the right number and type of Israeli-issued identity cards already mentioned, it remains only to note that entry into Egypt from Gaza has always been exceedingly difficult for Palestinians since the days when Egypt ruled the area, from 1948 to 1967. Finally, for Palestinians, whichever passport they carry, passage via Ben Gurion airport—the main air gateway into the country—generally involves a lengthy interrogation and search procedure by plainclothes security officers upon arrival, and a similar but often lengthier process on departure. These "arrival ceremonies" take place in a special room set aside exclusively for Palestinians.

Such experiences are so universal that a Palestinian wit has said that whenever an independent, sovereign Palestinian state with full control over its own borders is finally created, its border guards will be specially trained to show precisely the same exquisite courtesy as has so long been bestowed on Palestinians to citizens of all those countries which had singled them out for "special treatment." These border guards will be under strict orders to repeat to every citizen of these countries the same words that Palestinians have heard so often since 1948: "Step out of line and follow me."

At a time when internal and international barriers to the free movement of people and ideas are crumbling rapidly in many places, those barriers remain in place for Palestinians, and some have been newly erected, like those around Jerusalem. The fact that all Palestinians are subject to these special indignities, and thus are all subject to an almost unique postmodern condition of shared anxiety at the frontier, the checkpoint and the crossing point proves that they are a people, if nothing else does.

Ironically, it is Israel, the prime agitator for and beneficiary of the free movement of Soviet Jews, which has been responsible for many of these suffocating restrictions on the movement of Palestinians. There is clearly a paradox here. Its core is that Israelis, many of them descended from victims of persecution, pogroms, and concentration camps, have themselves been mistreating another people. We thus find that the sins done to the fathers have morally desensitized the sons to their sins toward others, and have even sometimes been used to justify these sins. (Many Lebanese would bitterly say the same thing about the behavior of the PLO in Lebanon between the late 1960s and 1982.)

This intertwined history, this counterpoint between two extraordinary narratives, and the interplay between two senses of identity which have certain things in common with each other, but are completely different in so many other ways, is one of the themes that stands out in any study of the emergence of Palestinian national identity. The fact that these two—and other—narratives are so intertwined, and often give completely different significance to the same places, events, and people in the same land, makes it harder to disentangle the Palestinian narrative, or to convey it to Western readers who are generally conversant only with the Jewish-Israeli one, or the Christian biblical one. The purpose of this book is to overcome these impediments, in order to explain how a strong sense of Palestinian national identity developed in spite of, and in some cases because of, the obstacles it faced.

II

This examination of the construction of the national identity of the Palestinian people is divided into eight chapters. Chapter 2 examines different narratives in their history and some of the constituents of Palestinian identity, in particular those relating to Jerusalem. It explores why it is so difficult to perceive the specificity of Palestinian nationalism. This is so partly because of the way in which identity for the Palestinians is and has always been intermingled with a sense of identity on so many other levels, whether Islamic or Christian, Ottoman or Arab, local or universal, or family and tribal. The chapter also explores how the Palestinian narrative intersects with other powerful narratives, religious and national, which focus on Palestine and Jerusalem, in some cases drawing on them and in others clashing with them. One of the main arguments of this book, first laid out in this chapter, is that the fierce conflict between the Palestinian and Zionist narratives which developed at an early stage in the history of both is among the reasons why Palestinian identity is so poorly understood. In addition, several over-lapping senses of identity are involved in the process of how Palestinians have come to define themselves as a people, which can lead to others misunderstanding or misintepreting them.

Chapter 3 examines the various constituents of Palestinian identity in the intellectual and cultural realms that theorists and historians of nationalism primarily focus on. Concentrating on Jerusalem before 1914, this chapter examines the elements that shaped the emerging identity of Palestinians in the late Ottoman era, when they had multiple loyalties to their religion, the Ottoman state, the Arabic language, and the emerging identity of Arabism, as well as their country and local and familial foci. Among the institutions involved were the press, schools, religious establishments, the organs of the Ottoman state, clubs, libraries and charitable organizations, and political groups. Other elements shaping identity included extended family linkages, traditional connections to other parts of Palestine, and the impact of foreign missions, diplomats, and visitors.

Chapter 4 moves to the specific, focusing on the lives of two individuals from this era and several of their compatriots who exemplify the shifting identities of Palestinians before World War I. These two men, Yusuf Diya' al-Khalidi and Ruhi al-Khalidi, uncle and nephew, were scholars, writers, and diplomats who served as representatives of Jerusalem in the Ottoman Parliament in 1876–78 and 1908–13 respectively. Through an examination of their lives and their writings, and those of colleagues and contemporaries of theirs such as Sa'id al-Husayni, Muhammad Hassan al-Budayri, 'Arif al-'Arif, and Musa al-'Alami, the choices open to their generation in terms of identity become clearer, and it is possible to understand more fully the matrix out of which Palestinian identity emerged in the early twentieth century.

Another aspect of the crucial role Zionism played in shaping Palestinian identity is examined in chapter 5. Rather than looking at ideology, where the encounter between these two emerging identities is so often examined, this chapter focuses on what happened on the land at the very outset of the interaction between the two nascent national movements. Palestinian peasant resistance starting more than a century ago was the first harbinger of a conflict which throughout has focused on control of land, and has been animated on the Palestinian side by a dynamic often propelled from below rather than from above. It was peasants driven off their farmland by Zionist land purchases, mainly from absentee landlords, in the late nineteenth and early twentieth centuries, who first understood the nature of the process of colonization affecting Palestine. Their struggle for their rights in turn alerted the urban intellectuals who thereafter played a prominent role in the opposition to Zionism, even as they helped to shape Palestinian identity.

The role of the press in the early Arab reaction to Zionism between 1908 and 1914 is covered in chapter 6, which carries further the examination of the interplay between Palestinian identity and Zionism, focusing on how newspapers in Palestine and other parts of the Arab world catalyzed attitudes toward Zionism while at the same time shaping ideas of identity. This chapter also shows how the press in neighboring Arab countries, particularly in Beirut, Cairo, and Damascus, focused on the issue of Zionism, in some cases playing a leading role in the opposition to it. This illuminates concretely the interplay between the Palestinian and the Arab elements, not only in the reaction to Zionism, but also in the constitution of Palestinian identity. Examining the press in this way also helps to correct the oversimplified view that this identity was primarily a response to Zionism.[6]

Chapter 7 deals with the crucial first years of British control of Palestine, from 1917 until 1923, when the Balfour Declaration and the League of Nations Mandate gave international legal sanction and great-power support to the claims of Zionism, and when the nascent Palestinian polity had to respond to this powerful concatenation of forces. The focus here is on the shift from Arab/Ottoman to Palestinian/Arab identity, which took place at the beginning of the period in response to these watershed events; and on the role of the press, education, and other elements of civil society in mobilizing the emerging Palestinian national consciousness. The chapter also examines the uneven development of this consciousness, and the strong divisive tendencies in Palestinian society—regional, familial, and social—which have lingered on since the 1920s.

In conclusion, chapter 8 eschews a straightforward historical narrative, taking as its focus first the reasons Palestinian identity did not simply disappear during the barren years of dispersion, exile, and control by others from 1948–1967, and the role of the PLO and its constituent groups in developing and shaping this identity in new ways until 1982. It also touches on an event which, like the peasant resistance to Zionism of the pre-World War I period, was animated by the grass-roots rather than by urban elites: the 1936–39 revolt. This seismic occurrence in Palestinian history, and its tragic sequel for the Palestinians, the war and expulsions of 1947–49, are examined here not primarily in terms of their causes, effects, and implications, but rather as they served to shape Palestinian identity as it emerged after 1949 into the bleak new dawn of occupation, expulsion, control by a variety of powers, and the attendant shattering of Palestinian society.

CHAPTER 2

Contrasting Narratives of Palestinian Identity

I

What are the limits of Palestine? Where does it end and where does Israel begin, and are those limits spatial, or temporal,[1] or both? More specifically, what delimits the modern history of the Palestinian people from that of the Israelis, who over the past half century have come to dominate the country both peoples claim? Finally, what is it that demarcates Palestinian history from the larger canvas of Middle Eastern and Arab history, and from the history of the neighboring Arab states, Lebanon, Syria, Jordan, and Egypt? In other words, what in Palestinian identity is specific and unique, and what must be understood in the context of broader historical narratives, whether those of Zionism and the state of Israel, or those of Arabism and the neighboring Arab nation-states, or those of Islam and the Muslims?

Although Palestinian identity undoubtedly involves unique and specific elements, it can be fully understood only in the context of a sequence of other histories, a sequence of other narratives. Stuart Hall and others have argued that this is true generally: that identity "is partly the relationship between you and the Other."[2] As Edward Said puts it in

the new afterword to *Orientalism*: " . . . the development and maintenance of every culture require the existence of another, different and
competing *alter ego*. The construction of identity . . . involves the construction of opposites and 'others' whose actuality is always subject to the
continuous interpretation and reinterpretation of their differences
from 'us.' "[3]

Clearly, this relationship between definition of the self and of the
other is characteristic of many peoples in the Middle East and elsewhere,
particularly those in the numerous nation-states established since World
War I. For all of these peoples, transnational identities (whether religious or national), local patriotism, and affiliations of family and clan
have competed for loyalty. The pull of competing loyalties has been considerably stronger for the Palestinians than for others, so that these multiple foci of identity are characteristic features of their history.

Why is this the case? Part of the answer is relatively simple: unlike most
of the other peoples in the Middle East, the Palestinians have never
achieved any form of national independence in their own homeland. In
spite of some success in asserting their national identity inside and outside Palestine, they have consistently failed over the years to create for
themselves a space where they are in full control or are fully sovereign.
The Palestinian "state within a state" in Lebanon from the late 1960s
until 1982 was a partial exception, but it was ultimately not a happy experience for any of those concerned, for it had no sovereign authority, was
not in Palestine, and existed at the expense of the Lebanese, many of
whom came to resent it bitterly.[4] The newly formed Palestinian Authority
in the West Bank and Gaza Strip is explicitly denied sovereignty in the
accords of 1993 and 1995 between the PLO and Israel which established
it, and has only the most limited forms of control over a fraction of the
territory of these two regions.

This absence of sovereignty throughout their history has denied the
Palestinians full control over the state mechanisms—education, museums, archaeology, postage stamps and coins, and the media, especially
radio and television—which myriad recent examples show is essential
for disseminating and imposing uniform "national" criteria of identity.
The new Palestinian Authority has control of some of these tokens of
self rule, but many others are still firmly under Israeli control, while
Palestinian self-determination and independence are currently excluded for at least a five-year interim period, which is supposed to end in
1999, but may well continue beyond that date. Explaining this failure
thus far to achieve statehood and sovereignty, in terms of both the

external and internal factors responsible, is a central problem of modern Palestinian historiography.

The Palestinians resemble a few other peoples in the modern era who have reached a high level of national consciousness and have developed a clearly defined sense of national identity, but have long failed to achieve national independence. In the Middle East, these include the Kurds and (until their recent achievement of independence) the Armenians. All three peoples had reason to expect the self-determination promised by Woodrow Wilson's Fourteen Points in the wake of the breakup of the multinational Ottoman state during World War I, and all were disappointed. In spite of the sufferings of Kurds and Armenians, however, they are now in some respects freer than the Palestinians, and less subject to domination by others. The Armenians finally have an independent republic, albeit one engaged in border conflicts with neighboring Azerbaijan, and located in only part of their ancestral homeland. The Kurds, although denied statehood, currently enjoy an ambiguous international protection in northern Iraq, while a decade-long conflict with the authorities in Turkish Kurdistan continues. In spite of these differences, all three of these Middle Eastern peoples are in some ways comparable. They have all been denied self-determination by the great powers in the settlements imposed on the Middle East after World War I,[5] they live in disputed homelands that overlap with those of other peoples, and the territory they claim has ambiguous and indeterminate boundaries.

Given these similarities, an exploration of Palestinian identity thus has the potential to clarify the specific history not only of Palestine and its people in the modern era, but also of others in the Middle East, including all those with whom the Palestinians have been so intimately involved. It touches as well on broader questions of national identity and the overlapping frontiers of national narratives, national myths and national histories that are relevant far beyond the Middle East. This can help us to understand how a polity which can be understood as a unified people for certain purposes can also be subject to fragmentation. It thus employs the history of a people that has still not fully or successfully defined itself in the eyes of others to illuminate the processes at work in the self-definition of more "successful" peoples, including the neighbors of the Palestinians themselves.

What follows is not a reinterpretation of the history of Palestine or the Palestinian people, grounded in new research in primary sources (although it is largely based on such research). It is, rather, an exploration of the interplay between the different narratives that make up Palestinian history, meant to illuminate aspects of the identity of a people about which much has been written and said, but little is understood. Beshara Doumani concludes his book, *Rediscovering Palestine: Merchants and Peasants in Jabal Nablus, 1700–1900*, with the words:

> until we can chart the economic, social and cultural relations between the inhabitants of the various regions of Palestine during the Ottoman period, we cannot have a clear understanding of the politics of identity, nor can we confidently answer the questions of when, how, why, and in what ways Palestine became a nation in the minds of the people who call themselves Palestinians today.[6]

This book does not purport to do anything so ambitious, although it delves into the cultural, social, and economic relations that Doumani correctly emphasises as the basis of identity. It is not even an attempt to define fully those much written-about and heavily contested terms, "Palestine" and "Palestinian people." One of the subjects it does explore, however, is why such a great deal of attention has produced so little useful scholarship, for the degree of heat that is often generated by the very mention of the terms "Palestine" or "Palestinian" is notable in itself. It is even more striking in contrast to the small amount of light cast on the subject by these copious writings.

The best explanation for this phenomenon of intense polemical heat combined with scant intellectual light is that in Palestine many powerful and contradictory views of self and of history are conjoined. These may be religious, whether Jewish, Christian, or Muslim; or secular, as for example the focus of Masonic ritual on the Temple in Jerusalem; or they may be national or supranational, whether Arab or Jewish. Whatever their nature, however, these narratives of self and history that focus on Palestine have an influence far beyond its boundaries, reaching millions who know of this land only through the texts produced by these various currents of thought and belief, or perhaps in consequence of brief pilgrimages. All of these people nevertheless feel that they know the country intimately, whatever name they give it, and however they visualize its boundaries.

Moreover, those who hold these views often do so with an intense passion combined with a dogmatic certainty about their beliefs, against a background of nearly complete ignorance of Palestine and its history. This unique combination of deeply held beliefs related to Palestine and little concrete knowledge of it helps to explain the level of conflict the country has witnessed in the past. To take a distant example, an otherwise almost incomprehensible sequence of events like the Crusades—a series of ultimately futile attempts over more than two centuries by northern Europeans to conquer and colonize part of West Asia—can be understood only in terms of a combination of passion and ignorance. Thus, the fervor of the Crusaders' yearning for Palestine, which was apparent in the willingness of so many to set off on such a daunting endeavor, was matched only by these northern European knights' obliviousness to the complex political, cultural, and religious realities of Palestine and adjacent parts of the Islamic world in the eleventh, twelfth and thirteenth centuries. The ignorance of the Crusaders, however, was no bar to their lengthy and intense involvement in the affairs of the region.

To this day, the Crusades have a powerful resonance in Palestine and far beyond its confines. For Palestinians and Israelis in particular, the Crusades have been invested with special meaning, for one people as representing the ultimate triumph of resistance to alien invasion and colonization, and for the other as an episode to be contrasted unfavorably with the more successful Zionist enterprise. Each side thus sees in the Crusades only what it wants to see, and indeed we shall see many direct and indirect references to the Crusades by Palestinians in the pages that follow.[7] This continuing resonance is a testament both to the ferocity of this two-century-long conflict, and to the power of self-contained and self-reflective narratives like those of the Crusades. Such accounts are grounded in the history of the country—for it was of course the Christian connection to Jerusalem and the holy land that originally provoked the Crusades—but they have an autonomous dynamic growing out of forces and passions whose original locus is elsewhere, and a raison d'être all their own, defined primarily in terms of medieval European history. Thus the story of the Crusades is often told in isolation from its context, neglecting the social implications of these massive military campaigns inside Europe as well as their powerful and often disastrous impact on the Jewish communities of Europe, the Byzantine Empire, and the Islamic societies of the Middle East.[8]

II

It is certainly not a coincidence that virtually all narratives about Palestine—religious and secular, Jewish, Christian, and Muslim, Palestinian, and Israeli—revolve around the city of Jerusalem, which has long been the geographical, spiritual, political, and administrative center of Palestine. Indeed, it is in and over Jerusalem, which has such great significance to so many people in so many different ways, that the contrasting narratives regarding Palestine come most bitterly into conflict. It is in Jerusalem as well that one sees the most extreme instances of the various local parties' attempts to assert physical control over the country, and to obtain validation of their conflicting claims to the space they share.

In Jerusalem, as elsewhere in Palestine, such validation is achieved notably by the act of naming. This process is already strikingly evident in the disputed naming of Palestine/Israel by the two peoples who contest the same land: most Israelis and Palestinians today have in mind essentially the same country, from the Mediterranean to the Jordan River, and from the deserts in the south to the southern foothills of the Lebanese mountains and Mount Hermon in the north, although they have different names for it. This process of seeking validation for conflicting claims is most fittingly symbolized, however, by the unremitting struggle over the naming of Jerusalem. The city is called *Yerushalaim* in Hebrew (a word derived from the Aramaic, meaning, ironically, "city of peace"). The English derivative of this Hebrew name is Jerusalem, while translated into Arabic it is rendered *Urshalim*. Since early in the Islamic era, however, Arabic-speakers have almost without exception called Jerusalem either *Bayt al-Maqdis*, meaning the House of Sanctity (a term that may itself be drawn from the original Hebrew term for the Temple), or most commonly *al-Quds al-Sharif*, the Noble Holy Place.[9]

But while Jerusalem might be expected to have different names in different languages, what is at issue here is an attempt to impose on one language a name based on usage in another. Thus in its Arabic-language broadcasts, Israeli radio refers to the city exclusively as "*Urshalim/al-Quds*," and this is the name found on all official Israeli documents in Arabic. Israeli television weather forecasts in Arabic shorten this to *Urshalim*. Those who have mandated this usage seem to want to force Palestinians to recognize the Hebrew name for the place, although speakers of Arabic have had a perfectly serviceable name of their own for the city for well over a millennium.

Although such measures may seem petty, they are related to the significant process of attempting to signal control by imposing place names. This has, for example rendered the West Bank as Judea and Samaria in the official terminology used for Israel's Hebrew, English, and Arabic pronouncements and publications. For the past few decades many such archaic or invented place names have been imposed throughout Palestine over the Arabic ones employed for many centuries and still used by most of the present-day population (many of these Arabic names, ironically, are based on earlier Hebrew, Aramaic, Greek, Latin, or French Crusader names for the same sites).[10] This process of naming is an attempt to privilege one dimension of a complex reality at the expense of others, with the ultimate aim of blotting the others out, or decisively subordinating them to Israeli domination.[11]

Another aspect of this process is visible in the sphere of archaeology. Attempts to privilege one archaeological stratum over others are predicated on a belief both that one stratum is "superior" or unique, and that the past can be manipulated to affect the present by "proving" this superiority. Thus, if one specific stratum of a city can be privileged, if one set of names derived from that stratum (or taken from the Bible or another ancient text and applied to that stratum) can be given pride of place over all others below or above it, then a certain contemporary "reality" claiming roots in the past can be imposed on the present, and further consecrated.[12]

This phenomenon is illustrated in the Arab neighborhood of Silwan, which has developed out of an ancient village adjacent to and immediately south of the walls of the Old City in Jerusalem. Israeli settlers who have occupied several homes in the midst of Silwan are attempting to impose exclusive use of the name "City of David" (after the hillside where King David is supposed to have built his capital alongside the earlier Jebusite city), thereby giving their current claims the patina, prestige, and legitimacy of a connection some 3,000 years old.[13] In this they are aided by various maps, tourist guides, and road signs produced by the Israeli government, the Jerusalem municipality, and the Israeli tourist authorities, which use the archaic name "City of David" wherever possible in place of Silwan, the name used for centuries by the Arab inhabitants (ironically, this Arabic name is derived from the biblical Siloam, site of the pool of the same name!).

This contest over names has in the past had dimensions other than the Palestinian-Israeli one. For example, books in Arabic published in Jerusalem by Catholic presses in the early nineteenth century referred to the place of publication as *Urshalim* (the name for the city used by Eastern Christian churches that utilize Arabic in their liturgy), rather than as *al-Quds al-Sharif* or *Bayt al-Maqdis*. A work published in Arabic by the Franciscan press as late as 1865 still uses the term *Urshalim* for the place of publication, even though the work is a petition presented to the local government, which is described in the text of the petition itself as that of "*al-Quds al-Sharif*."[14] Similarly, a book on the history of the Orthodox Church in Jerusalem, published in 1925 in Jerusalem, uses the term *Urshalim* in the title, and the term *al-Quds al-Sharif* to describe the place of publication.[15]

This vestigial reluctance to use the common Arabic name, with its Islamic overtones, even in works referring to that name somewhere on their title pages, represents the last flickering of a rivalry for control of Jerusalem between Islam and Christianity—a rivalry that began in the seventh century with the city's conquest by Muslim armies from Byzantium, was greatly intensified during the Crusades, and abated only in the early twentieth century.[16] More recently, the devotion of some fundamentalist Western Christians to Israel, and their visceral hostility to Islam and the Arabs, shows that a few embers of this ancient rivalry have not been entirely extinguished.[17]

The conflict over names in Jerusalem goes beyond the name of the city itself. Jerusalem's most prominent geographical feature, as well as its most important site historically and religiously, is the vast man-made plateau in the southeast corner of the Old City within its Ottoman walls. This spacious rectangular platform (about 480 by 300 m.) is located around a huge stone which is all that remains of the peak of Mount Moriah, where Jews, Christians, and many Muslims believe the prophet Abraham to have been commanded by God to sacrifice his son.[18] From this stone, Muslims believe, the Prophet Muhammad alighted on the miraculous night journey from Mecca to Jerusalem described in the Qur'an (17:1). The entire site, known in Arabic as *al-Haram al-Sharif*— the Noble Sanctuary—encompasses a number of strikingly beautiful Islamic structures, notably the al-Aqsa Mosque and the Dome of the Rock, which have dominated and adorned this space for the past thirteen centuries.[19]

The same site is known to Israelis and others as the Temple Mount. Six centuries before the advent of Islam, it was dominated by the great Temple built by Herod.[20] This structure, destroyed by the Roman general Titus, son of the Emperor Vespasian, in 70 A.D., was built in turn on what was believed to be the site of earlier structures, going back to the Temple described in the Bible as having been constructed by Solomon. Much of the outer enclosure wall of the Herodian Temple compound survives in its lower courses of finely finished cyclopean masonry, which constitute the foundations for the eastern, southern, and western walls of the *Haram al-Sharif* enclosure, built in its present form on the identical site by the Umayyads in the seventh century.

Needless to say, Arabs and Israelis recognize only their own respective names for this site, demonstrating that in much of what it does, each side chooses to be oblivious to the existence of the other, or at least pretends to be.[21] In a sense, each party to this conflict, and every other claimant, operates in a different dimension from the other, looking back to a different era of the past, and living in a different present, albeit in the very same place. These two peoples, however, live cheek by jowl perforce, and their awareness of this enforced coexistence is occasionally illustrated in striking and bloody fashion, ranging from the so-called Wailing Wall riots of 1929 (although sparked by clashes over the rights of the respective communities to this site, most of the violence took place elsewhere), to the October 1990 clashes in which Israeli security forces shot and killed 18 Palestinians and wounded more than 300 others inside the precincts of the *Haram al-Sharif*.[22]

The conflict over this site, and over its name, extends down to levels of even greater detail. Thus, as we have seen, the southernmost section of the western wall of the *Haram al-Sharif* includes in its lower courses part of the outer enclosure of the Temple compound built by Herod. Known as the "Wailing Wall" or the Western Wall, *ha-Kotel ha-Ma'ravi* in Hebrew, this site has been the scene of public Jewish worship since the sixteenth or seventeenth century, before which time such worship took place on the Mount of Olives overlooking the eastern walls of the *Haram*.[23] Precisely the same section of this western wall is considered by Muslims to be the site where the Prophet Muhammad tethered his winged steed *al-Buraq* on the night journey "from the *Masjid al-Haram* [in Mecca] to the *Masjid al-Aqsa* [in Jerusalem]" described in the Qur'an (17:1). As such, the spot has long been venerated by Muslims.[24]

The very same wall is thus among the holiest of sites to two faiths, and is naturally considered by each to be its exclusive property. Immediately inside the wall of the *Haram*, near the *Bab al-Magharib* gate, is a small mosque called *Jami' al-Buraq*, commemorating the spot where *al-Buraq* was supposedly tethered.[25] The entire area to the west of the wall, until 1967 a residential quarter called *Haret al-Maghariba*, or the Moroccan quarter, was established as a Muslim waqf, or inalienable pious endowment, in 1193 by al-Malik al-Afdal, the son of the Ayyubid Sultan Salah al-Din (Saladin), who retook the city from the Crusaders. A few days after Israel's occupation of East Jerusalem in 1967, the entire Moroccan quarter, including the four Muslim religious sites it encompassed, was demolished, and its approximately 1,000 residents evicted, in order to create the large open plaza that now exists west of the wall.[26] In addition to its frequent use for Jewish religious observances, this plaza has since 1967 become the site of Israeli national and patriotic mass gatherings, such as torchlight ceremonies celebrating graduation from training for recruits to elite army units, and political demonstrations by right-wing parties.

This disputed site thus displays elements of the various conflicting narratives—going back to those relating to the patriarch Abraham, venerated by followers of all three monotheistic faiths—that lie behind the complex identity of the Palestinians, the Israelis, and many others. This conflict is illustrated by the archaeological excavations carried out for many years after 1967 immediately to the south of the *Haram al-Sharif*, on a site immediately abutting the *al-Aqsa Mosque*, and the Western Wall/*al-Buraq* plaza. According to Meir Ben Dov, the Israeli field director of the dig, this site "contains the remains of twenty-five strata from twelve distinct periods."[27] Each stratum is part of the identity of the Palestinian people as they have come to understand it over the past century—encompassing the biblical, Roman, Byzantine, Umayyad, Fatimid, Crusader, Ayyubid, Mameluke, and Ottoman periods[28]. At the same time, several strata have special importance to others who revere Jerusalem (the Byzantine and Crusader strata for Western Christians, for example, or the stratum containing the southern steps of the Herodian temple—where Jesus encountered the money-changers—for Christians and Jews alike), and they are not treated equally by any means.[29]

Most importantly, central though Jerusalem is to the Palestinians and to their self-image, it is also central to the self-image of their Israeli adversaries. For both, it is important today as a space, and historically, over time, as an anchor for modern identity.[30] Yet the Israelis control Jerusalem, and are able to expropriate, excavate, label, and describe antiquities there as they please. They can thus put the stamp of authority on narratives that give extraordinary weight to selected strata, thereby successfully manipulating both the spatial and temporal aspects of identity, in pursuit of a clear nationalist political agenda. Their success can be seen from the tides of foreign tourists that choke the narrow alleys of the Old City for much of the year, most of them in groups led by Israeli tour guides propagating a specific version of the city's history.

It is interesting to speculate what a Palestinian version would look like (there are a few clues to this already), and even more interesting to contemplate the possibility of a multidimensional narrative that would reproduce all of Jerusalem's ambiguity and the overlapping traditions it represents, instead of reducing the complexity of the city's history to a single narrow dimension.

III

One of the central arguments of this chapter is that several overlapping senses of identity have been operating in the way the Palestinians have come to define themselves as a people, senses that have not necessarily been contradictory for the Palestinians themselves, but can be misunderstood or misinterpreted by others. As Palestinian identity has evolved over time, its elements have varied, with some eventually disappearing and others newly emerging. What follows is a discussion of this process, and of the ways in which both collective traumas and major obstacles have played a role in shaping and expressing a separate Palestinian identity, even while problems internal to Palestinian society have helped prevent—thus far at least—the realization of the Palestinian "national project."

It is characteristic of both time and place that the intellectuals, writers, and politicians who were instrumental in the evolution of the first forms of Palestinian identity at the end of the last century and early in this century, figures who will be discussed further in the chapters that follow (among them Sa'id al-Husayni, Ruhi al-Khalidi, Najib Nassar, 'Isa al-'Isa, Muhammad Hassan al-Budayri, 'Arif al-'Arif, Khalil al-Sakakini, and Musa al-'Alami), identified with the Ottoman Empire, their religion, Arabism, their homeland Palestine, their city or region, and their family, without feeling any contradiction, or sense of conflicting loyalties.[31]

By the late 1920s and the 1930s, the way in which such individuals or others like them related to these foci of identity had changed greatly. The Ottoman Empire had disappeared, the importance of religion in public life had declined somewhat, Arab nationalism and its association with Syria had suffered defeats at the hands of the French (whose troops drove an Arab nationalist government out of Damascus in 1920), and Britain had received a mandate for Palestine within fixed frontiers, wherein national rights had been promised for the Jewish minority, but not mentioned for the Arab majority. All these changes intensified and transformed the preexisting identification with Palestine of such people, their contemporaries, and the generation that followed them into politics, education, and journalism, although they still continued to identify with religion, Arabism, and their localities and families.

This process of identification with new entities—nation-states, or nation-states-in-embryo in most cases—was not particularly unusual for its time and place. The main difference was that that unlike Egyptians, Iraqis, Syrians or Lebanese, all of whom developed a loyalty to some form of nation-state nationalism over approximately the same period (albeit in different ways in every case, and with markedly different understandings of what the nation-state was, and how it related to the nation),[32] the Palestinians had not only to fashion and impose their identity and independent political existence in opposition to a European colonial power, but also to match themselves against the growing and powerful Zionist movement, which was motivated by a strong, highly developed, and focused sense of national identification, and which challenged the national rights of the Palestinians in their own homeland, and indeed the very existence of the Palestinians as an entity.

Although the Zionist challenge definitely helped to shape the specific form Palestinian national identification took, it is a serious mistake to suggest that Palestinian identity emerged mainly as a response to Zionism.[33] Important though Zionism was in the formation of Palestinian identity—as the primary "other" faced by the Palestinians for much of this century—the argument that Zionism was the main factor in provoking the emergence of Palestinian identity ignores one key fact: a universal process was unfolding in the Middle East during this period, involving an increasing identification with the new states created by the post-World War I partitions. In every case, this was based on the development of preexisting loyalties and the inception of new ones, just as with the Palestinians. In every case, these new identities can be shown to have been contingent, conjunctural, and dependent on circumstances rather than essential or primordial. As part of this universal process, moreover, Lebanese, Syrians, Egyptians, Iraqis and Jordanians all managed to develop their respective nation-state nationalisms during the same period without the dubious benefit of a Zionist challenge.[34]

The existence of overlapping senses of identity—including transnational, religious, local, family, and nation-state loyalties—is to be expected in such polities as these Arab states, where new national narratives have developed in the context of the existence of many separate loyalties. In some cases champions of different narratives of the nation have come into conflict, which has resulted in the absence of even a minimal consensus on national identity, as was long the case in Lebanon.[35] Most often, however, such a consensus has eventually emerged. Although the phenomenon of overlapping senses of identity characterizes all the neighbors of the Palestinians, including the Israelis, there is one vital difference: these neighboring peoples have lived for most of the past half century under the rule of increasingly strong independent states, which gave substance to their national narratives and propagated them domestically and internationally in an authoritative fashion.

In contrast, the lack of a strong state—indeed of any state of their own—has clearly had a great impact on the Palestinian sense of national identity. In other Arab countries under European colonial and semicolonial rule during the interwar period, a strong central state under at least nominal indigenous control was accepted as a given (and indeed was a required feature of the other Mandates conferred on Britain and France), although it was also generally a site of fierce contestation among local elites, and between them and the colonial power. In Palestine throughout the Mandate period, however, the power of the state accrued exclusively either to the British or to their Zionist protégés, and was rigorously denied to the Palestinians. We shall see in later chapters how being deprived of access to formal state power then and afterward has affected the growth of Palestinian identity, and what took its place, whether in the form of traditional social structures dominated by the old notable families, or parastate formations like the PLO.

The major currents that have swept the Middle East during the twentieth century, such as the Western powers' definition of state boundaries, as well as Arabism, Islamic trends, Zionism, and the growth of nation-state nationalisms in the Arab states, all affected the process of Palestinian self-definition, but so did several more parochial factors—among them a strong religious attachment to Palestine among Muslims and Christians,[36] the impact over time of living within long-standing administrative boundaries,[37] and enduring regional and local loyalties. These loyalties involved the intense attachment of the urban population to their cities and towns, of the peasantry to their villages and lands, and of both to their home regions.[38] While studies of Palestinian nationalism have concentrated on its evolution in recent decades, in fact most elements of Palestinian identity—particularly the enduring parochial, local ones—were well developed before the climactic events of 1948, although they continued to overlap and change both before and after that date. The existence of such local identities was not peculiar to Palestine, of course; but there, and elsewhere in the Arab world, these parochial loyalties served as the bedrock for an attachment to place, a love of country, and a local patriotism that were crucial elements in the construction of nation-state nationalism.

In 1948 half of Palestine's 1.4 million Arabs were uprooted from their homes and became refugees, while the traditional Palestinian political and social leadership was scattered and discredited. In addition, the political structures this class had dominated were pulverized, not to be replaced for over a decade and a half, during which time there existed a leadership vacuum. Although a very few members of the traditional notable families remained politically active in the years that followed, none of them has since played a prominent leadership role in Palestinian politics (Faysal al-Husayni may prove to be the first exception to this rule). Were a basic core sense of national identity not already in place among key segments of the Palestinian people, the catastrophic shock of these events might have been expected to shatter the Palestinians as a people, eventually leading to their full absorption into the neighboring Arab countries. This indeed was what many of their opponents hoped would happen.[39]

After 1948 the Palestinians in fact were to some degree integrated into the Arab host countries, whether socially, economically, or politically, as might be expected given the overlapping identities of the Palestinians with many of their neighbors. But instead of causing their absorption into these countries, the trauma of 1948 reinforced preexisting elements of identity, sustaining and strengthening a Palestinian self-definition that was already present. The shared events of 1948 thus brought the Palestinians closer together in terms of their collective consciousness, even as they were physically dispersed all over the Middle East and beyond. The catastrophic experience of 1948, and its impact on different segments of the Palestinian people, is still a common topic of discussion among Palestinians of diverse backgrounds and generations, and ultimately a potent source of shared beliefs and values.

The overt obstacles to the expression of a separate Palestinian identity in national terms are thus worth examining, alongside the ideologies that competed for the loyalty of the Palestinian people or exerted influence on them, from Ottomanism and Arabism, to Islam, to the nation-state nationalism of the neighboring Arab nation-states. Whether as elements of the Palestinians' overlapping sense of identity, or as obstacles to, or opponents of, the expression of this identity, all of these "others" contributed, albeit in markedly different ways, to the Palestinians' self-definition.

The main obstacles to the expression of a separate Palestinian identity included the external powers that have dominated the region during the twentieth century, Britain and the United States, both of which at different times perceived Palestinian nationalism as a threat to their interests. As we have seen, the Balfour Declaration and the League of Nations Mandate for Palestine (which governed British policy in Palestine for three decades), explicitly excluded Palestinian national rights, and did not even mention the Palestinians *per se*, whether as

Palestinians, Arabs, or Syrians. They were referred to instead solely in negative terms, as "the non-Jewish communities in Palestine." This negation was an important prerequisite both for the denial of self-determination to the Palestinians, and for the British decision to favor Zionism: for if the Palestinians had no determined identity,[40] they were unworthy of self-determination, or at least less worthy than the Jews, who clearly had a determined identity, now being posed in national rather than religious terms. At the same time as they denied Palestinian identity, both documents enshrined the establishment of a Jewish "national home" as Britain's primary responsibility in governing Palestine. Except for a brief period following the issuance of the 1939 White Paper, Britain remained essentially faithful to this dual approach until 1947–48, when it successfully colluded with Jordan (and indirectly with Israel) to prevent the emergence of the Palestinian state which was provided for in the United Nations General Assembly's plan for the partition of Palestine, embodied in resolution 181 of November 1947.[41]

As for the United States, although in 1947 it supported the partition of Palestine and the creation of a Palestinian state alongside Israel, it did nothing to help that state come into being against the machinations of Jordan, Britain, and Israel, but instead materially assisted the nascent state of Israel. Since 1948, the United States has followed essentially the same course as Britain, supporting Israel but never conceding the validity of Palestinian national rights or the self-determination and statehood that their implementation would entail, and indeed frequently making efforts to prevent their implementation. This policy was consistent, although different administrations edged ambiguously toward accepting certain Palestinian political rights, while invariably excluding the most important right, that of national self-determination. For example, while the 1978 Camp David agreement includes the phrase "the legitimate rights of the Palestinian people," it is clear from the context that these are less than full rights of self-determination and independence. Little has changed since then, whether in the U.S.-brokered framework for the Middle East peace negotiations which started in October 1991, or in the PLO-Israel Declaration of Principles signed on the White House lawn in September 1993, and the self-rule agreement that resulted from it signed in the White House in September 1995. All of these documents produced under American patronage fail to provide for Palestinian self-determination or statehood.

The obstacles to the achievement of Palestinian national rights also included the Zionist movement, which since its implantation in Palestine at the end of the last century has strongly opposed any expression of independent Palestinian nationalism, Palestinian claims to the country, and the exercise of Palestinian national identity. With few exceptions (Ahad Ha-Am and Judah Magnes stand out among them), early Zionist leaders, and Israeli politicians since the founding of the state, have tended to see their conflict with Palestinian nationalism as a zero-sum game.[42] Beyond winning most of the early rounds of this game on the ground in Palestine, they were able to carry their battle back to the international "metropolises," of the era, whether London and Paris before World War II or Washington and New York since then. In doing so, they succeeded in gaining world support for their own national aspirations, while at the same time they delegitimized those of their Palestinian opponents before key segments of international public opinion.

Since the early days of the Zionist movement, Palestinian intellectuals and political figures perceived that Zionism had objectives that could be achieved only at the expense of Palestinian aspirations, whether framed in Ottoman, Muslim or Christian, Arab, Syrian, or narrowly Palestinian terms, and they too generally came to hold a zero-sum view of the conflict.[43] One of the earliest recorded Palestinian reactions to Zionism was a letter sent to the first leader of the modern Zionist political movement, Theodor Herzl, in 1899 by Yusuf Diya' al-Din Pasha al-Khalidi [hereafter Yusuf Diya' al-Khalidi], former mayor of Jerusalem and deputy for the city in the 1877–78 Ottoman Parliament. In it, he warned that the Palestinians would resist the aspirations of political Zionism, which they understood could be achieved only at their expense, and concluded, "leave Palestine in peace."[44] We will discuss this letter further in chapter 4.

It may be asked why, given this early awareness, the Palestinians were not more effective in their resistance to the Zionist movement. For the effective and successful expression of Palestinian identity—meaning the achievement of a greater measure of independent national existence, up to and including sovereignty—was not obstructed solely by external obstacles, powerful and numerous though these were. Internal factors, resulting largely from the nature of the social structure of Palestine in the nineteenth and twentieth centuries, have also contributed to maintaining the Palestinians in a state of dependence until the present day.

The general outlines of this social structure, fragmented along regional, class, religious, and family lines, were not peculiar to Palestinian society: indeed they were common to many others in the Arab world in this period. Other Arab countries, however, generally succeeded in transcending these divisions, at least in times of national crisis. At similar times, the lack of cohesion of Palestinian society repeatedly hindered effective, unified responses to the challenges posed by the formidable foes of Palestinian nationalism.

It is illuminating to study the differences between the Palestinians and the Arab peoples who over the past century developed national frontiers and state structures and secured independence from the same Western powers that denied these things to the Palestinians. Both Egypt and Tunisia showed a high degree of cohesiveness, in spite of deep societal divisions, and managed to negotiate the difficult transition from foreign occupation to independence with limited instability, dissension, or domestic repression. In Syria and Iraq, the passage was stormier, with national consensus harder to build, and less mutual tolerance and pluralism in political life than in Egypt or Tunisia. The result was that before and after independence in Syria and Iraq, internal sectarian, social, and political tensions repeatedly exploded in bloody domestic strife, leaving both countries with repressive, authoritarian states as the price of this transition.[45]

In the Palestinian case, what had to be achieved was more difficult than in other Arab countries, for as we have noted, the opposition of both Britain and the Zionist movement had to be taken into account. But from 1918 until 1948, the Palestinians also demonstrated less ability to transcend local, family, and political rivalries and to unify their efforts against their common enemies than did Egyptians, Tunisians, Syrians, Iraqis, and even the religiously divided Lebanese. In all these cases, the respective national movements managed to display greater cohesiveness and solidarity at critical moments in the struggle with the colonial power than did the Palestinians: Egypt in 1919 and 1936; Tunisia in the mid-1950s; Syria in 1925–26 and 1936; Iraq in 1941 and 1946–48; and Lebanon in 1943. At times, the outcome was not an unequivocal victory, but in all cases the ultimate result was independence.

Certainly, the lack of access after 1918 to state structures (or indeed to any meaningful level of government: the top posts in the mandate administration were reserved for the British[46]) hindered the Palestinians by comparison with their Arab neighbors. Most other Arab countries either had a preexisting state with a degree of independence, as in Egypt or Tunisia, which had autonomous, hereditary regimes under the Ottomans before European occupation in the 1880s, and retained them afterwards; or the European powers were bound by the terms of League of Nations mandates to create such state structures and eventually to hand over power to them. We have already seen that this was not the case with regard to the Palestine mandate. Moreover, in Palestine the Zionists built their own exclusive, well-funded parastate structures with the blessing of the mandatory authority and in keeping with the terms of the Mandate, even while benefiting inordinately from the British-created administrative structures of the Government of Palestine.

But in addition to these special disadvantages affecting the Palestinians, it might also be argued that Palestine, and especially the hilly central Nablus-Jerusalem-Hebron axis whence came most of the political leaders, was simply less developed economically, and therefore had evolved less socially and politically, than had the urban areas of Egypt, Syria, Iraq, and Lebanon during this period.[47] Moreover, even in neighboring Lebanon and Syria, which were most similar to Palestine, political leadership tended to come not from the towns of the relatively isolated hill areas, but rather from the middle and upper classes of the larger and more socially, economically, and politically developed cities of the coast and the interior plains: Beirut, Aleppo, and Damascus. In 1942, these cities had populations of 233,000, 257,000, and 261,000 respectively, while the three largest cities in Palestine with Arab populations—Jerusalem, Haifa, and Jaffa—had populations of 143,000, 116,000, and 89,000, with only about 180,000 of the three cities' total population of 348,000 being Arabs.[48]

In Palestine, by way of contrast, while in the early part of the twentieth century Jaffa and Haifa were the fastest growing cities, and were the commercial and economic foci of the country, as well as centers of intellectual and cultural life and of press activity (and by 1948 had the largest Arab populations of any cities in the country—larger even than Jerusalem), Jerusalem, Nablus, and other cities and towns of the hills tended to dominate political life. The implication is that Palestinian politics tended to be most influenced by these hill areas where religious, clan, family and parochial perspectives were more prevalent, rather than by the coastal cities where working class associations, radical urban religious groups, commercial and business concerns, and intellectual and social organizations were most active.[49]

Certainly, political party organization, sustained mass political mobilization, a vigorous independent political press, and many other features of "modern" politics, which had burgeoned rapidly at this time in other Arab countries, were relatively underdeveloped in Palestine when the crucial test of the 1936–39 revolt arose.[50] Palestinians showed great solidarity in the opening phases of this revolt, which was started and sustained by the grassroots rather than the traditional political leadership. It is also true that the strong religious, family, and local loyalties that characterized this society were initially a great asset during the revolt.[51] Nevertheless, in the end the lack of organization, and of nation-wide structures, as well as the urban-rural, class, and family divisions that bedeviled Palestinian society reemerged, splintering the internal front even as the British mounted a fierce campaign of repression in late 1938. The result was a crushing military and political reverse for the Palestinians. This reverse was perhaps inevitable, since it is difficult to imagine the British Empire accepting defeat at the hands of the Palestinians, however sophisticated their leadership and organization, at this crucial juncture just before World War II, and in an area the British considered to be of vital strategic importance to them. The likely inevitability of this reverse made it no less devastating.

The decisive defeat in 1936–39 had fatally weakened the Palestinians by the time of their desperate final post-World War II struggle with the Zionist movement to retain control of some part of what they passionately believed was their country. In consequence, when expeditionary forces of four Arab armies entered Palestine on May 15, 1948, the Palestinians had already been militarily overwhelmed by the forces of the Haganah, the Palmach, and the Irgun in a series of sweeping routs which ended in the loss of Jaffa, Haifa, Acre, Tiberias, and many other cities, towns, villages, and strategic communications routes. The defeat created a political and military vacuum the nascent Israeli state rapidly filled, together with the armies of several Arab states, which proceeded to lose much of the rest of Palestine to the victorious Israelis.

It was not until the mid-1960s that the rebirth of Palestinian nationalism would put the Palestinians back on the political map of the Middle East. By this time, a new middle class leadership had emerged at the head of effectively organized political structures like Fatah and the Movement of Arab Nationalists, eclipsing the traditional leaders who had failed during the mandate period.[52] The legacy that those leaders left to their successors included the heavy burden of repeated political defeats culminating in the disaster of 1948, and the complete frustration of Palestinian aspirations for independence and sovereignty.

Yet this sequence of setbacks, far from weakening it, seems to have reinforced the sense of Palestinian national identity that had emerged over the preceding decades out of the disparate strands of religious and local attachments to Palestine, commitment to Arabism, and resistance to what Palestinians perceived was the creeping encroachment of the

Zionist movement on their homeland. The Palestinians held fast to this strong sense of identity after 1948, both those who became refugees, and those who remained in their homes inside Palestine. Even while it continued to evolve and change, this sense of identity remained the foundation upon which the Palestinian nationalist groups that emerged after 1948 were to build.

IV

Given this background, how has the way Palestinians define their identity changed over time? While it is difficult to date precisely when a distinct sense of Palestinian identity first emerged, there is little doubt that it emerged unevenly—in different ways among different groups and in different areas—and that it always coexisted with other forms of identification, such as religion or family. Important roots of this identity go back before the development of modern national consciousness. But there is considerable evidence that much of the population of Palestine came, in Benedict Anderson's term, to "imagine" themselves as a political community, with clear boundaries and rights to sovereignty, early in the twentieth century.[53] This section recapitulates some of the stages in this process, concluding with a warning of the pitfalls that threaten those who study the topic.

The incipient sense of community-as-nation can be seen in an article by Najib 'Azuri, a former Ottoman official in Palestine, in the newspaper *Thamarat al-Funun* on September 23, 1908. 'Azuri suggested that the newly restored Ottoman Parliament expand the existing *sanjaq* of Jerusalem northwards to include the northern regions of Palestine which at that time were part of the *vilayet* of Beirut, stressing that "the progress of the land of Palestine depends on this."[54] The idea of a clearly defined political unit called "the land of Palestine," with frontiers approximating those later given to the country under the mandate, must have been clearly present in 'Azuri's mind, and also in the minds of his readers, for him to have made such a proposal. His proposal specifies a primary unit of territory to which the residents of Palestine belonged and owed their loyalty, and through which they should be represented in the Ottoman Parliament. In 'Azuri's case, we know from his book *Le Reveil de la nation arabe*[55] that he had a clear sense of Palestine as a country—the book contains an entire chapter on the history, geography, population and administration of Palestine—and of the potential impact on it of the rise of the

Zionist movement. There are many other indications that such an "idea of Palestine" existed at this time, among them the founding in Jaffa in 1911 of the influential newspaper *Filastin* (meaning Palestine), which in the decades to follow was instrumental in spreading this idea.

Before the twentieth century, as we have seen, Ottoman Palestine had been subject to a variety of administrative arrangements. The existing sense of Palestine as a country, however, was little affected by Ottoman administrative changes, in part because this sense was based on the long-standing and firmly held religious idea common to all three monotheistic faiths that Palestine within generally recognized borders was a holy land. The importance of this idea for shaping the nascent nationalist consciousness of Palestinians in the late nineteenth century has been well traced by the late Alexander Schölch, in his masterful study, *Palestine in Transformation: 1856–1882*.[56] As he points out, for Muslims this sense of Palestine as a country went back to the *"Fada'il al-Quds"* (or "merits of Jerusalem") literature, which described Jerusalem and holy sites and places of note throughout Palestine, including Hebron, Jericho, Bethlehem, Nablus, al-Ramla, Safad, Ascalon, Acre, Gaza, and Nazareth for pilgrims and visitors to Palestine, and for the devout and inquisitive elsewhere.[57] These place names suggest that a clear idea of the rough boundaries of Palestine, as a sort of sacred—if not yet a national—space, already existed in the minds of authors and readers of this Islamic devotional literature. A similar idea existed for Christians, as well as for Jews.

This sense of Palestine as a special and sacred space recurs in the historical record. In 1701, the French consul in Sidon paid a visit to Jerusalem, an innovation never before permitted by the Ottoman authorities. This produced a strong reaction from the local Muslim population, whose representatives met in the *Haram al-Sharif*. There, more than eighty Muslim leaders representing the city's main families, together with several local military officials and large numbers of the populace "including poor and rich," deliberated and signed a petition demanding that the Ottoman ruler, Sultan Mustafa II, revoke permission for such a visit.[58]

The terms this document uses are telling.[59] The petitioners remind the Sultan that Jerusalem, called *Bayt al-Maqdis* throughout the document, is the first of the two *qibla*'s, or directions of prayer, and the third of the Islamic holy places.[60] They salute the Sultan using his various titles, prominently including that of protector of Jerusalem (*hami Bayt al-Maqdis*). They state that the consul carried with him an imperial document issued in Istanbul which gave him permission to remain in Jerusalem, something that had never been allowed to a foreign diplomat under Islamic rule since the conquest of the city by 'Umar Ibn al-Khattab in the seventh century, or its recovery from the Crusaders by Saladin in the twelfth.[61]

Those present at the meeting argued to the qadi and the governor that the consul's visit to Jerusalem violated the conditions imposed by 'Umar Ibn al-Khattab and later caliphs, and that his behavior was a great evil, "especially since our city is the focus of attention of the infidels," suggesting considerable concern that the events of the Crusades could be repeated. The petition warned that "we fear that we will be occupied as a result of this, as happened repeatedly in past times," another clear reference to the Crusades. The qadi and the governor agreed with those present and requested the consul to leave, which he did. In conclusion, the petitioners asked that foreign consuls continue to be posted in Sidon, as had always been the case in the past, and requested that the Sultan prevent the French consul from remaining "in this holy land" (*al-diyar al-qudsiyya*).[62]

This petition recapitulates the idea of Palestine as a special and sacred land with Jerusalem as its focus. Such a notion is found throughout the *fada'il al-Quds* literature, and shows that the sense of Palestine as an entity, whose importance Schölch stresses for the late nineteenth century, was in fact clearly present at least two centuries earlier. A careful reading of the petition shows that this idea of Palestine's special importance is, at least in part, rooted in the heightened Islamic concern for Jerusalem and Palestine that followed the traumatic episode of the Crusades. This idea was widespread, and persisted for centuries thereafter. One of the most eminent eighteenth-century religious figures in Jerusalem, Shaykh Muhammad al-Khalili, in a *waqfiyya* document of 1726 establishing an endowment that survives to this day, warned that the transfer of waqf property to foreigners in Jerusalem constituted a danger to the future of the city, which must be built up and populated if Jerusalem were to be defended against the covetousness of these external enemies.[63]

Thus the assertion that Palestinian nationalism developed in response to the challenge of Zionism embodies a kernel of a much older truth: this modern nationalism was rooted in long-standing attitudes of concern for the city of Jerusalem and for Palestine as a sacred entity which were a response to perceived external threats. The incursions of the European powers and the Zionist movement in the late nineteenth century were only the most recent examples of this threat.

— Muslim

These themes are reiterated during one of the earliest cases of organized opposition to Zionist land purchase in Palestine: the al-Fula (or 'Afula) incident of 1910–1911. Many newspaper articles written in opposition to this sale stressed the special place of Palestine, for it was one of the biggest purchases up to that point, and one of the earliest to lead to the eviction of large numbers of Palestinian peasants. In two anonymous articles in the Damascus paper *al-Muqtabas*, later reprinted in newspapers in Haifa, Beirut, and elsewhere, much is made of the presence on this land of the "fortress" of al-Fula, supposedly built by Saladin, and shown in an illustration accompanying one article.[64]

This ruin, located at the center of the present-day Israeli settlement of Merhavia, was what remained of the Crusader castle of La Fève. Although not built by Saladin, it was captured by his forces in 1187, and is not far from Mount Tabor, a site dominated in the twelfth century by a still-extant Crusader fortress. The important thing was not whether the ruin had originally been built by Saladin: it was that these newspapers' readers believed that part of the heritage of Saladin, savior of Palestine from the Crusaders, was being sold off (by implication, to the "new Crusaders") without the Ottoman government lifting a finger.

The government's alleged dereliction of its duty to restrict Zionist colonization was the focus of speeches made in Parliament on May 16, 1911, by Ruhi al-Khalidi and Hafiz Sa'id, deputies for Jerusalem. They were joined in their critique by Shukri al-'Asali, the newly elected deputy of Damascus and former *qa'immaqam* (district governor) of the Nazareth district, who had fought the al-Fula land sale in his previous post (and was probably the author of the anonymous articles in *al-Muqtabas* about it). In his Parliamentary intervention, al-'Asali specifically mentioned the fortress, saying that it had been captured by Saladin from the Crusaders. But while this use of the Saladin/Crusader theme evoked the danger of Zionism in the Palestinian and Arab press,[65] it produced only derision in the Ottoman Parliament, where other speakers demanded that the three deputies stop wasting the chamber's time with nonexistent problems such as that of Zionism.[66]

In Palestine, by contrast, such ideas were seriously received, for al-Khalidi was reelected the following year in an election rigged by the government to rid itself of opposition in the Arab provinces, even though government loyalists described the debate on Zionism that he initiated as an anti-governmental ploy.[67] He retained his seat at a time when other critics of the government lost theirs, at least in part because in his speeches on Zionism before Parliament, which were widely reprinted in the local press, al-Khalidi appealed to ideas that resonated with his Palestinian constituents.[68] These long-standing ideas about Palestine as a holy land under threat from without, to which these men and others appealed, offered a focus of identity that was central to the local Palestinian patriotism which was the forerunner of modern Palestinian national consciousness.

This local patriotism could not yet be described as nation-state nationalism, for the simple reason that the prerequisites for modern nationalism did not yet exist, notably the means for a political leadership to mobilize large numbers of people and rapidly win them over to a single set of ideas, especially the idea that they partook of the same fate and were a single community. Yet the ideas represented in the 1701 petition were not restricted to the elite, as is attested by the mass nature of the meeting at which it was adopted. This continuing attachment to Palestine in the face of an external threat constituted one of the bases upon which modern Palestinian nationalism was built when the prerequisites for its emergence—the press, historical novels, modern communications, the spread of education, and mass politics—appeared in the early decades of the twentieth century.

Following the 1908 Ottoman revolution, all these factors began to function together. As before, Jerusalem was the focus of concern for Palestinians,[69] and the center of their responses to all external challenges. As in 1701, many Palestinians feared the territorial ambitions of external powers, albeit with somewhat more reason than their eighteenth-century predecessors. In the 1911 Parliamentary speeches just mentioned, expressions of this fear were prominent: al-Khalidi warned that "the aim of the Zionists . . . is the creation of a Israeli kingdom [*mamlaka isra'iliyya*] whose capital will be Jerusalem," while al-'Asali declared that the Zionists intended "to create a strong state, for after taking possession of the land they will expel the inhabitants either by force or through the use of wealth."[70]

In spite of these early warnings, the Palestinians have been less successful in defending their country in the face of the external and internal challenges they have faced in the twentieth century than were their ancestors in 1701. Although Palestinian leaders in recent years have had access to newspapers and rapid means of communication and organization, while being able to wield new ideological tools giving them more power than their predecessors to mobilize people, these instruments of modern politics were not yet fully developed for most of the twentieth century, nor had society changed rapidly enough to respond to them fully. Moreover, even though in many ways the Palestinians had become a unified people, in others they were still fragmented, and understood their history in terms of a multiplicity of narratives. Finally, the Palestinians now faced foes with considerably greater abilities to organize and mobilize than those they possessed.

To obtain a nuanced understanding of Palestinian history, we need to comprehend how and why success in meeting these challenges eluded the Palestinians, and why, in consequence, the Zionist movement triumphed at their expense. In order to do so, we must give proper weight to all the factors of unity and diversity that affect them, and all the different narratives that intertwine to make up Palestinian identity. Our objective should be scholarship that respects the specificity of the Palestinian experience without sacrificing the sophistication derived from an appreciation of how all these disparate narratives interact. This may help prevent the study of Palestinian history from sinking to the level of shameless chauvinistic self-glorification prevalent in much nationalist-influenced Middle Eastern historiography, whereby the writing of much Arab, Turkish, Iranian and Israeli history has yielded to ideological distortion, and a blindness to the different strands that comprise the current reality of each modern nation-state in the region.

In the Arab world what has most often been lacking—partly as a result of the influence of early Arab nationalist historiography—is an appreciation of the Ottoman and Islamic heritage in the genesis of existing Arab nation-states. This deficiency is frequently combined with an overemphasis on even the most tenuous Arab connections, a tendency to "Arabize" much Islamic and pre-Islamic history, and an overemphasis on colonial influences. Turkish historiography has similarly slighted the Ottoman roots of the modern republic, as well as the Islamic and non-Turkish contributions to the Ottoman heritage, while rewriting earlier history in light of modern Turkish nationalist canons. Much Iranian historiography has minimized the influence of either non-Iranian or non-Islamic elements in Iranian history, while over-stressing that of either Iranian or Islamic factors (the Islamic revolution of 1979 is the demarcation line between these contradictory trends). Israeli historiography and archaeology have often looked obsessively for evidence of a Jewish presence in Palestine, the majority of whose population for millennia were non-Jews, while neglecting elements of the larger pattern, except as background to Jewish history.[71]

The possible pitfalls for the study of Palestinian identity include similar obsessions with the larger framework into which the Palestinian case fits, particularly the Arab or Islamic contexts. There is also often a tendency to see an essential Palestinian identity going well back in time, rather than the complex, contingent and relatively recent reality of Palestinian identity, and to stress factors of unity at the expense of those tending toward fragmentation or diversity in Palestinian society and politics. Another unique pitfall is the tendency to focus on the external reasons for the failure of the Palestinian people to achieve self-determination, to the exclusion of internal ones. The alignment between Britain and Zionism for thirty years of the twentieth century, and that between the United States and Israel since then, has unquestionably engendered a daunting set of external challenges. But these facts cannot absolve students of Palestinian history from asking whether the Palestinians could not have improved their chances to realize their national project at certain critical junctures, and if they could have, what structural or other reasons prevented them from doing so.

Focusing on Palestinian social dynamics, I have suggested answers to these questions, and while there are other possible avenues of investigation, this would seem to be a fruitful one. It is hard for historians who are part of a society still suffering from the direct effects of such a series of historic failures to look self-critically at that society's fissures and flaws, while the consequences of not doing so are obvious. Much of the historical writing on this subject has been done by Israelis and others who harbor little apparent sympathy for their subject. It is necessary for those with empathy, as well as that unique access to and understanding of sources that often go with it, to address such questions rigorously. Without rigor, the writing of Palestinian history risks being tainted by the same chauvinism and disguised emotionalism that have already affected the writing of much other modern Middle Eastern history. These factors are partly responsible for leaving the Middle East field behind others, mired in naked partisanship, engaged in provincial debates of little interest to others, and cut off from trends that affect the wider historical community. Although the study of Palestinian identity is far from a *tabula rasa*, perhaps it is not too late to avoid these pitfalls. In the following chapters we shall examine the genesis of this identity with these warnings in mind.

CHAPTER 3

Cultural Life and Identity in Late Ottoman Palestine: The Place of Jerusalem

I

Given its religious importance to Muslims, Christians, and Jews, it is easy to see why Jerusalem should have been a touchstone of identity for all the inhabitants of Palestine in the modern era as in the past. This was true although the ways in which this identity was framed and understood, and its relationship to Jerusalem, changed over time, and did so especially rapidly in the nineteenth and twentieth centuries. Jerusalem was also important to the inhabitants of Palestine as an administrative center, all the more so after 1874, when it became the capital of an independent *sanjaq*, which sent one deputy to the parliaments of 1877–78, and three to those of 1908–1918. But Jerusalem was also significant as a center of education, the press and other aspects of intellectual and cultural life. This became even more the case following the restoration of the Ottoman Constitution in 1908, which resulted in a greater degree of public and political freedom than ever before.

Although Jerusalem was important as the capital of the district of southern Palestine, its importance extended far beyond that. Its schools, newspapers, clubs, and political figures had an impact throughout

Palestine, even before the country's British mandate boundaries were established after World War I. This was partly a function of the religious importance of the city, and of the sense we have already examined of Palestine as a unit—albeit in religious terms, as a holy land, rather than in political terms at the outset. But it also drew on the fact that the city was a focus of the interests, aspirations and designs of foreign powers, and of their diplomats, spies, tourists, and businessmen, so that both the Ottoman authorities and the local inhabitants considered Palestine in general and Jerusalem in particular to be under threat from without.

Notwithstanding its undoubted local, regional, and international prominence, Jerusalem has, in the past century or so, not been the first city in Palestine in terms of population and economic importance. Although it was probably the biggest city in Palestine in 1800 and seems to have retained that position until some time in the first half of the twentieth century (when the Jaffa-Tel Aviv urban area overtook it), we have seen that by the eve of World War I, the port cities of Jaffa and Haifa were growing much faster, in keeping with the patterns of urban growth throughout *bilad al-sham* (the Arabic term for greater Syria, or the lands between the eastern Mediterranean littoral and the desert).[1] Increased trade with Europe, the building of new railways for which these ports were terminals, and the consequent stimulation of economic activity in their immediate hinterland, all contributed to their growth, and made them the commercial centers of the country.[2] By 1931, according to the second British census of Palestine's population, the Jaffa-Tel Aviv urban area had a larger population than Jerusalem,[3] and as already noted, both Jaffa and Haifa had a larger Arab population than Jerusalem by the end of the mandate period.

While this chapter will focus on cultural and intellectual trends in Jerusalem because of their impact throughout Palestine, it is important nevertheless to recognize that other centers in the country, notably the two main coastal ports, Jaffa and Haifa, but also Nablus, Hebron, Nazareth, and Gaza among others, were important foci of Palestinian cultural and intellectual life, as well as being political, administrative and economic centers.[4] Beshara Doumani indeed reminds us that during most of the nineteenth century, "Nablus was Palestine's principal trade and manufacturing center."[5] Beyond our focus on Jerusalem, we will thus have occasion in this chapter to refer to cultural developments in many of these other cities, particularly Jaffa and Haifa, whose dynamism in so many spheres significantly affected the shaping of Palestinian identity.

There was dynamism and change in Jerusalem as well, however. During the final half century of Ottoman rule in Jerusalem, as elsewhere in the region, a momentous shift took place from a long-standing and stable Islamic system of justice and education, and the traditional intellectual pursuits and ways of thought that went with this system, to Western-based forms in all these domains. In Palestine, this change had its biggest effect in Jerusalem, which had for centuries been the apex of the region's judicial system, and an educational center drawing scholars from the entire Islamic world. Before this shift took place, the Islamic religious court in Jerusalem, *al-mahkama al-shar'iyya*, near the *Haram al-Sharif*, had been the focus of legal matters, and the venue for mediating many of the most important social, economic and political affairs of Jerusalem and the surrounding districts. At the same time, the religious schools, the *madrasas* and *kuttabs*, surrounding the *Haram al-Sharif* were the venues where those among the city's Muslim population with access to education received their basic and higher learning. These same institutions were also the scene of the initial stages of training for a career within the Islamic legal, educational, and administrative system which prevailed throughout the Ottoman Empire and beyond. In the shari'a court, as in the schools and mosques, learned members of a number of prominent urban families held positions of varying prestige, power, and influence, often handing them down from father to son. The next chapter looks at examples of such personal trajectories.

Around the middle of the nineteenth century, the locus of power began to shift dramatically in Jerusalem and other provincial centers throughout the Ottoman Empire. New courts, administering laws based partly on Western models and staffed by personnel trained in Istanbul, were set up, and took over many of the legal tasks of the shari'a courts, which were gradually restricted to matters of personal status and inheritance. Similarly, secular schools that were open in principle to the entire population were rapidly introduced, and became the path to positions in the new, European-style bureaucracy of the Ottoman state. As a result of these trends, within a few decades the venue for local politics, in Jerusalem and elsewhere, shifted from the courts, schools, and religious institutions the old local elites had always dominated to new arenas governed by a completely different set of rules. Equally important, the new dispensation decisively tipped the balance between the central government and local centers of power in favor of the former. In consequence, the influence of formerly semiautonomous local elites in cities like Jerusalem rapidly became dependent on their relationship with the central authorities.[6]

Given the material and other resources of these notable families, and their experience in adjusting to the realities of power over the centuries, it should not be surprising that they accommodated rapidly to this shift from a system which had long been in place and from which they had benefited substantially, to a new one, and in doing so largely managed to preserve their standing and influence. Within a generation, most of the same families who had for centuries produced the judges, teachers, officials, and preachers who dominated the old system had secured privileged access to the modern educational institutions which were the path to positions in the new legal, administrative, educational, and political order. Although there they had to compete with others from more humble backgrounds trained like them in the new secular schools, or in the growing number of new schools run by western missionaries, they still retained many of their advantages, as we shall see in the next chapter.

This chapter will trace the changes in the cultural and intellectual life of Jerusalem and other centers in Palestine that resulted from these new circumstances, stressing both the important elements of continuity with the traditional order, and the rapid incorporation of components of the new one. Among the issues it will examine is how an elite whose prestige and position had for centuries been a function of the centrality of religion in public life reacted to the late-nineteenth-century decline in the importance of religion as an organizing principle of government. The chapter will also explore the extent to which cultural and intellectual life in Jerusalem—and by extension in the rest of Palestine—at the end of the Ottoman era was in tune with similar developments elsewhere in the Islamic world, particularly in neighboring Arab regions. It will conclude by assessing how these developments occurring within a relatively restricted circle of the elite in Jerusalem and other centers affected the broader populace in the cities and towns and in the countryside, and thus how these changes contributed to the shaping of identity in Palestine in the late Ottoman period and afterward.

II

During the nearly eight decades between the beginning of the *Tanzimat* reforms in the Ottoman Empire and the end of World War I, a profound alteration took place in the situation in the Arab provinces.[7] This was a function of momentous transformations in the structure and scope of government which resulted from the legal provisions of the *Tanzimat*, from successful efforts to strengthen the Ottoman central government, and from the intensive state-building activities of Sultan 'Abd al-Hamid II (1876–1909). These changes were both the culmination of a long-standing drive from within to reform and modernize the Ottoman state, and a response to external pressures which increased as the involvement of the European powers in the Middle East grew apace. We have seen that among the spheres most affected by these sweeping changes were law and education. Both were areas where Arab notables had traditionally held a certain advantage in the Ottoman system (as they had under the Mamelukes and Ayyubids before that), largely because of their command of the Arabic language. Arabic was naturally instrumental in both the mastery of all the branches of the shari'a, and in education, which before the nineteenth-century reforms was based almost entirely on religion.

Under the rapidly evolving new dispensation of the *Tanzimat*, education was to a large degree secularized and brought under control of the government, which established a network of new public schools throughout the country, starting with provincial capitals and gradually expanding the system. These schools were modeled in some ways on the foreign missionary institutions whose attractiveness to young students was feared by Ottoman reformers. Unlike these foreign schools, however, the state public schools taught most subjects in Turkish, and laid stress on Ottoman patriotism.[8] Many of the numerous remaining private Muslim religious schools followed the lead of government, Western missionary, and private schools in introducing modern methods and teaching foreign languages and other nontraditional subjects, all of this alongside their standard religious curriculum.

As has already been mentioned, Ottoman legal institutions were also transformed during this period, and a new network of law courts was established to administer the growing system of secular, western-influenced laws. This led to the gradual circumscription of the role of the shari'a courts, which had governed virtually all aspects of dispute-resolution in traditional Islamic societies (and usually also played a much broader role). Although they retained their exclusive control over inheritance and personal status matters such as marriage, divorce, and child-custody, and remained important for the registration and adjudication of many contracts, in other spheres the power of the shari'a courts fell away. This was particularly true as regards criminal law, much of civil law, and "political cases," all of which were increasingly dealt with in the new state courts on the basis of the newly drawn up legal code, the *Mecelle*, which although inspired by the shari'a, represented a codification of Ottoman law on European lines.[9] Consequently, the shari'a courts retained a role, but it became predominantly a local and parochial one. Increasingly, the new state courts became the locus of influence and prestige in the Ottoman legal system.

Alongside these developments, the rest of the state bureaucracy grew in size and changed radically in composition, absorbing more personnel, notably the many graduates of the expanded and modernized educational system. During the nineteenth century, the creation of a more powerful, pervasive, and thoroughly centralized administrative system, and of an expanded and strengthened army, both benefiting from the greatly improved communications made possible by the introduction of the railway, the steamship, and the telegraph, enabled the central government to extend its authority over broader areas of Ottoman society. These changes enabled the state in addition to exert much firmer control over the farflung provinces, many of which had long enjoyed a great degree of autonomy.

The impact of these measures on the Arab provinces and other remote areas of the Empire during the latter half of the nineteenth century was little short of revolutionary. Earlier, many desert, mountainous, and other outlying districts had been beyond the effective control of the Ottoman government, with such law and order as existed in the hands of local tribal, sectarian, and feudal leaders. Even in such provincial capitals as Damascus, Aleppo, Mosul and Baghdad, where the central government had always retained a significant presence, as well as smaller centers like Jerusalem, Nablus, and Hama, local notables had enjoyed a dominating position in urban society, with their influence often barely mediated by the representatives of the central government. As a result, their freedom of action was great, sometimes shading into overt insubordination, in which they were often joined by military officers and provincial officials.[10]

However, the new capabilities the development of modern state structures put at the disposal of the Ottoman central authorities during the nineteenth century changed all of this. And with these profound changes in power relationships came changes in ways of thought and career patterns. Under the old Ottoman order, which privileged religious learning, Arab notables were in many cases at the cutting edge of scholarship, and had great prestige because of their mastery of the traditional Islamic sciences. Arabs often reached the highest levels of the Ottoman judicial bureaucracy, serving in positions such as *Shaykh al-Islam* and *Kadiasker*, which were the pinnacles of achievement within the Ottoman religious bureaucracy.[11] Centers of Islamic learning such as Cairo, Damascus, and Jerusalem were visited by scholars from all over the Islamic world in search of great libraries, respected teachers, and the prestigious *ijaza*'s, or diplomas, which the latter could confirm on worthy students.

After the *Tanzimat*, these intellectual pursuits continued, and many Arab provincial notables with an Islamic education continued to enter the Ottoman religious bureaucracy and to rise within it. However, this bureaucracy rapidly ceased to be a locus of power, and Islamic learning gradually ceased to confer prestige and status in society as it once had. Instead members of the educated classes increasingly saw the Western-based study of Islam as the source of true scholarship about Islamic religion and culture. Great prestige came to attach as well to disciplines that had been revolutionized by Western methods in the sciences and mathematics, the social sciences and the humanities, all of which were accessible only in foreign languages, or in translation from these languages into Turkish and Arabic. This in itself was a major change: heretofore, throughout Islamic history, Arabic had been the medium of scholarly interaction in many fields of intellectual endeavor in the Islamic world, notably religion and law, with Persian paramount in literature and belles-lettres, and Turkish in government and military affairs. Suddenly, a new situation obtained; no longer were these three languages of classical Islamic learning those in which the most important intellectual issues of the day were being pursued, but rather French, English, and German. However, not all perceived this immediately.

This situation on the intellectual plane of course changed as the balance of power between the Ottoman Empire and the European states changed, and as the latter encroached ever more aggressively on the Ottoman dominions in the eighteenth and nineteenth centuries. Previously, it had been possible for Arab and other Ottoman notables to look down on Europeans, and to assume that while the latter may have benefited from certain material advances, on the cultural plane they remained inferior objects of contempt. Such an outlook on things Western was rooted in the belief that Islam was the last and most complete of the revealed religions. An example of this traditional attitude can be found in the message sent by the governor of Gaza to the qadi, the military commanders and the notables of Jerusalem, warning them that Napoleon's army had reached the outskirts of Palestine in January

1799. The language used to describe the French is revealing. They are called: "*kuffar al-faransa al-mala'in, damarrahum Allah ajma'in*" [the cursed French infidels, may God destroy them all].[12]

This attitude was necessarily modified as the nineteenth century wore on, with Europe's achievement of a decisive hegemony over the Ottoman Empire, and the attendant shifts in intellectual ascendancy. As members of notable families acquired Western educations or were trained in Western-influenced state, missionary, and private schools, they came to value Western intellectual traditions, which in turn deeply informed the growing number of Arabic- and Turkish-language newspapers and periodicals published in the Ottoman Empire and outside it in the latter decades of the nineteenth century.

The impact of all of these shifts on the plane of culture can be seen clearly in Jerusalem. Thus, a member of one Jerusalem notable family, Yusuf Diya' al-Khalidi, lamented in the conclusion to his 1880 edition of the verse of the pre-Islamic *jahili* poet Labid ibn Rabi'a that not one Arab scholar answered an appeal for help in collecting the poetry of Labid, which he had published in the leading Arabic-language journals of the time, *al-Jawa'ib, al-Jinan,* and *Hadiqat al-Akhbar*.[13] By contrast, he notes, foreign scholars of Oriental languages had been generous in providing him with material on Labid. Yusuf Diya' al-Khalidi concludes with the hope that the Arabs would soon regain their former glory, indicating a clear sense of Arab identity on the part of the author. Nevertheless, it is clear that for him and for many of his contemporaries, one would now have to look toward Europe and European science for models of true scholarship, even in the project so central to early Arabism of uncovering and reinterpreting the linguistic and literary roots of Arab culture.

The continuity between more traditional and the newer, European-style scholarship can be seen from an examination of a unique source for understanding cultural life during this period: the holdings of family libraries in Jerusalem. The most important of these in Jerusalem, and the most significant surviving collections of such materials *in situ* in Palestine, include the al-Aqsa Library, *al-Maktaba al-Khalidiyya* and *al-Maktaba al-Budayriyya*. The former, which is the largest, includes three main collections brought together relatively recently: that of the long-established *Dar Kutub al-Masjid al-Aqsa*, which originated in the manuscript repository of the al-Aqsa Mosque, and which included a valuable collection of old Qur'ans now kept in the adjacent Islamic Museum; part of the library of the renowned eighteenth century scholar, al-Shaykh

Muhammad al-Khalili, who was mentioned in the previous chapter; and part of the library of al-Shaykh Khalil al-Khalidi (1863–1941).

Established in 1899 by Hajj Raghib al-Khalidi, but based on family holdings of manuscripts and books that went back for many generations, *al-Maktaba al-Khalidiyya* was intended to be open to the public, with the aim of encouraging the spread of learning, and reviving interest in the classics of Islamic learning, as well as modern subjects. Although much smaller, in this respect it resembled the Zahiriyya Library in Damascus, whose founder, the prominent *salafi* Shaykh Tahir al-Jaza'iri, was a collaborator with Hajj Raghib in organizing the Khalidi Library during his period of service as curator of the libraries of the *vilayet* of Damascus. In this capacity, al-Jaza'iri helped to establish libraries both inside the *vilayet*—in Damascus, Homs, and Hama—and outside it, in Jerusalem and Tripoli.[14]

As an example of the continuation of the older forms of Islamic scholarship, published catalogues of the Al-Aqsa Library and the *Budayriyya* show the continued copying of religious, historical, and literary manuscripts into the nineteenth and even the early twentieth century, well after the time when printed books—primarily editions of the Islamic classics—were first being purchased by the custodians of these institutions. It is clear from an examination of the catalogues of these libraries that traditional Islamic scholarly pursuits still retained at least some of their vitality.[15] The manuscripts in *al-Maktaba al-Budayriyya*, which is located adjacent to the Haram al-Sharif, were mainly collected by Shaykh Muhammad ibn Budayr ibn Hubaysh (d. 1220/1805), and only a few were added after his death. As with the al-Aqsa Library, however, many of these additions are manuscripts copied in the late nineteenth and early twentieth centuries.[16] Similar results are emerging from the ongoing cataloging of the more than 1,200 manuscripts of *al-Maktaba al-Khalidiyya*, which shows both the continued copying of earlier manuscripts and the production of new religious and other texts in manuscript form late into the nineteenth century.[17]

Also revealing in this context is the appearance of printed editions of classic Islamic texts in these libraries. An examination of the contents of *al-Maktaba al-Khalidiyya* shows that even while the copying and collection of manuscripts continued, the members of the family whose personal libraries went to make up this collection were also buying copies of the printed texts of the major works of the traditional Islamic sciences.[18] In the field of history, for example, the oldest printed edition in this collection is a single copy of the 1274/1857 Cairo edition of Ibn Khaldun's *al-Muqaddima.*[19] More significantly, the library contains multiple copies of many of the classical Islamic historical texts.[20]

The significance of the existence of multiple copies of these earliest locally printed editions of major Islamic historical works is clear: several members of the al-Khalidi family considered it important to obtain printed versions of works of which they in many cases owned manuscript copies, in order to benefit from the relatively modern comparative scholarship these new editions represented. This is a typical example of the shift in the intellectual sphere which this period witnessed. Even as some members of this family continued to pursue the traditional religious sciences (the Library contains numerous multiple copies of printed editions of basic reference works in the religious sciences by authors and compilers such as al-Bukhari, Muslim, Qastalani, and al-Tabari, which constitute a considerably larger proportion of its total holdings than the historical works) others were becoming interested in history and other subjects which, although traditional in some respects, were increasingly influenced by Western scholarship and methodologies. This can be seen not only from the large number of standard Islamic history works in new editions, but also from the many works of contemporary European Orientalist scholars in the Library, ranging from Renan, Dozy, Carra de Vaux, Muir, and de Goeje, to E. G. Browne, Margoliouth, E. J. W. Gibb and Massignon.[21]

Perhaps linked to this renewed interest in Islamic history, whether based on traditional sources or more recent European scholarship, was the sympathy of many ulama' of this era for the *salafi* tendency, with its concern for the revival of Islam, a return to the original sources of religion, and the modernization of Islamic societies.[22] All of these interests are apparent in the holdings of printed books, periodicals, and pamphlets in the Khalidi Library. We have already noted that one of the most important leaders of the *salafi* movement in Syria, al-Shaykh Tahir al-Jaza'iri, played an instrumental role in helping to found *al-Maktaba al-Khalidiyya,* and indeed he was present at its formal opening, as is evidenced by a contemporary photograph.[23] Several of al-Jaza'iri's books, some in multiple copies, are found in the Library, together with many examples of the writings of other *salafis* such as al-Sayyid Rashid Rida.[24]

Numerous other Islamic reformers were also close to al-Khalidi family members whose collections went into the Library, notably Muhammad 'Abdu, one of whose autographed works is in the collection,[25] and al-Sayyid Jamal al-Din al-Afghani, whose photo, with a warm autograph to his close friend Yusuf Diya' al-Khalidi, is in the Library collection.[26] Yusuf

Diya's brother, al-Shaykh Yasin, was also a friend of the leading Tripoli *salafi* shaykh and reformer, Husayn al-Jisr, founder of *al-Madrasa al-Wataniyya* in Tripoli, whom Yasin met when he was qadi there. Several of al-Jisr's books are in the Library, some of them in multiple copies.[27]

Linked to this *salafi* tendency was a manifest interest in the latest writings of European positivist authors, especially the popularizers among them. One of those who seems to have particularly caught the fancy of the generation that came to maturity in the late Ottoman period was the prolific French writer, Dr. Gustave Le Bon. His books on the development of civilizations, the evolution of peoples, and political psychology found a wide audience in the Middle East, and were translated into Arabic by such leading intellectual figures as Taha Husayn, Ahmad Fathi Zaghlul Pasha, and 'Abd al-Ghani al-'Uraisi, and into Turkish by Abdullah Cevdet. It is therefore not surprising to find six of Le Bon's works in the Khalidi Library, five in translation and one a lavishly bound French-language volume, *La Civilisation des Arabes*.[28] Nor is it surprising to find new bookstores opening in Jerusalem and Jaffa at the end of the Ottoman period, catering to the demand for foreign books, periodicals, and other works in Arabic and foreign languages.[29]

Notwithstanding this evidence of interest in some kinds of modern scholarship, there were clearly gaps in many fields in the cultural life of Jerusalem. The editor of a Jerusalem newspaper, Sa'id Jarallah, complained bitterly in 1912 that although "the country of Palestine" ("*al-qutr al-filastini*"[30]) had a glorious past and deserved to have its history recorded, "in our libraries we find no good history." "The land of Palestine" ("*ard Filastin*"), he went on, was important because it was where Israelite civilization ("*al-madaniyya al-isra'iliyya*") existed, where Christianity started, and where the Crusades were fought; it was the first qibla, or direction of prayer, for the Muslims, even before Mecca, and it was the cherished objective of the Arab conquerors in the days of the fourth caliph, 'Umar. And yet, he complained, there exists no Arabic-language text on the history of Palestine except translations of European texts, and dated works like *al-Uns al-Jalil* and the travel account of 'Abd al-Ghani al-Nabulsi. In conclusion, the author called on Arab scholars to fill this gap, as the writing of history will help to civilize the country, move forward its affairs, and raise up its people, who are ignorant of Palestine's virtues, although others appreciated them.[31]

We can read between the lines of this harsh critique some of the public and patriotic purposes which the founders of libraries and other cultural and educational institutions in this period had in mind. Indeed, al-Hajj Raghib al-Khalidi, in his announcement of the founding of the Khalidi Library in 1900, began by stressing the linkage between libraries and culture going back to the era of the Greeks and the early Islamic era, for when "civilization and culture reached the Arabs, they founded libraries and schools." He affirmed that the spread of knowledge was the basis of progress and prosperity, adding that the Europeans had learned this from the Arabs. This had brought them to their present state of "wealth, happiness and greed for what belongs to other lands," continued al-Hajj Raghib al-Khalidi, sounding the same note of alarm about European expansion which we saw expressed as early as 1701 in the petition discussed in the previous chapter. He then lamented the deterioration of the great libraries that had been established in Jerusalem in the past, and stressed that he meant the Library he was founding to be an asset to "*al-diyar al-maqdisiyya*" [meaning here the Jerusalem region, and by implication the holy land], "for whatever we do, it will be hard to match what exists in the way of foreign institutions in these lands."[32]

The Khalidi Library was intended, in other words, to help restore the Arabs to prosperity by fostering knowledge, and to enable them to match the powerful cultural establishments created by foreign powers all over the region. Twelve years later, Sa'id Jarallah called for the Palestinians to write their own history, and not to depend on the narratives of others, since without an appreciation of history, it was impossible to achieve progress, or for the country's inhabitants to appreciate and therefore defend "the land of Palestine," which others coveted. For both Jarallah and al-Hajj Raghib al-Khalidi, the development of culture, whether via encouraging the indigenous writing of history or the founding of libraries, was clearly an important element in the preservation of their country, their culture, and by extension their identity, against the external dangers that threatened them.

III

Whatever the importance of such libraries and the activities that went on in them, books and scholarship were restricted to a very limited segment of Palestinian society, the vast majority of whose members were illiterate.[33] However, a shift was then underway from this well-established traditional intellectual pattern affecting only a tiny elite to a new one involving larger numbers of people and influenced by European models. The crucial elements in this shift were the development of new social formations, classes, and professional groups, and the impact of major new institutions established after the middle of the century.[34]

Central among these processes in their effect on society were the expansion of the educational system and the growth of the government bureaucracy. The traditional institutions of Ottoman government, education, and justice had been central elements in urban society in Jerusalem and other centers throughout the first three centuries of Ottoman rule. Not surprisingly, therefore, the new schools, courts, and government offices established during the *Tanzimat* period were crucial instruments in the transformation of society in terms of the formation of new social strata, professionalization along Western lines, and familiarization of large segments of society with the everyday routines of the modern, Western world.

This was true throughout the cities of *bilad al-Sham*, but it was particularly the case in Jerusalem, which was a governmental and educational center, and where those other vital engines of change, commerce, and industry, did not grow as fast as in the coastal ports. At the same time, the large numbers of tourists and pilgrims it attracted (more than 20,000 per year on average at the turn of the twentieth century) provided Jerusalem with a significant source of income and also with constant external stimuli. Their impact on the mores, values, and attitudes of Jerusalemites had both positive and negative aspects.[35]

We have already noted that the new schools founded to teach foreign languages and modern science and mathematics, as well as some traditional subjects, were particularly important in stimulating change, partly because they had an influence far beyond the narrow bounds of the existing traditional elite. Unlike the new courts and administrative institutions, which were in large measure initially filled with personnel brought in from the outside and followed a fixed imperial pattern, the new schools were mainly staffed with local teachers, frequently differed from one locality to another in nature and organization, and were often established as a result of local initiatives. This was not initially true of missionary schools, although they did eventually have local as well as foreign teachers, but it was the case for state schools and for the many private schools that were set up all over the Arab provinces in response to the desire for access to education of those Muslim and Greek Orthodox families wary of the mainly Protestant and Catholic missionary schools, and whose needs could not be met either by existing religious schools or by the rapid expansion of the state system.[36]

The need for such schools can be seen from figures provided in the Ottoman *Salnameh* [yearbook] for 1288/1871 for the vilayet of Syria, which at this time included all of Palestine. For a Muslim population of Jerusalem listed as 1,025 households, there were seven schools with 341 students, while the Christian and Jewish populations of 738 and 630 households respectively had between them nineteen schools with a total of 1,242 students.[37] There was thus nearly one school place per household for non-Muslims, and only one school place for approximately every three Muslim households. If one assumes similar family sizes per household— an arbitrarily chosen four children per household, for example, half of them of school age—it follows that only about one in seven of the approximately 2,000 school-age Muslim children in Jerusalem would have had access to schools, while nearly half of the more than 2,500 non-Muslim children of school age would have had such access. Moreover, this was the situation in the largest urban center in the country: it was undoubtedly far better than that in other cities and towns, not to speak of the villages.

According to another later source, around the turn of the century there were thirty-five local Christian and missionary schools in Jerusalem with more than 2,200 students and more than 150 teachers.[38] Although these statistics are not comparable with the preceding ones, and we have no analogous figures for private Muslim and state schools, several things are clear from this juxtaposition and from such other educational statistics as are available for this period. One is that educational opportunities had expanded greatly in Jerusalem for Christians and others willing to avail themselves of Christian and missionary schools. Another is that in the country as a whole things had improved somewhat by 1914, although only by comparison with the abysmal earlier situation.

According to the standard work on Arab education in mandatory Palestine, by A. L. Tibawi, by 1914 the Ottoman government had established 95 elementary and three secondary public schools throughout Palestine, with a total of 234 teachers and 8,248 pupils, 1,480 of them girls. The secondary schools were located in Jerusalem, Nablus, and Acre. At that time, there were additionally 379 private Muslim schools with 417 teachers and 8,705 pupils (only 131 of whom were girls).[39] State schools and private Muslim schools combined thus provided under 17,000 places for a total Arab school age population of about 72,000 in 1914. No pre-1914 figures are available for Christian missionary and private schools in Palestine (although one source puts the number of children in French and Russian schools throughout greater Syria including Palestine in 1914 at nearly 80,000[40]), but we can obtain an idea of the scale of such schools from the fact that in the 1920–21 academic year they had nearly 12,000 students.[41]

Although it is clear from these statistics that the Ottoman state established many schools in the decades leading up to 1914 (and indeed founded a higher secondary, or *sultani*, school in Jerusalem during World War I),[42] they also show that there were not enough places in these institutions, or in schools run by Muslim and Christian bodies, to meet the demand for education.[43] A number of private schools were eventually set up in Jerusalem and elsewhere to help meet this deficiency. One of them was *Rawdat al-Ma'arif al-Wataniyya al-'Uthmaniyya al-Islamiyya* (or the National Ottoman Islamic School), founded in 1324/1906.[44] It was typical of such schools in a number of respects, not only in having been founded by a cleric, Shaykh Muhammad al-Salih, but also in having a number of young men with Western educations from well-known families as teachers of modern subjects: thus we find the names al-'Alami, Dajani, al-Husayni, and Nuseiba among the teachers, as well as four foreign women who taught languages. The school was also typical in having leading notables as members of its Board of Directors, in this case the Mufti, Muhammad Kamil Effendi al-Husayni, and the Deputy for the city, Sa'id Bey al-Husayni.

There can be little doubt that this school played the same role in shaping the self-view of its students as did other similar private schools established at about the same time in Beirut, Tripoli, and Damascus by similar notables.[45] Tibawi states that *Rawdat al-Ma'arif* may have been "the earliest Muslim private school to develop a modern curriculum."[46] The name of the school indicates the different cultural tendencies the school embodied: patriotic, Ottoman and Islamic. In this too it was characteristic of many such schools. Muhammad al-Shanti, the Palestinian editor of the Cairo newspaper *al-Iqdam*, visited *Rawdat al-Ma'arif* as part of a trip to report on public and private schools (and the courts) in Palestine in 1914, and came away positively impressed by it.[47] The school, he noted in a long article on the educational and judicial systems in Palestine, had 350 day students, 40 boarders, and 13 teachers, and offered scholarships to 72 of its students. He predicted that this school, where the students were being taught that Zionism was a danger to their country, would be the "foundation stone to build the future of Palestine, and the premier cultural weapon to fight foreign schools and Zionist colonialism."[48] Clearly, the students in *Rawdat al-Ma'arif* were being exposed to ideas that were growing in influence in Palestinian society, and that helped to shape their sense of community and their patriotism.

Another school set up along similar modern lines was *al-Madrasa al-Dusturiyya* (the Constitutional School), founded in 1909 by the noted Jerusalem writer, journalist, and educator Khalil al-Sakakini, a passionate nationalist who enjoyed great public esteem.[49] Like *Rawdat al-Ma'arif,* al-Sakakini's school was intended to provide students with an education in the sciences, mathematics, and foreign languages, as well as teaching them a love of the Arabic language and Arab history. In this, it was characteristic of the private educational institutions of the era in inculcating an Arabist consciousness through encouraging love of the national language and literature, and through reimagining what had heretofore been taught as Islamic history as Arab history. Unlike other schools, both al-Sakakini's collaborators in the project and the students at *al-Madrasa al-Dusturiyya* were from different religious and social backgrounds. In his own words, "This was the first time in the history of our country that the sons of the different faiths meet in one school on one bench."[50] Here too can be seen the lineaments of the nationalist project, which attempted to elide, ignore, or resolve religious differences, or to bury them in a shared vision of an other. Among those who participated with al-Sakakini in the organization and management of the school, which thrived until the outbreak of World I forced its closing, were Muslims and Christians, including 'Ali Jarallah, Jamil al-Khalidi (who was also a newspaper editor), and Eftim Mushabbak, all active young educators from Jerusalem.[51]

A similar response to the growing demands of the population of Jerusalem for more and better education can be seen in the activities of Christian private and missionary schools. Perhaps the best-known such schools in Jerusalem were St. George's School, founded in 1899 by the Jerusalem and East Mission under the direct control of the Anglican Bishop of Jerusalem,[52] and the French Jesuit-run College des Frères, founded in 1875. Typical of the growth of these institutions was the expansion and transformation of the school of the Church Missionary Society (CMS) in 1904 from a free school established about 30 years earlier to teach religion and train missionaries, into a fee-paying preparatory school designed to feed students into the Syrian Protestant College in Beirut (later renamed the American University of Beirut), the most prestigious of the Protestant missionary institutions in the Arab world.

The pamphlet that announces these changes in the structure and syllabus of the CMS school stresses in its introduction that circumstances had changed in the country: "These days in the eyes of the citizens knowledge is given greater importance and its benefits are more appreciated. As a result, parents of every class are more eager to educate their children in the most modern ways, and want the doors to be opened for them to learn foreign languages and science . . ."[53] This is a clear expression of the strong demand for education that characterized many sectors of the population of Palestine, and that was to continue through the British Mandate period, when the rural population would pay to finance the building of schools in their own villages.[54]

Education was clearly a realm where there was profound ferment, growth, and change in the decades leading up to the end of Ottoman rule over Palestine, and afterwards. The impetus for these processes was both external and internal. On the external front, the Ottoman state and foreign powers were engaged in a silent but deadly battle for the minds of future generations. Although foreign missionary education was directed in some measure at the souls of the children affected, there was little doubt either on the part of the European governments, which financially subsidized and/or diplomatically supported such education, or on that of the Ottoman authorities, that questions of allegiance, influence, and ultimately power were also at stake. This could be seen most strikingly in the willingness of the aggressively secular and anti-clerical French Third Republic—which sought to limit the spread of Church-controlled schools inside France—to support religious education outside of France, where it was clear that such schools served as a potent instrument for the extension of French national influence abroad. And in this competition for young hearts and minds in the pre-World War I era, there was nowhere in Palestine, and few places in the Middle East, where the issue was more fiercely joined than in Jerusalem. This was at least in part because Jerusalem was unique as the focus of Western religious interest in the region, as a major consular, pilgrimage and tourist center, and as a symbolic site of importance in registering the competing influence of the great powers.

On the internal front, the improvement of Muslim schools, the founding of other private schools, the rapid expansion of the state system, and the high degree of acceptance of missionary education, increasingly even by Muslims, were a function of the demand from within Palestinian society for more and better educational opportunities for the younger generation. The citation from the CMS pamphlet above indicates that the local population fully recognized the vital importance of education. Another example of this recognition comes from a 1912 editorial in the Jerusalem paper *al-Munadi*, which faulted the government for not keeping the pledge made in the Constitution of universal free primary education in the local language. "The government has ordered all locally raised money for education to be spent locally," the writer noted, "but if more money were needed, the numerous *awqaf* originally founded for educational purposes produced income sufficient to fund as many as three schools." "Unfortunately," he added, "some families live off this wealth, and grow lazy, instead of which they should pay half of this income for education." The editorial concludes: "We still don't value knowledge enough; the poor and middle classes need education, but the rich teach their children to love power and wealth."[55]

There is evidence that some in Palestine and elsewhere in the Ottoman Arab provinces understood that they were pawns in a game between the great powers and the Ottoman state where education was concerned, as in so much else.[56] Some actively fought against insidious foreign influences via support for the state educational system, some tried to stay out of this game where possible, for example via the establishment of private schools, while others sent their children to foreign schools, either ignoring, accepting, or welcoming the political implications (which of course were different depending on which foreign power supported a given school: the American schools were seen as the most politically neutral). But in any case, the demand for a modern education was far greater than the number of places available in all the existing schools in Palestine, and many parents were willing to make extraordinary sacrifices to obtain a modern education for their children, especially one involving training in foreign languages, which they increasingly understood was a valuable asset.[57]

One of the inevitable results of these external pressures, combined with this barely quenched thirst for education, was the growth during the Ottoman period of a fissiparious and divided educational system—in fact, several systems, each using a different syllabus, teaching a different foreign language, and under the control of a different authority. Education retained much of this diversity during the Mandate, in spite of some efforts at standardization. Thus, in the absence of a unified educational system, offering obvious advantages for the uniform socialization of the population, for much of the past century the Palestinians, like others in the Arab provinces of the Ottoman Empire and its successor states, had to contend with a deeply divided educational sector, which served many interests besides their own. But unlike the peoples of the other Arab countries, which eventually achieved independence and created unified school systems, until the present day the Palestinians have suffered from an educational system that is divided and outside their control. The consequences of this situation for Palestinian self-conceptions and for a unified Palestinian identity have been great, although they were in some measure overcome through phenomena that transcended these divisions, such as a limited number of common elements of the curriculum under both the Ottoman and Mandate systems, and student involvement in nationwide student political activities, as occurred throughout the Mandate period, and came to a peak in 1936, when students playing a leading role in organizing the general strike of that year.

IV

Among the many influences on cultural and intellectual life during the last few decades of Ottoman rule, the press had perhaps the most widespread impact on society. As part of the cultural, educational and linguistic revival known as the *nahda*, which took place in *bilad al-Sham* and Egypt in the latter part of the nineteenth century, the daily press, as well as periodicals, flourished. Although much of this journalism was forced abroad by the censorship of the period of Sultan Abdul Hamid II in the years after 1878, it continued to prosper in Egypt, acquiring readers all over the Arabic-speaking world. An ever-growing number of newspapers, magazines, and technical and scientific journals were published there by Egyptian and other Arab writers, bringing their readers daily news as well as the latest trends in European and Islamic thought. After the 1908 revolution restored the Constitution, and with it press freedoms, in the Ottoman Empire, there was a blossoming of the press in *bilad al-Sham* in particular, with thirty-five new newspapers established in the first year after the reimposition of the Constitution throughout the region, and dozens more thereafter.[58] Palestine shared in this expansion of the press,[59] which provides us with an invaluable window on the self view of an important segment of society, and the development of ideas about politics, society, and identity.

It has been argued with regard to this period and this region that one cannot deduce too much from the press: we can read what was written in it, but we cannot be sure who was reading it at the time, or what impact it had.[60] Whatever the merits of this contention (and they seem limited indeed, inasmuch as this criterion could just as easily be utilized to dismiss many other categories of sources), we can certainly deduce some things if we find how widely distributed a given newspaper or periodical was. Ideally this would mean obtaining circulation figures, and even lists of subscribers, but such luxuries are unfortunately rarely available to the historian of the modern Middle East (although circulation figures for some pre-World War I Jerusalem newspapers do exist[61]). Nevertheless, we can get some idea of their circulation from the holdings of the major periodicals of the day in a number of private libraries.

What can be deduced in this regard from the three libraries which have been examined in Jerusalem, two of them grouping together at least three separate collections, is clear. In the Khalidi Library, for example, we find copies, usually bound and often multiple, of late Ottoman periodicals, from Ahmad Faris Shidyaq's *al-Jawa'ib*, founded in Istanbul in 1860; to Butrus Bustani's *Jinan*, founded in Beirut in 1870; to Ya'qub Sarruf and Faris Nimr's *al-Muqtataf*, published in Cairo starting in 1877; to later publications such as Jurji Zeydan's *al-Hilal*, founded in Cairo in 1892; al-Sayyid Muhammad Rashid Rida's *al-Manar*, founded in Cairo in 1897; and Muhammad Kurd 'Ali's *al-Muqtabas*, founded in Cairo in 1906 and two years later moved to Damascus.[62] While each of these periodicals had a different focus—*al-Jawa'ib* and *al-Manar* tended to be religious in emphasis, while the other four were more secular in orientation—all attempted to describe and interpret for their readers the latest developments in science and industry, to reassess Islamic and Arab history, and to examine the reasons for the rise of the West and the relative weakness of the Islamic world.

That this collection is not exceptional can be seen from the periodical holdings of the al-Aqsa Library, which contains runs of most of the same publications that are found in the Khalidi Library, like them frequently in fine old leather bindings and often carrying an indication of whom the original owner was. It contains *al-Muqtataf* from 1880 through the 1920s, *al-Hilal* from the first issue, also through the 1920s, and runs similar to those in the Khalidi library of *al-Manar* and *al-Muqtabas*.[63] These holdings in both libraries of the most important of the first Arabic-language periodicals, made up of volumes which largely predate the formation of both of the libraries in question, originated in the private collections of several different Jerusalemites. They constitute evidence of a deep interest on the part of these individuals, and presumably others like them, in the newest writings on Western science, history, and politics, as well as Islam, Arab history, and the politics of the region.[64] Having been placed in libraries open to the reading public, moreover, these periodicals were accessible to a wide range of readers.

In an announcement of its establishment, the founder of the Khalidi Library explicitly called it a "public library" (*maktaba 'umumiyya*).[65]

Interest in these same subjects can be followed in a different manner in the daily press, which in turn broadcast it to a wider audience than had access to such periodicals. Through serialization in daily newspapers, much of what was published in journals like *al-Hilal* and *al-Muqtabas* in particular was accessible to a broader readership, together with the news of the day. One can presume that the information reached an even more extensive audience by word of mouth. Such papers as *al-Mufid* in Beirut, published by 'Abd al-Ghani al-'Uraisi, *al-Muqtabas* in Damascus (the daily newspaper, with the same name as the periodical, and also published by Muhammad Kurd 'Ali), *al-Karmil*, published in Haifa by Najib Nassar, and *Tarablus al-Sham*, published in Tripoli by Muhammad Kamil al-Buhayri, regularly reproduced articles by leading *salafi* thinkers, as well as historical, literary, and scientific pieces, in serial form. Like many newspaper and periodical editors of the day, Kurd 'Ali, Nassar, and al-Buhayri each owned a press that published books by some of these same authors.[66] Rashid Rida had the same arrangement in Cairo with the press of his periodical *al-Manar*.

This practice was also followed by some publishers of newspapers and periodicals in Jerusalem. Two years before he began to publish the newspaper *al-Quds* in 1908, Jurji Hanania had established a printing press and publishing house.[67] Khalil Baydas, publisher of the popular periodical *al-Nafa'is al-'Asriyya*, also printed pamphlets and the occasional book (he used the printing presses of Jerusalem's Dar al-Aytam orphanage). Similarly, Muhammad Hassan al-Budayri, publisher of the short-lived but influential post-war nationalist newspaper *Suriyya al-Janubiyya*, and his cousin Muhammad Kamil al-Budayri, publisher of its successor as the leading nationalist daily, *al-Sabah*, used to publish books and pamphlets on the press their papers were printed on, which was located in a room adjacent to the *Haram al-Sharif* which today houses *al-Maktaba al-Budayriyya*.[68] On balance, however, Jerusalem in the late Ottoman period was too small a market, and too provincial a city, to be a major publishing center.[69] Instead, it depended for its intellectual sustenance mainly on the newspapers, periodicals, and book publishers of the cities of the Palestinian coast, especially *Filastin* in Jaffa and *al-Karmil* in Haifa, as well as those of the Syrian littoral and interior like Beirut and Damascus, and the major regional centers, Cairo and Istanbul.

Several newspapers were nevertheless published in Jerusalem during this period, although some of them were relatively short-lived. Jurji

Hanania noted in a 1913 editorial that the number of papers being published in the city in that year was fewer than when his newspaper, *al-Quds*, started publishing in 1908, adding that many papers founded after the 1908 revolution had been forced to close, and others to reduce their frequency of publication, including his own. He ascribed this phenomenon to the unwillingness of some subscribers to pay their subscription fees, and the tendency of others to share their copy of the newspaper with "fifty other readers."[70] While helping to explain the limited nature of the Jerusalem market for the daily press, this remark also enables us to get an impression of how widely diffused the material in each issue of a given newspaper might have been, particularly if we take into account oral transmission to a yet broader circle than that of these "other readers."

Among the main Jerusalem papers were the official *al-Quds al-Sharif/Quds Şerif*, which appeared irregularly in both Arabic and Turkish; Hanania's *al-Quds*; al-Shaykh 'Ali al-Rimawi's *al-Najah*; Iliya Zakka's *al-Nafir*; Sa'id Jarallah's *al-Munadi*; Khalil al-Sakakini and Jamil al-Khalidi's *al-Dustur*; and Bandali Mushahwar's *Bayt al-Maqdis*.[71] We can assume that due to the limitations of their printing facilities, the press runs of most daily newspapers in the region were small, and that of the Jerusalem papers even smaller, and that their readership was quite limited (the largest circulation appears to have been that of *al-Quds*, with 1,500[72]). Indeed, most newspapers appeared only once, twice, or three times a week, and we know that the size of the newspaper-reading public was severely restricted by widespread illiteracy and poor transportation outside the urban centers.

The small size of the market for "quality" newspapers is the subject of a lament by the editor of *al-Munadi*, Muhammad al-Maghribi. In an article entitled "The Death of Literature in Palestine" he argues that Arab civilization once reached great heights in Palestine, then declined. It was shameful that "in this country the illiterate are many times the number of the literate, that few go to school, and only hundreds of Arabs buy newspapers." Moreover, he complained, people buy frivolous publications, rather than literary or scientific ones. Readers of *al-Muqtataf*, *al-Hilal*, and *al-Muqtabas* in the land of Palestine ("fil-bilad al-Filistiniyya") are counted in the dozens, while the satirical *al-Himara* and *al-Nafa'is al-'Asriyya* have hundreds or thousands of readers.[73]

Nevertheless, a number of factors have to be weighed against these constraints in measuring the influence of the press in this early period. The first is that newspapers were commonly posted in public places and circulated freely from hand to hand (as the laments of publishers like

Hanania over lost revenues demonstrate). The Khalidi Library sub-
scribed to a number of newspapers, as did other libraries, and we can
assume that they were available to all those who used these facilities. We
know from a number of sources, moreover, that people were accustomed to having the newspapers read aloud to them at home and in public places, so that the low level of literacy, while a barrier to the influence
of the press, was not an insurmountable one.[74]

In addition, people, particularly those living outside the cities, were
accustomed to news reaching them after a delay. Thus, news in a paper
which reached a distant town or village days late was still devoured
eagerly by the reading and listening public. Some newspaper editors
realized their potential impact in the countryside, and took advantage of
it. The editors of *Filastin* sent free copies of their paper to the *mukhtar* of
every village in the Jaffa district with more than 100 inhabitants. The
objective, they wrote in an editorial, was to "acquaint the *fallah* with what
is happening in the country, and to teach him his rights, in order to prevent those who do not fear God and his prophets from dominating him
and stealing his goods."[75] These newspapers were apparently eagerly
awaited in the villages, for in the same editorial, 'Isa and Yusuf al-'Isa
asked those *mukhtars* with complaints about delays in delivery of the
newspaper to direct them to the office of the *qa'immaqam* of the district,
which had agreed to deliver copies via the local gendarmes. There is no
indication that any Jerusalem newspaper followed this practice, although some expressed similar populist sentiments.[76]

There are in addition various indications in the press itself and elsewhere of its growing influence in Palestine and other parts of the Arab
world as the twentieth century wore on, particularly in the larger cities.
One of them was the tendency of those in authority to close down newspapers when they published articles that offended them, a step which
surely would only have been taken because these papers had some effect
on their readers and in shaping a newly configured public sphere. As will
be shown in chapter 6, one of the most forceful instances of the impact
of the Palestinian and Arab press was the role newspapers played in the
opposition to the Zionist movement, a fact recognized by both Zionists
and Palestinians at the time, and amply demonstrated in the available
issues of the pre-1914 Palestinian daily press.

Not all newspapers and periodicals were anti-Zionist. While *al-Munadi*
frequently carried articles attacking the Zionist movement, and the most
widely read Palestinian papers, *Filastin* and *al-Karmil*, were strongly hostile
to Zionism, *al-Quds* and *al-Nafa'is al-'Asriyya* generally took a muted tone

on the subject, although they did carry an occasional article disparaging Zionist colonization or critically describing a specific incident involving settlers. The main exception to the general rule was Iliya Zakka's *al-Nafir*, which in the words of an Israeli historian of the Palestinian press, "published articles praising Jewish colonization in the country when it received payment for them, but launched attacks on it any time the payments were interrupted."[77]

As the Ottoman era drew to a close in Palestine, what can be seen in the press, as in few other sources, is the increasing usage of the terms "Palestine" and "Palestinian," and a focus on Palestine as a country, of which we have already seen a few instances. The newspaper *Filastin* was one of the primary venues for this orientation, with its very title evoking the centrality of Palestine in the outlook of its editors. In a characteristic item, which echoed many others published in this period, *Filastin* analyzed the differing trends at the 1913 Zionist congress, asserting that both of the main tendencies represented there intended to collect as many as possible of the Jews of the world in Palestine. It concluded its report with a poem by al-Shaykh Sulayman al-Taji al-Faruqi entitled "The Zionist Peril," and the editorial comment: "Do you accept to see our country stolen?"[78]

Filastin was by no means alone in this orientation, as most other Palestinian papers also referred to Palestine and the Palestinians as their primary concern. We have seen above two examples from *al-Munadi*, whose masthead bore the words "Giving particular coverage to local news and to study of conditions in Palestine":[79] one article stressed the importance of Palestinians writing the history of Palestine, and the other focused on the decline of culture in Palestine since the classical period, which marked the zenith of Islamic history.[80] The authors of both articles assume that Palestine is the central focus of their readers' loyalty, and evince a strong sense of patriotism and love of country. Noticeably, in neither article is Zionism mentioned, whether directly or indirectly. Even *al-Quds*, far less polemical or outspoken than most other newspapers of the day regarding Zionism (although its editor criticized Iliyya Zakka for his support of Zionism, and indeed won a court case against him[81]), constantly referred to Palestine, for example in an article surveying commerce, industry, and agriculture as main means for building up Palestine.[82] Indeed, every one of ten issues of *al-Quds* sampled at random over the period 1909–1913 included articles mentioning Palestine or "our country" (*biladuna*).

Muhammad al-Shanti, the editor of *al-Iqdam* whose description of the *Rawdat al-Ma'arif* school as the "foundation stone to build the future of

Palestine" has already been quoted, neatly summed up the way he understood Palestinian identity as fitting into other identities. In an article warning "Palestinian youth" of the danger of Zionism, al-Shanti declaimed: "Let the country become an Arab, Ottoman country, not a Zionist country" (*"wa tisbah al-bilad biladan 'arabiyya 'uthmaniyya wa la bilad sihyuniyya"*).[83] In directing his remarks to "Palestinian youth," and warning them about the dangers to "their country," al-Shanti had clearly defined the focus of his concern as Palestine; in stressing the country's Arab and Ottoman character, he was referring to established elements which were part of Palestinian identity. In expressing these sentiments, he was perhaps more outspoken than some of his journalistic colleagues working in Palestine, as befitted the director of a newspaper published in far-off Cairo, but he otherwise seems to reflect the outlook of most of them—and perhaps also, we may surmise, that of their readers.

V

There were other important centers for cultural and intellectual life in Jerusalem at the end of the Ottoman period, such as political parties and organizations, and religious and social clubs. We can follow some of their activities through the press, and it is clear from even a superficial examination of its coverage of these domains that while Jerusalem was by no means as active a center as were larger cities in the Ottoman Arab provinces, previously unheard of types of political and social organizations there were growing rapidly. Press coverage of politics is particularly important, for it reveals the same orientations regarding identity, and particularly the centrality of the idea of Palestine as the country to which its population belonged, and which belonged to its population.[84] Other sources reveal to us the operation of secret societies and political groupings,[85] and the workings of private and family endeavors.[86]

It remains to mention the circles around foreign diplomats, scholars, and missionaries, and the growing institutions of the Jewish *yishuv* (or the Jewish community) in Palestine, which were clearly the foci of much cultural and intellectual activity in Jerusalem. Of a total Jewish population of Palestine of approximately 60,000 before 1914,[87] between 25,000 and 30,000 lived in Jerusalem, where they constituted about half the population.[88] Much intellectual and cultural ferment occurred among this relatively large population, as well as among the many European merchants, missionaries, and consular officials posted in Jerusalem. With a number of exceptions, however, it appears that both of these important groups were very largely isolated from most of Palestinian society, as a result of language and religious barriers, and in some cases by choice. They thus had a relatively limited impact on the intellectual and cultural life of most of the Arab inhabitants of Jerusalem (with the important exception of the schools run by Christian missionaries and the Alliance Israélite Universelle, which attracted a number of Christian and Muslim students, especially from the upper classes).[89] Some members of the elite were nevertheless influenced in some measure by their contacts with both European missionaries, tourists and diplomats and Jewish residents and settlers in this period, as we will see in a number of cases in the next chapter.

Jerusalem and the rest of Palestine were in a nearly constant process of transition during the last half century of the Ottoman period. As these transformations in government, administration, education, justice, communications, and transportation took place, and as the security situation in the country improved, the population grew, and the economy responded positively to these changes and to the blessings of the last lengthy period of uninterrupted peace in the country's modern history. As the Ottoman era drew to a close, the first signs of the Palestinian-Zionist conflict which was to consume the country for most of the twentieth century were already apparent, notably in the press and in those parts of the countryside where Zionist settlements founded in the wake of the second *aliya* (or wave of Jewish immigration to Palestine, 1904–1914) had expanded at the expense of the indigenous peasantry. Nevertheless, only the most prescient contemporary observers would have pointed to this as the issue that would completely dominate the future of Palestine.[90] Most others would probably have looked to the momentous changes we have focused on for clues to the future.

In the intellectual realm, much changed during the decades preceding World War I, although some things stayed the same. Under the *Tanzimat* religion had lost much of its centrality to the processes of governance, and the religious institution was marginalized as a pillar of daily administration of justice and much else.[91] However, during the 33-year reign of Sultan 'Abd al-Hamid II, popular religion was perceived by the Ottoman authorities as a useful tool for establishing legitimacy and justifying their control by appealing to ideas that were widespread and popular among much of the population, although most of the *Tanzimat* reforms were kept in place.[92] On the local level in Jerusalem, this shift back toward religion, albeit in a situation where the religious establishment was robbed of much of the substance of real power it had once enjoyed, meant a shift by the state away from favoring the families, such as the al-Khalidi's, associated with reform in government and liberal *salafi* thought in religion, and toward favoring those like the al-Husayni's with a more conservative political bent, and a greater involvement with popular religion.[93] After the 1908 Constitutional Revolution, this trend of state reliance on more conservative notables was temporarily halted, but it was to be resumed during the British mandatory period.

One of the other crucial changes of this period, however, was that these issues of notable infighting were beginning to matter less, as the realms of culture, politics, and government were no longer the exclusive preserve of such families, although they were adept in maintaining much of their old influence in the very different new circumstances. Now, hundreds of educated individuals were needed as teachers, government officials, military officers, journalists, telegraph operators, and railway employees, all relatively well-paid and prestigious professions which either did not exist before the nineteenth century, or had changed and expanded greatly.[94] Thus, as we have seen, in Jerusalem around the turn of the century Christian and missionary schools alone employed more than 150 teachers, most of them locals. Elsewhere, the Syrian Protestant College in Beirut in 1912 employed 34 local instructors, exclusive of foreigners, in prestigious, high-paying jobs.[95] This massive expansion of opportunities gave ample scope to individuals of both non-notable and non-Muslim backgrounds to achieve status.

At the same time, the economic expansion that half a century of peace, rapid population growth, and improvements in security, communications, and transportation made possible opened up opportunities for many individuals of these and other backgrounds to prosper. As a result, Palestine was in a state of ferment that increased in the years leading up to 1914, a state that was pregnant with possibilities, many of them positive. Its promise was not to last. As the Ottoman era in Palestine ended with the capture of Jerusalem by General Allenby's troops in December 1917, there passed with it not only sovereign dominion—transferred from one power to another—but also the possibilities of autonomous development for the indigenous population, and of unfettered economic, social, and intellectual interaction between Palestine and other parts of the region. These possibilities would not be replicated for many decades, and indeed are far from being assured today.

In the next chapter, we will examine some of the political, intellectual, and ideological options that appeared to be open at the end of the Ottoman era in Palestine, via a detailed look at the lives of two individuals of this period.

CHAPTER 4

Competing and Overlapping
Loyalties in Ottoman Jerusalem

I

When a movement, or a leader, or an ideology triumphs, historians are understandably disposed to look at what went before as the inevitable run-up to this triumph. So it was initially with the study of the French Revolution, Napoleon, and communism, and so it was for many decades with the treatment of nationalism in the Middle East. The precipitous collapse of the Soviet Union over a period of a few years and the ensuing recent reexamination of modern Russian history, however, illustrates another common phenomenon: an equally strong tendency toward strident iconoclasm as soon as a formerly dominant ideology declines. A similar trend is underway in the analysis of nationalism in the Middle East, with writers from Islamic, Marxist and western perspectives vigorously questioning the inevitability, and indeed the importance, of the rise of Middle Eastern nationalisms over the past century or so, now that they seem to be in decline in many parts of the region.

This is perhaps truest of the recent historiography of Arab nationalism.[1] This ideology triumphed with the disappearance of the Ottoman

Empire, and has been hegemonic for most of the twentieth century throughout the Arab world. Today, however, it is heavily burdened by the weight of its own failure to achieve its objectives and by the degeneration of the regimes which rule and have ruled in its name, and is visibly on the defensive before the dramatic onslaught of Islamic radicalism and the growth of nation-state nationalism. After many decades when the history of the region was composed—both in the Arab world and often elsewhere—in light of the orthodoxies of Arab nationalism, this history is now being rewritten in light of its recent decline.

Unfortunately, much of the revision of the standard version of events is as flawed as the Arabist nationalist canon itself once was. Where the historiography of the modern Middle East generally repeated the assessments by the post-World War I generation of Arab nationalists, who regarded the Ottoman era in Arab history as one of unrelieved gloom, and the Arab leaders hanged for treason by order of an Ottoman Military Court in Aley in 1915 and 1916 as noble martyrs, more recent works take a completely different tack. One example of this about-face can be seen in a 1981 Beirut re-edition of a history written by the Egyptian nationalist leader Muhammad Farid before World War I as a panegyric to the Ottoman state. The reprint includes a new preface noting that this classic corrects false concepts about the Ottoman era which had been generally prevalent, showing the Ottoman Empire in its true light, as a worthy example of an Islamic state.[2] Similarly, the Lebanese historian Wajih Kawtharani's revisionist work *Bilad al-sham* takes a critical view of the Arab nationalist World War I "martyrs," reprising the Ottoman government's view of them at the time of their execution as no more than agents of foreign powers.[3]

Distortions of the history of the late Ottoman era in the Arab world from an Arabist perspective have thus given way to similarly reductionist Islamist and other anti-Arabist views of more recent periods, which draw on an equally biased set of assumptions for guidance. As a consequence, analysts of modern Arab history who rely on scholarship that uncritically accepts the grandiose self-assessments of the power and pervasiveness of Arab nationalism throughout the twentieth century are incapable of explaining the striking recent ascendancy of Islamic radicalism and nation-state nationalism in many parts of the Arab world, neither of which fits pan-Arab paradigms.

However, the new "revisionism" does little better than did nationalist historiography at portraying the complexity and subtlety of the network of affiliations and loyalties characteristic of most Arabs in the late nineteenth century, when nationalism first began to spread in the Middle East.[4] The Ottoman Empire, while far from being an ideal Islamic state, as some recent Islamic-oriented historians would have it, was hardly the den of iniquity portrayed by earlier nationalist historians, Arabs and others. And it was possible for an Arab notable of this era to be both a loyal supporter of the Ottoman state and a fervent believer in Arabism, a possibility excluded by extreme views in both schools.[5] Reintroducing some complexity into our portrayal of the politics of pre-World War I Palestine, with its amalgam of local, national, transnational, and religious loyalties, will thus hopefully correct our view not only of the late Ottoman era, but also of succeeding ones. This chapter will do so by examining the lives of two individuals whose careers illustrate this complexity, and will thereby shed light on some of the varied pre-World War I sources of Palestinian identity.

II

The last chapter touched on how the *Tanzimat* reforms and the intensive state-building activities of Sultan 'Abd al-Hamid II and the constitutional regime that followed his reign led to sweeping changes in the power and reach of the central government. This consequently led to shifts in the career patterns of notables in the Arab provinces during the last decades of the Ottoman era.[6] The change in the power balance in these provinces involved two different processes, if the Palestinian case is typical. The first, starting in the mid-nineteenth century after the end of the Egyptian occupation,[7] was the reduction by the state, often through the use of military means, of the influence of powerful families with a base in the Palestinian countryside. These included the Abu Ghosh family in the area west of Jerusalem, the 'Amr family of Dura in the Hebron district, and the 'Abd al-Hadi family in the Nablus area.[8] The second process, which took place somewhat later, involved the diminution of the dominating position in urban society of notable families in Jerusalem and other cities as a result of major changes in the way the government was structured.[9]

In the case of Jerusalem, we can find an apt illustration of the power that accrued to local notables under the old system in the career of one of them. This was al-Sayyid Muhammad 'Ali al-Khalidi (1781–1865), who succeeded his father in the powerful position of *ra'is al-kuttab wa na'ib* (chief secretary and deputy[10]) to the qadi of the Jerusalem shari'a court in 1220/1805. He held this position for most of the sixty years until 1281/1865 with a few interruptions, during which one or another of his sons often held the post.[11] As such, he deputized for the qadi in his absence, or during the interim period between the tenure of different qadis, and throughout he presided over the permanent court personnel and the archives of the court.[12] Thus, for the better part of three generations he was the senior local official in a court crucial to mediating economic, social, and other power relationships in Jerusalem and much of the surrounding district.[13] This gave him much influence in a situation where qadis appointed from Istanbul served for a single year, without developing local attachments or much familiarity with the region.[14] Having served at one point as qadi of Erzerum, Muhammad 'Ali al-Khalidi knew what that job entailed, and presumably preferred remaining in this position in Jerusalem to the vicissitudes of service elsewhere in the imperial religious establishment.

This key post had been held by Muhammad 'Ali's great-great-grandfather, al-Shaykh Muhammad San'allah al-Khalidi (d. 1139/1727),[15] for several decades between 1087/1676 and 1134/1722, and by several other members of the family after him, including Muhammad 'Ali's father, al-Sayyid 'Ali, who occupied it for nearly two decades starting in the late eighteenth century. The advantages conferred by holding such a position can be determined from even a cursory examination of the more than 250 *hujaj* (legal documents and records) originating in the *mahkama shar'iyya* and located among the collection of family papers preserved by San'allah, 'Ali, Muhammad 'Ali and their descendants.[16] More than 150 of these documents—it is difficult to tell whether they are chancery copies or originals, although the latter is most likely—cover the sixty years during which Muhammad 'Ali almost continuously held the post of *na'ib* (about thirty of them refer to the earlier periods during which San'allah and later 'Ali held the post). The very fact that so many individuals in a single family could hold such a position, handing it down from father to son, both highlights and helps to explain the autonomy and influence of the provincial notables.[17]

These 250 documents, dating from the mid-seventeenth century to the early twentieth, are mainly in Arabic, with some in Ottoman Turkish, and cover a wide range of subjects, including legal cases that came before the court, as well as petitions, inheritances, and other matters generated or certified by the court. They seem to have been papers of importance to those who collected them, some of them having to do with family-controlled properties and *awqaf,* and others concerning important political or social issues of the day. They appear to have served as a personal reference collection for the individual who as *ra'is al-kuttab* had control over the flow of paper in the court. A long-serving chief secretary was clearly able to keep copies of the documents he considered most important (chancery copies of all documents that passed through the *mahkama shar'iyya* were kept in its archives, while another copy of the most important ones was sent on to Istanbul). They were thereupon carefully preserved and handed down in the family,[18] giving any of its members who came to hold this post an inestimable advantage in terms both of understanding matters of precedent, and knowledge of important past cases decided in the court.

By the time of Muhammad 'Ali's death in 1865, the changes we have been discussing in the structure of provincial government, and consequently in career patterns, were already well under way, and the notables of Jerusalem were actively adjusting to them.[19] Muhammad 'Ali's eldest son, Yasin (d. 1318/1901), received a traditional Islamic education and followed his father into the ranks of the 'ulama, serving as *ra'is al-kuttab* in Jerusalem after his father's retirement on several occasions, as *na'ib* in Nablus, and as qadi of Nablus and Tripoli.[20] A supporter of the *Tanzimat* reformers, he was elected as a member of the General Council of the *vilayet* of Syria from 1867–1875 when the reformer Mehmed Reşid Paşa was Vali, and served as a qadi from 1878–1880 when Midhat Paşa, the father of the Ottoman constitution, became Vali of Syria. After a period in disfavor under 'Abd al-Hamid, he was elected as a member of the Jerusalem Municipal and Administrative Councils, and was appointed Mayor of Jerusalem in 1898.[21] Two of Yasin's brothers also became 'ulama, often deputizing for and ultimately succeeding their father in his posts in the Jerusalem shari'a court, and one served as qadi of Jaffa.

However, the third of Muhammad 'Ali's sons, Yusuf Diya' al-Din Paşa al-Khalidi [Yusuf Diya'] (1842–1906), took a completely different educational and career path, initially without his father's blessings. Muhammad 'Ali al-Khalidi was a still vigorous eighty years of age, and was still serving as *na'ib* and *ra'is al-kuttab*, when at the age of eighteen his son Yusuf Diya' went off to study at the Malta Protestant College, after he had received a thorough grounding in the traditional Islamic sciences from his father and his father's colleagues in the religious establishment of Jerusalem. Yusuf Diya' stayed in Malta for two years, thus becoming the first in his family to study foreign languages and other modern subjects (which he had begun earlier by attending the British Diocesan Boys School founded in Jerusalem by Bishop Gobat). At the instigation of his older brother Yasin, he went on to study for nearly three years in Istanbul at the Imperial Medical School and then at Robert College, until his father's death in 1865 interrupted his education and brought him back to Jerusalem to start his career.[22]

The careers of Yusuf Diya' and his nephew Ruhi serve to illustrate some of the transformations in the Ottoman system that we have mentioned, and the changes in ideology that went with them. An examination of the lives of these two individuals will show the different elements that constituted the identity of Palestinian notables in this transitional phase of the late Ottoman era, and will hopefully cast some light on issues of identity for others in Palestinian society, who were not part of the notable class, to which they belonged.

The careers of these two men can be summed up briefly. Yusuf Diya' al-Khalidi was an outspoken liberal member of the first Ottoman Parliament, three times Mayor of Jerusalem, an Ottoman diplomat, an instructor and then a professor at the Imperial-Royal Oriental Academy in Vienna[23], and author of several scholarly works, including the first Kurdish-Arabic dictionary (and one of the first examinations of the Kurdish language on modern linguistic principles[24]). After this long and varied career, he died in Istanbul in 1906. Like Yusuf Diya', his nephew Ruhi (the second son of Yusuf Diya's eldest brother Yasin) also first received a traditional Islamic education and then Western schooling; was also an Ottoman diplomat, a prolific author, a modern linguist and a lecturer at a major European university (in his case the Sorbonne); was also an outspoken representative of Jerusalem in the Ottoman Parliament, and also died in Istanbul, barely seven years after his uncle.

Yusuf Diya' and Ruhi al-Khalidi are broadly representative of the notables of Jerusalem, and to some degree those in the rest of the Arab provinces. Coming from families that had specialized in religious learning and provided 'ulama to staff the provincial, and occasionally the imperial Ottoman, religious establishment, they are typical of a new generation that shifted to modern educations and government service. This assertion, which is supported by the work of other scholars who have studied them,[25] is borne out by examination of the education and careers of many of their contemporaries. A typical example would be Ruhi al-Khalidi's fellow representative of Jerusalem in the Ottoman parliament, Sa'id Bey al-Husayni (1878–1945), members of whose family had held the important posts of Hanafi mufti of Jerusalem, *shaykh al-haram*, and *naqib al-ashraf* almost continuously since the late seventeenth or early eighteenth century.

The change over time is mirrored in the shift between Sa'id al-Husayni and his father, Ahmad Rasim al-Husayni (1823–1880), who in some sense straddled this generational divide. Although Ahmad Rasim al-Husayni received a traditional training in *fiqh*, he went into commerce and became head of the new commercial court of Jerusalem, rather than joining the corps of 'ulama as had his father and his grandfather, who was Hanafi mufti of Jerusalem at the turn of the nineteenth century. Only later in his career, after the death of the incumbent, did he become *naqib al-ashraf.* Sa'id al-Husayni, by way of contrast, received a modern education from the outset, culminating in a time at a school run by the Alliance Israélite sufficient for him to learn Hebrew. He went on to become a government official in Jerusalem, serving as a censor of the Hebrew press, and after being elected Mayor of Jerusalem in 1905, was elected to Parliament in 1908 as a deputy for the Jerusalem district.[26] The shifts in education, career, and presumably outlook, leap out from photographs of individuals of different generations during this era, with the fathers shown in traditional 'ulama garb, and the sons in impeccable western suits.

The men we will focus on are of interest as well because, in addition to their various achievements during active lives of administration, scholarship and politics, each was in touch with leading intellectual figures of the age, both in the Ottoman Empire and the rest of the Islamic world, and in the larger European academic sphere where the organization and systemization of knowledge about "the Orient" was proceeding rapidly. An examination of these figures is thus of more than merely biographical interest, and holds out the prospect of shedding light on the affiliations, loyalties, and outlook of a broad range of individuals prominent during this era, as well as others about whom we may know less, but can reasonably infer conclusions.

III

Yusuf Diya', the third of al-Sayyid Muhammad 'Ali al-Khalidi's five sons, was born in 1842, after his father had already served for decades as the senior local official in the shari'a court of Jerusalem, and three years after the *Hatt i-Şerif* of Gulhane had inaugurated the *Tanzimat*. We have seen that Yusuf Diya' was the first and only one of eight siblings to obtain a western education.[27] By present-day standards, the little more than five years spent in three different western-style schools may seem a modest amount of education, and indeed some Europeans were scornful of his attainments.[28] It must be remembered, however, that Yusuf Diya' had a thorough traditional Islamic education, that the schools he attended were the most advanced ones extant for their time and place, and that in the 1850s and 1860s even in Europe and America schooling had not yet developed into the decades-long odyssey it has since become.

It is tempting to see in this new departure a conscious attempt by a Jerusalem notable family to diversify its options in view of the sweeping changes that were affecting the Empire. However, the existing evidence indicates that it was Yusuf Diya' himself who sought Western-style education, for reasons he set out in an autobiographical sketch: upon reflection, he found that the Europeans were able to dominate others because of their superior learning, combined with the ignorance of their opponents. Thinking about these matters drove him to seek knowledge, which he initially tried to do in the Egyptian schools established by Muhammad 'Ali and his successors, to which his father tried but failed to gain him admission. Thereupon, after his father refused to allow him to travel to *bilad al-Afranj* [the lands of the foreigners] to study, Yusuf Diya' ran off with a cousin to Malta, where by the intercession of Anglican Bishop Gobat of Jerusalem, he was admitted to the Malta Protestant College. Later, his eldest brother, Yasin, helped him gain admission to the Imperial Medical School in Istanbul.[29] Unlike Yusuf Diya', all of his brothers—the older two, Yasin and 'Abd al-Rahman, as well as Khalil and Raghib, who were younger than him—received religious educations and followed in their father's footsteps, and as we saw they eventually served in various posts as members of the Muslim religious establishment in Jerusalem and other parts of the Empire.[30]

Nevertheless, if a shift from traditional career patterns was what was intended by this change in education, it was eminently successful in the case of Yusuf Diya.' Through his studies in Jerusalem, Malta, and Istanbul, he learned French, English, and German,[31] and knowledge of foreign languages (for which he appears to have had an aptitude) opened up a number of opportunities for him, although the high-level connections his family and class background made possible were instrumental in shaping these opportunities. While in Istanbul as a student at the Imperial Medical Academy and Robert College, Yusuf Diya' became the protégé of reformist *Tanzimat* statesmen such as Midhat Paşa and Reşid Paşa, with the latter of whom his older brother Yasin was already on good terms. These powerful men were to prove helpful in advancing Yusuf Diya's career at the outset, although his associations with them were to hurt him in later decades after they lost power and Sultan 'Abd al-Hamid II established his absolute rule.

All of this was still in the future when Yusuf Diya' returned to Jerusalem in 1865, at the height of the implementation of the *Tanzimat* reforms in the provinces. Yusuf Diya's return to Jerusalem, occasioned by the death of his father, coincided with the appointment of Reşid Pasha as Vali of Damascus (which during this period briefly included the Jerusalem *sancak*). In keeping with his life-long belief in the importance of education if Ottoman society were to be transformed, Yusuf Diya's first activity in Jerusalem was the founding of a state middle school (*ruşdiyye*) on the premises of an old *madrasa*, in 1284 (1867–68). Counting perhaps on his older brother Yasin's connections, Yusuf Diya' apparently expected to be appointed director of this school, but instead "they brought a Turkish teacher from Istanbul" to take the post. Any disappointment he may have felt at this turn of events was probably assuaged soon afterwards, when he was appointed as Mayor of Jerusalem, in his own words "by the people of Jerusalem and the Turkish Government."[32] He held this post for five years (and on two other occasions later in his career for several more years), and is described in a number of sources as an active mayor. His efforts, supported by Reşid Paşa in Damascus (Jerusalem was not separated from the Damascus *vilayet* until 1872), included helping to initiate the construction of the first carriage road from Jerusalem to Jaffa, and improving the water supply of the city.[33]

When his patron, Mehmed Reşid Paşa, returned to Istanbul upon his appointment as Foreign Minister in 1874, Yusuf Diya' followed him "at the request of the late Grand Vizier, Mehmed Ruşdi Paşa."[34] He first was assigned to the Ministry's Translation Bureau, and later in the same year obtained an appointment as Ottoman Consul in Poti, a Russian port on the Black Sea. This consular posting to a small, provincial Russian town apparently involved little of the glamour often associated with diplomacy—indeed, his correspondence shows him to have been left considerably poorer as the result of a robbery and by incurring official expenses, for which he had the greatest difficulty in prevailing upon the Foreign Ministry to reimburse him after his patron, Reşid Paşa, lost his post.[35] After this assignment in Russia, which ended abruptly after only six months, Yusuf Diya' traveled to Vienna, spending two months visiting different parts of Russia including Odessa, Kiev, Moscow, and St. Petersburg along the way.[36] In Vienna, Mehmed Reşid Paşa was now Ambassador—a clear demotion from Foreign Minister, and a sign that his star was waning. Through his intercession, Yusuf Diya' nevertheless was able to obtain a post as an instructor of Arabic and Ottoman Turkish at the Imperial-Royal Oriental Academy in Vienna, which he held for eight months before returning to Jerusalem. There, after another short term of office as mayor, he was elected to the Ottoman Parliament in 1877.[37]

Until this point, Yusuf Diya' al-Khalidi had been a protege and supporter of the leading Ottoman statesmen of the late *Tanzimat* era. His achievements—such as initiating the building of the road from Jaffa to Jerusalem—had been in furtherance of their modernizing, reforming program, and had been made possible in part by the support in high places which they were able to provide him, and which was so essential in the Ottoman system (and probably in any system). But upon his election to Parliament at the age of thirty-five, Yusuf Diya' al-Khalidi came into his own. Educated in the West and acquainted with a number of Western Orientalists, he knew several foreign languages, was relatively widely traveled, and was apparently a public speaker of some skill. Indeed he was described by the American Consul-General in Istanbul as having made "a sensation in the Parliament by his eloquence and boldness," and by another American diplomat as "the finest orator and ablest debater in the Chamber."[38] He was thus thoroughly conversant with entirely new dimensions of modern politics which some of the older *Tanzimat*-era statesmen who were architects of the Constitution, and who had been brought up in an earlier tradition, had not mastered.

Having imbibed heavily of liberal ideas, Yusuf Diya' was an active figure during both sessions of the parliament elected during the brief first Ottoman constitutional period from 1876–1878.[39] He proved himself one of the parliament's strongest supporters of constitutional government, and was an outspoken opponent of the Sultan 'Abd al-Hamid's absolutism in his speeches, statements, and letters both inside and outside the parliamentary chamber. Not surprisingly, this prominence did little to endear him to the Sultan, who had no use for liberalism, constitutions, or public speeches. His ire was directed at Yusuf Diya' in particular, since he had repeatedly attacked specific actions of 'Abd al-Hamid, once protesting in Parliament against his unconstitutional choice of the President of the Chamber during its first session with the words: "The member of Istanbul, His Excellency Ahmed Vefik Effendi, tells us that he is our President. Who made him so?"[40] In February 1878, after suffering through two sessions marked by such parliamentary criticism of his policies and his chosen ministers, the Sultan finally felt strong enough to suspend the constitution and prorogue parliament, thereby instituting thirty years of direct, absolute rule.

As a result of his outspoken opposition to the Sultan's autocratic predilections, Yusuf Diya' al-Khalidi was exiled from Istanbul immediately after Parliament was suspended, together with nine other active opposition members of that body, five of whom were from the Syrian provinces. He was described by one source close to the Palace as among the four of these ten "considered most dangerous."[41] Undoubtedly chastened by the way his experience as a deputy had ended, Yusuf Diya' returned to Jerusalem in April 1878, where he once again took up his duties as mayor, but once more fell foul of the Sultan and his officials. After a clash with the *mutasarrif* of Jerusalem, Ra'uf Paşa, who was determined to curb the power of both the al-Khalidi and al-Husayni families (but ended up weakening mainly the former[42]), Yusuf Diya' was removed from his post in October 1879 and, in what was to become a routine for opponents of the Sultan, went into exile. He left Palestine for Vienna, where he returned to the Imperial Oriental Academy, this time as a Professor of Arabic. In 1880, he published his edition of the poetry of Labid ibn Rabi'a al-'Amiri, author of one of the famous pre-Islamic *mu'allaqat*.[43] Yusuf Diya' apparently felt secure enough to brave the Sultan's displeasure, for he returned home soon thereafter, and we find him in 1881 serving as *qa'immaqam* of Jaffa, where he remained for a number of years, and after that in a number of minor provincial posts.

It was unlikely that this outspoken liberal (he was described by the American Consul General in Istanbul as "almost as liberal as a French Republican"[44]), a man who throughout his life remained in close touch with foreign scholars and diplomats,[45] would ever enjoy the full confidence of a suspicious autocrat such as 'Abd al-Hamid.[46] After the abrupt termination of his parliamentary career he never seems to have done so—even though in 1893 he was raised to the rank of Paşa. It is perhaps no coincidence that his Kurdish-Arabic dictionary, *al-Hadiyya al-hamidiyya fil-lugha al-kurdiyya*, published in the same year, refers obsequiously to the Sultan's name in its title, while its introduction includes a reference to the Sultan preceded by a string of complimentary titles so exaggerated as to verge on the sarcastic.[47] Notwithstanding this promotion, most of the posts he served in after 1878 were honorific and meaningless, or remote and amounted to internal exile. Thus he was named *qa'immaqam* of a district in Bitlis *vilayet* in the mid-1880s and later of other districts at Hasbayya and in Jabal al-Duruz. In 1307/1890, he is listed in the Ottoman state yearbook as heading the Ottoman Embassy in Belgrade, although whether he ever took up this posting is not clear.[48] What appeared to be the sole exception to this pattern was a brief appointment in the 1890s as Ambassador in Vienna, a post Yusuf Diya' was uniquely suited for, but was never allowed to take up.

For most of the last ten years of his life, Yusuf Diya' was in effect kept in enforced residence in Istanbul by the Sultan, who appointed him to ambassadorships he was not allowed to fill, to a consultative council that never met, and later to another similarly meaningless post, all of this with the objective of preventing him from going abroad, and thereby keeping a potential opponent under surveillance and control. In the late Hamidian period, for an official to travel without permission, especially to Europe (which was not generally given to liberals or others under suspicion like him), was construed as abandoning one's post—even a meaningless one—and thus equivalent to treason.[49] Thus, while he was allowed to visit Jerusalem occasionally and Cairo once during the last few years of his life,[50] this cosmopolitan scholar was never again allowed to travel abroad, and was obliged to spend most of his time in the capital.

While in Istanbul, Yusuf Diya' became a close friend and companion of another virtual prisoner of the Sultan whose ideas were too dangerous to allow him to go free, al-Sayyid Jamal al-Din al-Afghani (Yusuf Diya' was at his bedside when Jamal al-Din died[51]). At the same time, through foreign post offices beyond the reach of the Sultan's spies (notably the Austrian, which he was able to use freely, as a former faculty member at a Hapsburg imperial institution and recipient of a Hapsburg honor[52]), he was able to keep in contact with friends and colleagues such as the great poet Ahmad Shawqi and Shaykh Muhammad 'Abdu in Egypt, and with European scholars far and wide. After being allowed by the Ottoman authorities to publish his Kurdish-Arabic dictionary and grammar in 1893, Yusuf Diya' Paşa never again managed to publish, although a number of apparently complete manuscripts are located among his papers,[53] and the fact that he was being held in a gilded cage perhaps inevitably came to affect his health, which gradually began to decline.

His regular letters to his brother and nephew are increasingly full of mention of his failing health toward the end of the century,[54] and it is clear that life in Istanbul under the watchful eyes of Abdul Hamid's spies did not agree with him, notwithstanding the constant reading in several scholarly and literary fields in a number of languages which we know him to have engaged in from the marginal notations in books in his library, and from his extensive correspondence.

Among the highlights of these communications with a variety of European and Middle Eastern scholarly and public figures was Yusuf

Diya' Paşa's 1899 letter to Theodore Herzl via the medium of Zadok Kahn, the Chief Rabbi of France, mentioned in chapter 2. In this letter, he warned the Zionist leader that while Zionism was "in theory a completely natural and just idea" as a solution to the Jewish problem, and might work elsewhere, Palestine was a part of the Ottoman Empire, was heavily populated by non-Jews, and was venerated by 390 million Christians and 300 million Muslims. He asked: "By what right do the Jews demand it for themselves?" Wealth cannot purchase Palestine, "which can only be taken over by the force of cannons and warships." He warned that the day would never come "when the Zionists will become masters of this country," and concluded: "For the sake of God, leave Palestine in peace."[55]

Yusuf Diya' had closely followed the progress of the Zionist enterprise from its earliest days, when as Mayor of Jerusalem and *qa'immaqam* of Jaffa he had witnessed it from close quarters. While in Vienna in 1875, he wrote two letters to the *Jewish Chronicle* in London on the Jewish community in Jerusalem, one commenting on an article by the newspaper's correspondent there, and the other on the visit to Palestine of the Jewish philanthropist Moses Montefiore.[56] At some stage in his career he learned some Hebrew, partly out of his interest in what we would today call comparative religion, and partly so as to follow the activities of the Zionist movement. In later years he maintained a correspondence with Zionist leaders such as Norman Bentwich, a few traces of which are preserved among his papers.[57]

In his enforced residence in Istanbul, one of Yusuf Diya' Paşa's greatest consolations was the education of his nephew Ruhi, for whom he had the greatest affection. The aging statesman and scholar clearly saw Ruhi as his spiritual heir (Yusuf Diya' was married and had a daughter, but no sons), and indeed he left him all his books and papers. Much of the correspondence between the two has survived—mainly Yusuf Diya's letters to Ruhi—and is marked by a striking warmth and constant encouragement to Ruhi in his studies and in his career, first as a scholar, then as a diplomat.[58] Yusuf Diya' Paşa frequently sent his nephew money, and also helped him with his career by giving him advice and drawing on the many connections in the Ottoman hierarchy that he had developed over a quarter century of service to the state, and that he knew from his own experience were vital to bureaucratic advancement.[59]

In his old age, stricken by infirmity, and obliged to spend much of his time in Istanbul, Yusuf Diya' Paşa lost none of his fiery liberal spirit or his hopes for reform, in spite of their frustration for decades by the regime of Sultan 'Abd al-Hamid, according to observers who knew him well.[60] To his death, the man who in his youth had described himself as elected as Mayor of Jerusalem in 1868 by "the people of Jerusalem and the Turkish Government," always maintained that in spite of the suspension of the Constitution, he continued to hold the Parliamentary seat for Jerusalem. Berating his fellow liberal in the first Parliament, Khalil Ghanem, for writing "ex-Deputé" on his visiting card (his own defiantly described him as Deputy for Jerusalem) Yusuf Diya' Paşa is reported as saying: "the description of deputy is by the will of the nation and by its election, and only ceases upon the election of another."[61]

Two years after the death of Yusuf Diya' al-Khalidi in 1906 at the age of sixty-four, the officers of the Committee of Union and Progress [CUP] carried out a military *coup d'etat* that ended the Sultan's absolute regime and reinstated the 1876 Constitution. In the elections that followed, Ruhi al-Khalidi was elected to the seat representing Jerusalem which, until his death two years earlier, his uncle had staunchly insisted he continued to hold.

IV

Born only twenty-two years after Yusuf Diya', in 1864, Ruhi al-Khalidi nevertheless came to maturity in a different age than had his uncle, and this affected considerably the educational opportunities open to him. He grew up, in Jerusalem and the other places his father Yasin's career took his family, at a time when religious education no longer commanded the same prestige it once had, and when the state school system, missionary schools, and modern western education in general were seen as the keys to knowledge and advancement. In spite of his reputation as a reactionary, Sultan 'Abd al-Hamid II's three decades of absolute rule witnessed a massive expansion of the modern educational system at every level and in most regions.[62] In the *vilayet* of Beirut, for example, 359 state schools were established between the passage of the 1869 Ottoman Education law and 1914, most of them during the Hamidian period,[63] and we saw in chapter 3 that by 1914 there were a total of 98 state schools in Palestine.

Ruhi al-Khalidi went to several of these new state schools, including the *ruşdiyye* schools in Jerusalem and Tripoli, followed by several years at the *Sultaniye* school in Beirut (where he graduated at the top of his class in most subjects[64]). In 1887 he went to Istanbul to undertake the difficult course of study at the prestigious *Mekteb-i Mülkiye* school, which he completed in 1311/1893 with equal distinction,[65] after which he went to France to complete his studies (doing so against the will of his parents, who wanted him to obtain a government job in Palestine). Before studying in state schools, however, Ruhi began his education at traditional religious schools in Jerusalem, and later spent periods of time in such schools in the various places where his father was posted. It is not surprising therefore that in later stages of his education he did so well in the religious subjects which were still an important part of advanced schooling and the training of an Ottoman civil servant. Nor is it surprising that his father, who had received only a traditional religious education, but was a committed reformer, should have seen to it that his son obtained the best of both systems.[66]

We know the details of Ruhi al-Khalidi's education both from an autobiographical sketch which he wrote immediately after his election to Parliament in 1908, and from other papers and books of his which have survived.[67] Perusal of this material reveals that as a young man of twelve to fifteen he purchased numerous books in Tripoli, Nablus, Beirut, and Jerusalem, indicating his wide-ranging interests in religion, law, languages, literature, and history.[68] Among the extant documents is an *ijaza* in which one of Ruhi's teachers, al-Hajj Yusuf al-Sadiq al-Imam al-Husayni, the Shafi'i mufti in Jerusalem, certified that he had successfully completed training in all the classical subjects of the Islamic curriculum, listing as well his various other teachers.[69] From a young age, al-Khalidi was evidently well enough versed in Islamic learning that when his uncle 'Abd al-Rahman took him along on a visit to the *Shaykh al-Islam* in Istanbul in 1297/1879, he impressed this dignitary sufficiently to cause him bestow on Ruhi the scholarly rank of *R'us Brusa*, one of the lower grades in the Islamic religious hierarchy of the Ottoman Empire. At the time he received this honor, which nominally entitled him to teach certain religious sciences, Ruhi was only fifteen years old.[70]

While he was receiving elements of both a secular and a religious education, Ruhi also studied at the Alliance Israélite school in Jerusalem, where he began to learn Hebrew,[71] as well as at the *Salahiyya* school (Ste. Anne) of the Pères Blanches, where he continued the study of French he had begun several years before. During his father's tenure as qadi in Tripoli, Ruhi al-Khalidi had attended *al-Madrasa al-Wataniyya*, a private school founded by Shaykh Husayn al-Jisr, mentioned in chapter 3, which taught foreign languages and other modern subjects along the lines first developed by the missionary and state schools. The influential Shaykh

Husayn was one of a group of modernizing educators rooted in the reformist *salafi* religious tradition who had a profound influence on several generations of students in the late Ottoman period.[72] A strong supporter of reform of the state apparatus and the extension of its power, we have seen that al-Jisr was a close friend of Ruhi's father Yasin, and Ruhi became a student at the new *Sultaniyya* school in Beirut soon after al-Jisr was named to the post of director there.

After successfully completing his studies in Istanbul Ruhi departed for France to study political science in 1893, a departure which was made hastily since the Ottoman secret police had him under surveillance because of his involvement in the circle of Jamal al-Din al-Afghani.[73] He had met the shaykh through his uncle Yusuf Diya'.'[74] After a three-year course in political science, Ruhi al-Khalidi entered the Ecole des Hautes Etudes of the Sorbonne, where he did advanced research in the Islamic field under the French Orientalist Hartwig Derenbourg, who was director of the section devoted to religion. Derenbourg, an acquaintance of Yusuf Diya' Paşa from the latter's days at the Oriental Academy in Vienna, seemed to appreciate the breadth of knowledge of the young Ruhi al-Khalidi. In an attestation appended to the young man's *ijaza* from Jerusalem Derenbourg noted that he had taken his courses on the Qur'an, on al-Hariri, on Saladin, and on Himyarite inscriptions, noting that "il s'est bien initié aux méthodes européennes sans pour cela rien perdre de sa science orientale, et je souhaite qu'il rapporte dans son pays et qu'il y répand nos procédés et nos habitudes d'enseignement."[75] Derenbourg appointed him a *conferencier* at the Sorbonne, and used his influence to help Ruhi to advance in the world of European Orientalism.

One of the high points in this regard was his presentation of a paper on the spread of Islam in the modern world to the 1897 Orientalist Congress in Paris, which was later published in both French and Arabic.[76] The paper utilized much of the training Ruhi had obtained, both at the *Mülkiye* and at the Sorbonne, particularly to analyze the statistics on the Muslim populations of the countries of the world, an analysis which constitutes the bulk of the 65-page booklet as it was finally published. He came to the conclusion, based on a careful country-by-country assessment, that the number of Muslims in the world at the time was far larger than the 175–180 million estimate given by most sources. He reports that his figure, of more than 285 million, or one-fifth of the human race, provoked the response from some of those present at the Congress that this was another instance of "Oriental exaggeration."[77]

The implied slur apparently spurred Ruhi al-Khalidi to expand his talk for publication with forty-seven pages of statistics on Muslim populations in every country in the world.[78]

Ruhi al-Khalidi published many books and articles in Arabic and French thereafter, including works on Arabic literature, early Arab scientists, political history and a variety of Islamic subjects.[79] Notable among them was his edition of the manuscript of a work of *fiqh* by a fourteenth-century ancestor of his, Sa'd al-Din al-Dayri al-Khalidi, which he had found in the Khalidi Library.[80] This consisted of an annotated forty-page edition of the text of a treatise on the conditions in which imprisonment is acceptable according to the shari'a, followed by several heavily annotated biographies of the author, three of them copied from biographical dictionaries in manuscript in Istanbul and Jerusalem.

After his appointment as Ottoman Consul-General in Bordeaux in 1898, al-Khalidi continued to publish, but because of the constraints imposed by his official position (and the regime's dislike of those who published even the most innocuous materials at home or abroad), he had to do so under the pseudonym of "Maqdisi" [Jerusalemite] with articles appearing in periodicals and newspapers in different parts of the Arabic-speaking world and Europe. During this time, Ruhi Bey al-Khalidi (the title Bey had come with his Consular appointment) married a Frenchwoman, by whom he had a son, continued his activities as a Mason,[81] and presumably continued his liberal political activities—which we can conclude by his having a rare copy of the first published rules of the Committee of Union and Progress among his papers.[82]

The stress laid on the significance of education in the discussion of Yusuf Diya' and Ruhi al-Khalidi in this chapter deserves explanation. Education was clearly important in the eyes of both men, who devoted a large part of their lives to teaching and scholarship. We can see this in many ways: Yusuf Diya' begins his Kurdish-Arabic dictionary with a passage on the importance of learning languages and the significance of the great expansion of science, learning and education under 'Abd al-Hamid: "the educational programs are crowded with subjects, the barriers to learning are breaking down, the rich and poor desire it . . . yes, indeed this is necessary in all civilized countries."[83]

Similarly, well over half of Ruhi al-Khalidi's eight-page autobiographical note cited earlier is devoted to the details of his education,[84] and he too laid stress on the importance of knowledge: he relates how during his childhood he saw how knowledgeable about the Holy Land were members of a party of Europeans at Jericho, and contrasted the respect for knowledge and freedom in the West with the ignorance and oppression that prevailed in the East.[85]

For members of most notable families in the Arab provinces, education was traditionally accorded a high priority, for obvious reasons: it was crucial for maintaining a position in the elite, as well as being central to a fuller understanding of the Islamic religion, and for the sake of knowledge itself. While ambition, the desire for status, and material motives cannot be ignored, love of knowledge should not be underestimated: many members of this class were devoted and serious scholars, who were clearly deeply committed to their research and writing. From his private papers, for example, we can see that Ruhi al-Khalidi, who was in effect a perpetual student, teacher, or scholar for nearly thirty years, until his appointment as Consul-General in Bordeaux in 1898, was sincerely interested in what he studied, taught, and wrote about. He occasionally sought appointments in government service during this period, but at other times turned down good job offers for a chance to study, as when he want off to France in 1893, and for many years seemed as content as had been his uncle Yusuf Diya' to remain a scholar.

With his election to parliament as a representative of Jerusalem following the 1908 Revolution and his reelection in 1912, Ruhi Bey was once again following the career pattern pioneered by his uncle. He eventually became Vice-President of the Chamber, and was generally considered a staunch member of the governing CUP. Ruhi al-Khalidi came to public attention in Palestine and all over the Arab provinces of the Empire on one notable occasion during his parliamentary career. This occurred when in May 1911 he raised the issue of Zionism in the Chamber, starting the debate mentioned in chapter 2 in which he was supported by his colleague from Jerusalem, Sa'id al-Husayni, and opposition leader Shukri al-'Asali, the newly elected deputy from Damascus.[86]

Ruhi al-Khalidi began his long, prepared speech by noting that as Deputy from Jerusalem, he represented a large number of Jews who had demonstrated their loyalty to the homeland, but that he was against Zionism, which was working to establish a Jewish state ("*mamlaka isra'iliyya*") with its capital at Jerusalem, and to take control of Palestine. He discussed the writings and statements of a number of Zionist leaders, showing that their objective was fostering national spirit among the Jews, "in order to create a nation [*umma*] in Palestine and to colonize the promised land, to which they are returning twenty centuries after they departed from it."[87] Undoubtedly sensitive to the possibility that his remarks could be interpreted as anti-Semitic,[88] he concluded by once again affirming that he was warning only of the danger of Zionist settlement in Palestine: "The Jews [*al-isra'iliyun*] are a great people and the country benefits from their expertise, wealth, schools and knowledge, but they should settle in other parts of the Empire and should acquire Ottoman nationality."[89]

Explicit in this speech is the urgent sense that Palestine was in danger from Zionism—in fact the speech exaggerated this danger, by inflating the number of settlers and their achievements—and that it was the obligation of the Empire to help protect this important part of its domains. In spite of the care he took to avoid being misunderstood, some members of parliament took offense at Ruhi's speech. After Ruhi's fellow-deputy from Jerusalem, Sa'id al-Husayni, had risen to support his colleague, arguing that the objective of the Zionists was the creation of a new nationality in Syria, a Jewish CUP deputy from Izmir, Nisim Mazliah, intervened in the debate. He defended the Zionist movement, demanded a government inquiry to show the falseness of some of the accusations made against it, and attacked Ruhi Bey fiercely, asking what was the sin of the Jews if the Torah promised them resurgence and strength? "Ruhi Bey al-Khalidi can burn the Torah, but the Qur'an is there to prove what is in it," he stated angrily, adding: "I warn him against this seed he has sown in the chamber, for the plant it will produce will not be good. He and his friends wish by their words only to oppose the government . . ."[90]

The last of the Arab speakers was Shukri al-'Asali. In the speech already mentioned in chapter 2 (and described in the Damascus newspaper *al-Muqtabas* in a first-page article as "resonant") he strongly criticized the activities of the Zionist movement in Palestine, and described at length his fruitless efforts to stop the al-Fula purchase while he was *qa'immaqam* of Nazareth. Shukri al-'Asali then accused the Zionist movement of having ambitions beyond Palestine, indeed as far as Mesopotamia, and concluded by urging the passage of legislation he had already proposed limiting Jewish settlement in Palestine.[91]

There is a major difference in tone between al-'Asali's speech and that of Ruhi al-Khalidi, specifically as regards the open hostility to the CUP government of the former (al-'Asali responded at one point to an interjection by CUP leader Talat Bey with the sarcastic words, "So you say"), and his more exaggerated estimations of the power of the Zionists. But al-'Asali's speech was peppered with anecdotes drawn from his own service as a government official in Palestine which illustrated the effects of land settlement on the peasantry, and the high degree of internal organization of the new Jewish colonies. By contrast, the speeches of both Ruhi al-Khalidi and Sa'id al-Husayni appear to have been drier, more abstract, and more boring.[92]

We know that Zionism had long been a matter of intense interest to Ruhi al-Khalidi, and that he approached it in the deliberate, scientific fashion which he acquired as a result of his academic training. Ruhi Bey's notebooks are full of notes, tables, and other data on the Zionist movement, while he had several scrapbooks full of press clippings on the same subject. Both he and his uncle, moreover, owned numerous works on Zionism, Jewish history, the history of anti-Semitism, and related matters. Like his uncle, we have seen that Ruhi Bey was interested enough in this subject to learn some Hebrew, and he too had many Zionist and non-Zionist Jewish acquaintances.[93] His 1911 speech is notable for its scholarly references to the history of Palestine and of the Jewish people, amply buttressed with biblical quotations, and by a disquisition on the genesis of Zionism. All of this was more appropriate to a classroom or a published article than to the raucous chamber of the Ottoman parliament. Indeed, as Ruhi was speaking, one deputy interjected, "Mr. Speaker, we are discussing the budget. I beg you, let us not waste time listening to these tales from history!," and another said, "Let the speaker publish his words in the official gazette and stop wasting our time!"[94] Perhaps for these reasons, his speech seems to have had even less impact on his colleagues than that of al-'Asali, although none of the three Arab speakers seems to have been particularly effective.[95]

At the time of his death, Ruhi al-Khalidi was finishing a piece of research he seems to have worked on for many years, probably since before he left France in 1908: an analytical study of Zionism, entitled "Zionism or the Zionist Question," examining the roots of Zionist ideology in ancient and modern Jewish history, and surveying the genesis of the modern Zionist movement.[96] Like his speech before Parliament, this 146-page manuscript laid out the threat to both Palestine and the Ottoman Empire which Ruhi al-Khalidi perceived in the Zionist movement. The aim of the Zionist movement, he states, is "to establish a Jewish state in Palestine to which all Jews suffering the persecution called anti-Semitism would emigrate, to create in Palestine a national home (*watan*) for them alone according to the rules of their nation (*milla*), and which would be recognized by the civilized nations."[97]

Zionism, Ruhi al-Khalidi argued, grew out of a radically new reading of the Torah, the Talmud, and medieval and modern Jewish writings which calls upon the Jews "to return to Palestine and stresses that worldly and religious happiness consist in possessing Zion and ruling it."[98] In hindsight, these seem perfectly straightforward conclusions, and indeed much of al-Khalidi's work (like the earlier essay on the subject by Najib Nassar[99]) is buttressed with sections from a long article on Zionism translated from the *Encyclopedia Judaica*. But in the context of the public debate of the time in the Ottoman Empire, when these very objectives of the Zionist movement were being strongly denied by its partisans (indeed defenders of Zionism denied them during the debate in the Ottoman parliament in May 1911), these were revolutionary conclusions, although al-Khalidi deliberately stated them in a low-key manner.

Ruhi al-Khalidi was quite aware of the differences within the Zionist movement regarding how to go about achieving its objectives, and noted the fact that most of its leaders now understood that they would have to "colonize Palestine little by little." He pointed out to his readers that the movement also understood the value of favorable publicity, and was liberal in providing subsidies to journalists and newspapers who supported it. He declared that the Ottoman paper *Iqdam*, the French-language Istanbul papers *Aurore, Orient*, and *Le Jeune Turc*, as well as the Arabic-language papers *al-Nasir* in Beirut, *al-Nafir* in Jerusalem, and *al-Akhbar* in Jaffa, were all subsidized by the Zionist movement in order to provide it with favorable publicity,[100] a subject discussed further in chapter 6.

In his analysis, al-Khalidi relied on more than his research in European and Ottoman sources, and his experience in the rough world of Ottoman politics. The last chapter of the work, which consists of a settlement-by-settlement examination of the progress of Zionist colonization throughout Palestine, is clearly based on visits by Ruhi al-Khalidi to many of these settlements. In the wake of what he saw there, as Walid Khalidi points out in his analysis of this work, it is apparent that Ruhi was torn by divided feelings: on the one hand, "he admired the achievements of the Jewish colonists and their modern methods; on the other he was embittered by the backwardness of the Palestinian country-side, and angered by Arabs who sold land and by the middle-men and Ottoman officials who facilitated the purchases."[101]

The conclusion to all of this was grim, in Ruhi al-Khalidi's view. Against the disclaimers that the true objectives of Zionism involved no ill intentions toward the Arab population of Palestine, and against the rosy descriptions by supporters of Zionism of how much good they were doing for Palestine and its people, he set this bleak panorama of what he argued was actually happening in Palestine: "the policy of the Zionists is to provoke the government to repress and debase the influential people in the country, bring about their extinction, and then win over the thinking of the simple peasants, bringing them under their financial power and using them to cultivate their land as they take possession of it, village by village."[102]

This work, incomplete though it was, nevertheless appears to be the fullest assessment until that time of what Zionism portended for the Arab population of Palestine. While clearly motivated by a sense of alarm at the danger to the country and its indigenous population posed by the Zionist movement, it is neither alarmist nor extreme in tone, but rather analytical and deliberate. It embodies, moreover, one of the first explicit, overt expressions of the relationship between local patriotism and opposition to Zionism which were to play such a large part in the shaping of Palestinian identity over the rest of the twentieth century. It appears that this manuscript was in the process of being copied for the printer (only a few pages of the first draft remained to be copied from the author's hand into a clear, double-spaced copy) when in July 1913 Ruhi al-Khalidi traveled to Istanbul, where he suddenly fell sick, and died after an illness of only a few days at the age of forty-nine.[103]

V

How did these two individuals, whose careers span the last half century of the Ottoman period, reconcile their commitment to the Ottoman framework with other loyalties and affiliations? Among these other allegiances were Islamic solidarity, Arabism, Palestinian patriotism, opposition to Zionism, party political affiliation, local Jerusalem loyalties, and family linkages, as well as a commitment to liberal constitutionalism, administrative reform of the state apparatus, the expansion of education, and the spread of learning.

There is little sign that Yusuf Diya' and Ruhi al-Khalidi (or colleagues of theirs like Sa'id al-Husayni) felt that their different loyalties conflicted fundamentally with one another, or with their wholehearted acceptance of an overarching Ottoman political structure. There were naturally conflicts between different commitments, as when Ruhi al-Khalidi's outspoken criticism of the government's policy toward Zionism brought down on him the opprobrium of some of his CUP colleagues in Parliament, who accused him and his fellow anti-Zionists of opposition for opposition's sake, and of fomenting sectarian discord and thereby weakening the Empire. There is no sign, however, that he perceived such an accu-

sation as having any foundation, and he answered his detractors by arguing that his objective in making such criticisms was to strengthen the
Empire.[104] It is nevertheless possible to discern in the last pages of Ruhi
al-Khalidi's manuscript on Zionism the beginnings of a disenchantment
with the CUP, the constitutional government, and perhaps the Empire,
because of their dereliction of duty in the face of what he perceived as
the deadly menace to Palestine and the Empire posed by Zionism.

For both Yusuf Diya' and Ruhi al-Khalidi, Arabism, Palestinian patriotism, local Jerusalem loyalties, and Ottomanism were overlapping
identities which complemented one another, and could be reconciled
when a contradiction between them arose. Schölch cites a letter from
Yusuf Diya' to the German Orientalist Wahrmund in 1878, in which he
called Jerusalem his homeland (*watani al-Quds al-Sharif*), but stressed
his loyalty to the Ottoman nation ("*milla*") and state.[105] That Yusuf
Diya' was an Arabist, in the sense of a cultural nationalist, cannot be
doubted: the references, already noted, in his autobiographical sketch
of 1875 to "a Turkish teacher from Istanbul" obtaining the post he coveted, and to his election by "the people of Jerusalem and the Turkish
government," are clear signs of his awareness of the ethnic facts of life
in the Empire. Moreover, in his 1880 edition of the *diwan* of the pre-
Islamic poet Labid ibn Rabi'a, Yusuf Diya' is explicit in expressing his
hopes for the revival of the Arabs. After quoting a line of Imru al-Qays's
poetry evocative of past glories ("*qif bil-diyar fa hathihi atharuha . . .*"), he
adds: "However, we have the strong hope that the Arabs will soon
recover the place among civilized nations they lost in the centuries of
darkness, since this nation [*milla*], may God protect it, is still numerous,
has many kingdoms [*mamalik*], high ideas and many sources of wealth
drawn from its language . . ."[106]

Nevertheless, there is no hint of a contradiction between such clear
expressions of cultural nationalism and their author's loyalty to the
Ottoman framework. Indeed a year after this book was published in
Vienna, 'Abd al-Hamid appointed Yusuf Diya' *qa'immaqam* of Jaffa, his
first official post since he had angered the Sultan with his speeches
before Parliament a few years earlier.

In a later generation, Ruhi al-Khalidi's Arabism, which like that of
his uncle was cultural rather than explicitly political in nature, was no
bar to his being one of the leading Arab members of the CUP, in spite
of the Turkish nationalist orientation of some of its leaders.[107] The key
to explaining Ruhi al-Khalidi's continuing adherence to the CUP when
many other Arab leaders—including his ally in the debates on Zionism,

Shukri al-'Asali—were increasingly alienated from it, lies in his agreement with its views on the position and role of the Sultan, and on the need for reform of the state administrative system. Ruhi al-Khalidi, like his uncle and other liberals of their day, was deeply marked by the experience of opposing the autocratic rule of the Sultan for more than three decades.

For these men and others like them, the Ottoman government dominated by the CUP represented the best vehicle for championing constitutionalism and opposing the arbitrary exercise of power, and for carrying out the administrative modernization necessary to restore the strength of the Empire, and to enable it to resist strong external pressures. These were clearly ideas in which they and others of their generation believed deeply. Both had suffered personally from censorship and the arbitrary exercise of power by a near-absolute monarch,[108] both were strong supporters of constitutionalism and parliamentary government, and both had spent much of their lives furthering the centralization and modernization of the government apparatus with which the CUP was identified.[109] They saw these things as essential if their homeland were to escape falling under foreign control.

For such members of the elite of the Arab provinces of the Empire who had spent their careers in service of the state, their Ottomanism was natural and ingrained. Whether as members of the religious establishment (where many members of notable families still sought preferment, while others moved away from this field),[110] or as officials in the modern state bureaucracy, members of this elite looked to the Ottoman state as a barrier against the incursions of aggressive foreign powers with designs on the Arab provinces. Such individuals could be more or less liberal— Sultan 'Abd al-Hamid had little trouble finding politically conservative members of notable families with a secular modern education to hold key posts in Palestine and other parts of *bilad al-sham* in the decades after he purged the liberal supporters of Reşid Paşa and Midhat Paşa such as Yusuf Diya' al-Khalidi in the 1870s and 1880s.[111] But as a group, they remained loyal to the Empire and committed to it as a political framework at least until 1914, notwithstanding their differences with a given Sultan, or regime, or government. In this there is little difference between pro-CUP Arab notables and leading Arab political figures who left the CUP and joined the opposition such as Shukri al-'Asali, Shafiq al-Mu'ayyad, or 'Abd al-Hamid al-Zahrawi, all parliamentary colleagues of Ruhi al-Khalidi in the 1908–1912 Parliament who were defeated in the "big stick" election of the latter year.[112]

They found no contradiction between a firm commitment to Ottomanism, and taking pride in their Arab heritage (Ruhi al-Khalidi made a point of stressing that he had delivered the first lecture in Arabic at the Sorbonne),[113] defending Palestine against what they perceived as the danger of Zionist colonization, and opposing the government party on this issue. However, if there was one area where a certain dissonance appears in their beliefs some time after the turn of the twentieth century, it was over the issue of Zionism. For Ottoman liberals, and even for others, it had long been possible to accept that many things wrong with the Ottoman system were caused by the absolutism of 'Abd al-Hamid, or the lingering effects of his reign. But by 1911, and all the more so by the time of Ruhi al-Khalidi's death in 1913, it must have begun to seem that the problems in Palestine could not be ascribed solely to the ill-effects of the rule of a long-deposed Sultan. The increasingly sharp tone of the Arabic press after 1908 (which we will examine in a later chapter), of the speeches by al-Khalidi, al-Husayni and al-'Asali in the Ottoman Chamber in May 1911, of Najib Nassar's 1911 essay on Zionism[114], and of Ruhi al-Khalidi's book on Zionism, with its bitter concluding words about the role of the government in supporting Zionism, all point to the beginnings of a shift in this regard, prompted by local developments in Palestine.

Nevertheless, even while helping to rewrite Islamic, Ottoman and Arab history in ways that were to lay the foundation for modern nationalist interpretations,[115] it is apparent that for the most part Ruhi al-Khalidi, Yusuf Diya' al-Khalidi, and others of their generations and their class before 1914 could still feel that they were operating within a framework flexible enough to contain the incipient contradictions between the various ethnic groups, nationalities, and "imagined communities"[116] it encompassed.

Perhaps Ruhi al-Khalidi was fortunate to die when he did, before World War I. The wrenching changes the war brought in its wake shattered this framework, and opened the Middle East to a brave new world of aggressive, assertive new nationalisms. He and others of his generation were nonetheless central in laying the intellectual groundwork for Arabism, Palestinian patriotism, and other ideologies that came into full flower after 1918. Their lives illustrate fully the tapestry of loyalties that constituted identity for them, and illuminate how the various trends that comprised this identity came to evolve in the following decades, and came to have an impact on larger and larger segments of the population. For through the medium of the press, parliamentary politics, and the speedier and broader diffusion of ideas made possible by the expansion of the educational system, their understanding of identity came to be shared with far wider circles of their fellow-citizens than would otherwise have been the case.

The next two chapters will show how this occurred over the issue of Zionism, with chapter 5 exploring the first early clashes between Zionist settlers and Palestinian peasants, and chapter 6 examining how the debate over Zionism played out in the pages of the Arabic-language press in Palestine and elsewhere. In Palestine in particular, what Anderson describes as "print capitalism" thereby helped shape a broad community of interest, an imagined community that came to describe itself as Palestinian, and that saw itself as under threat from Zionism, and from other directions. In this fashion, ideas like those expressed by Ruhi al-Khalidi, Sa'id al-Husayni, and Shukri al-'Asali in this chapter, and those of others—peasants, notables, and newspaper editors—whom we will encounter in the next two chapters, were placed before ever wider audiences and gained greater and greater currency.

CHAPTER 5

Elements of Identity I:
Peasant Resistance to
Zionist Settlement

I

It is a commonplace that history is written by the victors. And it follows that it is more likely to be written about the strong than the weak, and that the views and exploits of those able to read and write are perhaps naturally more frequently recorded by historians, with their tendency to favor written records, than those of the illiterate.

All of these inherent historical biases have complicated the modern historiography of Palestine. Their effect has been magnified by the fact that over the past five decades, much source material for writing the modern history of the Palestinian Arabs has been lost, destroyed, or incorporated into archives in Israel, where it was long inaccessible to many Palestinian and Arab historians. The unsettled situation of the Palestinian people since 1948, whether under occupation or in the diaspora, has meant that when Palestinian archives, research institutions, and universities could be created, they were often denied the stability, continuity, and possibilities for long-term planning necessary to provide the requisite support for sustained research and scholarship. Also harmful has been the absence or weakness of unifying central Palestinian national institutions, and the support such institutions can provide for education, research, scholarship, libraries, and state archives.

The PLO'S Palestine Research Center and the independent Institute for Palestine Studies (IPS), both founded in Beirut in the mid-1960s, amassed considerable library and documentary collections and produced some significant research, until Israel's 1982 invasion of Lebanon disrupted their functioning, and indeed much Palestinian intellectual production. The Center's historical archives were seized by occupying Israeli forces, and although they were returned as part of the November 1983 prisoner exchange with the PLO, for more than a decade they could not be reopened. The IPS archives were moved to safety after the 1982 war, and some of them are still inaccessible. The 1982 war also disrupted a UNESCO project for a Palestinian Open University, as well as the academic atmosphere at the five Beirut universities where many Palestinian scholars had become established since 1948. Similarly, the Israeli occupation has caused severe problems for the six West Bank and Gaza Strip universities, which were exacerbated by the Israeli closure orders which were in effect in most of them throughout the Palestinian *intifada*, from 1987 until 1992, and afterwards in some cases.[1]

Partly in consequence of these circumstances, there has been a dearth of sound historical scholarship by Palestinians.[2] Most writing about modern Palestinian history has been done by non-Palestinians, who have by and large lacked an intimate familiarity with the indigenous sources, the individuals concerned, and the social and cultural context of Palestinian politics. Irrespective of any bias such foreign scholars may have had, this situation has naturally had a major effect on what has been written, and particularly the perspective from which it is written. While a cross-cultural approach is often extremely valuable, and can provide insights otherwise unavailable, obviously nothing can substitute for people writing their own history, and indeed the two processes can and should be complementary.

Thus, the purview and perspective of much work on the history of Palestine has paid more attention to certain sources and subjects than to others. One example is Yehoshua Ben Arieh's *Jerusalem in the 19th Century: The Old City*, much of which treats the city's Arab population (according to Ben Arieh, Arabs were a majority of its population during most of the period he covers) relying mainly on European traveler's reports and European Jewish accounts, but using no Arabic or Ottoman sources.[3] Similarly, Isaiah Friedman's *The Question of Palestine 1914–1918*, subtitled *A Study of British-Jewish-Arab Relations,* in practice deals only with the British and Jewish sides of this triangle, again using no Arabic or Ottoman sources.[4]

Further, even when the Arabs have been the primary focus of a work, the urban and literate sectors of the population have perhaps naturally tended to be the focus of attention, as in the respected works on Palestinian political history during the 1920s and 1930s by Yehoshua Porath and Ann Mosely Lesch, which depend on a judicious selection of Arabic, Zionist, and Western sources.[5] In other works of history, more use has been made of Zionist sources than Arab ones. This is true even with examples of sound scholarship and great originality focusing primarily on the Palestinians such as Neville Mandel's *The Arabs and Zionism before World War I,* which relies mainly on press reports preserved in the Central Zionist Archives, rather than on the Arabic newspapers themselves, for an analysis of the Arab press.[6]

There are justifications for some of these apparent methodological and historiographical weaknesses. As has already been pointed out, Israeli and Western archives contain more material and tend to be better organized than many existing Arab ones. In other cases, accessibility and convenience have perhaps wrongly determined which sources were used. The problem is made more difficult by the fact that the population of the countryside was poor, illiterate, and largely inaccessible for much of the modern era, and as such left few records of its own. Moreover, it is to be expected that the Arab urban population, which was the most visible and politically active, and the most extensively represented in the existing written record, would be the object of the most intense scholarly scrutiny. All of this is aside from any biases in favor of a focus on the elite that might have affected historians.[7]

But regarding issues crucial to the modern history of Palestine like the overall economic and social effects on the Palestinians of land sales to Zionist purchasers, the scope of peasant dispossession and resistance, the degree of politicization of the rural population, and the impact of Zionist settlement on the Palestinian Arab rural majority, some of these justifications ring hollow. While the British and Zionist records are necessarily central sources for any such analysis, and while attention must be paid to the newspapers and activities of the elite Arab urban population, in looking at issues such as these, what happened at the village level should be the primary focus, and sources that reflect this local reality should be sought out. It is possible to follow developments at this level utilizing nontraditional sources, as did Ya'kov Firestone in his pioneering work using material from outside the formal archives,[8] or through using these archives with special attention to the rural areas, as did Ylana Miller in her *Government and Society in Rural Palestine, 1920–1948.*[9]

Such an approach is essential in any work dealing with demography, land, and the peasantry in Palestine. It is absent in many popular works, such as Joan Peters's *From Time Immemorial,* which makes sweeping and unsubstantiated assertions regarding all these subjects, with the aim of proving the nonexistence of the Palestinian people. A book like this, which is based on the selective and tendentious use of sources, systematic misquotation, and other unscholarly methods, would not deserve mention here, but for the prominent figures who praised it, the noted scholars whose aid was acknowledged by the author but who refrained from disassociating themselves from it, the respected publications that reviewed it but failed to reveal its shoddy scholarly underpinning, and the impact it has had in reinforcing crucial stereotypes regarding Palestine in American public discourse.[10]

Such an approach is absent as well in nominally more serious works that reiterate Peter's themes. Thus, Arieh Avneri's *The Claim of Dispossession,* subtitled *Jewish Land Settlement and the Arabs 1878–1948,* purports to show that there was no dispossession of Palestinians, in large part because the "Palestinians" did not exist in the commonly accepted sense of the word.[11] He asserts rather that much of the Arab population of the country drifted into it in recent times, an old and persistent canard which has been disproved by all recent demographic research.[12] Slightly more coherent than Peters, Avneri too treats this subject using Western and Hebrew sources, to the exclusion of Arabic or Ottoman ones. In three hundred pages, moreover, he never dignifies the indigenous population or the sovereign authority until 1918 with so much as a single quotation from a source generated by them.

It is clear that in works such as Peters's and Avneri's, the society being described is an object rather than a subject of history. It can be described by others, but cannot describe itself. For the assertions of polemicists such as these are tenable only from a perspective that denies any credibility to the sources produced by the society being studied. In the words of Edward Said, for such writers the Palestinians do not have "permission to narrate."[13] From these authors' perspective, of course, such a denial is rigorously logical, since the Palestinians don't exist![14]

While it is impossible at this temporal remove, and in the absence of much essential data, to record in detail what took place between Arab peasants and Jewish settlers in the Palestinian countryside before 1914, what follows is an attempt to reconstruct certain key interactions from a variety of sources, with the objective of providing a perspective too often absent. Far from being "history from below" or subaltern history for its own sake, however, it constitutes an attempt to suggest that these scattered early incidents were important not only in defining the terms of the Palestinian-Zionist conflict, but also in the genesis of Palestinian identity.

II

According to a once widely held view, Arab opposition to Zionism began only some time during the Mandate period, and since then this opposition has been artificially fostered by a succession of self-interested protagonists for a variety of reasons.[15] In fact, both a relatively widespread Arab awareness of Zionism and a fear of its potential impact on the Arabs of Palestine go much further back in time, and are much more deeply rooted, than this view would have it. During the pre-World War I period, Zionism became the subject of extensive journalistic comment and public controversy in Palestine and other Arab regions of the Ottoman Empire, and ultimately became a major issue in both local and Ottoman politics. Some of this has already been briefly described in the discussions of the growth of the press in chapter 3, and of the 1911 parliamentary debates in chapter 4.[16]

The extent of the opposition within Palestine itself to Zionist immigration before 1914 has been examined by several studies.[17] Less attention has been paid to the effect of developments in Palestine during this period on the thinking of the elites of the rest of Syria, Egypt, and the other Arab lands under Ottoman sovereignty, at a time when Arabism, the forerunner of Arab nationalism, was developing into an effective political movement.[18] This took place against the background of the flourishing of political, intellectual, and journalistic activity throughout the Empire beginning with the reimposition of the Ottoman Constitution in 1908 and continuing until 1914, during which time, as we have seen, there was a major expansion of the Arabic language press in Palestine and other parts of greater Syria.

Simultaneous with these developments, the Arabs of Palestine were dismayed by the impact of increasing Zionist colonization, as the mounting persecution of Eastern European Jews sent large numbers of new settlers to Palestine in the second *aliya,* or wave of Jewish immigration to Palestine, from 1905 to 1914.[19] From around the turn of the century to

1914, the Jewish population of the country appears to have doubled, from about 30,000 to 60,000, during which time the total population grew much less quickly.[20] Besides increasing Jewish numbers significantly, most of these newcomers were more deeply imbued with political Zionism than earlier Jewish settlers, and more intent on creating a new, purely Jewish society in Palestine. As we shall see, many of them also had other beliefs, which made friction with the Arab peasantry all the more severe.

The Palestinian reaction to this increased Zionist activity was strong, particularly during the years from 1908 to 1914 when it could express itself more freely, and was encouraged by the activities of political leaders like Ruhi al-Khalidi and Sa'id al-Husayni, and by articles in newspapers like *Filastin* and *al-Karmil.* For the first time, many Arabs realized that Zionism aimed ultimately to create a Jewish polity in Palestine in place of the existing Arab one. This realization was intensified by the fact that in the Palestinian countryside after the turn of the century, increased land purchases and the replacement of Arab wage-laborers on Jewish estates by Jewish workers angered many *fellahin.* The intensity of these reactions, combined with the new political and press freedoms, helps explain the impact of the Palestine question on Arab politics at this time. And while it was understandably the response of the literate urban Palestinian upper and middle classes as expressed in the press, in the Ottoman Parliament, and elsewhere, that most affected thinking in other Arab countries, we shall see that at the root of the fears of many of these urban Palestinians about Zionism was the experience of the *fellahin* who were the first to clash with the Zionist settlers.

As Roger Owen and Charles Issawi have shown, economic and social change in the lands of the Eastern Mediterranean was increasingly rapid in the late nineteenth century.[21] Underlying many of these changes was the gradual expansion of the market economy over a long period of time, and the tendency it fostered toward the privatization of land ownership and its concentration in fewer hands. This was particularly the case after the promulgation of the Ottoman Land Code in 1858, which was put into effect in Palestine very slowly, over a period of decades, and appears to have had a differing impact on different regions.[22]

In the hill regions of Palestine, where small plots and individual ownership and/or usufruct had long been common, the law seems to have had considerably less effect as far as alienation of peasants from their land and the concentration of landed property in a few hands.[23] In lowland areas favorable to grain cultivation, however, the new law facilitated registration in the name of individual owners of agricultural land, most

of which as state land, or *miri*, had never previously been privately registered and most of which had formerly been treated according to traditional forms of land tenure, generally *musha'*, or communal usufruct.[24]
The new law meant that for the first time a peasant could be deprived not
of formal title to his land, which he had rarely held before, but rather of
the right to live on it, cultivate it, and pass it on to his heirs—rights that
had formerly been inalienable if taxes on miri *land* were paid regularly.

Under the provisions of the 1858 law, as it came to be implemented,
communal rights of tenure were often ignored, particularly in lowland
and *musha'* areas, as many peasants with long-standing traditional rights
failed to register out of fear of taxation and other state exactions,
notably conscription. Instead, village shaykhs, tax-collectors, and urban
members of the upper classes, adept at manipulating or circumventing
the legal process, registered large areas of land as their personal property.[25] As far as lands in Palestine were concerned, three areas were most
affected: the fertile central coastal region; the Marj Ibn 'Amir, a broad,
extremely rich valley running southeast from Haifa to Beisan (also
known as the Plain of Esdraleon and the Jezreel Valley); and eastern
Galilee, all of which were less heavily populated than the hill regions,
since they had suffered most from the depredations of nomads in the
late eighteenth and early nineteenth centuries before the Ottoman government reestablished its authority.

The biggest beneficiaries of this process of consolidation of land ownership through registration were the newly prosperous merchants of the
coastal cities of Beirut, Haifa, Jaffa, and Gaza. Their new wealth was a
byproduct of the incorporation of the region into the world economy,
with the attendant opening up of new means of communications, and the
growth in trade and in agricultural production related to the improvement in security in the countryside in the 1870s and 1880s. They invested
much of this new wealth in land in Palestine, as happened in other parts
of *bilad al-Sham*, with the difference that in Palestine the market for land
was soon to be fundamentally transformed by the demand produced by
Zionist colonization. In the middle of this new situation lay the peasantry,
in some cases with long-standing traditional rights as cultivators which
were swept away by the new laws, and in other cases with grazing and other
rights which were equally in jeopardy under the new legal dispensation.

Given these rural trends, and such indicators as the growth of the
press and the spread of education, it is clear that the society within which
Jewish immigrants settled around the turn of the twentieth century was
far from stagnant, and indeed was changing rapidly. Although the most

visible changes could be found among the urban notables and a small but growing middle class, change was taking place as well among the peasant majority of the Palestine population. Some scholars have argued that "for all practical purposes the masses were politically, socially and intellectually non-existent," and that it was "the reactions of the political elite among the Arabs to Zionism, . . . and not those of the peasant masses, which was significant."[26] Contrary to these views, it can be argued that from the beginning, the reaction of the peasantry was central to the struggle over Zionist colonization in Palestine.[27]

Although most peasants were illiterate, they were aware of events in their immediate region and often farther afield. Certainly land sales involving the physical removal of the traditional Arab cultivators in favor of newcomers, a process that became increasingly frequent after the turn of the twentieth century, would have been widely noticed by the rural population in a given locality. The illiteracy of the peasants nevertheless meant that in order for them to have an effect beyond their own district, others would have to record their responses. We are thus left with little direct record of these responses, except as they were passed on by the literate urban members of the community (who rarely perceived them first-hand), or via the paper trail left by outbursts of peasant violence against Jewish colonists. From a study of both sets of reactions, and the interaction between them, it is clear how and why events in the Palestinian countryside aroused such widespread concern in the rest of the country and farther afield in the Arab world.

III

There are no precise or reliable figures regarding the population of Palestine just before World War I, which the best estimates—those of Justin McCarthy, based on official Ottoman data—place at over 720,000.[28] According to studies based on contemporary Zionist sources, the Jewish population of the country was by then about 85,000, but McCarthy's estimates, based on the careful examination of all the available Ottoman and western statistics, indicate that a figure of about 60,000 is more likely.[29] According to all sources, before 1914 the great majority of the Jewish population of Palestine lived in the cities and towns, notably the four "holy cities" of Jerusalem, Hebron, Safad, and Tiberias; only 10,000–12,000 lived on the land, nearly all of them in the more than forty agricultural colonies that had been established since 1878.

It is this rural minority of the Jewish population that concerns us most, however. Unlike most of the urban majority of Jews in Palestine at this time, who were generally religiously-oriented and apolitical, a great many of those in the countryside were committed Zionists with explicit political objectives. Additionally, it was this rural settler population which came into the closest contact with the majority of the Arab population of Palestine, the peasantry. This naturally occurred because, as can be seen from any map showing the location of the Jewish colonies established before 1914,[30] these were sited mainly in the fertile lowlands of the coastal plain, in the Valley of Jezreel, or in eastern Galilee. By and large these areas were already fairly heavily populated by Arabs, although often less so than the hill regions.

The situation in the different lowland areas where the main collisions between Arab and Jew first took place must be explained. In the coastal plain, running from Gaza north to Haifa, much of the soil was sandy and was not easily brought under grain cultivation, while in other areas there were marshes and swamps, and much of the region had therefore been relatively sparsely populated before the mid- to late nineteenth century. With sufficient investment, however, it proved ideal for the citrus culture for export made possible by rapid steam navigation and the growing incorporation of Palestine and other parts of the Eastern Mediterranean littoral into the world economy. This labor- and capital-intensive form of agriculture, which expanded rapidly in the decades after the 1850s, drew workers to these areas, and by 1914 was producing Palestine's most valuable export crop. In the best pre-war year, 1913, 1.6 million cases of oranges, valued at nearly £300,000, were shipped from Jaffa, figures not exceeded until 1923–24.[31] American consular officials in 1880 estimated that there were about 500 orange groves between two and six acres each in the Jaffa region, an overall area of about 2,000 acres, and that the land devoted to oranges had tripled since 1850.[32] It increased rapidly in the following years, reaching about 30,000 *dunums* (or 7,500 acres) by the outbreak of World War I, most of it owned and cultivated by Arabs.[33]

Meanwhile, in the years after the 1860s, the same processes of population growth and expanded cultivation also took place in fertile lowland regions such as the Marj Ibn 'Amir and eastern Galilee. This came about as the imposition of strong central government control, which limited both bedouin depredations and factional fighting, allowed the more stable neighboring hill villages to expand regular cultivation into the lowlands, where previously they had been able to grow crops only in those periods when the precarious security situation permitted it. In many cases, of course, the peasants' "title" to such land, in the modern western legal sense of the word, was unclear.

Prosperous urban merchants from Beirut, Damascus, Haifa, and Jaffa were quick to realize the opportunities resulting from the expansion of cultivation made possible by the greater degree of security in Palestine, combined with the increased possibilities for establishing ownership over land in this category after passage of the 1858 land law.[34] In the succeeding decades, many of them managed to acquire title to large areas of these fertile lands. In some cases they settled new Arab cultivators on them, and in others they established their new rights at the expense of the claims of peasants who cultivated the land or nomads whose livestock grazed on it, turning the former into tenant-farmers. Soon afterwards, Zionist land purchase and settlement bodies were drawn to these same regions because of their fertility, because they were less heavily populated than the hills, and because ownership of large parcels was often in a few hands, facilitating transfer of title.[35] The resulting N-shaped pattern of Jewish settlement—running north up the coast, southeast along the Marj Ibn 'Amir/Valley of Jezreel axis, and then north along the shores of Lake Tiberias—was pointed out as early as 1907 by Arthur Ruppin, later to be the senior official of the Zionist movement in Palestine. This pattern of settlement in effect created the strategic and demographic backbone of the *yishuv* in succeeding years, and of Israel since 1948.[36]

By 1914, therefore, Palestine's Arab population of more than 650,000 was spread relatively densely over most of the fertile and cultivable parts of the country, in the hills as well as the lowlands, as a result of a process of rapid population growth, and the expansion and what Schölch calls the "filling" of existing villages starting in the 1860s.[37] Thus from a very early stage in the process of Zionist colonization, the establishment of a new Jewish colony frequently led to confrontations with the local populace. The process would begin with the purchase of land, generally from an absentee landlord, followed by the imposition of a new order on the existing Arab cultivators—sometimes involving their transformation into tenant-farmers or agricultural laborers, and sometimes their expulsion—and finally the settlement of new Jewish immigrants.

There were some exceptions to this pattern when the land concerned had formerly been sparsely populated or uncultivated (though, even in such cases, it may have been subject to customary grazing rights which the inhabitants were naturally unwilling to surrender). But most of the land purchased, especially after the turn of the twentieth century, was

fertile and therefore inhabited, and *fellahin* with long-standing traditional rights of tenure frequently stood in the way of the close settlement
of Jewish farmers on the land. The *fellahin* naturally considered the land
to be theirs, and they would often discover that they had ceased to be the
legal owners, and/or that they no longer had rights of usufruct on the
land, only when the land was sold by an absentee landlord to a Zionist
settlement agency. The situation was particularly acute if the agency concerned did not require their services as hired laborers or tenant farmers,
and intended to replace them with Jewish settlers, as was increasingly the
case after the turn of the century.

If the land were purchased or otherwise acquired by an Arab landlord, the result was much the same insofar as title was concerned, but
very different in other respects, since both the old and the new Arab
landlords needed the *fellahin* to cultivate their land. As Charles Kamen
points out, when the purchasers were Arabs, "the effects of such purchases were almost identical with those resulting from Jewish acquisi-
tions. The principal difference was that the Jewish owners would sooner
or later evict the Arab cultivators in order to settle Jews on the land,
while Arab owners would retain them as tenants."[38] With the creation of
Zionist land purchase and settlement agencies, committed to the principle that land purchased became the inalienable property of the Jewish
people, and could not be purchased or leased by Arabs, these distinc-
tions grew even greater, and the impact of land sales more acute.

This entire process, and the difference between earlier sales, which
rarely involved expulsion of the Arab cultivators, and those after about
1900, which often did, can be seen from examining three sets of conflicts
following land purchases, the first at Petah Tiqva in 1886, which will be
briefly recounted, and two others which we will look at more closely, one
in the Tiberias region running from 1901 to 1904 (which had a bloody
sequel in 1909), and the incidents at al-Fula in 1910–11, which have
been alluded to in previous chapters.

In the Petah Tiqva incident, which was settled by the intervention of
Ottoman troops and the arrest of many *fellahin*, a Jewish settler was killed
and several others wounded in an attack launched by peasants from the
neighboring Arab village of Yahudiyya who were aggrieved because land
they considered theirs had been sold to the colony after they forfeited it
to Jaffa money lenders and the local authorities.[39] According to one
source, the money lenders "had sold the Jews more land than was actually theirs to sell," while another indicates that "the Arab tenant farmers
were very likely entitled to the possession of 2,600 dunams" of the entire

parcel of 14,200.[40] As Mandel's account makes clear, it was only some years after the purchase had taken place that "for the first time some of the peasants were confronted with the fact that they no longer owned the land."[41]

The example of Petah Tiqva in 1886 confirms that there was a pattern stretching back to the early years of Jewish colonization in Palestine. Mandel mentions four similar incidents during the same period involving disputes over ownership. These culminated in settlers at Gedera being "harassed for years" from 1884 on; in a raid on Rehovot in 1892 "reminiscent of the attack on Petah Tiqva," followed by another attack in the following year; and in lengthy property disputes at Nes Ziyyona and Hadera. However, Mandel notes that in most of these early cases, Arab animosity eventually died down when the *fellahin* were able to lease back some of their lands from the new owners, and obtained permanent or seasonal work in other parts of their former properties.[42]

It is important to note that after these initial clashes during this early period of settlement, in most areas the pragmatic and relatively un-ideological settlers of the first *aliya* (1882–1903) in effect came to treat the *fellahin* little differently than had their former Arab landlords. They disappropriated the *fellahin*, but in most cases they did not fully dispossess them, as they integrated them into plantation-style colonies, characterized by a large number of Arab laborers and a few Jewish overseers. This uneasy, but at least temporarily manageable, situation changed definitively with the second *aliya* starting early in the twentieth century. This involved a new wave of immigrants, many of whom had fled Russia after vicious pogroms in Kishniev in 1903 and all over the country in October 1905. The newcomers brought with them the more radical socialist and nationalist ideas of the "conquest of labor"—which in practice meant replacing Arab workers with Jewish ones—and the "conquest of the soil," and a much greater willingness to take arms in defense of newly acquired lands, which translated into a more aggressive, forceful attitude to the Arabs. With these new immigrants and their novel ideas, a new, more exclusivist form of colonization began.[43]

The twentieth-century incidents in the Tiberias region and at al-Fula, especially the latter, are significant because of the major effect they were to have in the context of Ottoman and Arab nationalist politics and in the coalescence of Palestinian identity. Moreover they were also apparently the first cases where the replacement of Arab laborers with Jewish ones and the dispossession of the former was a major source of friction—for as we have seen, such a complete displacement of Arabs had not generally occurred in earlier cases. Both incidents are unusual in that they became the subject of serious disturbances and major public controversy at the time, and are among the few for which sufficient data are readily available from a variety of sources (there are very few Arab sources for the incidents before the turn of the century). Although they mark an escalation of the process, they nevertheless appear to form part of a clear existing pattern of peasant resistance to Zionist colonization, as the clash at Petah Tiqva and the four others just mentioned indicate, and as will be apparent from some of the details of these two incidents, cited below.

In the early years of the Zionist movement, many of its European supporters—and others—believed that Palestine was empty and sparsely cultivated. This view was widely propagated by some of the movement's leading thinkers and writers, such as Herzl, Bialik, and Mandelstamm, with Herzl never even mentioning the Arabs in his famous work, *The Jewish State*.[44] It was summed up in the widely-propagated Zionist slogan, "A land without a people for a people without a land." However, whatever Zionists in Europe may have chosen to believe, things looked different on the spot. There was little doubt in the minds of most Jewish settlers and of the officials responsible for purchasing land for settlement that the actual situation in Palestine was quite different from what this slogan indicated. And a brief visit to Palestine usually sufficed to show even the most ardent Zionist abroad that reality was more complicated than the movement's propaganda might lead some to believe. In the words of the famed writer Ahad Ha-Am in an essay entitled "Truth from the Land of Palestine," written after a three-month visit to the country in 1891:

> We abroad are used to believing that Eretz Israel is now almost totally desolate, a desert that is not sowed, and that anyone who wishes to purchase land there may come and purchase as much as he desires. But in truth this is not the case. Throughout the country it is difficult to find fields that are not sowed. Only sand dunes and stony mountains that are not fit to grow anything but fruit trees - and this only after hard labor and great expense of clearing and reclamation—only these are not cultivated.[45]

The situation Ha-Am described had inevitable consequences in terms of what had to be done with the Arabs who tilled land the Zionists coveted after the principle of the "conquest of labor" was slowly established as a basic element of Zionist ideology in the years following 1900. For this principle carried with it the necessity not simply to disappropriate the tillers of the land by moving in Jewish farm managers to supervise Arab *fellahin* who did the actual work (in the traditional colonial pattern that had generally obtained in the earlier settlements) but also to dispossess utterly the *fellahin* in order to make room for Jewish tillers of the soil. This harsh reality was clearly perceived by Dr. Arthur Ruppin, the foremost land expert of the Jewish Agency, who declared: "Land is the most necessary thing for our establishing roots in Palestine. Since there are hardly any more arable unsettled lands in Palestine, we are bound in each case of the purchase of land and its settlement to remove the peasants who cultivated the land so far, both owners of the land and tenants."[46]

We have seen that "removal" of the owners of the land was usually accomplished quite easily since, as a result of the accumulation of title to much fertile land in the hands of a small number of urban merchants and notables in the later nineteenth century, the tiller of the land was often different from the owner, and the latter often regarded land as no more than a commercial investment. But the resistance of *fellahin* to being uprooted from the land on which they and their ancestors had often worked and lived for generations was not so easily overcome. In their eyes, the transfer of formal, legal ownership—under a new system of property relations in land which they may or may not have comprehended or accepted—did not mean they could be deprived of what they believed were inalienable rights of usufruct. Given their understandable perspective, neither abstract legal principle, nor compensation, which was offered at times, were very convincing.

Sometimes, the *fellahin* accepted compensation from Jewish settlement bodies, presumably feeling themselves unable to stand up to the new owners of the land and their official backers. But at other times, they resisted their dispossession, on occasion with violence. In such cases, it was necessary for the purchasers to depend on the power of the state, whether the Ottoman, or, later on, the British Mandatory authorities, to enable them to take control of the land. In this new situation, lingering resentments remained, often expressing themselves in continuing acts of violence against the new settlements which, unlike the incidents of the 1880s and 1890s already described, did not dwindle as the former Arab cultivators found work as laborers or tenants on Jewish-owned land.

Starting in 1901, the Jewish Colonization Association (JCA) attempted to "remove the peasants who cultivated the land so far" from tracts totaling about seventy thousand dunums in the Tiberias district which it had purchased beginning in 1899 (the largest area of land thus far bought for

Jewish settlement in Lower Galilee). These efforts met with stiff resistance from the Arab inhabitants of the villages of al-Shajara, Misha, and Malhamiyya, who were to be dispossessed by this purchase, and other neighboring villages such as Lubiyya and Kafr Kanna, which lost some of their land as part of the transaction. Of the total area, more than 60,000 dunums had been purchased from the big Beirut merchant family of the Sursuqs, and their business partners, the Twaynis and Mudawwars. Some 700 dunums had been bought from local landlords, and 3,000 from some of the *fellahin* themselves.[47]

From the beginning, there was trouble. In 1901, *fellahin* from several villages, alarmed by news of the purchases, "molested JCA's surveyor on a number of occasions when he came to measure lands for sale."[48] According to the account of Chaim Kalvarisky, an official of the JCA, in the first stages of the dispute in 1901–1902, the *fellahin* not only refused to be removed from their lands after "Mr. Ossovetsky, who acted as agent, and the landlords paid no regard to the fate of these tenants, and insisted on their eviction, as the land had already been bought and paid for." Thereafter, "Ossovetsky was shot at; troops were brought and many tenants were arrested and taken to prison." Through the forcible intervention of the authorities, lands cultivated by inhabitants of the Arab villages were seized and they were prevented from tilling them.[49] Between 1901 and 1904, the Jewish agricultural settlements of Sejera, Kfar Tavor, Yavniel, Menehamia, and Bet Gan were set up on these lands, and others were established there later.[50] Expansion by these settlements in 1903 into lands purchased in 1899, but temporarily leased to Arab villagers from Lubiyya, led to further clashes, resulting in the death of a Jewish settler in 1904.[51]

Although this was ostensibly a routine conflict between new landowners and the traditional occupants of the land, with the state naturally intervening decisively on behalf of the possessors of legal title, there were several unusual factors involved. The first was that the new owners of the land were seen by the *fellahin* as foreigners and strangers, rather than just another set of local or absentee landlords whom they knew how to deal with. Secondly, the new settlers were increasingly motivated by the radical ideologies that animated immigrants of the second *aliya*, and fully intended to supplant the indigenous tenant farmers. Finally, these newcomers were supported by a regime that many among the local population were beginning to see as alien for the first time.[52]

Thus, in a situation where an Ottoman government that was beginning to be seen as Turkish-dominated forced Arab peasants to accept the sale and transfer of their land to Zionist colonists, it was of some significance that the Arab *qa'immaqam* of the Tiberias district, Amir Amin Arslan, should oppose the transaction on nationalist grounds.[53] This he did, Kalvarisky noted, in spite of the indifference to the issue's national aspects of his Turkish superior, Ruṣdi Bey, the *Vali* of Beirut. Ruṣdi Bey acted according to the letter of the law in ultimately seeing to it that the new owners of these lands were able to take possession of their property. But the opposition of an Arab government official presaged Arab opposition in the years that followed to both Zionist settlement endeavors, and to a Turkish-dominated government which took no apparent interest in a question of vital and growing interest to the Arabs of the Empire.

According to Kalvarisky's account, even after implementation of the *Vali*'s orders, Arslan continued to "resist the de-Arabization of the district"; he perhaps also gave discreet encouragement to the small bands of peasants angry at the loss of their land who afterwards harassed the new settlers.[54] For the time being there was little else he could do besides insisting that compensation be paid to the evicted tenants, whose will to resist had been broken by the Ottoman government's repression on behalf of the JCA. Within a few years, such aggrieved *fellahin*, who had found their former Arab landlords, the Ottoman state, and the new Jewish settlers backed by influential and affluent settlement bodies like the JCA, all ranged against them, were to find public advocates for their mute resistance.

The Ottoman Revolution of 1908 precipitated the change. Among the deputies elected to represent the Beirut *vilayet* in the Ottoman Parliament after the reimposition of the Constitution was the former *qa'immaqam* of Tiberias, Amir Amin Arslan, who won a 1909 by-election. In the Ottoman Parliament he became an active member of the large group of deputies representing the Arab provinces, who as time went on grew increasingly sensitive to the questions of Zionism and Arab nationalism, as we saw in the last chapter. At the same time, with the lifting of press censorship, and the flowering of the Arabic-language press, ideas that had long been long suppressed came to the surface and spread. The issue of Zionism soon became a subject of extensive comment, and a focus of criticism of the Ottoman authorities in the newly free press.[55]

Perhaps encouraged by the atmosphere of greater freedom, and the lifting of the heavy hand of the previous government, after 1908 there were more attacks on Jewish settlements, particularly those in the Galilee around al-Shajara which had been the scene of the 1901–4 incidents involving Amir Amin Arslan. Here new problems arose in the spring of

1909 as disputes over land which had "persisted for years" erupted, and the Arab former cultivators, perhaps emboldened by the Revolution, "challenged boundaries which had been agreed upon a decade earlier." In the resulting clashes in April 1909, four people were killed, two Arabs and two Jews, and several wounded on both sides over the course of a few days. In the aftermath, although two had been killed on each side, eleven Arabs were arrested by the authorities.[56]

The increased tension led to a consequence of great import for the development of the *yishuv* and for Jewish-Arab relations. In response to the escalating violence, in April 1909, a secret Jewish organization called *Bar Giora*, founded in 1907, publicly established a paramilitary organization called *Ha-Shomer* ("the guardian"), which was sent to guard the fields of these new Galilee settlements after the settlers received permission from the Ottoman authorities to arm themselves. *Bar Giora* was "a self-selected elite group in which 'Hebrew Labor,' settlement, and guarding all occupied pride of place," which "expressed a tendency to respond with force to clashes with the Arabs."[57] Its offspring, *Ha-Shomer*, combined an aggressive ideology with a swaggering addiction to weapons, ammunition belts, and Arab dress, as if in emulation of both their current Arab antagonists and those of the past, the Cossack oppressors of the Jews in Russia.[58]

The formation of this public paramilitary organization in April 1909 was the culmination of a process that had been going on for several years, and also fell under the rubric of the "conquest of labor," whereby the more assertive Jewish immigrants of the second *aliya* had gradually been taking over duties as armed watchmen at Jewish settlements, replacing the Arabs who had formerly performed these jobs. One of the first sites where this had occurred was in 1907 in the settlement of Sejera, on the disputed former lands of the village of al-Shajara. There, Mandel notes, as a result of this takeover "the former watchmen were disgruntled, and another source of friction had been created."[59] In taking over these jobs, Jewish settlers were not just signifying their empowerment after long years of powerlessness in the diaspora, nor merely depriving the Arab watchmen of their livelihood. Most importantly, they were taking on the defense of newly acquired land against its dispossessed former cultivators, many of whom firmly believed they still had rights to it: this incident and others like it can thus be seen as representing the conflict in Palestine in microcosm.

On both sides, the patterns established by these early clashes were lasting ones. In *The Making of Israel's Army*, Gen. Yigal Allon describes

Ha-Shomer as the nucleus of the *Haganah,* itself the forerunner of the Israeli armed forces.[60] This is a consistent trope that runs through the self-presentation of the Israeli military down to the present. The roots of the military institution which has been central to the Zionist enterprise throughout most of its history therefore lie in the active defense of newly acquired lands against those who still claimed rights over them. While much has been written about the founding of *Ha-Shomer* and what it signified, the simmering armed peasant resistance to Jewish settlement on land the *fellahin* stubbornly persisted in considering theirs was necessarily mute, inarticulate, and unsung. It was considerable enough, however, at least in areas of extensive land purchase from absentee landlords like the lands around al-Shajara in 1901–1904, to necessitate the creation of what Ze'ev Schiff, in his history of the Israeli army, calls a "highly disciplined" armed force, and like Allon describes as the precursor of that army.[61]

And on the Palestinian side, later armed movements, whether in the 1930s or the 1960s, harked back to what was described as the heroic resistance (*muqawama*) of these first *fellahin* to confront the newcomers with arms. Both the peasant headdress (the *kaffiyya*) and the term "resistance" were picked up by these later movements as symbolic of their continuity with these first armed opponents of Zionist settlement in Palestine.[62] Although we do not know the names of most of those involved on the Arab side in these incidents, and although there are few Arab records of them, we can attempt to read between the lines of the sources based on the ample contemporary Zionist and Western records, and discern something of their aims, motivations, and outlook.[63] In doing this we must take account of the fact that in these sources their actions are generally portrayed in a highly uncomplimentary and distorted light, often colored by both ignorance and hostility.

Important as had been the al-Shajara incidents in 1901–4 and their bloody sequel in 1909, which repeated the pattern of the earlier clashes in Petah Tiqva and elsewhere while taking the conflict to a higher level, a far greater impact was created by events in al-Fula, which were touched on in chapters 2 and 4. The village of al-Fula was only some fifteen miles away from al-Shajara in the neighboring district of Nazareth. There, as in al-Shajara a few years earlier, an Arab *qa'immaqam* supported *fellahin* threatened with dispossession, and unsuccessfully resisted his Turkish superior in opposing the transfer of land legally sold by an absentee landlord to the Zionists, and there too the Sursuq family of Beirut were the vendors of the land. Although the end result for many of the *fellahin* involved was the same—dispossession and homelessness—the al-Fula purchase marked the beginning of an overt and articulate anti-Zionist campaign, which was based on the widely publicized details of this case of dispossession. This campaign developed over the next two years until it had encompassed the provinces of *bilad al-Sham*, the Arabic press, and the Ottoman parliament.

The details of the al-Fula transaction are simple. The village lands totaled under ten thousand dunums situated in the middle of the fertile Marj Ibn 'Amir. Halfway between Nazareth and Jenin, al-Fula was only a small part of the vast ownings in various parts of this broad valley of the Sursuqs of Beirut, who in 1872 had purchased some 230,000 dunums from the Ottoman Government for the paltry sum of £T 20,000, and altogether seem to have owned well over a quarter of a million dunums. According to one source, the family's annual returns from its properties in Marj Ibn 'Amir equaled their original purchase price, while another put their annual income from these properties in 1883 at $200,000.[64]

In late 1910, Elias Sursuq agreed to sell the lands of al-Fula to the *Keren Kayemeth Leisrael*, the Jewish National Fund (JNF), a new institution of the Zionist movement devoted to land purchase and headed by Arthur Ruppin.[65] According to Mandel, this was "some of the best agricultural land in Palestine,"[66] and the JNF set about immediately occupying and settling its new property. There was strong resistance, however, from the *fellahin* of al-Fula, their resolve apparently stiffened by the changing mood in Palestine and other parts of the Empire regarding Zionism, and by the effect of earlier examples of dispossession in nearby parts of Lower Galilee over the preceding years. In addition to the first five settlements established between 1901 and 1904 on the land whose sale Amir Amin Arslan had opposed, another five had been set up in the same area between 1905 and 1910, and all were settled mainly by immigrants of the second *aliya*.

Another factor encouraged the resistance of the peasants of al-Fula: this was the support of the Arab *qa'immaqam* of Nazareth, to which we have already had occasion to refer. Shukri al-'Asali was a member of a prominent Damascus family who had received his higher education at the *Mülkiye* in Istanbul, and had thereafter held a number of government posts in different parts of *bilad al-Sham*. He was also an accomplished orator and an experienced journalist. Upon hearing of the sale, al-'Asali refused to hand over the title deed to the property to the new owners, in spite of a directive to comply from the *Vali* in Beirut, where the transaction had been arranged. The *qa'immaqam*'s refusal to go along with the sale led to further representations in Beirut, this time by Ruppin himself, and to a renewal of the order from the *Vali* to hand over title of the al-Fula lands to its new owners.

At this point al-'Asali went much further than had Arslan a few years earlier: he took advantage of the new opportunities opened up by the Constitutional era by writing an open letter bitterly critical of Zionism under the pseudonym of "Salah al-Din al-Ayyubi" (Saladin), which was published in two parts in the important Damascus opposition paper *al-Muqtabas* in December 1910.[67] This and succeeding articles about al-Fula by al-'Asali published in February 1911 accused the Zionists of separatist objectives in Palestine, and hinted strongly that they were prompted by motives incompatible with loyalty to the Ottoman Empire. All three articles had a large readership, as they were reprinted in the Haifa paper *al-Karmil,* and in the Beirut dailies *al-Mufid, al-Ittihad al-'Uthmani,* and *al-Haqiqa,* where they helped fuel the ongoing controversy over Zionism. In these and other articles on the subject by al-'Asali, the issue of peasant dispossession was prominently featured and linked to patriotic themes: there are historical connections linking the people to the land going all the way back to Saladin, and thus expelling its original peasant tenants and replacing them with foreigners is treason, al-'Asali wrote in one of his articles.[68]

Shukri al-'Asali's next step was even more radical. He was informed that at the orders of the local agent of the JNF, Yehoshua Hankin, a band of thirty armed members of *Ha-Shomer* had been sent to occupy the lands of the al-Fula villagers. This was part of what Shafir describes as "a new method of Jewish presence through 'conquest groups' that initially settled and prepared newly purchased land until it had been handed over to its permanent Jewish owners."[69] The *qa'immaqam* immediately sent a large body of troops to the scene to drive them away. This was all he could do, for the new owners had both the law and their potent financial capabilities on their side, and the Turkish *Vali* in January 1911 overruled al-'Asali's insubordinate actions and expelled the *fellahin,* allowing the establishment in that month of the settlement of Merhavia on the disputed lands.

The resistance of the dispossessed peasants of al-Fula, whose land and homes had been sold out from under their feet by the Sursuq family in Beirut, continued even after the sale had been completed. Attacks on Merhavia by the former cultivators of the land were frequent. In the words of an authority on Zionist land purchase, Alex Bein, these attacks were due to "the natural resentment of the former cultivators."[70] In an armed clash in May 1911, an Arab was killed near the settlement by a *Ha-Shomer* watchman, provoking angry elements of the local population to lay siege to Merhavia for two days until the local authorities moved in and jailed several of the settlers.[71]

Shukri al-'Asali's role did not stop there. Basing his election campaign on the al-Fula affair (which in the press was often referred to as the " 'Afula affair," in reference to the neighboring town of 'Afula), he ran for and won a seat for Damascus in a hotly contested January 1911 by-election. His electoral platform pledged him to fight Zionism "to his last drop of blood," on the basis of his experience in the al-Fula case. Once elected, al-'Asali was to play a key role not only in the opposition to Zionism in the Ottoman Chamber and outside, but in galvanizing members of the Arab parliamentary bloc in its opposition to the nascent Turkish nationalism of the ruling CUP.[72] He had all the more impact because he was one of the editors and part-owner of the Damascus newspaper *al-Muqtabas*, one of the most influential Arabist journals of its day thanks to his efforts and those of its other co-owners and editors, Muhammad and Ahmad Kurd 'Ali.

In large part as a result of al-'Asali's actions, the al-Fula incident became a cause célèbre in *bilad al-Sham*, with dozens of articles appearing in newspapers in Damascus, Beirut, Haifa, and elsewhere over a period of over a year. In the press and during debates in the Ottoman parliament after al-'Asali's arrival there, it served as a striking illustration of charges regarding the ruling CUP's failure to take into account Arab concerns made by Arabs restive over what increasingly seemed like Turkish domination of the Empire. From the press accounts and descriptions of al-'Asali's speeches during the election campaign and later on in the Ottoman Parliament, it is clear that it was the spectacle of Arab peasants resisting expulsion from their homes and lands to make room for foreign colonists which gave this incident its potent impact for most Arab audiences.

Again and again in the press coverage, the voices of the illiterate *fellahin* who cultivated the land come through in descriptions of the al-Fula affair. This is true even in an article defending his actions in ordering the handing over of the land to its new owners by the Vali of Beirut, Nur al-Din Bey. He stated that after Elias Sursuq began proceedings to sell the land, the peasant proprietors begged him to urge the government to exercise its right of eminent domain, or failing that to "sell it to the inhabitants of the villages for a similar price." This was refused by higher authorities in Istanbul, he stated, on the grounds that Sursuq had the absolute right to dispose of his property as he chose.[73]

Similarly, the lasting bitterness caused by the expulsion of these *fellahin* is visible in small local news items in the following months in *al-Muqtabas*, noting that settlers in the Tiberias area, including those of al-Fula, had sent telegrams to the authorities, accusing the local inhabitants of being motivated by a spirit of hostility, accusing the government of weakness, and demanding action.[74] Another article, in *al-Karmil*, argued that it was only because the government failed to do its job in resisting foreign colonial penetration that hostility to the settlers had developed among the Arabs of Palestine. When the Zionists took over lands, it added, there was naturally resistance to this, with the peasants fighting back, and the colonists killing them in the resulting clashes and then sending telegrams of protest to the authorities.[75] The peasants' continuing resistance to their dispossession is visible in other incidents reported in *al-Karmil*, such as one in June 1911, months after the al-Fula transaction had been completed, in which settlers there accused the inhabitants of a neighboring Arab village, which included some *fellahin* who lost their homes and lands as a result of the sale, of destroying crops and property to the value of 3,100 Turkish pounds.[76]

The sharp, continuing controversy sparked off by the al-Fula sale, an otherwise minor incident, underlines the importance of the dispossession and consequent resistance of the Palestinian peasantry in making the issue of Zionism a central one in Arab political discourse before 1914. As has been shown by Mandel and others, there were many other reasons for this strong response to political Zionism among the Arabs of Palestine and neighboring lands. But the intensity of the post-1908 reaction can be explained only by the cumulative effect of a series of land purchases from absentee landlords involving expulsions of *fellahin* and ensuing clashes. This is what brought important elements among the Arab urban elite to a realization of the full import of Zionism: not only was land being purchased, but also its Arab cultivators were being dispossessed and replaced by foreigners whose ultimate political objective was the domination of Palestine.

This phenomenon was particularly important in Galilee after the turn of the twentieth century, where twelve of the fifteen Jewish settlements established in Palestine between 1901 and 1912 were located. We have seen that in this fertile region much land had recently come into the hands of absentee landlords, most of them newly prosperous Beirut merchants, for whom land was an investment, and who were willing to sell when the price was right. Tension rose also because of the new freedom of expression in the Empire after 1908, which encouraged open expres-

sions of hostility to Zionism, and to the Ottoman authorities for their lax-
ness in dealing with it. It also increased after 1904 with the arrival of
immigrants of the second *aliya*, committed to the "conquest of labor"
and the replacement of Arabs by Jews in as many occupations as possible.
The coalescence of all these factors made the al-Fula clashes between
Arab *fellahin* and Jewish settlers more significant than the many others
that preceded it and that involved a few of the same elements.

Nur al-Din Bey had stated in his response to al-'Asali over the issue of
al-Fula that "property which is at the disposal of someone can be used by
him as he wishes, if there are no legal obstacles; this right is guaranteed
by the basic laws of all states."[77] For the Ottoman state, this was a simple
matter of property rights: Elias Sursuq had the absolute right to dispose
of his land to whomsoever he pleased. The fact that the Ottoman citizen
he was selling the land to was an intermediary for the Zionist movement,
and that many of the settlers who would occupy it were not Ottoman citizens was in effect not the business of the state, any more than was the
fate of the dispossessed peasants, or the alleged historic nature of the
parcel in question (we have seen that al-'Asali had quoted medieval Arab
historians to the effect that al-Fula was the site of a fortress erected by
Saladin after his defeat of the Crusaders at nearby Hittin in 1187).

All of these considerations combined with mounting concern among
the elite of Palestine and other Arab regions of the Empire over the
growth in the power and coherence of the Zionist movement in Europe
(there was intensive coverage in the press in *bilad al-Sham* and Egypt of
the Zionist congresses, particularly the tenth held at Basle in August
1911).[78] The result was a volatile mix, made all the more incendiary by
the growth of Arabist sentiment among that elite. Zionism, it was
charged, was being tolerated and even encouraged by the Turkish-dominated CUP because of the CUP's lack of concern for the Arab provinces.
These charges may or may not have been justified: some leaders of the
CUP, such as Cavid Bey, the Minister of Finance, were apparently sympathetic to the Zionists, while others were less so. However, they were
widely believed, and constituted a potent weapon in the conflict between
the Arabist tendency among the Arab elite and the CUP.

IV

To conclude an assessment of the significance of peasant resistance to
land sale and dispossession, it is necessary to attempt to establish some

facts about land sales to the Zionists before 1914. The majority of sellers are often described simply as "absentee landlords," and a controversy marked by fierce polemics has grown up around this point. A table listing land purchased according to former owners (the most authoritative published source extant) is contained in *The Land System in Palestine* by the eminent Zionist land expert, Dr. Avraham Granott. He was Managing Director of the JNF (the main land purchasing agency for the Zionist movement) from 1922 until 1945, after which he became Chairman of its Board of Directors. Based on incomplete Jewish Agency figures, the table gives details regarding 682,000 dunums purchased to 1936, or about half of Zionist land purchases in Palestine until 1948.[79]

As for the period before 1914, which concerns us here, Granott's table provides figures regarding 245,581 dunums purchased between 1878 and 1914 (59 percent of the total of 418,100 dunums acquired by Jews in Palestine by World War I). Granott divides the purchases into four categories according to "previous owners," as follows: 25% from "large absentee landlords," 25% from "large resident landlords," 37.5% from "various sources" (such as the Ottoman Government, large foreign companies and churches) and 12.5% from the *fellahin.*[80] For the entire period covered by the table (1878–1936) the figures are even more heavily weighted toward absentee and large landowners: in the same four categories the percentages are 52.6, 24.6, 13.4 and 9.4 percent respectively.

It would appear that for the period until 1914 the trends indicated by Granott were even more pronounced, and more heavily weighted toward non-Palestinian absentee landlords. This emerges from parcel-by-parcel pre-World War I land sale figures in a table in the unpublished work on Zionism written by Ruhi al-Khalidi, which was referred to in the previous chapter. Covering sales to Jewish institutions from 1878 to 1907, it can be supplemented by data from newspapers of the period, and other published sources.[81] The resulting figures are considerably more detailed than Granott's. They list by name the vendors of a total of 247,466 dunums, or 60 percent of all the land purchased to that point, and the twenty-two Jewish colonies established on this land, including many of the oldest and largest ones, and every one of those which were the scenes of the cases of peasant resistance discussed in this chapter. These sources yield the following results regarding those selling land:

Non-Palestinian absentee landlords: 143,577 dunums (58%).

Palestinian absentee landlords: 88,689 dunums (36%).

Local landlords and fellahin: 15,200 dunums (6%).

The first group includes foreigners, foreign diplomats, Beirut merchants, as well as Turkish government officials. This and the second group sold 94 percent of the land that changed hands before 1914 for which we have detailed figures. If these figures are representative (and Granott's similar figures strongly indicate that they are), they show that a far higher proportion of land sales were undertaken by absentee landlords, both Palestinian and non-Palestinian, than some scholars have indicated. It would furthermore seem that the role of non-Palestinian absentee landlords was decisive in this regard in the pre-1914 period.

Extrapolating from the two sets of partial pre-1914 figures on land sales presented above, and adding to them further figures for the succeeding decades, it is possible to come to tentative conclusions about land sales for the entire period to 1948. In his book *The Land System in Palestine 1917–1939*, Kenneth Stein lays particular stress on sales of land to Jews by Palestinians, particularly notables who often played a prominent role in nationalist opposition to Zionism. There can be little doubt that under the kind of economic pressure combined with financial inducements that Stein describes, Palestinian landlords, both absentee and resident, as well as *fellahin* cultivators, often sold land. Nevertheless the overall picture is in fact more complex than he paints it.[82]

Stein himself notes that "during the 1920s more than 60 per cent of the land purchased by Jews was bought from Arab absentee landlords residing outside of Palestine."[83] The actual proportion is very likely much higher, as more than 240,000 dunums, or nearly half of the total of 510,000 dunums sold during the period 1920–29, was made up of an enormous piece of land encompassing most of the fertile Marj Ibn 'Amir, which was sold by the Sursuq family of Beirut and a number of their Lebanese partners in 1924–25. Together with the other lands in the Marj Ibn 'Amir (such as al-Fula), sold to the Zionists before 1914 by the Sursuqs and their business partners in a few Beirut families related to them (such as the 'Aryans and the Twaynis), this single bloc in one region amounts to 313,000 dunums, or more than 22 percent of all the land purchased by Jews in Palestine until 1948. This would seem to contradict Stein's assertion that the Marj Ibn 'Amir sale had "important significance, but certainly not the political value given it by many writers."[84] And these figures on the size of this sale do not even touch on the purchase's vital importance in terms of the territorial continuity of Jewish settlement in Palestine, which was first pointed out by Ruppin in 1907, and is correctly emphasized by Gershon Shafir.[85]

More importantly, for the more than 400,000 dunums sold before 1914 and the more than 500,000 thousand dunums sold in the 1920s, the available figures (which, it must be repeated apply to only a portion of these totals) suggest that well over 60 percent of the land acquired by the Zionists before 1930 was sold by non-Palestinians. Inasmuch as these 900,000 dunums are the bulk of the total of 1.39 million dunums purchased and registered by the Zionist movement until the end of the Mandate,[86] these partial figures have major implications for the whole question of land sales from the beginning of modern Jewish settlement in Palestine and until 1948. Although it is true that many Palestinian landlords and *fellahin* sold land, whether out of greed and lack of patriotism, or because of need and without knowing who would ultimately control it, the conclusion is inescapable that the great bulk of land would indeed seem to have been sold by non-Palestinian absentee landlords, for whom these were no more than straight-forward commercial transactions.

V

In light of the evidence presented in this chapter, it is clear that opposition to land sales to the Zionists, particularly sales by absentee landlords (both Palestinian and non-Palestinian), was an important shared element in cementing the link between members of the Palestinian elite who opposed Zionism on grounds of principle, and the *fellahin* whose resistance caught the popular imagination and thereby played a vital role in mobilizing opinion both in Palestine and the Arab world. This opposition united the peasants, who tried desperately to cling to their land, or retaliated against the Zionist settlers in a violent fashion if they lost it, together with the urban intellectuals and notables, some of whom realized what Zionism implied only when they beheld the dispossession that Shukri al-'Asali, Ruhi al-Khalidi, Najib Nassar, 'Isa al-'Isa and others decried.

The result was a new shared urban-rural perception among Palestinians of a new type of Zionist settlement, beginning with the second *aliya*, which for the first time witnessed Jewish settlers taking over not just ownership, but also cultivation, of the land on a large scale. This new phenomenon not only was the basis for the first systematic, public expressions of anti-Zionism in Palestine and Arab world. It also constituted an element of shared identity between those in the cities and towns of Palestine and those in the countryside, who now felt that in some way they shared the same fate, face to face with an external force whose

power at this stage they may perhaps have overestimated, but were genuinely afraid of.

We can see that many of those in the cities who warned against the
dangers of Zionism made a conscious effort to build this shared sense
of destiny between city and countryside, city-dweller and *fellah*. One
example of such an effort is the initiative of the editors of *Filastin*, mentioned in chapter 4, to distribute their strongly anti-Zionist newspaper
to every village in the hinterland of Jaffa—a region which was one of
the prime targets of Zionist colonization. This initiative was motivated
by an explicit sense that it was essential for the peasantry to be aware of
events throughout the country, particularly those related to Zionism on
which *Filastin* focused. Another example was cited in the last chapter,
in the reference to one of the last passages of Ruhi al-Khalidi's unfin-
ished manuscript on Zionism, which stresses the negative impact of the
Zionist movement both on "the influential people in the country" and
on the peasantry, as "they take possession of their land, village by village."[87] Similarly, Najib Nassar focused intensely on events in the rural
areas in his newspaper *al-Karmil*, and is described in Zionist sources as
being personally involved in helping the *fellahin* to resist the al-Shajara
sale of 1909.[88]

Such a pattern of interaction between rural resistance and urban
opposition to Zionism has already been established for the Mandatory
period. Thus, the funeral in Haifa in November 1935 of the first articulate public apostle of armed rural resistance, the Syrian Shaykh 'Iz al-Din
al-Qassam, who lived and worked for fifteen years among landless *fellahin* who had migrated to the Haifa slums, and died in combat with
British troops, became an enormous public demonstration.[89] This in
turn helped to spark the 1936 general strike and the 1936–39 Palestinian
Arab revolt. In the words of the author of the best study of al-Qassam,
Abdullah Schleifer, his death "electrified the Palestinian people."[90] Al-
Qassam appealed in particular to the uprooted landless peasants who
drifted from Galilee into the northern port city of Haifa. These first
recruits to organized armed resistance were in many cases the same people who had been dispossessed or displaced by earlier Zionist colonization activity in Galilee. In Schleifer's words: "Many of his followers were
former tenant farmers recently driven off the land by the land purchases
and Arab labor exclusion policies of the Jewish National Fund."[91] At the
other end of the social scale, urban leaders of the secular nationalist
Istiqlal Party like Akram Zu'aytir were deeply affected by al-Qassam's
huge funeral procession, as he recorded in his diary at the time.[92] We

115

have now seen that this pattern of *fellahin* resistance affecting the rest of Palestinian society, and of the latter in turn having an impact on the peasantry, already clearly established for the Mandatory period, in fact stretches back before 1914.

Because those we have focused on could not speak for themselves in the sources which are left to us after nearly a century, we have seen their actions through a glass darkly, largely via records left by foreigners who did not speak their language or understand their culture, who had little sympathy for them, and who often were their enemies. As for their countrymen, the urban elites of Palestine, they too have left us with all too little that can help us to establish a full picture of what was happening on the land in Palestine at the very outset of the conflict between Zionist settlers and Palestinian Arabs. Even regarding some issues where more information should be available, such as land purchase, we are forced to use fragmentary and incomplete data.

But it has been possible to discern a broad pattern of alienation of land from its cultivators, sometimes into the hands of Arab absentee landlords, and sometimes from them to Zionist land purchasing agencies. A largely mute process of resistance arose, particularly where land alienation and disappropriation was followed by dispossession. In the older Jewish colonies which were initially less affected by political Zionism, as the settlers were transformed into gentlemen farmers employing Arab labor, some Arab resentment had been appeased as the *fellahin* found jobs or were able to rent back the lands that had previously been theirs as tenant farmers. But a new and more serious process began with the second *aliya* in 1904 and the concomitant effort to establish an exclusive Jewish economy in Palestine.[93]

After 1908, peasant resistance was echoed by members of the urban upper and middle classes, many of whom were newly conscious of their identity as Arabs, chafing at what some increasingly were coming to perceive as Turkish control, and newly able to express themselves in the press and in party politics. This potent mix thus established a pattern that was already firmly set by 1914. All the elements were already in place for the bitter and protracted disputes over the questions of land sales and peasant dispossession and the resulting violence, which were the main features of the Mandate period.

Although only further research in the Ottoman, British, and Israeli archives and in Palestinian and other Arab sources can produce conclusive results as far as some of these questions are concerned, there is ample evidence to show that Arab attacks on early Jewish settlements were more than just "marauding" or "banditry" as some writers would have it (although banditry there surely also was on occasion).[94] Frequently, they were rather the result of a real process of dispossession which, in the cases for which we have evidence, can be conclusively documented not in the words of the victims but rather on the basis of contemporary Zionist sources and recent research based on them. We are forced to tell their story, like that of many of the powerless in history, in the words of those who victimized them. This does not make it any less vivid, or less valid as a picture of what was happening in Palestine before 1914. In the next chapter, we will examine in detail how this newfound sense of solidarity and of common identity between different segments of society in the face of a common external threat was expressed, reflected, and shaped in the press in the years after 1908.

CHAPTER 6

Elements of Identity II:
The Debate on Zionism
in the Arabic Press

I

It has now been generally established
that the Arab reaction to Zionism antedated the Balfour declaration of
1917, and was both a local Palestinian and a generalized pan-Arab phenomenon almost from its inception. Chapter 5 touched on the way in
which Zionism became an issue in Arab political discourse beyond the
confines of Palestine itself from the first stages of active Arab opposition
to Zionist colonization early in the twentieth century. This was especially
true, and can be perceived especially clearly, after the Ottoman Revolution of 1908 when, as we have seen, the reimposition of the 1876 Constitution resulted in the freeing of party political activity and the growth of
the press throughout the Empire.

As was mentioned in chapter 3, newspapers and periodicals founded
after 1908 in Beirut and other centers of Arab intellectual life played a
major role in the politics and cultural life of the period, drawing on the
model provided by the thriving Egyptian press, in which Syrian emigrés
were extremely active.[1] Thanks to the proliferation of newspapers after
1908, it suddenly becomes possible for the researcher to find a wealth of

source material regarding virtually all the important political issues of the pre-World War I period,[2] among them the problem of Zionist settlement in Palestine. With the appearance of this plethora of newspapers and periodicals, a society which until that point seemed almost opaque in many respects is suddenly illuminated to the historical observer.

Although it is hard to discern much about popular or even elite sentiment given this opaqueness engendered by the censorship and political repression that prevailed before 1908, some elements of the very earliest reactions to Zionism, both in Palestine and in the Empire as a whole, are clear. They seem to have focused mainly on the problems caused for the local population and the government by the arrival of large numbers of Jewish immigrants fleeing persecution in Eastern Europe who carried foreign passports, mainly Russian and Austro-Hungarian, with all that implied for increased European interference in the affairs of the Empire. This was a function not only of the tenuous nature of Ottoman relations with these two eastern European empires, but also of the fact that Britain had established itself as the protector of the Jews of the Ottoman empire (among other minority groups, such as the Druze), and like other European powers used the situation of its various protégés as a pretext for intervention in Ottoman domestic affairs.[3] The potential problems posed by the continuous increase in the number of foreigners in Palestine, many of whom violated Ottoman regulations and remained after their three-month permits had expired, and the reluctance of many of these immigrants to adopt Ottoman nationality, are constant themes in the early reactions to Zionism. These complaints were almost independent of any political ambitions the immigrants might have harbored, and these ambitions indeed may not have been fully apparent to most Ottoman and Arab observers at the outset.

But with the first Zionist Congress in 1897, and with the concomitant launching of modern political Zionism in an institutionalized form, this was to change. Gradually, as more was learned about the nature and objectives of the Zionist movement, mainly from reports of the statements and speeches made by its leaders in Europe, and partly from its activities in Palestine, and as Zionist settlement and land purchase accelerated in the first years of the twentieth century, many throughout the Empire came to fear the creation of yet another Ottoman "nationality problem." Given the extent of the problems caused for the Empire by similar problems in other regions, particularly the Balkans, such concern on the part of many Ottomans was understandable. The reaction among some was even more extreme: particularly among Palestinians, the fear grew that the country's existing Arab population might be swamped in a tide of newcomers and that Palestine might one day cease to be an Arab country. And with the growth of peasant resistance, especially after the turn of the twentieth century, which was examined in the previous chapter, there was considerable evidence from the Palestinian countryside that appeared to substantiate these fears.

The press played a central role in the development of these Arab attitudes to Zionism, as we have already begun to see. Newspapers informed their readers not only of the day-to-day details of the progress of colonization in the independent *sanjaq* of Jerusalem and the southern *sanjaqs* of the *vilayet* of Beirut, but also explained to them the aims and extent of the Zionist movement as a whole, sometimes in an exaggerated or distorted fashion, and reported news of the movement's activities throughout Europe. Thus, beginning in 1908, Arabic-language papers began to reflect a mounting concern about the dangers posed by Zionist colonization to the indigenous population of Palestine, and ultimately to that of surrounding regions. This is among the central conclusions that emerge from a survey of several hundred articles on Zionism published in a number of the most important Arabic-language newspapers during the Ottoman Constitutional period, 1908–14, on which this chapter is based.[4]

This survey shows that although this concern about Zionism was naturally intense in the Palestinian press, it was also considerable in many papers in Cairo and Beirut, the leading publishing centers of the Arabic-speaking world, as well as in newspapers in other cities, such as Damascus. The founding of the Zionist movement, and the establishment of 32 settlements in Palestine between 1897 and 1914[5] (21 others had been established before the first date), seem clearly to have been perceived regionally, and not just in Palestine itself, as an ominous and potentially threatening phenomenon. Indeed, it was often the press in Cairo, or Beirut, or Damascus, which first raised a concern or expressed a theme, only to have it picked up by newspapers in Palestine, which would write editorials of their own or reprint the original article. Similarly, articles from Palestinian papers were often reprinted elsewhere, first alerting readers far beyond the confines of Palestine to a new trend or an important event relating to Zionist settlement.

Given the overlapping identities and the fluid boundaries of the period, none of this should be surprising. Northern Palestine was of course part of the Beirut *vilayet*, and the press in Beirut was therefore writing about events in a province of which it was the capital when it described the progress of Zionist settlement in Marj Ibn 'Amir or eastern Galilee. Many Beirutis, moreover, had important commercial interests in Palestine, among them a number of major landowners. In Cairo, many of the newspaper editors, and many of their readers, were what we would today call Palestinians, Lebanese, and Syrians, although they were then all called Syrians—or *shawam*—by Egyptians (indeed this term is still in use), and many of them were deeply concerned with events throughout what they thought of as their home region of *bilad al-Sham*, including Palestine. Finally, for Damascenes and other Syrians, events in Palestine were on their doorstep, as many Syrians owned land there, and many Damascus families were related by marriage to others in Jerusalem, Nablus, and elsewhere in Palestine. The press reflected this pre-World War I reality, before the European partitions of the postwar years imposed hard and fast frontiers where before there had only been looser Ottoman administrative boundaries.

II

Ideally, a study of the early treatment of Zionism in the Arab press would survey the published issues of papers from all parts of *bilad al-sham*, as well as Cairo and Istanbul, and perhaps beyond, for the entire Constitutional period of 1908 to 1914, and where possible even before that. Many issues of some newspapers published during this period are unavailable, however, while others paid varying amounts of attention to the subject of Zionism. In the end, the survey on which this chapter is based examined in detail the issues published over at least three years of the two most important Palestinian newspapers of the era, the two major Cairo papers owned and edited by individuals originating in Syria and which devoted attention to affairs in that region, as well as five newspapers published in Beirut, and one in Damascus, the most widely read of its day in that city. In addition to these ten newspapers surveyed for at least three years of this six-year period, available issues of several other newspapers and periodicals from other cities of the region were also examined, but less intensively. The result offers sufficient diversity, geographically and otherwise, to be considered broadly representative of the treatment of Zionism by the Arabic press from 1908 until 1914.

A total of 22 newspapers and periodicals were thus surveyed in whole or in part for purposes of this analysis, of which ten newspapers were available in continuous runs of at least three years during times when the issue of Zionism was the subject of lively debate, and could therefore be used for purposes of comparison. These ten include the leading Palestinian paper to focus on Zionism, *al-Karmil*, edited in Haifa by Najib Nassar, as well as *Filastin*, published in Jaffa by 'Isa and Yusuf al-'Isa, both of which were discussed briefly in chapter 3;[6] *al-Mufid*, edited by 'Abd al-Ghani al-'Uraisi and Fuad Hantas;[7] the Damascus paper *al-Muqtabas*, edited by Muhammad Kurd 'Ali and his brother Ahmad, to which extensive reference has already been made;[8] the two leading Cairo dailies, *al-Muqattam*, owned by Ya'qub Sarruf, Faris Nimr, and Bishara Taqla, and *al-Ahram*, edited by Dawud Barakat; and five Beirut papers: *Lisan al-Hal*, owned by Khalil Sarkis; *al-Ittihad al-'Uthmani*, edited by Shaykh Ahmed Hassan Tabbara; *al-Haqiqa*, edited by Kamal 'Abbas; and *al-Iqbal*, edited by 'Abd al-Basit al-Unsi. All were dailies except the latter two, which appeared biweekly and weekly respectively, and *al-Karmil* and *Filastin*, which were biweeklies during this period.[9] The remaining twelve newspapers and periodicals, which were available only for periods of under three years, or for which many issues are missing among the surviving copies, are referred to selectively in the course of this chapter.[10]

A total of well over 10,000 issues of these ten papers were examined for this study, yielding more than 600 articles on Zionism (more than 650 articles on Zionism were found in all 22 publications). The greatest interest in the question of Zionism is apparent in the years 1911–13, when more than 450 of these articles were published, notwithstanding the extensive press coverage given first to the Libyan and then to the Balkan wars in those years. The year 1911, during which 286 such articles were published in these ten papers, in many ways marked the high point in the press controversy over Zionism. Thereafter, interest continued in the subject, with escalating warnings about the dangers inherent in Zionist colonization, and reports on its progress and on the actions of Zionist bodies abroad, but without the same frequency.

The only exception to the uniformly negative reaction to Zionism of all 22 publications surveyed was *al-Muqattam*. Their correspondent in Palestine was Nisim Malul, an Egyptian Jewish newspaper editor fluent in Arabic who had earlier founded two short-lived papers in Egypt, *al-Nasr* in Alexandria in 1903, and *al-Salam* in Cairo in 1910, and later was to publish *al-Salam* briefly in Jaffa in 1920.[11] Malul worked for the Palestine Office of the Zionist Organization founded in Jaffa in 1908, writing reports on the Arabic press for the Central Office of the Organization in Cologne and later in Berlin which are cited extensively in Neville

Mandel's *The Arab and Zionism before World War I.*[12] Even in the columns of *al-Muqattam,* however, which was the only paper of all 22 examined to carry more pro-Zionist than anti-Zionist articles, numerous writers vigorously opposed Zionism, supported by letters to the editor from anti-Zionist readers.

A word is in order on how an evaluation of a newspaper's position on Zionism was made. To make an assessment, articles on the subject were classified according to three broad categories: "pro-Zionist"; "anti-Zionist"; and "other," the last category including numerous articles primarily of an informative nature. Although these classifications are far from rigid, and are by no means precise (e.g., apparently "pro-Zionist" articles in a strongly anti-Zionist paper were often merely reprints of material by Zionists published for the information of the readers), a clear picture of the intensity of a newspaper's position on the Zionist issue could be obtained. While the results will be referred to throughout the newspaper-by-newspaper survey that follows, the most striking conclusion to emerge from this assessment is that with the one exception just mentioned, *all* the newspapers surveyed were anti-Zionist. Together with the information on the frequency of appearance of articles on Zionism in these papers, these data give the broad outlines of the importance of the Zionist question in the Arab press during this period, as it is reflected in the ten papers intensively surveyed, and twelve others.

The following section analyzes each of these ten papers in terms of its position on the Zionist issue, after which the chapter concludes with an assessment of some of the broad trends discernible in the treatment of this question in the Arab press before World War I.

III

Al-Karmil

Of the ten Arabic-language newspapers for which issues covering more than three years were available, *al-Karmil* was by far the most outspoken in its opposition to Zionism. Named for Mount Carmel, which overlooks Haifa Bay, it was first published in December 1908, and almost immediately became the primary vehicle of an extensive campaign against Zionist settlement in Palestine. That campaign, which involved many organs of the Syrian press, came to a peak in 1911. During that year alone, *al-Karmil* carried 73 articles on Zionism, or an average of one in nearly every one of its almost 100 issues. In the total of 330 issues surveyed, *al-Karmil* published 134 articles on Zionism, including 45 editorials or leading articles.

The owner and editor of the newspaper, and often the writer of much of its contents, Najib Nassar did not depend on sheer volume to convince his readers of the extent of the danger the Zionist movement represented to Palestine.[13] In addition to news items from Galilee and other parts of Palestine, and his own persuasive editorials (a remarkable number of which were reprinted in other Syrian papers, as we shall see), he re-published articles on Zionism from *al-Muqattam*, *al-Ahram*, *al-Mufid*, *al-Ittihad al-'Uthmani* and other Cairo and Beirut newspapers, as well as the Damascus paper *al-Muqtabas*, *al-Hadara* of Istanbul, and *Filastin*—all, except *al-Muqattam*, being strong opponents of Zionism.

Not content with his own and other editors' arguments against the Zionist movement, Nassar covered in detail the activities of the various branches of the Zionist colonization movement in Palestine, and of their parent organizations abroad. As a result, other anti-Zionist papers soon came to depend on *al-Karmil* for much of their information on these activities. At the same time, the owner-editor of *al-Karmil* attempted to give his readers extensive background information on the history, objectives, and significance of the Zionist movement. For this purpose he published condensed translations of a lengthy article on Zionism from the *Encyclopedia Judaica.* Nassar eventually issued this sixteen-part series, published from March until June 1911, as a 65-page booklet under the title *al-Sihyuniyya: Tarikhuha, gharaduha, ahamiyyatuha* [Zionism: Its history, objective and importance].[14] It concluded by describing the efforts of Theodor Herzl on behalf of Zionism, provoking the observation by Nassar to his readers that what Palestine needed in opposing Zionism was "sincere leaders like Herzl who will forget their private interests in favor of the public good." Nassar went on: "We have many men like Herzl; all they lack is a realization of their own abilities, and the courage to take the first step. Let such men appear, and not hesitate, and circumstances will favor them, for men's ideas have matured and we are ready."[15]

Nassar's opposition to Zionism was linked to a strong feeling of patriotic devotion to Palestine. In an editorial in August 1913, for example, he commented on the recent Zionist Congress, calling for a simultaneous conference to be held in Nablus "while others are meeting to take over our country and our farms."[16] This and many similar instances of local patriotism were matched by Nassar's parallel devotion to Arab nationalism in its broader pan-Arab sense. Some of the motivation for this orientation in Nassar's case and that of many other Arabist thinkers of this period was what was perceived as the bias of the ruling CUP in favor of Zionism.[17] Thus Nassar, whose newspaper in 1908 and 1909 reflected a positive approach to the CUP, by 1911 had become a fervent opponent of the ruling party and supporter of the Ottoman opposition with which most Arabists were by this stage affiliated.[18] Such a development in the overall political line taken by *al-Karmil* appears to have followed closely, and probably to have been largely influenced by, Nassar's increasingly uncompromising opposition to Zionism. In this respect, Najib Nassar's evolution can be seen as representative of that of numerous other Arab political and intellectual figures during this period, although in other respects, such as the sophistication and tenaciousness of his opposition to Zionism, he was definitely a pioneer among Palestinian and Arab journalists.

Filastin

Although it did not commence publication until January 1911, more than two years after *al-Karmil, Filastin* soon became its rival both inside and outside Palestine as an opponent of Zionism, and indeed during the Mandate became the more important newspaper of the two, and one of the country's main dailies. While Zionism was one of the central issues on which the newspaper's owners and editors, Yusuf and 'Isa al-'Isa, focused, others were also important. These included the encouragement of education,[19] the struggle of the Arab Orthodox to free their church from domination by the Greek higher clergy,[20] and the poor condition of the peasantry.[21] In many cases, these other issues came to be connected to Zionism, whether in terms of the local patriotism which engendered much of the editors' concern for education, the questions of religious and national identity which were raised by the struggle within the Orthodox church, or the problem of rural poverty with its inevitable linkage to land-sales to the Zionist movement and the consequent dispossession of the *fellahin.*

In its opposition to Zionism, *Filastin* rapidly became quite as uncompromising as *al-Karmil.* The concern for the lot of the peasantry expressed in articles on rural conditions, and shown also in the paper's policy of sending a copy of each issue to every village in the Jaffa region, was at the root of the editors' fears regarding Zionism. While in early issues of the paper problems such as the Ottoman authorities' failure to control Jewish immigration and the large numbers of foreigners entering the country were at the center of the critique of Zionism in *Filastin*,[22] in time the problems of peasant dispossession by Zionist land-purchase, and the possibility that the entire Arab population of Palestine might in time be dispossessed by the newcomers, came to the fore. From publishing only a few articles on Zionism every month in its first year, this biweekly was soon publishing an article or more per issue on the subject.

Very soon, *Filastin* came to be relied upon by newspapers throughout the region for news of Zionist colonization in Palestine, and eventually enjoyed the same high regard as did *al-Karmil*. Articles from the paper were reprinted widely, and appear to have had a major impact in shaping how Palestinians and other Arabs came to see Zionism. Through stress on this issue, and others which concerned the population of the Jerusalem *sanjaq* and the country as a whole, *Filastin* played a role in shaping a sense of Palestinian identity, which clearly was one of its main aims, given that its title means "Palestine." At the same time, through the influence of its articles reprinted in Beirut, Damascus, and Cairo, *Filastin* helped to establish the question of Zionism as one that concerned all Arabs. Like Najib Nassar, 'Isa al-'Isa and his cousin Yusuf can thus be seen as pioneers of an unwavering Palestinian and pan-Arab opposition to Zionism, which was to continue and intensify in later years.

Al-Mufid

The newspaper that perhaps came closest to the fervor of *al-Karmil* in its opposition to Zionism was *al-Mufid*. As unofficial mouthpiece of the Arab nationalist secret society *al-Fatat*,[23] it had an influence greater than might at first appear, over a region that stretched far beyond the borders of the Beirut *vilayet* (which of course included northern Palestine). Although issues of the paper are only available for three years, it is clear that *al-Mufid* was, together with *al-Karmil, Filastin,* and *al-Muqtabas,* the most persistent and determined opponent of Zionism in the Arabic-language press of the period. This is borne out by the relatively large number of articles it carried on the subject—a total of 71, 52 of them in 1911 alone—and by the fact that 22 of the newspaper's editorials were devoted to it, most of them also in 1911. For a period of nine months during the latter year, *al-Mufid* carried almost one article on Zionism every three days, many of them violently opposing the sale of state lands to foreigners or their agents, who it was feared were working for the Zionist movement. A large proportion of these articles and others in the Arab press in 1911 dealt with a proposal by Dr. Najib Asfar to buy up Ottoman state lands, a project which was thought to be backed by the Zionists.[24] These fears were almost surely misplaced, but they indicate the degree of alarm Zionism had already aroused in certain circles by 1911. During the Mandate, as well as after 1967 in the occupied West Bank and Gaza Strip, the issue of the limits and status of former Ottoman "state lands" and control over them continued to be a vital one.

Together with *al-Karmil* (the two papers frequently reprinted one another's editorials and news reports),[25] *al-Mufid* laid great emphasis on the importance of protecting the indigenous Palestinian peasantry from being expelled from its ancestral farmland to make way for colonists from Europe.[26] And like the Haifa paper, it was scathing in its condemnation of those Arab landlords who sold their land to the Zionists. Not surprisingly, however, given its Arabist political orientation, al-Mufid's greatest ire was reserved for the CUP-dominated government, which it described as being at best lax in its enforcement of laws hindering Zionist immigration and land-purchase, and at worst as being in complicity with the Zionists, a charge that came to be widely believed in many Arab circles. Soon after the CUP government's fall in 1912, *al-Mufid* wrote:

> . . . all we said about the Zionist question was totally ignored while the Unionists held power over the nation and accommodated the Zionists. Then we raised cry after cry with no response. Now things have changed and the new government should pay attention to what the previous one ignored. The people of the country emigrate to America, while the Zionists immigrate into our country: one day, if things go on like this, the Arab in his own country will become worse off than an orphan at the tables of the stingy.[27]

Perhaps the main significance of *al-Mufid's* opposition to Zionism lies in its linking of the Arabism that it championed so staunchly with resistance to what it described as an alien colonizing movement that threatened to split the Arab world in half. The fiery editorials of its young owner-editors, together with the many articles written for it by older leaders of the Arab movement such as Shukri al-'Asali and Rafiq al-'Azm, undoubtedly had a potent effect on the paper's strongly Arabist readership, and inculcated them with an intense wariness of Zionism. This connection between Arabism and anti-Zionism was to continue in later years in the Arab nationalist press of Lebanon and Syria and beyond. Significantly, it emphasized the linkage between Arabism and the problems posed by Zionism, which might otherwise have been seen as solely a Palestinian concern.

Al-Muqtabas

Edited by the noted literary and political figure Muhammad Kurd 'Ali and his brother Ahmad, *al-Muqtabas* was one of the era's most active opponents of Zionism, carrying the largest number of articles on Zionism of any newspaper surveyed, with the exception of *al-Karmil*. These included fifteen articles reprinted from the latter, three from *Filastin*, and numerous other articles reprinted from other papers. This is doubly important because of the wide influence of *al-Muqtabas*, which was described by French consular reports as the most important Damascus paper.[28] Closed down by the Ottoman authorities repeatedly for its Arabist political line, it was forced to change its name, once to *al-Umma* in 1909–10, and once to *al-Qabas* in 1913–14. During the latter period, Shukri al-'Asali is listed as its owner, and he seems to have collaborated with its editors, Muhammad and Ahmad Kurd 'Ali, throughout, except in 1911–1912, when he was in Istanbul representing Damascus in the Ottoman Parliament.

Two related themes stand out in the many articles on Zionism carried by this newspaper: the first is the complicity with the foreign colonizers of Arab landowners who sell land to Zionist settlers; and the second is the acute observation that Zionist successes are before anything else a function of the failure of the Arabs to organize themselves for resistance. In the first context, *al-Muqtabas* carried many articles, some reprinted from *al-Karmil* and some based on the experience of al-'Asali, detailing how large Arab landowners were involved in sales of land to the colonizers.[29] In one such article, Najib Nassar wrote that those who should be leaders themselves are selling their country cheaply.[30] He added in another article, in which he held up Saladin as a heroic example of unbending resistance to invasion, that if the current generation had half the patriotism, enthusiasm, and love of country as that which had faced the Crusaders, the Zionists could not dream of regaining Palestine.[31]

The second theme, that of self-criticism for Arab failures, is important because of the way it contrasts with many articles in other papers which ascribe the success of Zionism in Palestine solely to superior financial resources, foreign support, or the laxity of the Ottoman authorities. These are mentioned frequently as factors by *al-Muqtabas*, but the newspaper leaves its reader with the unmistakable impression that Arab complacency, disunity, greed, and self-interest were more important reasons for Zionist success and Arab failure than the strength of the settler movement itself. Commenting on a report of Zionist activities in 1911, Muhammad Kurd 'Ali wrote: "Our slowness to resist the Israelites makes one envious of their vigor."[32] Two years later, an article reprinted from *Filastin* made a similar point, praising the way in which the Zionists evinced solidarity, and bemoaning the lack of it among the Arabs.[33] Like *al-Mufid*, *al-Muqtabas* adhered to an Arabist political line during this period, and like the Beirut newspaper, it forcefully espoused the argument that Zionism constituted a shared Arab problem, and that resisting it was a joint Arab cause.

Al-Muqattam and al-Ahram

Although neither of these two newspapers carried as many articles on Zionism as the four we have just discussed—and in relative terms carried far fewer—both *al-Ahram* and *al-Muqattam* played a central role in the controversy over Zionism in the Arabic press during the constitutional period. This was because these two Cairo dailies had a readership and prestige far greater than that of the papers published in Syria, most of them founded after the 1908 Revolution. Established in 1876 and 1889 respectively, each of these two papers had press runs of well over 5,000 copies according to some sources.[34] Their prestige derived both from their age and journalistic professionalism, and from the fact that during the censorship of the Hamidian period they had remained free to write without hindrance about the political events of the day from their base in Cairo. Even after the 1908 Revolution and the growth of a vigorous local press in the cities of Syria, both papers retained an extensive readership there, and remained very influential. In addition, the identification of *al-Ahram* with France's Middle East policy, and of *al-Muqattam* with that of Britain, made them all the more necessary reading for the politically aware in a region that was exposed to the ambitions of both powers.

While the two newspapers published a similar number of articles on Zionism from 1908 until 1914—65 in *al-Muqattam* and 63 in *al-Ahram*—there were major differences in their treatment of this issue, and indeed in their general political line. The most noticeable difference was the tendency of *al-Muqattam*, particularly pronounced at the beginning of this period and less so at the end, to justify and show sympathy for the Zionist movement. As has already been explained, this was largely the effect of the articles written for the paper by Nisim Malul in Jaffa. In addition to Malul, *al-Muqattam* had a number of correspondents—many of them apparently Egyptian Jews committed to Zionism such as a certain "Jacques Levy" of Tanta—who wrote regularly to the paper in support of Zionism and in answer to articles opposing it which had appeared in *al-Muqattam* and other papers.[35] But even *al-Muqattam* appears to have been affected by the trend in the rest of the region insofar as Zionism was concerned, for beginning in 1909 and 1910, and growing more numerous in the following years, articles appeared that strongly opposed the Zionist movement, several of them by Palestinian authors. At the same time, the editorial line of the paper vis-à-vis the CUP underwent a gradual transformation from support to opposition, with a corresponding increase in sympathy for Arabism and the growing demands for reforms and decentralization in the Arab provinces of the Empire.

Beginning in 1911, *al-Muqattam* developed into a forum for a heated dialogue between several of its pro-Zionist contributors and a number of prominent Arab writers and political figures such as Rafiq al-'Azm and Shakib Arslan.[36] It also received articles from Dr. Shibli Shmayyil and 'Isa al-'Isa, co-editor of *Filastin*, supporting the opponents of Zionism in this ongoing controversy. Ironically, some of the strongest and most coherent arguments against Zionism in the pre-World War I period can be found in the pages of *al-Muqattam* from 1911 until 1914, in the context of these varied responses to the claims made by Malul and other Zionist sympathizers in their own articles in the paper. These were claims that were to be heard for many years, some of which have been touched on in our discussion of the 1911 Ottoman parliamentary debate on Zionism, and Ruhi al-Khalidi's manuscript on Zionism: Zionism, these writers asserted, was good for Palestine, would bring in much-needed capital, would provide employment for the indigenous population, and had no ulterior political aspirations to rule over the country.

Among the most notable responses to these claims is an article by Shakib Arslan in January 1912, in which he pours scorn on Malul's claim in an earlier article that ruin will befall Palestine if Zionist colonization is halted. The Zionists, he went on, are benefiting from the country far more than it is benefiting from their presence, and Malul is guilty of gross exaggeration when he describes the blessings of Zionism for Palestine.[37] An article in 1914 by Muhammad 'Abd al-Rahman al-'Alami alluded to another side of the problem, pointing out that the Zionists are able to buy up land in Palestine only because of the dereliction of its duty by the local government, which he emphasized was made up of rich men willing to sacrifice the whole of Palestine for their own personal benefit.[38] A third article by the noted writer Shibli Shmayyil a few days later emphatically stressed that the Zionists were outsiders and aliens (*dukhala' ghuraba'*) engaged in stealing the land from its rightful owners. He added that while opposing Zionism, the Arabs must learn from it, competing with it in developing the land and in cultural work.[39]

Other articles by al-'Alami and 'Isa al-'Isa in May 1914 show that at least the Palestinian opponents of Zionism were well acquainted with the objectives of the Zionist movement as defined by its leaders, and were not taken in by the honeyed words of Malul and others regarding the benign nature of Zionist political objectives in Palestine. Thus, al-'Alami cited the resolutions of the Basle Congress of the movement as well as a declaration by Max Nordau, a close collaborator of Herzl, regarding Zionist aims in Palestine, while 'Isa al-'Isa quoted not only the resolutions of the Basle Congress, and the words of Nordau regarding the undesirability of integration with the local population of Palestine, but also an inflammatory statement by the Russian Zionist leader Menachem Ussishkin in direct contradiction to the conciliatory tone found in articles by Zionist writers in *al-Muqattam*.[40]

Thus even in the columns of the only major Arabic-language paper surveyed that showed any sympathy for the Zionist cause, the reader of the day could find compelling arguments refuting those adduced by the Zionists to prove the harmlessness of their enterprise in Palestine to the country's Arab inhabitants. In spite of the numerous articles by Malul and others, it is hard to avoid the impression that by 1914 the anti-Zionists were getting the best of the argument, even in the pages of *al-Muqattam*.

Al-Ahram's editorial line, by contrast with that of *al-Muqattam*, was generally anti-Zionist, with occasional pro-Zionist articles, usually from readers reacting to editorials or articles from its correspondents critical of Zionism. This newspaper appears to have been the first during our period to raise the question of Zionism, with two articles in December 1908. The first, with the ominous title "The Ambitions of the Zionists in Palestine," reported a speech by a Zionist leader in Cairo in which the speaker expressed the hope that two million Jews would settle in Palestine.[41] The second article, a week later, stated that the Zionists did not want to establish a separate government for themselves in Palestine, but only desired to live in equality with its inhabitants. *Al-Ahram*'s editors commented warily on these declarations, saying that Zionist immigrants would be welcome only if they abandoned their foreign citizenship and became loyal Ottoman citizens. They added that concentration of the immigrants in one area was also unacceptable.[42]

Both of these complaints—that most immigrants retained their foreign nationality, and that they were concentrated in a few areas—were in fact old objections by the local Palestinian population to the Zionist colonization movement, and continued to be central themes of the opposition to Zionism during the Constitutional era. The far-sightedness of the editors of *al-Ahram* can be deduced from their response in July 1909 to a letter from Jacques Tantawi (presumably the same Jacques Levy of Tanta who wrote repeatedly to *al-Ahram* and *al-Muqattam*), who protested that the Zionists were loyal Ottoman patriots. Their answer—that any Jew was welcome to settle in the Empire, as long as the colonists were not concentrated in one region, for that "might lead them to aspire to establish a state within a state, even if that was not part of their plans on the day they immigrated"—sounds strangely prophetic in view of subsequent events.[43]

Notably, although the press of *Bilad al-Sham* appears to have begun to take the Zionist issue seriously in 1909—spearheaded by *al-Karmil*—more articles were carried during that year in both *al-Ahram* and *al-Muqattam* than in any of the other papers surveyed for this study. For all the importance of *al-Karmil* in sounding the alarm against Zionism, it indeed seems clear that these two prestigious Cairo newspapers, with their wide circulation in Egypt and far beyond its borders, played an important vanguard role in awakening readers throughout the Arab world to the earliest stages of a problem that has played such a central part in its political life since then.

Seen in this light, even the pro-Zionist articles carried in these papers played a positive function in terms of Arab opposition to Zionism. Such articles seem to have provoked and aroused Arab readers, particularly those in Palestine, who could see with their own eyes what the Zionists were in fact doing, and set that against the honeyed words of writers favorable to Zionism. At the same time, they could compare the soothing arguments of pro-Zionist writers in the two papers who sought to assure them of the benign nature of Zionist intentions, with the blunt and disturbing words of Zionist leaders directed to European and Zionist audiences. Although this was a different function from that of the four newspapers previously surveyed, it was in many ways more important, for the heated dialogues in these two papers are on the whole more convincing rebuttals of Zionist arguments than many of the one-sided anti-Zionist diatribes in the pages of the Syrian press.

Lisan al-Hal

Of the remaining papers surveyed, four were published in Beirut and were anti-Zionist in their editorial line, although all printed an occasional pro-Zionist article. However, two major differences separate *Lisan al-Hal* from the other three—*al-Ittihad al-'Uthmani*, *al-Haqiqa*, and *al-Iqbal*. It was a strong supporter of the CUP, and its editor was a Christian. It might be added that *Lisan al-Hal* was the oldest of the four papers, having been founded in 1877, and also probably had the largest circulation of any Beirut daily, and perhaps the largest of any daily in the Arab provinces of the Ottoman Empire.[44]

Mention of the religion of the owner of this paper requires some explanation, for the owners or editors of four of the six papers we have discussed (*al-Karmil*, *Filastin*, *al-Ahram*, and *al-Muqattam*) were also Christian, but no reference has been made to this fact. The point has been raised here because of a serious misconception to be found in Neville Mandel's book, regarding the relations between the religious affiliation of a newspaper's owners or editors, and its pro- or anti-Zionist editorial line. From the regular monitoring of the Arab press by the Palestine Office of the Zionist organization in Jaffa, which was begun in 1911 by Nisim Malul, and specifically citing his analysis of the Beirut and Damascus press in the first half of 1912, Mandel concludes that "in Beirut and Damascus, a newspaper's stand in respect of Zionism was as much a function of its editor's religion as of his politics."[45]

Mandel claims that in these two cities, anti-CUP papers—"almost invariably edited by Muslims"—were anti-Zionist as well as anti-Christian, while papers edited by Christians were generally pro-CUP and either friendly or neutral toward the Zionists: "In other words, Muslim editors in Beirut and Damascus tended to be averse to everything that was non-Muslim and non-Arab."[46] Leaving aside the casual bigotry of the last statement (whose falseness can be proven via a perusal of *al-Mufid*, *al-Muqtabis*, or *al-Ittihad al-'Uthmani*, with their absence of the slightest hint of religious intolerance, their many articles by Christian writers, and in the case of the former, al-'Uraisi's outspoken admiration for European culture[47]), Mandel would appear to be completely wrong in his assessment. Whatever conclusions Malul and the Zionist Organization's Palestine Office in Jaffa may have come to on this subject, it is absolutely clear from the ample evidence available in the extensive number of issues of the Arabic-language press of the period still extant that pro-CUP papers edited by Christians were generally as outspoken in their opposition to Zionism as anti-CUP ones edited by Muslims.

It is true that no final conclusion can be reached about the Arabic press as a whole on the basis of the limited sample of newspapers discussed here for several reasons: only one of the ten papers surveyed in full was published in Damascus; of the Beirut papers only one was edited by a Christian; and of the remaining twelve papers not discussed in detail, all were either unavailable for a sufficiently long period, or did not publish a significant number of articles on Zionism. Nevertheless, Mandel himself has not utilized any Beirut or Damascus daily newspaper (as noted, he relies mainly on Malul's press reports), and his usually reliable contemporary Zionist sources seem in this case to have done him a disservice. For not only was *Lisan al-Hal*—edited by a Christian—firmly anti-Zionist, publishing nine articles against Zionism and only three in favor over the period examined; but also three other Syrian papers edited by Christians of which the available issues were checked for purposes of this study showed no pro-Zionist bias, and if anything tended to be anti-Zionist. Of these, one was a Beirut paper, *al-Barq*, edited by Bishara al-Khuri (later the first president of an independent Lebanon); another a Tripoli biweekly, *al-Hawadeth*, edited by Lutfallah Khlat; and the third was the Aleppo paper *al-Sha'b*, owned and edited by Leon Shawqatly and Fathallah Qastun.[48]

While al-Khuri's paper was firmly pro-CUP, the latter two opposed the Unionists, with the first supporting the reform and decentralization movement, and the second openly espousing a strongly Arabist line. As for their position on Zionism, it is clear that none of them was favorable to it, even from the limited number of issues available to us. A 1910 article in *al-Sha'b*, for example, warns against a large-scale project to develop state lands in Palestine which, it was feared, was backed by Zionist and other foreign interests. The article pointed out that the British had originally gained control over India via a commercial company that developed a privileged position for itself in the country.[49] Yet another article in the same paper, written by Rafiq al-'Azm and reprinted in February 1911 from the Arabist Istanbul paper *al-Hadara*, warned against Zionist colonization of Palestine for fear that the country would be lost to the settlers. It emphasized the poor state of the Muslim and Christian villages in the country when compared with the Jewish settlements.[50] A third article, printed four days later, reported the speech of an Aleppo deputy in the Ottoman Parliament, Nafi' al-Jabiri, who strongly opposed the land-development project in Palestine mentioned above, for similar reasons.[51] The other two papers similarly show no pro-Zionist bias.

As for *Lisan al-Hal*, perhaps the most important pro-CUP organ in the Arab provinces, it contains little to bear out Mandel's contention, based on Malul's reports, that the Christian-edited pro-CUP press was necessarily any less anti-Zionist than Muslim-edited anti-CUP papers. A 1911 article in Lisan al-Hal reported a speech by the opposition leader Isma'il Bey in the Ottoman Chamber warning that the objective of the Zionist movement is the establishment of a separate government in Palestine.[52] A further article a few months later by Jubran Matar, writing from Palestine, described the progress of Zionist colonization in alarmist tones, and concluded by declaring: "If we observe all this heady activity, and we realize the great extent of the accumulated power it represents, don't we begin to wonder whether Palestine will soon belong to them?"[53]

Another article in *Lisan al-Hal*, written in 1914 by 'Abd al-Ra'uf Khayyal of Gaza, declared that the blame for what is happening in Palestine should be shouldered by the citizens themselves, and not ascribed to the Zionists or the government. They should act instead of talking and writing, imitate the industriousness of the Zionists, and work to oppose their settler movement, which is on its way to taking over Palestine. He went on to warn the nation to beware: "Otherwise you will become the foreigners, and the foreigners will become the citizens."[54] While *Lisan al-Hal* is clearly trying to deflect criticism over the issue of Zionism from the CUP government it supported with this article—what is happening in Palestine, it argues, is not the government's fault, but that of the citizens themselves—the newspaper's stance critical of Zionism is nevertheless unmistakable.

From this brief review of only a few papers edited by Christians, it should be clear that Mandel's sweeping generalizations rest on limited and misleading evidence, and are in the main incorrect. There was little correlation between journalists' religion and their position on Zionism, and only somewhat more between their stand vis-à-vis the CUP and their attitude to Zionism, although in general anti-CUP papers were strongly anti-Zionist, pro-CUP papers slightly less so. Moreover, there is no apparent reason why their religion should affect editors so much in Beirut and Damascus, and so little in Cairo, Haifa, and Jaffa. Mandel admits that both *Filastin* and *al-Karmil*, as well as *al-Ahram*, all edited by Christians, were anti-Zionist, but claims this was the result of special factors.[55]

In fact, irrespective of the religions of their editors, newspapers in Palestine were virtually all anti-Zionist—and Ya'qub Yehoshua, the leading Israeli historian of the Palestinian press before 1914, notes that most Palestinian newspaper owners were Christians.[56] The point is that the same thing can be said in almost every case about Arabic-language newspapers outside Palestine, whether in other parts of Syria, or in Cairo or Istanbul, and whether their owners and editors were Christian or Muslim. The key to anti-Zionism clearly does not appear to be the religion of the journalists concerned. Indeed, there may well be no trend to be discerned here, for as we noted in chapter 3, virtually the only newspaper editor in Palestine to write consistently in favor of Zionism, Iliya Zakka, editor of *al-Nafir*, was himself Christian, while most of the country's other newspaper owners and editors in this period, mainly Christians, with a few Muslims, were hostile to Zionism.[57] Perhaps a more extensive survey covering all the important papers throughout Syria, as well as in Cairo and Istanbul, for the entire period could settle the question conclusively. But the evidence cited above would seem to rule out religion as the determining factor insofar as a newspaper's stand on Zionism was concerned.

al-Ittihad al-'Uthmani, al-Haqiqa and al-Iqbal

It remains for us to conclude our discussion of the last three of the five Beirut newspapers surveyed. Of them, *al-Ittihad al-'Uthmani* was both the most influential and the most intense in its concentration on the Zionist issue. Like 'Abd al-Ghani al-'Uraisi, its editor-owner, Shaykh Ahmed Hassan Tabbara, was an important political figure in his own right. He too played a prominent role in the First Arab Congress held in Paris in June 1913, and like al-'Uraisi, was hanged by the Ottoman authorities for his Arab nationalist activities (indeed, of the 31 most prominent Arab "martyrs" executed in 1915 and 1916, 16 were journalists[58]). He was in addition one of the leaders of the Beirut Reform Society established in 1913, and after his paper was closed by the Ottoman censor in May of the same year, he changed its name to *al-Islah*, which it remained for the next seven months.

Like *al-Mufid*, *al-Ittihad al-'Uthmani* printed a large number of articles on Zionism by correspondents and contributors from various parts of the Arabic-speaking world, including Egypt, various parts of Palestine, Istanbul, Damascus, and towns like Marja'youn in what is today southern Lebanon. This journal in addition occasionally reprinted articles on the subject from other papers, notably *al-Karmil* and *Filastin*, printing three from the former and one from the latter over a period of three years.[59]

Combined with evidence drawn from an examination of *al-Mufid* and *al-Muqtabas*, this shows that Najib Nassar and 'Isa and Yusuf al-'Isa were able to reach a wide audience as a result of the reprinting of their articles in the Beirut and Damascus press, in itself a clear indication that their influence spread far beyond the frontiers of Palestine. Thus, three of Nassar's articles were also published in *al-Mufid* during the three years for which issues are available, and one in *al-Haqiqa*,[60] in addition to the fifteen printed in *al-Muqtabas*, which have already been mentioned.

In one of the articles printed in *al-Ittihad al-'Uthmani* in 1910, Nassar warned that the objective of the Zionists was to take over Palestine, a dream he claimed was cherished by the Jews since Roman times. He went on to remind his readers of the danger of apparently innocent projects for commercial development in Palestine, which in fact concealed activities of the Zionist organizations.[61] In another article, printed in both *al-Ittihad al-'Uthmani* and *al-Mufid* in February 1911 (and apparently written specially for the two papers) Nassar responded to the claims by a defender of the Zionist movement, Sulayman Effendi Yellin, in the columns of the former paper that Zionism meant no harm to the people of Palestine, and was only a humanitarian movement to relieve the suffering of oppressed Jews, while the settlers in the Zionist colonies were all Ottoman subjects. Nassar's response was that a true humanitarian movement would not cause hardship to the people of the country so as to relieve the oppression of others. He added: "Sulayman Effendi says that the farmers in these colonies are all Ottoman subjects, and we believe him, since most of them have Ottoman identity papers in their hands and foreign passports in their suitcases. . . . How many of them remained Ottoman when they were called up for military service??"[62] Nassar concluded by affirming that there could be no legitimate objection to Jewish immigration to Palestine *per se*, as long as the immigrants avoided segregation from the local population, treated them well, and became loyal Ottoman citizens. In such a case no Ottoman citizen would oppose them, nor would anyone fear their immigration into the Ottoman territories. Belying these reassuring words, however, was the clear implication that Nassar fiercely opposed Zionism because most Zionist immigrants to Palestine did none of these things.

Another leader of the anti-Zionist movement in the Syrian provinces was Shukri al-'Asali, who as we have already seen was elected to the Ottoman Parliament in 1911 as a representative of Damascus after he had failed to prevent the sale of the lands of the village of al-Fula to the JCA. al-'Asali went on to become one of the leaders of the Arab opposition to the CUP, and was one of those hanged in 1916 for his prominent role in the Arab nationalist movement.[63] We saw in chapter 5 that al-'Asali actively used the pages of the Syrian, Palestinian, and Istanbul press as platforms for his opposition to Zionist land purchases, writing under the pseudonym of "Salah al-Din al-Ayyubi" (Saladin) while he was still a government official in 1910, and under his own name afterwards. We thus find articles on this subject by al-'Asali in the Istanbul paper al-Hadara, edited by Shaykh 'Abd al-Hamid al-Zahrawi, another prominent Arabist leader,[64] and numerous others in al-Muqtabas (3), in al-Karmil (3), al-Mufid (2), and the Beirut papers al-Ittihad al-'Uthmani (2), al-Haqiqa (2), and al-Iqbal (1).[65]

One of al-'Asali's most widely published pieces appeared in al-Ittihad al-'Uthmani in February 1911 (as well as in al-Mufid and al-Haqiqa).[66] Its subject was the 10,000 dunum plot of land in al-Fula in the Marj Ibn 'Amir purchased a few months earlier by the Zionists, and whose transfer al-'Asali had unsuccessfully tried to block a few weeks earlier, a transaction we have referred to several times. In this article, al-'Asali described the ruins of an old fortress on the land dating back to the Crusader era, which he said had been captured after a battle in 1187 by Saladin (whence al-'Asali's pseudonym in his earlier articles). The article described in detail the negotiations whereby the JCA, together with the original owner of the land, Elias Sursuq of Beirut, had removed the peasant inhabitants of the land, and then attempted to have the transfer officially registered by al-'Asali in his capacity as qa'immaqam. He included a summary of the texts of several official communications which had passed between him and the Vali in Beirut, wherein the latter took the side of the Zionists, and al-'Asali did his utmost to block completion of the transaction. Emptying this land of its original peasant tenants, and their replacement with foreigners is treason, al-'Asali concluded, and something which he refused to have any part in facilitating.

Building on the emotive connotations of Saladin's reputed connection with the site (which al-'Asali supports with a quotation from the twelfth-century Arab historian Ibn al-Athir) and on the fact that the nearby Haifa branch of the Hijaz Railway was meant to carry Muslim pilgrims to Mecca and Medina, the article strongly impresses its readers with the power, wealth, and persistence of the Zionists, the venality of the Arab landlords willing to sell their land to them, and the complicity of the authorities, or at least their dereliction of duty. It is no surprise therefore that this article should have been so widely reprinted, or that the Vali of Beirut should have seen the need to reply in the columns of the same newspapers, setting off a controversy that went on for weeks.[67] Nor is it particularly surprising in light of this incident that, as we have already seen, al-'Asali should have campaigned in the 1911 by-election in Damascus on a platform pledging him to oppose Zionism, or that in the Chamber after his election he became one of the most outspoken opponents of Zionism.[68]

Although the three remaining Beirut papers—*al-Ittihad al-'Uthmani*, *al-Haqiqa*, and *al-Iqbal*—were strongly anti-Zionist, all also carried an occasional pro-Zionist piece, usually a letter to the editor or an article reprinted from another journal followed by editorial comment. Nisim Malul, for example, sent five letters to *al-Haqiqa* in 1911, provoking angry responses from other readers critical of Zionism.[69] Similarly, in 1913, at the time of the First Arab Congress in Paris, *al-Ittihad al-'Uthmani* briefly changed its line, calling for a more understanding attitude to the Zionists.[70] This shift was apparently motivated by hopes of an agreement with the CUP in the summer of 1913 before and after the Paris Congress, which would have provided for a measure of decentralization and local self-government, and thus would have enabled the local population to regulate and thereby reduce the potential danger of unlimited Zionist immigration. At the same time, contacts had begun in Cairo between Arabist leaders and representatives of the Zionist Organization with a view to exploring the possible grounds for agreement between the two sides. As a result of these two sets of developments, the anti-Zionist tone of the majority of the Syrian and Cairo press lessened noticeably in the late spring and early summer of 1913.

Soon afterwards, however, things changed, after the hopes for an Arab-Turkish entente faded, and after a shift by the Zionist Executive which, in the words of Mandel, "judged it inappropriate for Hochberg [the Zionist envoy to the contacts with the Arabs] to make a secret entente with the Arab nationalists."[71] Thus in late 1913, *al-Ittihad al-'Uthmani* (after being closed down by the authorities, and now appearing under the title *al-Islah*) carried further articles warning against the situation developing in Palestine as far as Zionist land purchase and immigration were concerned. 'Isa al-'Isa is quoted in one article reprinted from *Filastin* in November 1913 as asking what will be the result "if the Zionists arrive in Palestine on every boat and the citizens emigrate on every other?"[72] Another article ten days later ended with the warning that Zionist immigration, with its attendant expulsion of the indigenous peasant population from their lands, posed a serious threat to the country both from the economic and political angles.[73]

Although their coverage of Zionism was less extensive than that of the other newspapers surveyed, *al-Ittihad al-'Uthmani*, *al-Haqiqa*, and *al-Iqbal* all reflected the same unyielding attitude to Zionism of most of the rest of the Arabic press of this period. That they should have done so is evidence that this issue was one which, although animated largely by the Palestinian press, and by Palestinian journalists and letter-writers, aroused concern far beyond the confines of Palestine itself.

IV

By implication, *al-Muqtabas'* critiques of the weakness of the Arab resistance to Zionist colonization in this early phase pointed out the path to fellow: greater understanding of the aims of the Zionist movement, more unity and better organization on the part of the Arabs in resisting it, and so forth. But rarely did the Arab press critics of Zionism go much further. In no article among the more than 650 examined for this analysis of the press and Zionism was there a call for armed resistance to the colonizers, although we have seen that in a few areas the peasants had already spontaneously engaged in such resistance. Nowhere was the much-lamented failure of the Ottoman government to solve the problem cited as justification for extreme measures against it on the part of the Arabs. In spite of the scathing criticism by many writers of land sales by individual landowners, and of the upper classes in general for dereliction of their duty, these analyses never went on to critique the new form of European-derived property relations that made such land sales possible, or to demand a wholesale social transformation as a precondition for success in the conflict with Zionism.

Clearly, in spite of the alarm Zionism aroused among a large section of the Arab intelligentsia, such radical solutions were not yet seen to be necessary, nor perhaps was the time ripe for their propagation. We have nevertheless noted in the preceding chapter that in the countryside, the peasants themselves had begun to react violently to the seizure of what they understood to be their land by its new Zionist owners, after its purchase from absentee Arab landlords. In the pre-World War I period, as afterwards, the literate upper classes were occasionally to show themselves to be ahead of the rest of Arab society in terms of perceptions, but lagging behind when it came to action and, with several notable exceptions,[74] can thus be judged guilty of a certain degree of failure of leadership—and, at the same time, unwillingness to follow the lead of the *fellahin*.

In spite of these inconsistencies, and the difficulties of translating the Arab critique of Zionism into an effective program for action, in the course of our survey of the treatment of the Zionist question in the Arab press, based on a close investigation of the ten papers discussed above and a cursory examination of a dozen other newspapers and periodicals, a number of major themes have emerged. One of the first in importance was strong opposition to the laxity of the Ottoman central authorities in restraining Zionist colonization, a stand linked to an intense feeling that local needs, desires, and wishes were being ignored. We have here, in the varied forms in which it emerged before 1914, the embryo of the Palestinian demand for self-government and self-determination, one that would continue to be asserted for a long time to come. This theme, moreover, hints at the beginnings of an identity rooted in Palestine which, while not separate from other overlapping elements of identity at this stage, had its own specificity and its own unique characteristics.

Among other important themes are opposition to unrestricted Zionist immigration and land-purchase, and resentment at the self-imposed segregation of the immigrants and their failure to become loyal citizens of the country they settled in. Looming behind all of these concerns is the fear, expressed in dozens of articles, that the Arabs in Palestine would one day be reduced to a minority in the country, and become strangers in their own land. This, it was feared, would be the result of the Zionists' achievement of their objective of winning exclusive sovereignty over Palestine, an aim frequently denied by defenders of Zionism, but perceived as being the real, unavowed aim of the movement by most Arab writers at this time. If anything, this is one of the most striking conclusions to emerge from a study of the Arabic press and its treatment of Zionism: by 1914 most editors and writers in the papers examined were fully aware that the seemingly innocuous activities of the Zionist movement were directed at the ultimate establishment of a Jewish state in Palestine, with its necessary concomitant of the dispossession of the Arab population.

In chapter 4 we saw an expression in 1899 by one Jerusalem notable, Yusuf Diya' al-Khalidi, of an explicit awareness that this was what was ultimately at stake in Palestine: Jewish sovereignty and Arab dispossession. And we have seen in the last chapter how the friction on the land between settlers and peasants came to affect wider and wider circles in Palestine. The period from 1899 to 1914, and in particular the years after 1908, provide us with hundreds of examples drawn from the daily press of the growth of such an awareness, presented to tens of thousands of readers, whose letters to the newspapers concerned reveal that this was a dialectical process, with newspaper readers as well as journalists contributing to a growing awareness of this subject. This is a perfect example of the kind of "imagined community," mediated and shaped by the press, whose members did not know one another, but who shared a certain body of knowledge, a certain understanding, and a joint sense of grievance, which Benedict Anderson has written about.[75]

We have seen that the first Arabic-language newspapers to devote great attention to this issue after 1908 were those of Cairo, followed closely by *al-Karmil* (whose first two articles on the subject were reprinted from *al-Muqattam* with critical comment by Nassar).[76] Thereupon the initiative seems to have passed to the Palestinian and Beirut press, which in late 1910 and 1911 subjected the Zionist enterprise to minute investigation and scathing criticism. The Tripoli and Balkan wars of late 1911–1912 and late 1912–1913, as well as the CUP's occasional repression of the press, caused a temporary lull in attention to Zionism from late 1911 to 1912, but by 1913 the press was once again focusing on the matter. Although faint hopes of agreement with the CUP and the Zionists in 1913 caused some shifts in this general trend, by the end of the year the same resolute tone of concern about Zionism and criticism of the government was again apparent in the press, and it would continue until the outbreak of World War I.

Thus in the newspapers of Palestine, of Beirut, of Damascus, and of Cairo, we can already discern during the Ottoman Constitutional period a vivid awareness of the significance and implications of the Zionist movement for the population of Palestine and for the Arab world. The reader of the hundreds of articles on this subject cannot fail to be impressed, not only by the prescience of many of the arguments presented by their authors, but also by the degree to which what they were saying foreshadowed the main lines of Palestinian and Arab nationalist rhetoric about Zionism in the succeeding years.

And in the way in which Cairo, Beirut, Damascus and Jaffa, Haifa, and Jerusalem newspapers played off one another in addressing the question of Zionism, expressing slightly different perspectives in every case, we can see an example of the complex interpenetration between Ottoman, Arab, Syrian, and local Palestinian elements in the framing of this issue, an interplay that came to be central to the definition of Palestinian identity. While a chauvinist modern-day Palestinian nationalist perspective would perhaps stress the role of *al-Karmil, Filastin,* and other Palestinian newspapers in shaping the Arab response to Zionism, it is clear from our survey of the press in this chapter that the reality was considerably more nuanced. Syrians and Lebanese in Cairo, Beirut, Damascus, and Istanbul, as well as Palestinians in Jaffa, Haifa, and Jerusalem, all played a role in developing the public understanding of what Zionism meant for Palestine and the region. And while these conclusions had the most relevance for Palestine itself, they were shaped by considerations, whether national or religious, that extended far beyond the frontiers of Palestine.

In the succeeding chapter we will explore how this new and more widely held understanding of Zionism, and other new factors engendered by the momentous events of World War I, were to influence the self-view of the people of Palestine, and to contribute conclusively to the shaping of their identity.

CHAPTER 7

The Formation of
Palestinian Identity:
The Critical Years, 1917–1923

I

When did a significant proportion of the
Arab inhabitants of Palestine begin to think of themselves as Palestinians?
What are the constituent elements of this sense of identification with
Palestine, and how does it relate to other forms of identity, whether
national, religious, or otherwise? These and other basic questions touching on Palestinian identity have generated an extensive polemical literature.[1] They have also produced some valuable scholarship.[2] These questions have informed our consideration of the identity of Palestinian Arabs
in the pre-World War I period. These same questions are the primary
focus of this chapter, which argues that the answers to them can be found
largely in the years at the end of World War I and immediately afterwards.

As with the identity of the peoples of many other Arab countries (and
indeed other countries) in the modern period, we have seen that the
case of Palestinian identity is complicated by the difficulty of explaining
its interrelation with broad, powerful transnational foci of identity, in
particular Arabism and Islam, and with other potent regional and local
loyalties. People in the Arab world throughout most of the twentieth

century (including the Palestinians themselves), understood that these and other elements simultaneously constituted the identity of a Palestinian Arab. This interrelation is particularly difficult to explain to those who think of national identity in ahistorical, unidimensional terms, generally with reference to models derived from an idealized and simplified version of the Western European experience.[3]

Thus, while in most cases the identity of a Frenchwoman would today be determined both by herself and by others *primarily* in terms of her identification with the French nation (notwithstanding important differences among the French of region, religion, politics, race, gender, class, and broader European affiliations), it would be normal for a Palestinian today to identify *primarily* as an Arab in one context, as a Muslim or Christian in another, as a Nabulsi or Jaffan in yet another, and as a Palestinian in a fourth.[4] The Frenchwoman would refer her identity in some measure to a powerful, generations-old "historical" narrative of Frenchness, propagated with authority since some time in the nineteenth century by a unified school system and other means at the disposal of the French state. In contrast, given the lack of such a state or such a unified educational system, the Palestinian would be more likely to refer identity to a number of "historical" narratives, each carrying a different valence and a somewhat different message. The same pattern of multiple foci of identity of course applies to the populations of other Arab countries in the modern era, with the major difference that in their cases there exist authoritative official "historical" national narratives (most of them fairly recent) propagated vigorously for several generations by their respective nation-states, which usually would take pride of place in the self-description of these populations.

However, unlike that of the other Arab peoples—indeed, perhaps uniquely—the Palestinian case is further complicated by the intimate intertwining over the past century (and in some senses for much longer) of the Palestinian narrative with one of the most potent narratives in existence, that of Israel and the Jewish people, a circumstance touched on in chapter 2.[5] The interweaving of these two narratives reaches the point that in much public discourse about the Palestinians in the United States, their narrative can be considered only in terms of the other,[6] and as a rule such discourse is constructed in terms of a rigid polarity between the two narratives. This polarity is sometimes justified, but at other times it is artificially imposed: it often means that permission cannot be granted for a Palestinian voice to be heard—even on matters having absolutely nothing to do with Israel—without the reassuring presence of its Israeli echo. The opposite, of course, is not true: a Palestinian voice is not necessarily required when exclusively Israeli or Jewish concerns are aired.

Clearly, within this paradigm, the Palestinians exist not as an independent entity with an independent narrative, but only in relation to another entity and another narrative. In view of the compelling claim we have already cited—that self-definition takes place with reference to an "other" (as Stuart Hall puts it, "only when there is an Other can you know who you are"[7])—discussions of contentious questions of national identity understandably tend to gravitate in the direction of such polarizations. But over the past few decades the intertwining of, and the tension between, the Palestinian and Israeli national narratives may have reached a level of intensity in Palestine itself, and in American and European public discourse, that is unique.

This overlap of the two narratives has primarily affected that of the Palestinians. In recent decades, the resounding success of the Zionist political project, and the resultant successful grafting of modern political Zionism onto Jewish history, with the former coming to be considered the logical and inevitable outcome of the latter, has legitimized the resulting synthesis of the two, such that there is a perceived continuity, a seamless transition, between ancient, medieval, and early modern Jewish history on the one hand, and the history of modern Zionism and Israel on the other.[8] Palestinian identity, by contrast, never having enjoyed such success, has since its beginnings struggled for acceptance and legitimacy in the outside world,[9] and even for recognition of its very existence as a category of being. Israeli Prime Minister Golda Meir's widely disseminated dismissive remark that "There was no such thing as Palestinians. . . . They did not exist" was significant not only for its broad impact on public discourse, but also as expressing a common view that over time has come to be widely held among westerners generally.[10]

All of this has complicated what might otherwise have been a relatively straightforward story. In the case of the national identities of the peoples of other Arab countries which came into being in their modern form in the wake of World War I, similar processes of the construction of new identities building on elements of old ones as part of a novel synthesis (for this is what we are talking about in the Palestinian case and most other cases of the development of new national identities in the modern era) have occasioned relatively little attention, and limited controversy, whether within these countries or elsewhere. The main exception was Lebanon. And in the instance of Lebanon, the resulting debate has been primarily an internal one among Lebanese, for whom the definition of Lebanese identity proved to be a bitterly contested subject throughout the twentieth century, contributing significantly to the civil strife that afflicted the country in 1958, and again much more severely from 1975 until the early 1990s.[11] Although the question of Lebanese identity has occasioned some scholarly attention outside of Lebanon, this was restrained and unpolemical by comparison with that devoted to the Palestinian case.

While issues of Palestinian identity are hotly disputed in the United States and Israel, they occasion controversy as well in the Arab world and among Palestinians. From a radical Arab nationalist perspective, the very existence of nation-states in the Arab world is suspect: from this purist point of view, they are seen as a contrivance imposed by western imperialism, and as utterly lacking in legitimacy. Although rapidly waning in force in recent years as pan-Arabism declined, such a view lingers on to this day in corners of Arab popular consciousness. It has at various times in the past been taken by, among others, the Ba'thist regime in Syria as a pretext for arguing that the Palestinians (and for that matter the Lebanese and Jordanians) should accept Syrian hegemony. The Syrian Ba'thist position at times suggested that Palestine is part of Southern Syria, a small segment of the great Arab homeland whose legitimate representative is none other than the Ba'th party, headed by Hafiz al-Asad. While often cynical and manipulative, and perceived as such by many in the Arab world, such views benefited from a certain popularity and credibility as long as pan-Arabism retained its power, particularly when put forth by a rhetorical and tactical master such as Egyptian President Gamal 'Abd al-Nasir during the decade or so when he was at the height of his pan-Arab power and prestige, from the mid-1950s until the 1967 war.

Similarly, from a radical Islamist perspective, Palestinian-centered nationalism is tantamount to heresy, splitting as it does the Islamic *umma*—a word which can mean community, or people, or nation in different contexts—into warring nations, a view in support of which various more or less canonical sayings of the Prophet Muhammad are adduced. Such a view, which has been growing in popularity lately, is espoused by Palestinian Islamist factions such as *Hizb al-Tahrir al-Islami*, the Islamic Liberation Party, an almost entirely Palestinian radical organization dating from the 1950s, as well as the Palestinian branch of the Muslim Brotherhood and its offspring of the late 1980s, Hamas, and the equally recent Islamic Jihad movement. All subsume Palestinian nationalism within one or another form of Islamic identity, although all are primarily Palestinian organizations in terms of membership, organization, and goals, and it is not clear how they resolve the tension between their universalist Islamic message and the particularist Palestinian reality in which all of them are firmly grounded.

In contradiction to these Arabist and Islamist views, there is mainstream secular Palestinian nationalism, grouped together under the umbrella of the PLO and represented for the past three decades by a variety of its constituent organizations including Fateh, the Popular Front for the Liberation of Palestine (PFLP), and others.[12] These groups, which have probably represented the views of a majority of Palestinians since some time in the mid- or late 1960s, emerge from a relatively recent tradition which argues that Palestinian nationalism has deep historical roots. As with other national movements, extreme advocates of this view go further than this, and anachronistically read back into the history of Palestine over the past few centuries, and even millennia, a nationalist consciousness and identity that are in fact relatively modern.[13] While not denying the Islamist or the Arabist dimensions of Palestinian identity outright, they tend to give precedence to the purely Palestinian aspects.

With this background in mind, this chapter attempts to reconstruct the formative period in the genesis of Palestinian national identity, specifically the years immediately after World War I. It builds on the assumption that many of the constituents of this identity—patriotic feeling, local loyalties, Arabism, religious sentiment, higher levels of education and literacy, and other factors we have examined in the preceding chapters—were already widespread before World War I, and were probably even then coalescing into a sense of community among the people of the country as Palestinians, without yet constituting the primary focus of identification for most of the Arab inhabitants of Palestine.

The main thesis of the chapter is that under the impact of rapid, momentous, and unsettling changes during the period from the outset of World War I to some time early on in the British mandate for Palestine, at the outside in 1922 or 1923, the sense of political and national identification of most politically conscious, literate, and urban Palestinians underwent a sequence of major transformations. The end result was a strong and growing national identification with Palestine, as the Arab residents of the country increasingly came to "imagine" themselves as part of a single community.[14] This identification was certainly not exclusive—for Arabism, religion, and local loyalties still remained extremely important, and continued to make it possible for Arabs in

Palestine to also see themselves simultaneously as part of other communities, both larger and smaller ones. And this identification certainly did not include all sectors or classes of the population. But it did constitute a new and powerful category of identity that was simply nonexistent a generation or two before, and was still novel and limited in its diffusion before World War I.

In succeeding decades, this identification with Palestine was to be developed and refined significantly, as Palestinian nationalism grew and developed during the mandatory period and after 1948. Equally important, it continued its slow spread beyond the relatively narrow elite which was initially affected by these ideas to broader sectors of the population—outside the upper and middle classes in the cities, and in the countryside. The acceleration of ongoing social and economic trends, which can be traced back to the years before World War I, such as the growth in the urban population, and of wage labor, the expansion of the press and of the educational system, and the spread of literacy, played a major role in this process. So profound a transformation of the sense of self of the Arab population of Palestine, which began during the years immediately before World War I and intensified immediately after it, resulted in the emergence of a Palestinian national identity where a few decades before no such thing had existed.

II

Among the factors that caused the Arab population of Palestine to identify with the country in the years immediately before World War I, several stand out. We have already touched on many of these, but it is worthwhile reiterating and redefining them before going on to look at the years after World War I when so much changed so fast. First among these factors was a religious attachment to Palestine as a holy land on the part of Muslims and Christians (as well as by Jews, of course), which we have glimpsed repeatedly in earlier chapters. This attachment was felt by followers of both faiths elsewhere, but it was particularly strong for those Christian and Muslim Arabs who lived in Palestine.

Although Muslims and Christians had somewhat different conceptions from one another of what made Palestine a holy land, and of its boundaries and extent, they shared a similar general idea of the country as a unit, and as being special and holy. In the Christian case, as Alexander Schölch has pointed out most clearly (in the context of ascertaining "the extent to which it is at all meaningful to write a history of Palestine during a certain phase in the nineteenth century when there was no administrative unit with this name and when this area's 'borders'—in other words, the area's historical-geographical identity—were contested"), this conception was firmly based on the biblical definition of the country as running from "Dan to Beersheba."[15] It was reinforced by the boundaries of the jurisdiction of the Greek Orthodox and Latin Patriarchates and the Protestant Episcopate of Jerusalem, all three of which included the entirety of Palestine irrespective of the Ottoman administrative divisions, which changed from time to time.

Both Schölch and Yehoshua Porath have described how the Muslim perception of Palestine as a holy land—it is indeed called "*al-ard al-muqaddasa*" [meaning "the holy land"] in the Qur'an (5:21)—developed over time.[16] This took place notably through such genres as the "*Fada'il al-Quds*"literature referred to briefly in chapter 2, which praised Jerusalem, Hebron, and other parts of Palestine, and which was widespread before, and even more so after, the Crusades.[17] This literature reinforced the sense for Muslims in which Palestine was an entity, albeit a sacred rather than a political one. Also important in this regard were annual seasonal pilgrimages to local holy sites, notably the Nabi Musa celebration, which traditionally attracted thousands of Muslim pilgrims from all over the country to a site identified with Moses by Muslims, at a twelfth-thirteenth century shrine located halfway between Jerusalem and Jericho.[18]

Various authors have also described how two more factors helped to shape the local inhabitants' conception of the country: the first was Ottoman administrative boundaries, and the second was the ambitions and aspirations of the European powers in Palestine. As far as the first is concerned, we have seen that from 1874 onwards, the *sanjaq* of Jerusalem, including the districts of Jerusalem, Bethlehem, Hebron, Beersheeba, Gaza, and Jaffa, was a separate unit administered independently from any other Ottoman province, and as such was under the direct authority of Istanbul. In earlier times, Jerusalem had briefly been capital of a larger province, a *vilayet* of "*Filastin*," which encompassed all of what is now Palestine, including Nablus, Haifa, and the Galilee. More frequently in the period before 1874, the Jerusalem *sanjaq* was included with other regions within the province of Damascus.[19]

The way in which these administrative arrangements affected local conceptions of the country can be seen in recommendations for action by the new Ottoman Parliament published in the Turkish and Arabic press in 1908 by a former official of the Jerusalem *sanjaq*, the Lebanese

Najib 'Azuri. Among the recommendations in this article (mentioned in chapter 2) was the expansion of the *sanjaq* of Jerusalem, and raising it to the rank of a *vilayet*, which 'Azuri argued was necessary "since the progress of the land of Palestine depends on it."[20] 'Azuri had earlier aroused the ire of Sultan Abdul Hamid for his outspoken opposition to government policies, notably regarding Zionism. He had been sentenced to death for treason *in absentia* after his flight to France, where in 1905 he wrote the prophetic book *Reveil de la Nation Arabe*, which predicted a momentous conflict between Zionism and Arab nationalism. His opposition to Zionism was undoubtedly one of the bases for his argument that Palestine should be a separate province, but it was clearly predicated on the assumption that there was such a thing as a "land of Palestine," an idea that must have been shared with the readers of *Sabah* and *Thamarat al-Funun*.

This bears out Schölch's statement that "the administrative experiments and facts mentioned here, especially the elevated position of the *sanjaq* of Jerusalem (which lasted for almost half a century), doubtless contributed to the emergence of the concept of Palestine as an administrative entity."[21] Porath goes further: " . . . at the end of the Ottoman period the concept of *Filastin* was already widespread among the educated Arab public, denoting either the whole of Palestine or the Jerusalem *sanjaq* alone."[22] This resulting local consciousness of Palestine as a discrete entity, based on religious tradition and long-standing administrative practice, was only enhanced by the second factor, the fact that foreigners also recognized it as such.

The covetousness of the European powers regarding Palestine, and in particular their constant efforts to expand their influence and standing there throughout the nineteenth century,[23] naturally affected the self-view of the inhabitants of the country. We have noted that the inhabitants of Palestine had long perceived that control of the country was a prize of value to the Western powers, and it can easily be seen that such a consciousness did much to cement a sense of community and belonging, and to spur patriotic feeling regarding Palestine. Such a feeling was originally particularly strong among Muslims, and had been widespread among them at least since the Crusades, as was clear from the 1701 petition by notables and other inhabitants of Jerusalem to Sultan Mustafa II protesting the visit of a French Consul to Jerusalem, discussed at length in chapter 2. It is worth recalling that the petition mentioned that "our city is the focus of attention of the infidels" and that "this holy land" could be "occupied as a result of this, as has happened repeatedly in earlier times." The meeting which produced this petition was attended by both notables and common people, testimony to the prevalence of such feelings among all sectors of urban society.[24] In the nineteenth century, many Palestinian and other Arab Christians came to share this fear of European imperialism, while at the same time many Christians were among the first local inhabitants to be affected by Western notions of nationalism and patriotism obtained in missionary schools and through other contacts with Europeans.

In looking at the factors that caused the Arab population to identify with Palestine, an obvious one has already been mentioned and deserves reiteration: this was a powerful local attachment to place. As in other Islamic cultures, in the cities of Palestine there was a strong tradition of what might be called urban patriotism. Jerusalemites, Nabulsis, Gazans, and Khalilis (inhabitants of Hebron—al-Khalil in Arabic) all took pride in their cities, as can be seen from the profusion of local histories devoted to cities and regions of Palestine.[25] This can be seen also from the frequency of the use of the name of a city—al-Maqdisi, al-Nabulsi, al-Ghazzawi, al-Khalili, and so on—as either a family name or as an identifier in addition to a family name. Outside of the cities, there was also a deep attachment to place, including pride in the village as special and better than others, and a related pride in family and lineage which was shared by city-dwellers, villagers, and nomads.[26]

With the spread of a broader notion of patriotism as modern education reached wider circles of the population, and with the increased ease and speed of travel in the late nineteenth and early twentieth centuries as roads and railways were constructed, these local loyalties were gradually supplemented by a sense of belonging to an entity larger than a city, town, or village and its immediate environs. Local loyalties have never been completely superseded, however, and they still retain their vitality in the cities and villages of Palestine.[27] It is difficult to convey how dense can be the associations with place in a society like that of Palestine, and especially difficult to do so when the referent is American society, in much of which mobility has greater value than rootedness. In Palestine and other Arab countries, these local associations are still meaningful to the degree that people can often be easily identified as to their place of origin by their family name, and to some degree remain identified with these places, even if they have never lived there. This can be seen particularly clearly among residents of Palestinian refugee camps who, to this day, identify with their villages and towns of origin even if they have lived in exile from them for two or three generations.[28]

We have seen in chapters 5 and 6 that the reaction of the Palestinian Arabs to modern political Zionism drew upon all these preexisting elements: religious attachment to what both Muslim and Christians saw as a holy land, the conception of Palestine as an administrative entity, the fear of external encroachment, and local patriotism. Before going into the details of the Palestinian reaction to Zionism, it is worth stressing that these elements of attachment to Palestine all antedated the encounter with Zionism. It is necessary to stress this obvious fact because of the common assertion that Palestinian identity was no more than a reaction to Zionism, and the attachment of Palestinian Arabs to the country no more than a response to the attachment to it of those inspired by Zionism. There is a kernel of truth in these assertions: in some measure, as we have already seen, identity develops in response to the encounter with an "other." But for the Palestinians there were always other "others" besides Zionism: among them were the covetous European powers and the country's Turkish rulers before World War I, and the British Mandatory authorities and other Arab peoples after that. In any case, it is clear from the abundant evidence, much of which we have surveyed, that the Arab population of Palestine had a strong attachment to their country—albeit an attachment expressed in pre-nationalist terms—long before the arrival of modern political Zionism on the scene in the last years of the nineteenth century.

We have seen in earlier chapters that there was a widespread and sophisticated opposition to Zionism among educated, urban, and politically active Palestinians from a very early stage in the implantation of the Zionist movement in Palestine. Chapter 5 analyzed the crucial role in engendering this opposition played by the strong resistance to Zionism among the peasantry in areas where Zionist colonization led to the displacement of *fellahin* from their lands. All of this was reflected in the press, which had a broad impact on public opinion, and helped to shape both Arab views of Zionism, and the conception of Palestine as a land under threat. At the same time, it has been apparent that the issue of Zionism was a defining one for many Palestinian papers, notably Najib Nassar's *al-Karmil,* and *Filastin,* published by 'Isa and Yusuf al-'Isa. As was pointed out, the very titles of these two papers, as well as others like *al-Quds,* named for Jerusalem, are indicative of the local patriotism that inspired their establishment.

One of the clearest pre-war examples of this conception of Palestine as a land under threat from the Zionist movement, and of the Palestinians as an entity, indeed a national entity, can be seen from the opening words of a full-page editorial in a special one-page broadsheet issue of *Filastin* in 1914 entitled "An Open Letter to Subscribers." In it, the editors began by commenting sarcastically on an attempt by the Ottoman authorities to close down the newspaper in May 1914 in response to their published attacks on the Zionist movement: "Dear readers, it seems we have done something serious in the view of the central government in warning *the Palestinian nation* [*al-umma al-filistiniyya*—my italics] of the danger which threatens it from the Zionist current."[29] This brilliantly written editorial is full of pungent attacks on the government, ridiculing it for defending the Zionist movement and trying to shut down *Filastin*, even though the newspaper was only doing its patriotic duty by warning against a clear danger to the country. The editorial writers stress repeatedly that nothing the government can do will change the belief that "we are a nation [*umma*] threatened with disappearance in the face of this Zionist current in this Palestinian land [*fi hathihi al-bilad al-filistiniyya*]." As significant as the sentiment that the Palestinians were endangered by Zionism was the repeated use of the term "Palestinian nation" in this context. Perhaps equally significant, Yusuf and 'Isa al-'Isa fought the government closure order in a local court, won the case, and were described in contemporary French consular reports as having been carried from the courtroom on the shoulders of a delirious throng of well-wishers.[30]

Much else in this editorial is worthy of note. Its authors mention that a Zionist leader, a certain Dr. Orbach, had stated to a Jewish audience in Haifa that the Zionists should oppose the Arabs, and scatter them from their lands, because this would be a service to the Turks, who would thank the Zionists for this. Such statements were foolish, the authors of the editorial argued, since they inspire hatred in the heart of the Arab nation (*al-umma al-'arabiyya*), and wake it from its stupor, and make the Zionists, who claimed disingenuously they were "cousins of the Arabs," look like liars. The authors continued:

> Let the central government learn that Zionism is not a mere "ghost" or a "bogey-man," as its supporters claim. Today it is a palpable danger. If it succeeds in silencing us . . . it cannot prevent the eye from seeing, or the hand from touching what is before it and around it. If it silences us, how can it suppress this resurgence which has touched all the patriotic newspapers, reaching as far as the Nile Valley. . . . Even if they defeat *Filastin* in court, patriots will arise to found tens of newspapers like it to serve the same principles, and to mount the same defense of the

body of this poor nation which is threatened in its very being by expulsion from its homeland.[31]

In view of these powerful sentiments, which clearly distinguish among, while accepting, loyalty to Ottomanism, belonging to an Arab nation, and Palestinian patriotism, it can be understood that, although other foci of loyalty were still operative for most of the Arab inhabitants of Palestine before World War I, the idea of Palestine as a source of identity and as a community with shared interests had already taken root. It competed with and complemented loyalty to the Ottoman state and to the Muslim and Christian religious communities, the growing sense of Arabism fostered by the spread of education and the expansion of the influence of the Arabic press, and other more local loyalties—to regions, cities, villages, and families.

In this context, the growing problem of dealing with Zionism provided Palestinians with the occasion to feel part of a larger whole, whether Ottoman or Arab, which they hoped might help them to deal with an opponent whom they had already begun to fear they could not resist alone. This tendency was encouraged by the extent to which the question of Zionism was addressed in Ottoman politics, in parliament, and in the press, and by the degree to which Arabist politicians and newspapers stressed their opposition to Zionism. However, as time went by, the problems posed by Zionism contributed to the tendency for Palestinians to feel separate and abandoned, for in the end the Ottoman authorities failed to take seriously the complaints of the Palestinians regarding Zionism (the same editorial noted bitterly: "government officials in the provinces do not understand the Hebrew of those like Orbach, . . . and if we translate their words the government does not trust our translations, and lets it all pass lightly, laughingly."),[32] while even those Arabist politicians who initially seemed sympathetic in the end proved equally ineffective.

The overlap between these various loyalties, and the way in which one developed from another, can be seen from remarks of 'Isa al-'Isa about the motives that led him to found *Filastin* in 1911. In a speech many years later at the Arab Orthodox club in Jerusalem, he stated that at the outset his main aim had been to defend the Arab Orthodox cause.[33] Very soon afterwards, however, he said that he found himself in the midst of a national conflict on two fronts: one Arab-Turkish, and the other Arab-Jewish, and he joined in both, without ever abandoning the Orthodox cause.[34] Clearly, for an individual such as 'Isa al-'Isa, all of these loyalties were fully compatible with one another, and notable among them was the sense of Palestinian identity which his words in the *Filastin* editorial cited above show clearly to have been prominent even before World War I.

World War I changed many things as far as Palestinian identity was concerned, however. Of the elements of identity for Palestinians and other Arabs whose attraction had waned by the end of the war, two stand out: they were Ottomanism and religious affiliation. The reason for the collapse of Ottomanism as a focus of identity is obvious. Beyond the defeat of the Ottoman army and the withdrawal of Ottoman authority from the Arab provinces by the end of 1918, Ottomanism as an attempt at a transnational ideological synthesis was rendered obsolete by the outcome of World War I. Among Turks and Arabs, Armenians and Kurds, its place was taken by the national principle. That principle had already asserted itself forcefully in the decades before 1914, as it dissolved many of the bonds that held the multinational Empire together. Its appeal was greatly strengthened during World War I, when President Wilson made national self-determination one of his Fourteen Points. Although the Ottoman heritage was to continue to have a powerful influence on the Arab world in the following decades (one that has been unjustly ignored and insufficiently examined),[35] in a period of a few years, Ottomanism as an ideology went from being one of the primary sources of identification for Palestinians, and many others, to having no apparent impact at all. We have touched on some of the ways in which Ottomanism bound Arab elites to the Empire, in looking at the careers of Yusuf Diya' and Ruhi al-Khalidi. For others, the Ottoman bond was a simple religious one: the Ottoman Sultan was the Caliph, and the Empire the greatest Muslim state of its day.

In regard to the Arab provinces, it can be argued in hindsight that even before the war the Ottoman synthesis was gravely undermined because of what many Arabs and others came to perceive was the rise of Turkish nationalism as the governing principle of the Ottoman state and the party that dominated it from 1908 until 1918, the CUP.[36] Similarly, the decline of religion as the governing principle of the Ottoman state in the waning years of the Empire, and what was perceived by many as the cynical exploitation of Islam by the highly secular CUP from 1908 to 1918, accelerated a decline in the saliency of religious identification in the Empire before and during the War. This complemented and enhanced a growing shift to secularism and secular nationalism on the part of some of the younger segments of the Ottoman elite, but this shift was by no means as definitive as the eclipse of Ottomanism.

For many sectors of the population, and perhaps for most people in the successor states of the Ottoman Empire, religion has remained the most important single source of identification and community feeling. This has been true not only of the lower classes and the rural populace, but also of many members of the upper classes and among city dwellers, particularly the older ones.

The end result was nevertheless that two of the central pillars of identity before 1914, Ottomanism and religion, were seriously diminished in importance by the end of World War I. This left the field open for nationalism, the ideological rival of both, which had been growing rapidly in influence in the late Ottoman period. The only question, in Palestine and elsewhere, was not whether nationalism would supplant other forms of loyalty, but rather which specific form of nationalism would do so. And, at the outset, the answer to that question seemed to be clear: Arab nationalism appeared to be the obvious successor to Ottomanism as the hegemonic ideology throughout the former Arab provinces of the now-defunct Ottoman Empire.[37] However, in Palestine, as elsewhere in the Arab world, matters were to prove to be not quite that simple.

III

> A nation which has long been in the depths of sleep only awakes
> if it is rudely shaken by events, and only arises little by little. . . .
> This was the situation of Palestine, which for many centuries had
> been in the deepest sleep, until it was shaken by the great war,
> shocked by the Zionist movement, and violated by the illegal pol-
> icy [of the British], and it awoke, little by little.[38]

These were the words used in 1925 by the eminent Jerusalem writer and educator, Khalil al-Sakakini, the co-founder of the *al-Madrasa al-Wataniyya* school in Jerusalem whom we met in chapter 3, to describe the situation in Palestine in the immediate aftermath of World War I, a period during which rapid and crucial changes in consciousness and perception took place among much of the population.

Each of the factors listed by al-Sakakini had a major impact on Palestine. The war initially brought with it a massive Ottoman military presence to support the campaigns across the Sinai desert against the Suez Canal launched by Cemal Paşa's Fourth Army. Three years of Ottoman military campaigns against Egypt from bases in Palestine, and of grave dislocations caused by the British naval blockade to an economy that had become in large part dependent on foreign trade, were followed by the arrival of the allied army commanded by General Allenby, fighting its way north through the country in 1917 and 1918. Parts of Palestine were devastated by combat, notably the Gaza region, many trees throughout the country were cut down to fuel steam locomotives, draft animals were requisitioned by both armies, famine prevailed in some areas, and virtually all the draft-age men were inducted into the Ottoman army, many never to return. Others were arrested, executed, or exiled by the authorities on suspicion of aiding the allies.[39] The economic results of the war were debilitating, as was its demographic impact, which has been estimated in the most careful assessment of the demography of Palestine during this period as leading to a population decrease of over 6 percent in little more than four years, a particularly grave decline given that the population of Palestine had been growing by about 2 percent per year before the war.[40]

However serious was the material impact of the war on Palestine, its political and psychological consequences were even greater.[41] The effect of the collapse of the Ottoman state, within whose framework some twenty generations of Arabs had lived for four centuries in the countries of the Fertile Crescent, has already been mentioned. This event left a huge vacuum in political consciousness, particularly for the older generation, one made all the greater by the occupation of the region by the British and the French, an eventuality much anticipated and much feared by most of the population even before the war.[42] As the quotation from al-Sakakini indicates, the issuance of the Balfour Declaration and the revelation of the Sykes-Picot accords by the Bolsheviks—both in November 1917, only weeks before Jerusalem fell to Allenby's forces— had an enormous impact in Palestine.[43] Suddenly, the Palestinians found that their country was being occupied by the greatest imperial power of the age, Great Britain, which had made secret arrangements for its disposition with France, and had publicly proclaimed its support for the national aspirations of the Zionist movement in Palestine—aspirations some Zionist spokesmen had denied,[44] but many Palestinians feared.

During the war, and unbeknownst to the Palestinians at the time, Britain had in fact entered into three international engagements respecting Palestine. The first was the Husayn-McMahon correspondence, an exchange of letters in 1915 and 1916 between the British High Commissioner in Egypt, Sir Henry McMahon, and the hereditary ruler of Mecca under the Ottomans, the Sharif Husayn Ibn 'Ali, in which the

British promised to support Arab independence within extremely ill-defined frontiers, if the Arabs would revolt against the Ottomans. The question of whether or not Palestine was included within those areas in which Britain had agreed to support Arab independence was one of the most vexed issues of the interwar period (it was ultimately addressed at an international conference in London in 1939) and of Middle East historical scholarship since then.[45]

The other two engagements were the Sykes-Picot accords of 1916, whereby Britain and France divided the Arab provinces of the Ottoman Empire between them into spheres of influences and zones of direct control, and the Balfour Declaration, whereby Britain promised to support the establishment in Palestine of a national home for the Jewish people. Of the three, only the latter was made public at the time, although the Bolshevik Commissar for Foreign Affairs, Leon Trotsky, revealed the Sykes-Picot accords and other secret inter-Allied agreements to the world in November 1917, immediately after the Russian Revolution.

These upheavals in the world around them, upheavals that impinged directly on the structure of the lives of the entire population, made possible, and at the same time necessitated, extremely rapid changes in attitudes and consciousness on the part of the people of Palestine. The speed and magnitude of these changes is striking. It is essential to emphasize this point, particularly since the upheavals of the war itself were followed by several more years of equally rapid, equally momentous changes as the Versailles peace conference and other postwar gatherings of the European powers disposed of Palestine, Syria, and other Arab lands, and as an independent Arab kingdom was established in Damascus and then eliminated by the French.

By way of contrast with the rapid changes in attitude made necessary by the upheavals of the war and the years immediately afterwards, mentalities and ideology appear to have evolved relatively slowly in Palestine in times of peace and stability, such as the decades stretching from the late 1860s through 1914 (and in this respect Palestine appears to have been similar to other Arab regions of the Ottoman Empire). We have seen in earlier chapters that there were important transformations in government, social structure, education, and ideology over this period. But the pace of change, at least as regards attitudes, mentalities, and self-view, appears to have been fairly sedate.

It is clear, however, from the evidence for the years after 1914 that in this time of crisis, when the population was subjected to great stress, their attitudes and identities were transformed very rapidly, and with only minimal apparent dislocation for those whose self-view was thus transformed. It would appear that this propensity of peoples to reassess fundamental attitudes and beliefs at times of major historical shifts is a general pattern, and not one exclusive to this time and place.[46] Clearly, more must be involved than simply a situation of crisis, great stress, and a threat to existing values and attitudes: there also must be a vision or a goal, or at least a viable alternative for people to be drawn to, since stress and crisis by themselves could simply lead to the shattering of a community.[47]

For primary material providing Palestinian perceptions of events for the war years and the first year afterwards, we are unfortunately restricted to memoirs, private papers, a limited number of published documents,[48] and the occasional pamphlet or interview in the press outside of Palestine. Both British and Zionist sources are of course available in abundance for the early years of the British occupation of Palestine, but they are of extremely limited utility for purposes of studying Palestinian attitudes. Indeed both the level of ignorance of Palestinian society and politics, and the prejudices, of most British and Zionist officials on the spot in Palestine, particularly in the first few years after the war, drastically diminish the value of many of their observations about the beliefs and attitudes of the Arab population during this period.[49]

Perhaps the most crucial source for evaluating Palestinian public attitudes and perceptions for most of twentieth century, the local press, was shut down by the Ottoman authorities at the outbreak of the war and only reappeared slowly afterwards, starting in 1919, when it began operating again under strict British military censorship. The postwar delay can be explained in part by the fact that the country was under military rule—under the rubric Occupied Enemy Territory Administration (South)—until 1920, and indeed was an active scene of combat for most of 1917 and 1918, until the armistice in November of the latter year. During much of the hard winter and spring of 1917–1918, moreover, a near-famine reigned in many parts of Palestine.[50]

The British military regime was superseded by a civilian one in July 1920, which itself maintained tight control over newspapers and other publications. This can be seen from two letters from the Military Governor of Jerusalem, Sir Ronald Storrs, to the journalist Mustafa al-Budayri, both dated August 16, 1921, one refusing permission for publication of a new newspaper entitled *al-Amal,* and the other refusing permission to open a printing press. A third letter dated six days latter requested in a peremptory manner that Muhammad Kamil al-Budayri, publisher of the nationalist newspaper *al-Sabah*, come into the Governorate the following morning for an interview.[51]

Many established pre-war publications, such as 'Isa al-'Isa's Jaffa newspaper *Filastin*, did not resume publication until well after the war ended, following many delays in reopening.[52] In al-'Isa's case, this did not take place until March 1921 because of his exile from the country by the Ottoman authorities during the war, his service with Faysal's government in Damascus for two years thereafter, and what appears to have been a British ban on his reentry into Palestine for several months after that.[53] Najib Nassar's *al-Karmil*, another important pre-war Palestinian paper, resumed publication in Haifa only in February 1920, while Iliya Zakka's much less influential *al-Nafir* reappeared in the same city in September 1919.[54] Although the press was hampered by censorship, beset by the problems of restarting in a society ravaged and impoverished by war and famine, and with its ranks thinned by the death of many journalists and the disappearance of many papers during the 1914–1918 period, it remains a crucial source for us in devining attitudes toward identity in Palestinian society.

IV

In the years immediately after the war, the first new newspaper to be established in Palestine was *Suriyya al-Janubiyya*, published in Jerusalem beginning in September 1919 by the lawyer Muhammad Hassan al-Budayri, and edited by 'Arif al-'Arif.[55] This paper was important in several respects: it appears to have been the most influential organ of opinion during its short lifetime; it was highly political and intensely nationalist; and its articles were extremely vividly written—for many years indeed only *Filastin* among Palestinian papers could approach *Suriyya al-Janubiyya* for the pungency and power of its prose, and as we have seen, it was nearly two more years before *Filastin* reopened. That this new newspaper should have attracted such talented writers is not surprising, given that it was affiliated with the Arab nationalist club *al-Nadi al-'Arabi* in Jerusalem, that the Arabist movement had been a magnet for talented journalists since well before the war,[56] and that during this period Arabism benefited from the prestige that attached to the new (albeit short-lived) Arab state in Damascus.[57]

The newspaper was certainly taken seriously by the British authorities, as was evidenced by their closing it down for a month after the first ten

issues, and then shutting it down permanently following the disturbances of April 1920, after it had appeared for less than a year. The first
issue after the initial closure in November 1919 reports the paper's
reopening after a month of enforced silence, while insisting staunchly
that it will not change its "Arab principles," and calling on God to bring
good to the "umma" [nation], and success to the "watan" [homeland].
This issue shows a slight softening of its normally militant nationalist
tone by comparison with earlier numbers, a softening that does not continue in the later issues of the paper.[58]

The newspaper's title, meaning "Southern Syria," was indicative of
the political temper of the times: at this stage, many in Palestine and elsewhere were motivated by the hope that all of Syria (here meaning
greater Syria, or *bilad al-Sham*, including the modern-day countries of
Syria, Lebanon, Jordan and Palestine/Israel) would remain united
under the state established by Amir Faysal, third son of Sharif Husayn, as
a first stage toward a larger Arab unity, a hope that was to wane in succeeding years, although it remained alive. The initial salience of this
hope, and its diminution over time, can be traced from the varying frequency of the employment of terms reflecting it in the slogans found at
the top of the pages of nationalist newspapers like *Suriyya al-Janubiyya*
and its successor as the leading organ of patriotic opinion, *al-Sabah*. It
can be seen as well from the names chosen for conferences, meetings,
and political parties and clubs in Palestine, the wording used in com-
muniqués and statements, and the letters and papers of Palestinians during the first few years after the war.

Thus, while *Suriyya al-Janubiyya* printed the words "*biladuna lana*" [our
country/countries are ours] across the masthead of every issue, the slogans at the top of the inside pages on issues ranging from October 1919
to March 1920 were either overtly Arabist ("we live for the Arabs and die
for the Arabs") or expressed general nationalist sentiments (such as
"there is no majesty, no glory, no honor and no life except in independence"). By contrast, *al-Sabah* employed the more general—and more
ambiguous—"*bilad al-'Arab lil-'Arab*" ["the Arab countries are for the
Arabs"] on its masthead. While an unexceptionable sentiment in Arab
nationalist terms, this slogan also represented a tacit adjustment to the
new realities of 1921, with its implicit recognition that there are many
Arab countries.

The background and import of the commitment to southern Syria at
this time in Palestine requires some explanation, and is illustrative for
our exploration of the emergence of Palestinian identity. The new Arab

Syria

state in Syria was seen quite differently by different constituencies. For the British, the entity headquartered in Damascus was not a legitimate state; it was no more than a temporary military administration, under overall British military command, of one area of a region where Britain had multiple commitments and interests. Great Britain in fact never recognized this state, or Amir Faysal in his capacity as King of Syria after his coronation by a Syrian congress. When in London, and at the Versailles Peace Conference, Faysal was received by both Britain and France as the representative of his father, Sharif Husayn, whom the British recognized as King of the Hijaz. Ultimately, of course, in July 1920 the British gave in to insistent French demands that they honor their commitments to France embodied in the Sykes-Picot agreements, and allowed French forces to take over Syria, expel Faysal, and dismantle the Arab state he headed.[59]

In contrast, for many Arabs, this state was a harbinger of a new era of Arab independence and unity, the first stage in the reconstruction of an Arab polity whose roots were seen as going back to the earliest era of Islam, and fittingly, to the great Umayyad state, whose capital was Damascus.[60] The boundaries of this new Syrian state were always problematic. The linguistic lines separating the mainly Arabic-speaking areas of Syria from the mainly Turkish-speaking areas of Anatolia served as rough boundaries in the north, the separation of Syria from Egypt to the west and the Hijaz to the south was generally recognized, while the relation of Syria to Iraq was settled by Iraqi representatives at a congress in Damascus that called for a separate Iraqi state linked dynastically to Syria. The precise status of Lebanon and Palestine, however, was less clear.

These coastal areas of greater Syria, or *bilad al-Sham*, were the ones Britain and France coveted the most. It was there that they had the most extensive interests, and where they had agreed in the Sykes-Picot accords during the war to establish their direct control. The Arab state in Damascus nevertheless claimed sovereignty over the littoral, and although Arab troops were expelled from Beirut by the French in 1918, and the British never allowed this state to extend its authority to Palestine, both Lebanese and Palestinians sat in the Syrian Parliament, and many of them served as ministers in the Syrian government.[61] While elections were held for deputies in other parts of Syria, since this was not possible in Lebanon and Palestine due to French and British obstruction, they were represented in the Syrian Parliament by the surviving deputies for these regions who had served in the Ottoman Parliament originally elected in 1914.

For the Palestinian elite, therefore, a commitment to seeing their country as southern Syria was in large measure an indication of devotion to Arabism, and to its incarnation, the first modern Arab state of Syria with its capital in Damascus. As with Palestinian identity, there is little in the pre-war period to indicate an intense commitment to Syria as a primary focus of identity on the part of the great majority of Syrians, including Palestinians, while, as in the Palestinian case, there is much evidence of a general consciousness of Syria as an entity, and of the existence of strong local loyalties that were sometimes transmuted into Syrian patriotism. The encroachments and ambitions of foreign powers, in particular France, whose government explicitly and publicly declared its desire to control Syria from 1912 onwards, had had a potent cumulative impact in Syria, but until World War I, the response to this external challenge more often took an Ottomanist or Arabist cast than a Syrian one.[62]

The idea of Southern Syria as a post-war focus of identity among the Arab inhabitants of Palestine was therefore almost entirely new, its emergence as rapid as that of Palestine as a focus of identity. Like Palestinian identity, it overlapped with Arabism, albeit to an even greater degree during the two brief years when Syria was the location of the Arab state that seemed the incarnation of Arab nationalist aspirations. Unlike Palestinian identity, however, for inhabitants of Palestine it did not rest on a pre-war substratum of religious, administrative, local, and other loyalties going back many generations. With the crushing of the independent Syrian state by the French in 1920, Syria was to fade rapidly as a focus of identity for Palestinians, although it remained important for many Lebanese, particularly Sunnis and Greek Orthodox.[63] Thus, less than a month after the fall of Faysal's government in Damascus, Musa Kazim Paşa al-Husayni, who was the preeminent nationalist leader in Palestine until his death in 1934, declared: "Now, after the recent events in Damascus, we have to effect a complete change in our plans here. Southern Syria no longer exists. We must defend Palestine."[64]

We can observe an example of the centrality of Syria for Palestinians soon after the war in the earliest extant issue of *Suriyya al-Janubiyya*, dated October 2, 1919, where the focus is clearly on Syria, and in particular on news about developments relating to the country at the Paris peace conference. Already at this early date, a note of alarm emerged as to the possibility that Syria would be partitioned at the behest of the European powers: an article by 'Arif al-'Arif reported rumors that the Versailles peace conference was going to confirm the separation of both Lebanon and Palestine from the rest of Syria and the right of the Zionists to immigrate to the latter.[65] Another article in the same issue, reprinted from the newspaper *al-Istiqlal al-'Arabi* in Damascus, gloomily concluded that after Iraq had been forgotten by the Arabs and abandoned to the British (who at this stage were intent on imposing direct rule there on the Indian model) now it was the turn of Palestine, which would be separated from the rest of the Arab lands, and abandoned to the "shadow of Zionism."[66]

The same notes of defiance are struck even after the paper's closure by the British. In the first issue after it was reopened, in November 1919, one article commented on news from Paris regarding the likely partition of Syria, arguing that "we are residents of Southern Syria, we do not want partition, we want an independent Syria, and we are against Zionist immigration."[67] A second article, reporting a public speech by Sir Herbert Samuel at the London Opera House on the second anniversary of the Balfour Declaration, categorically stated that the Arab nation had awakened from its sleep, and that "our country is Arab, Palestine is Arab, and Palestine must remain Arab."[68] This passage is interesting in that it combines local patriotism, focused on Palestine as "our country," with a strong commitment to Arabism—a combination that was to become characteristic, and that we have already seen in pre-war editorials in *Filastin.* Such an assertive response can be understood in light of the content of Samuel's speech, in which he said that while the Zionist movement did not intend to turn Palestine into a "purely Jewish state" immediately, its aim was to create as soon as possible "a purely self-governing Commonwealth under the auspices of an established Jewish majority."[69] Not entirely surprisingly, this "moderation" on Samuel's part failed to reassure Palestinians suddenly faced with the spectre of sooner or later becoming a minority in a country they naturally assumed was their own.

The focus on Syria continued through 1919 and into early 1920 in *Suriyya al-Janubiyya,* which by this time had established itself as the most influential newspaper in Palestine.[70] A December 1919 article entitled "Warning, Warning!" cautioned against meetings between Arab leaders and the Zionists at which deals were made at the expense of Palestine: it stressed that any agreement which does harm to "the Arab grouping (*al-jami'a al-'arabiyya*) and Syrian unity" would be opposed by the people.[71] Similar language was used in a March 1920 article stating that Amir Faysal knew better than to make an agreement with the Zionists at the expense of Arab rights, for the Arabs, especially "the people of Southern Syria," knew their history and their rights.[72] Such a stress on Arabism and on the unity of Syria (while at the same time underlining the special place of Palestine—"Southern Syria" in the rhetoric of the moment) was to be expected at a time when the elected First Syrian General Congress, including representatives from Syria, Palestine, Lebanon, and Jordan, had just concluded its meetings in Damascus in early March 1920 with radical resolutions proclaiming Faysal King of a united Syria, rejecting a French mandatory, as well as both the Sykes-Picot agreement and the Balfour Declaration, and stressing the unity of Syria as a part of the Arab homeland.

In fact, as Muhammad Muslih and other historians have shown, by this stage many Palestinians, including the most devoted Arabists among them who were in Damascus serving the new Sherifian state, had grown disillusioned with Faysal's willingness to compromise with the Zionists, and with the lack of concern shown by many Syrian leaders regarding the issue of Zionism.[73] This disillusionment can indeed be read without difficulty between the lines of the articles just cited. It became clear to these Arabist Palestinian intellectuals and political leaders in Damascus that, for some Damascene politicians, the survival of an independent Arab state in Syria in the face of French imperialist ambitions would require great sacrifices, including perhaps a sacrifice of Palestine to Britain and the Zionists, who might then support Syrian independence against the incessant pressures from the French.[74]

This can now be seen to have been a shortsighted calculation, for neither the British nor the Zionists had the ability to deter France from its drive to control Syria, even had they wished to. In any case, within a few months these were rendered moot questions, as the entry of French troops into Damascus ended Syrian independence and delivered a crushing blow to Arab and pan-Syrian aspirations. The effects of these momentous events were naturally felt strongly in Palestine: just as the destruction of the Ottoman Empire forced a fundamental rethinking of questions of identity on Palestinians, so did the destruction of Faysal's much shorter-lived kingdom in Damascus. Within a period of less than three years beginning in 1917, occurrences outside Palestine and circumstances that were completely outside their control thus forced Palestinians to confront repeatedly fundamental questions of identity.

Even before this, however, and before *Suriyya al-Janubiyya* was shut down for good by the British in the wake of the Nabi Musa riots of April 1920, the paper had begun to reflect other ideological trends than its original defiant Arabism. Side by side with a continuing commitment to Arabism, and with it to a unified Syria, this important organ of opinion showed a growing concentration on purely Palestinian matters. A remarkable article by Hajj Amin al-Husayni (later to become Mufti of Jerusalem) argued that the Arabs should take heart from the experience of a people ("*qawm*") long dispersed and despised, and who had no homeland to call their own, but did not despair and were getting together after their dispersion to regain their glory after twenty centuries of oppression (nowhere are the Jews or Zionism mentioned by name, although the meaning is unmistakable). While ostensibly addressed to the Arab people as a whole, the fact that this exhortation was directed primarily at a Palestinian audience is indicated by comments like: "you can see others with far less then yourselves trying to build their house on the ruins of yours," an unmistakable reference to Zionism and Palestine.[75]

More blatant than the subtle argument of Hajj Amin was a piece published in January 1920 over the signature "Ibn al-Jazira," meaning "Son of Arabia," a pseudonym perhaps for 'Arif al-'Arif, entitled "*Manajat Filastin*" [meaning a confidential talk or spiritual communion with Palestine] which began with the fulsome peroration:

> Palestine, oh stage of the Prophets and source of great men; Palestine, oh sister of the gardens of paradise; Palestine, oh Ka'ba of hopes and source of fulfilment; Palestine, oh beloved of millions of people; Palestine, oh lord of lands and pride of worshippers; Palestine, oh source of happiness and spring of purity; Palestine, my country and the country of my forefathers and ancestors; Palestine, only in you do I have pride, and only for you am I ashamed; Palestine, oh maiden of nations and desired of peoples; Palestine, my honor, my glory, my life and my pride.

This remarkable paean was followed by a lengthy series of further declarations of loyalty to Palestine and love for it, stressing in particular the "patriotic bonds and national rights" which tie the people of Palestine to their country. Noting that these were the sorts of expressions of the love of Palestinians for their country by which they proved to all how attached they were to it, the piece concluded with the words "Long live dear Palestine and its honest, sincere sons."[76] This is classical, full-blown nationalist rhetoric, notable for the fact that it referred solely to Palestine, and not the whole of the Arab lands, and solely to the people of Palestine, and not all the Arabs.

While these were no more than the words of "Ibn al-Jazira"—presumably 'Arif al-'Arif—and represented no more than his own ideas, their appearance in the most popular Palestinian newspaper of the day, one profoundly Arabist in orientation and whose very title proclaimed its commitment to the idea of greater Syria, is indicative of a shift in the direction of expressions of Palestinian patriotism, and of a growing identification with Palestine alone. While one such article does not constitute a trend in and of itself, it signifies a phenomenon not previously present, and one wholly unaccounted for by the conventional ascription of Palestinian identity and Palestinian nationalism to a much later period.

Even more striking than this example of overripe romantic nationalism is the terminology employed in news articles in *Suriyya al-Janubiyya* like one in March 1920. The article discussed the newfound unity between Christians and Muslims in Gaza "after all old sensitivities and frictions had been removed from spirits and hearts." This unity, the author of the article noted in conclusion, was demonstrated by the establishment of a Muslim-Christian Society in Gaza aimed at building a united front against Zionism and against attempts by the British and the Zionists to divide the Arabs on religious lines. The Gaza branch of this society described in this article was one of a series of such branches established in cities all over Palestine at this time which represented a new form of organization of Palestinian Arab politics in response to the British occupation and the boost it gave to the fortunes of the Zionist movement.[77] The article concludes that, God willing, this Society would have a positive effect in terms of "*al-wataniyya al-Filistiniyya khususan wal 'Arabiyya 'umuman*" (Palestinian nationalism/patriotism in particular, and Arab nationalism/patriotism in general).[78]

This crucial distinction between Palestinian and Arab patriotism, while ostensibly putting the two forms of patriotism on the same level, in fact privileged the former, for it was necessarily this form that was operative in practice in the day-to-day political activities of Palestinians in this period and afterwards. Isolated within the frontiers imposed on them by the British, and having to deal with their own specific problems, just as other Arab peoples were isolated within their own foreign-imposed frontiers and had to deal with their own problems, the Palestinians necessarily had to adjust. Inevitably, larger Arab concerns quickly began to fade by contrast with pressing Palestinian ones. This distinction between the two forms of patriotism, in exactly the same terms, formed the practical basis of nation-state nationalism in Palestine and other countries of the Arab *mashriq* in the years that were to follow, as commitment to Arab nationalism continued, but over the decades eventually declined into little more than lip-service.

It was only a matter of time before this change could be seen in small but significant shifts in political terminology, visible in the daily press. In the same March 1920 issue of *Suriyya al-Janubiyya*,[79] Damascus was described as "the capital," a description that was routine in that period, while Faysal's government and an independent Arab state were still in existence there. However, the newspaper *al-Sabah*, which became the successor to *Suriyya al-Janubiyya* as the leading nationalist organ in Jerusalem after the closure of the latter in April 1920, in its first issue in October 1921 mentioned that it was being published in Jerusalem "the capital of Palestine."[80] Minor though this difference in wording may seem, it bespoke a subtle but important change in focus in little over a year and a half for many Palestinians, who now saw that Jerusalem was the center, not Damascus.

Such a shift was not necessary for the main journalistic competitor of *Suriyya al-Janubiyya*, *Mir'at al-Sharq*, whose lead editorial in its first issue makes no reference to Arabism (the term *umma*, "nation," used frequently in its columns, is not further specified as being the Palestinian or the Arab nation, and could be understood in most cases as referring to either), while it stresses that it is being published "*bayna qawmina*" ("among our people") in Jerusalem, with the clear implication that the paper is Palestinian in focus.[81] While there is no evidence that the British directly supported *Mir'at al-Sharq*, they certainly looked with considerably more favor on it than on its nationalist rival, as is evidenced by the fact that when Maj. Gen. Bols, the Chief Administrator of Palestine, sought to respond to nationalist agitation in February 1920, he chose to do so via an interview with *Mir'at al-Sharq*.[82] It would not be surprising if the paper did receive British support, since providing subventions to local newspapers was an old British policy in Egypt, where Storrs had served before the War as Oriental Secretary, in which capacity he was responsible for such activities. We have seen from documents quoted earlier in this chapter from the archives of *Suriyya al-Janubiyya* and *al-Sabah*,[83] that Storrs exercised a personal surveillance over both papers, peremptorily calling in their editors when he saw fit.

This "South Syrian" interlude has been examined by a number of historians, notably Muhammad Muslih and Yehoshua Porath, although both tend to focus on broad trends of political history, and neither seems to have examined the press particularly closely.[84] This interlude marked a crucial hiatus between pre-1917 political attitudes of the Palestinians, and those that were to last for the rest of the Mandate period and beyond. As we have seen, the Southern Syrian idea was linked to and mainly espoused by fervent Arab nationalists. In the immediate aftermath of World War I, as the idea of independence for the Arabs, via the creation of a federation of three large states—Syria, Iraq, and the Hijaz—linked together by a Hashemite dynastic connection, seemed to be on the brink of realization, the initial optimism among Arabs that allied policy would allow such an outcome was encouraged by a combination of factors. These included what was known of the British promises to Sharif Husayn in 1915 and 1916, combined with public declarations by the allies such as the Anglo-French statement of November 7, 1918, promising the Arabs of Syria and Iraq liberation from Turkish rule and freely chosen governments;[85] the reassuring confidential counsels of British advisers and officials to various leading Arab figures such as Amir Faysal;[86] and a strong dose of wishful thinking.

While such hopes for independence and some form of unity animated many Arabs, in Palestine from the very outset of the post-Ottoman period the spectre of the Balfour declaration clouded these bright expectations. During General Allenby's ceremonial entry into Jerusalem in December 1917, which was attended by a host of French and Italian military and political representatives and contingents of their armed forces, the British had purposely excluded Arab forces, Arab military flags, and representatives of the Arab army.[87] This was in striking contrast to the situation elsewhere in Syria, where Arab forces were often given pride of place, as for example in the capture of Damascus and the entry of allied troops into the city.[88]

And in violation of the principle of strict maintenance of the *status quo ante bellum* as regards the holy places and the rights and privileges of the various communities, which Allenby proclaimed as the basis of the military government soon after the occupation of Jerusalem, important changes were soon made in favor of the Jewish community, such as the use of Hebrew as an official language.[89] Not surprisingly, this important change, which concerned language, so important where issues of identity and nationalism are salient, deeply disturbed the Palestinians. The behavior of representatives of the Zionist movement, some of whom apparently initially assumed that the Balfour Declaration meant that they would rapidly become the rulers of the country, and who soon began to arrive in Palestine in large numbers, only increased these initial concerns.[90] Within a short time, many Palestinians came to believe that the British intended to carry out their pledge to facilitate the establishment of a Jewish national home in Palestine, and that this meant

Jewish dominion over them, although others continued to hope that this was not the case.

Against the background of a growing understanding between Britain and France regarding the partition of the Arab lands, their disregard for Arab claims in Palestine, the unwillingness or inability of Faysal and other Syrian leaders to act against Zionism, and the failure of both the Arab and the Syrian ideas as practical vehicles either for the organization of political life or for obtaining support against the British and the Zionists, the Palestinians found themselves all alone. They were confronted by a Zionist movement that seemed to move from strength to strength. In this precarious situation, the Palestinians were obliged to find a satisfactory basis for their resistance to a multiplicity of external threats.

In view of developments in Palestine before World War I and the experiences of all the other Arab countries in similar situations—Syria, Iraq, Lebanon, and Jordan—[91] it seems almost certain that a Palestinian particularist response would have emerged eventually, irrespective of the goad of Zionism, and would eventually have developed into a separate sense of Palestinian identity, and ultimately a territorially based nation-state nationalism. Certainly that is the logic of every other entity in the eastern Arab world within the frontiers drawn by the imperial powers, without exception. But in the event, Palestinian identity crystallized much more rapidly than it might otherwise have done due to the urgency of the threat the Zionist movement was perceived as posing, and the already existing high level of Palestinian entity-consciousness. Indeed, it is apparent that within a few years of the end of the First World War, a well-developed sense of Palestinian identity had already emerged, at least among those sectors and strata of society whose views we are able to ascertain.

This can be seen in a variety of places, notably in the pages of the press, which both shaped opinion and reflected it. Thus, the nationalist successor of *Suriyya al-Janubiyya* in Jerusalem, *al-Sabah*, explained in its first issue in October 1921 that while one of its purposes was to defend the Arab cause, its main aim was "to serve the cause of the Fourth Palestinian Arab Congress, and to support the objectives of the delegation of the nation which is defending the Palestinian Arab cause in Europe, as part of the general Arab cause."[92] This delegation represented a coalition between various Palestinian political forces with a view to expressing their opposition to the Balfour declaration and other aspects of British policy to British policymakers in London. Through the thicket of the various qualifications and caveats about the Arab cause in the passage quoted, it is apparent that the practical focus of *al-Sabah*, and of the broad political trend in Palestinian society represented by the delegation it supported, had narrowed to Palestine itself.

In *al-Sabah* and other nationalist papers, and in general Palestinian political discourse in the years that followed, the "general Arab cause" would continue to be mentioned, but this was increasingly lip service: what really mattered was the "*Palestinian* Arab cause." If this was the line of the Arabist *al-Sabah*, it should not be surprising that *Filastin*, which even before the war had stressed Palestinian particularism, should be even more emphatic in stressing a separate Palestinian identity after its reappearance. Its lead editorial in its first issue after a hiatus of six years, in March 1921, explicitly talks of "Palestine and its sister Syria," thereby making clear that each is a separate country.[93] This terminology—"sister Syria"—represents the mature discourse of Arab nation-state nationalism. This is the discourse in which for over half a century now, independent Arab states have been referred to as brothers and sisters, implying that they are members of one family out of respect for the myth of the existence of one Arab nation, even while it is perfectly clear to all concerned that they generally act almost completely independently of one another.[94]

And beyond the press, beyond political discourse, this separate nature of Palestine was being emphasized and established in myriad ways. Among the most important was education, for our discussion so far of the growth of Palestinian national consciousness applies mainly to the urban, literate upper and middle class and highly politicized segments of the population, which were a minority in the early 1920s. However, contrary to the condescending views of most British colonial officials and Zionist leaders regarding the majority of the population (for G. S. Symes, Chief Secretary of the Mandatory government from 1925 to 1928, the Arab peasantry "obviously *couldn't*. . . manage their own affairs satisfactorily"),[95] some degree of politicization had already affected other strata, notably parts of the rural population. This could already be seen many years earlier from the clashes between peasants and Jewish settlers in the countryside before 1914 discussed in chapter 5, above.

The growth of the educational system in Palestine, and the attendant spread of nationalist concepts through this system, greatly facilitated the politicization of the countryside, and provided a sort of conveyor belt whereby the ideas we have been examining rapidly became widespread beyond the cities and the literate population in the following years. By 1947 nearly half the Arab school age population was enrolled in schools:

in that year 147,000 of an estimated Arab school-age population of 330,000 (or 44.5%) were being educated in government and private schools, with 103,000 in the former and the rest in the latter.[96] While these are modest figures by modern standards, they represent a significant shift in little over two decades: just over 20 percent of Arab school-aged children were in schools in 1922–23. And in the towns in 1945–46, 85 percent of boys and 65 percent of girls were in school; the problem was in the countryside, where only 65 percent of boys and 10 percent of girls were in school, a problem caused in part by the fact that only 432 of about 800 villages had schools.[97] It is nevertheless striking that by the end of the mandate a majority of Arab boys in both city and countryside, and of Arab girls in the cities, were in school.

The salience of Arab nationalism in the educational system in Mandatory Palestine has already been noted by many authors: the Peel Commission Report of 1937 claimed in somewhat exaggerated fashion that Arab teachers had turned the government schools into "seminaries of Arab nationalism."[98] What has been less noticed is the degree to which the system fostered a specifically Palestinian national consciousness, even though the teaching of history, normally the most potent entry-point for nationalist ideas, was closely monitored by the British to prevent the spread of such "subversive" thinking.[99] One example will suffice to illustrate how the educational system served this purpose, in spite of British attempts to orient it otherwise. As early as 1923, Sabri Sharif 'Abd al-Hadi, who taught geography in the Nablus secondary school, had published a book entitled *Jughrafiyyat Suriyya wa Filastin al-Tabi'iyya* (The natural geography of Syria and Palestine).[100] This is an otherwise unremarkable text, which discusses the natural features, agriculture, communications routes, demography, and administrative divisions of Syria and Palestine. Its importance lies in the fact that all over Palestine, students were already in 1923 learning that Palestine was a separate entity, a unit whose geography required separate treatment. Clearly, no one who disputes the widespread existence of Palestinian identity, and the emergence of a Palestinian national consciousness during the Mandate period, can have examined the press or the country's educational system during this early phase in even a cursory manner.

What this chapter has attempted to show is that even before the mandate for Palestine had been formally confirmed on Britain by the League of Nations in July 1922, important elements of the country's Arab population had already come to identify primarily with Palestine. This Palestinian identity was to remain strongly tinged, and to overlap with, elements of religious sentiment and Arabism (it will be recalled that the delegation to London in 1921 described itself as a Palestinian *Arab* body, and the most common self-description of political groupings during the mandate was as Palestinian Arab), both of which had been among its precursors. It was to spread significantly in succeeding years to broader segments of the population outside the cities, primarily via the growing influence of the press and the expansion of the educational system. Nevertheless, this early period saw the emergence in a relatively complete form of the basic self-identification of Palestinians as Palestinians which has characterized them until the present day.

CHAPTER 8

The "Disappearance" and Reemergence of Palestinian Identity

I

One of the most common tropes in treatments of issues related to Palestine is the idea that Palestinian identity, and with it Palestinian nationalism, are ephemeral and of recent origin. This is most commonly expressed as the assertion that both of these phenomena are in some sense artificial—the implication being that they must be distinguished from "real" identities and "real" nationalisms—and that they emerged only in the 1960s.

Such a distorted vision of the Palestinian national narrative denies the complex genesis of this identity over many decades around the turn of the twentieth century, which the previous chapters have chronicled. Beyond that, it obliterates memory of two subsequent periods that were decisive for the shaping of Palestinian identity. The first included the thirty years of the British Mandate, which were marked by the desperate, losing struggle of the newly formed Palestinian national movement against the greatest imperial power of the age, Great Britain, and its protégé, the Zionist movement. This first period ended in a crescendo of violence, as fighting inside Palestine between Arabs and Jews intensified from November 1947 until May 1948, culminating in the first war between the Arab states and Israel from May 1948 onwards. These traumatic events of 1947–49, which cost the Palestinians their majority status in Palestine and their hope of controlling the country, and cost half of them their homes, land, and property, are inscribed in Palestinian memory and historiography as *al-Nakba*, "the catastrophe."[1] The second period consisted of the "lost years" between 1948 and the emergence of the Palestine Liberation Organization in 1964,[2] during which time the Palestinians seemed to many to have disappeared from the political map as an independent actor, and indeed as a people.

Of the many partial explanations for this trope of Palestinian nonexistence before the 1960s, one is straightforward: there *was* a hiatus in manifestations of Palestinian identity for a period after 1948. During the 1950s and early 1960s there were few indications to outside observers of the existence of an independent Palestinian identity or of Palestinian nationalism. This hiatus is partly explained by the fact that Palestinian society had been devastated between November 1947 and mid-May 1948 as a result of a series of overwhelming military defeats of the disorganized Palestinians by the armed forces of the Zionist movement. These forces— the Haganah, the Palmach, and others that had grown out of the seed of the *Hashomer*, which we observed germinating in chapter 5—were transformed in 1948 into the core of the Israeli army. Their decisive victories over the Palestinians brought about the wholesale flight and expulsion of much of the Arab population of Palestine, beginning a demographic transformation of the country with long-lasting consequences.

This sequence of Palestinian defeats before May 15, 1948 is little known when compared with the events that took place after that date. Then, several Arab armies entered Palestine, and proceeded to lose much of the rest of the country to the new Israeli army in what came to be known as the first Arab-Israeli war. In many ways the earlier phase was more important to the Palestinians, because it resulted in the loss of major cities like Jaffa and Haifa (which by then had become those with the largest Arab population, and were the most dynamic centers of Arab economic and cultural life), and of hundreds of Arab towns and villages and vast tracts of land. These crushing defeats ended any hopes that the Arab state called for in General Assembly Resolution 181 of November 29, 1947, which provided for the partition of Palestine into an Arab and a Jewish state, would ever come into being. Instead the Arab state was strangled at birth, victim of the total failure of the Palestinians, the military triumph of the new Jewish state, and the collusion of a number of

Arab leaders.[3] May 15, 1948 thus marked not only the birth of the state of Israel, but also the decisive defeat of the Palestinians by their Zionist foes, and an approximate midpoint in the expulsion and flight of roughly half of Palestine's Arab population of 1.4 million. This process of population displacement continued until the conclusion of the armistice agreements between Israel and Egypt, Jordan, Syria, and Lebanon in 1949, although the precise numbers of those who became refugees are much disputed and are difficult to ascertain exactly even today.[4]

In the wake of this disaster for the Palestinians, and the division of their country among Israel, Jordan, and Egypt, it was difficult for outsiders to pick up the strands of a single narrative, and to identify where the focus of Palestinian identity was, or whether in fact it had survived the debacles of 1947–49. Indeed, during these "lost years" there no longer appeared to be a center of gravity for the Palestinians. The largest single group of Palestinians, those in Jordan, to which the region of central Palestine which came to be called the West Bank was annexed in 1949, received Jordanian nationality. They began an uneasy relationship with a country where they have formed a majority since 1949 , but where political power is out of their control. Less than 200,000 Palestinians remained in those parts of Palestine which were incorporated into the new state of Israel. These obtained Israeli citizenship,[5] but were to remain muzzled under military rule until 1966, and were barred for long after that from any expressions of Palestinian identity. Other Palestinians, in the Gaza Strip under Egyptian military administration, in Syria, Lebanon and elsewhere, obtained differing categories of refugee status, and faced different barriers to political organization, free expression, and manifestations of their identity.

Given the centrality of attachment to place characteristic not only of Palestinians, but also of others in traditional and semitraditional societies, it can be imagined how powerful an impact these events must have had: by the end of the process of dispossession in 1949, more than four hundred cities, towns, and villages in Galilee, the coastal region, the area between Jaffa and Jerusalem, and the south of the country had been depopulated, incorporated into Israel and settled with Israelis, and most of their Arab inhabitants were dispersed throughout the region as refugees.[6] However, even amidst the appalling conditions that affected the Palestinians, and the fragmentation that had beset them following their loss of their homes, the first stirrings of a reconstitution of an independent Palestinian identity were already taking place. In the refugee camps, the workplaces, the schools, and the universities where Palestinians congregated in the years after 1948, we find the beginnings, the pre-history as it were, of a new generation of Palestinian nationalist groups and movements which started clandestinely in the 1950s and emerged into the open in the mid-1960s.[7]

A student union at Cairo University, *Ittihad Talabat Filastin* (The Union of Palestinian Students), was founded in 1950 by a young, clean-shaven engineering student who had fought in the Palestine war of 1947–49 and was later to become known as Yasser 'Arafat,[8] together with a few close student colleagues including Salah Khalaf (later best known as the head of Fateh intelligence, under the *nom de guerre* Abu Iyyad). A student grouping at the American University of Beirut was founded about the same time by a medical student named George Habash and a few of his comrades. Other grassroots militant organizations also emerged in the Gaza Strip, such as that established by Khalil al-Wazir (a founder of Fateh later known as Abu Jihad[9]). By the mid-1950s these small beginnings had developed into a network of Palestinian national-ist organizations. Each had its own political agenda, and all were small and vulnerable, but they tapped a powerful vein of nationalist sentiment among Palestinians. The Arab governments and Israel soon learned that they had to deal warily with them.

Even a cursory examination of these new groups and their ideology reveals that they represented a continuation of the Palestinian national movement as it developed from the roots we have examined into the Mandate period, until its defeat and collapse in the wake of the 1948 war. There is the same use of the theme of historic Palestinian rootedness in the land, the same symbols signifying Palestinian identity, and the same obsession with Zionism, further accentuated by the traumatic impact of the events of 1947–49 on the Palestinians. This is true despite the major differences between the pre-1948 and post-1948 movements, among them the fact that in no case did the new movements include members of the leadership drawn from the old Palestinian elite, which was considered in some measure as being responsible for having "lost" Palestine. That class indeed disappeared utterly from the political scene, discredited by its fail-ures, and crippled by the loss of much of its lands, businesses, and prop-erties.[10] At a stroke, the older members of families like the al-Husaynis, Nashashibis, and al-Khalidis, who had dominated Palestinian politics from the 1920s through the 1940s, were replaced by very young men who were educated in the new schools that had sprung up in Palestine during the Mandate, were often graduates of universities in Cairo, Beirut, and Damas-cus, and generally came from poor or middle-class backgrounds.[11]

It must be admitted that both the continuities between these new, clandestine groups and the Palestinian national movement of the Mandate period, and the significance of these small, mainly underground groups of the 1950s and 1960s are easier to see in hindsight, and might well not have been fully apparent to many observers at the time. This hiatus thus in some measure appeared to substantiate the assertion that Palestinian identity emerged for the first time in the 1960s: for many years it could plausibly be argued that there did not appear to be a Palestinian identity, just as there was no Palestinian entity that could be pointed to on the map. It may thus have seemed, or could be made to seem, that, to quote Golda Meir once again, "There was no such thing as Palestinians. . . . They did not exist."[12]

Another important reason for the trope of Palestinian nonexistence before the 1960s was a paradoxical one: this was the power of the ideology of pan-Arabism, which in some measure obscured the identities of the separate Arab nation-states it subsumed. The potency of pan-Arabism can be understood on two levels: that of the Arab world itself, and that of the outside world, especially the West, where the representation of Arabism came to take on an almost mythical life of its own, for reasons that relate in part at least to the Palestinians. Within the Arab world, Arabism was the hegemonic ideology of the first half of the twentieth century, reaching its apogee in terms of political power in the 1950s and 1960s with the rise of Egyptian President Gamal 'Abd al-Nasir, who seemed to many to incarnate the Arab resurgence.

The ideology which 'Abd al-Nasir mastered and helped mightily to further had resonance throughout an Arab world profoundly frustrated for generations by its inability to shake off foreign rule or to achieve true independence and real economic development.[13] Its basic premise was that the Arabs were a single people with a single language, history, and culture, divided not by centuries of separate development of widely separated countries, but by the recent machinations of imperialism, and that all they had in common was more powerful than whatever separated them. This ideology was strong enough at a few times and in a few places to transcend the iron realities of the nation-state in the Arab world in this era, notably during the union of 1958–1961 between Egypt and Syria. The new Arab nation-states, many of which had first emerged after World War I, and which had only recently obtained even nominal independence, were nevertheless exceedingly strong and growing stronger. Even though most of them did not enjoy the ideological legitimacy of pan-Arabism, they nevertheless benefited from the fact that real material power and significant influence attached to these "artificial creations of Western imperialism," to use the disparaging rhetoric of pan-Arabism for the Arab nation-state.[14]

The Palestinians were deeply attracted by the pan-Arabism of 'Abd al-Nasir. Beyond the obvious fact that Arabism had been an important element of the Palestinian self-view for many decades, in its potent new pan-Arab form it promised, as had the other regional or transnational ideologies the Palestinians had identified with in the past—whether Ottomanism, Arabism or pan-Syrianism—to multiply their limited forces and give them support from outside Palestine against the Israeli foe they knew from bitter experience to be far stronger than they were. It also gave the Palestinian refugees, who were poorly treated in many Arab countries, a larger sense of identity, which gave the promise of protecting them from such pressures. Thus for a time, 'Abd al-Nasir's picture was on the walls of many homes in the Palestinian refugee camps; and in Israel, in Jordan, in the Gaza Strip, as well as in all the countries of the Palestinian diaspora, the Egyptian radio, *Sawt al-'Arab*, ("Voice of the Arabs"), with its intoxicating Arab nationalist message, was listened to avidly.

For many young Palestinians who joined pan-Arab organizations like the Movement of Arab Nationalists (MAN—*Harakat al-Qawmiyyin al-'Arab*),[15] the basic motivation was to benefit from the pan-Arab mobilization 'Abd al-Nasir promised, in order to facilitate their main objective, the liberation of Palestine. But the MAN, although it took an Arab nationalist form, and included numerous members from several Arab countries, was almost exclusively Palestinian in its leadership and its basic objectives. Not surprisingly, in the wake of the 1967 war it transmuted almost instantaneously from being an ostensibly pan-Arab organization, with branches all over the Arab world, into one of the main Palestinian political/military formations, the Popular Front for the Liberation for Palestine (PFLP). It did so in the wake of its rapid loss of support in the mid-1960s to Fateh, its main rival for loyalty among Palestinians, which from the start had taken on an overtly Palestinian configuration, barely paying even lip-service to the shibboleths of Arabism.

Thus among the Palestinians, although they certainly understood themselves to be Arabs, at least some of their devotion to pan-Arabism in the 1950s and 1960s was instrumental as regards their larger objective, which was the "return" to Palestine (*al-'awda*, a term used in the names of several of the groups that emerged in this period, such as *Abtal al-'Awda*, "The Heroes of the Return").[16] This was to take place via the "liberation" of Palestine which was the aim of all the clandestine groups that started in the wake of 1948, and that had emerged from the shadows by 1967. However, for many Palestinian activists, particularly those living under Egyptian military administration in the Gaza Strip, the encounter with Nasirism was less than edifying from the very beginning. The bitter experience of being hounded, jailed, and interrogated by the Egyptian *mukhabarat* (intelligence service), as happened to many of them suspected of carrying out attacks on Israel, naturally tended to make these individuals cynical about the Egyptian regime's highflown rhetoric about its commitment to the Palestine cause.[17]

For many other Palestinians, however, whether members of the MAN, unaffiliated Nasirists, or supporters of the Ba'th party, which was influential in Syria from the early 1950s onwards and has been in power there continuously since 1963, pan-Arabism retained its appeal both as an ideal that had long been popular among Palestinians—why after all should the Arab people not be united?—as well as what appeared to be a practical means to the achievement of their shared goal of the liberation of their country. However, pan-Arabism failed spectacularly in 1967, with Israel's crushing defeats of the armies of 'Abd al-Nasir and the Ba'thist regime in Syria (as well as that of Jordan), and the occupation by Israel of the Gaza Strip and West Bank, the only parts of Palestine that had remained under Arab control after 1948, as well as the Egyptian Sinai Peninsula and the Syrian Golan Heights.

In consequence of this failure of pan-Arabism, many of these Palestinians looked to groups like Fateh which from the beginning had espoused a Palestinian particularism with which they were both familiar and comfortable. These groups, the long-standing rivals of the MAN, the Ba'th and other Arabist formations, had already been gaining ground at the expense of the latter in the mid-1960s. And after the Arab debacle of 1967, with its ranks rapidly swelled with recruits and their coffers with contributions, Fateh swiftly achieved the dominance over Palestinian politics it has retained to this day.

But if pan-Arabism was dead—or at least moribund—as a political force among most Palestinians living in the real world of Middle East politics after 1967, it lived on as a convenient myth in the West, where its impact lingered on far longer than in the Arab world. This requires an explanation, and several are possible. The most charitable is that it was hard for westerners, weaned on their own myth of unitary nationalism we have already touched on, whereby a Frenchwoman is a Frenchwoman before all else, an American an American, and so forth, to understand the *this is my line*

multiple, layered identities so characteristic of the Arab world in general, and of the Palestinians in particular. Put simply, this view applied to the Palestinians as follows: these people could either be Palestinians or they could be Arabs, but they could not be both. In support of this explanation, it can be argued that confusion about such multiple, layered identities persists to this day among Westerners, even educated and knowledgeable ones, and about nationalities far beyond the Palestinian case.

There are two less charitable explanations for why the myth of Arabism lived on after its demise as a political force in the real world in 1967. The first is that Arab nationalism, especially in the form represented by 'Abd al-Nasir, had become a powerful symbolic bogeyman, representing all that was objectionable in the Arab world to those outside it. This was true for British colonialists like Anthony Eden, who could never forgive the Egyptians for freeing themselves from British control (and indeed Eden apparently suffered paroxysms of irrational rage in his hatred of 'Abd al-Nasir, comparing him to Hitler[18]); French colonialists like Guy Mollet, who could never forgive the Egyptians for their support of the Algerian revolutionaries and of Tunisian and Moroccan nationalists in the 1950s and afterwards; and American anti-Communists like John Foster Dulles, who could never forgive 'Abd al-Nasir for the 1955 Czech arms deal with Egypt, whereby the Soviet Union first obtained a foothold in the Arab world. To this powerful coalition of enemies must be added Israel and its friends, who were deeply uneasy at the prospect of a new Egyptian-led Arab coalition capable of challenging the results of the war of 1947–49.

Some of these enemies were to combine in the tripartite Israeli-British-French Suez invasion of 1956, whose failure ultimately shattered the power of Britain and France in the Middle East, and brought about the downfall of Eden's government. But the other enemies 'Abd al-Nasir had acquired at this stage were to stay with him: to ideologically oriented American policymakers, he continued to symbolize a hostile force allied with the USSR; and to Israel's leaders and supporters, he clearly appeared to be that country's most dangerous potential opponent. With powerful enemies such as these for well over a decade and a half, it is no wonder that so much should have been invested in the myth of the power of pan-Arabism. Particularly galling for American policymakers, 'Abd al-Nasir appeared to have much support in the region, while such American allies as King Faysal of Saudi Arabia and King Husayn of Jordan appeared to be in danger of losing power to revolutionaries inspired by pan-Arabism, as had happened to the monarchies in Iraq, Yemen, and Libya.

The last reason for some of the perceived force of pan-Arabism in the eyes of those who opposed it was that the existence of such an ideology was convenient for them. For pan-Arabism, which proclaimed the kinship of the Arabs as a single people, and purported to aim to unite them in a single state, made it easier for some to argue that in view of this ideology, there was no reason why the Palestinians, who could be shown to be such fervent Arab nationalists, and so devoted in following 'Abd al-Nasir, shouldn't simply dissolve in the larger Arab world. Such a solution, which at least a few of its proponents must have put forward in good faith and honest ignorance, had the unmatched merit in their eyes of removing the most legitimate Arab claimant to Palestine, leaving the Israeli claim to the country unchallenged.

The logic of this analysis can be perceived if one were to postulate the nonexistence or the extreme weakness of Arabism. In such a case, the Zionist claim to Palestine, which since even before the establishment of the state of Israel had depended in some measure on arguing that there was no legitimacy to the competing Arab claim, would have been much weaker. For if those others who claimed Palestine were *not* just generic Arabs, part of a larger Arab people with many wide lands to live in, who could and should go to the Arab countries where they belonged (and whence Joan Peters and others preached to the gullible that they had come), if in other words they had no other identity than as Palestinians, and were a people whose identity was rooted in Palestine, then they had a much stronger claim than would otherwise have been the case to this land in which the state of Israel had successfully established itself.

None of this is to say that pan-Arabism had no force of its own, or that it was entirely a bogeyman concocted by Anglo-French imperialists, American anti-communists, and Israelis intent on delegitimizing their foes. But it does help to explain the extraordinary strength of the hostility of many in the West to pan-Arabism for so many years, indeed well beyond the time it had ceased to be a dynamic force in Arab politics. In other words, this caricature of pan-Arabism was useful to its enemies as a mobilizational tool, even after the real movement on which it was based had lost its potency. This was directly relevant to the issue of Palestinian identity, since the strength or weakness of pan-Arabism was seen as inversely proportional to a separate Palestinian identity. This is not as far-fetched as it may sound, in view of the intensity of the passion and commitment attaching to the competing claims to Palestine this issue impinged on. A great deal was invested in the Israeli claim, and given that the legitimacy of Israel was denied in the Arab world in the name of the Palestinian claim, it was not surprising that the response should have been to add to the old argument that there were no Palestinians, the new one that these people were just part of the vast, undifferentiated Arab world, which was simply exploiting a nonexistent "Palestinian" claim in order to delegitimize Israel.[19]

All of this was suffused with ineffable emotion in Israel and the West, because from its inception and at least until 1967, Israel seemed to its supporters to be existentially threatened. In such a situation, the stubborn Arab denial of legitimacy to Israel, and the absolute refusal to recognize its existence, or even its name ("the Zionist entity" was the favorite term for Israel in the Arab world in those days), were seen as especially sinister. The wide gap between Arab rhetoric and actual Arab intentions, not to speak of the even wider one between Arab rhetoric and pitifully limited Arab capabilities, was rarely assessed rationally or calmly, nor were the broad differences of opinion on this matter in the Arab world (which had produced a number of initiatives for a settlement with Israel in the first years after 1948[20]) closely examined. Instead, the most extreme Arab rhetoric was taken for the only reality, and was often taken out of context, misunderstood, or mistranslated.[21] There resulted a fantastic but barely plausible representation of the Palestinians as no more than pawns for a huge, united Arab world deliberately waiting to pounce on tiny Israel and drive its population into the sea, a heady if fanciful representation that has evocative power to this day.

II

What may be called the hiatus in manifestations of Palestinian nationalism from 1948 until the mid 1960s, and the potency and utility of the myth of pan-Arabism to some of its enemies in the West and Israel, help to explain the trope of the late emergence of Palestinian identity which we have been examining, but these two explanations are not sufficient to elucidate it fully. At least one other factor must be adduced: the impact of the *failure* of the Palestinians on themselves and others.

The broad dimensions of this failure should be amply clear by now. Even before World War I, it was possible to detect a deep undercurrent of frustration among many Palestinians about their inability to bring their society's concerns about Zionism to the attention of the Ottoman government in a way that produced the required response. In spite of peasant resistance and rural unrest, in spite of the futile efforts of Palestinian deputies to raise the matter in Parliament, and in spite of news-paper editorials and local protests, the Ottoman government failed to act to rein in the growth of the Zionist movement. Thus a 1914 editorial in *Filastin* which has already been cited complained that although Ottoman government officials who do not understand Arabic refuse to accept the newspaper's translations of inflammatory Zionist statements, the government "is able to find a few words we wrote about the Zionists on page three of our newspaper next to the advertisements, and builds a court case on it, and punishes the paper with closure!"[22]

This inability to affect the Ottoman government was made all the more galling by an inability of activists and political leaders to affect their own society. The very first newspaper articles on the activities of the Zionist movement in Palestine which we have surveyed exhibit an awareness that were it not for the willingness of absentee and local land-lords to sell land to the newcomers, there would be little problem. Similarly, as we have seen, Ruhi al-Khalidi laid great stress on the issue of land sales in his book on Zionism, as did Najib Nassar in the pages of *al-Karmil*, and 'Isa and Yusuf al-'Isa in *Filastin*. Some of the blame could be placed on the Ottoman government, for example for failing to implement the laws restricting land sales to foreigners, or the visa restrictions on Jewish immigrants, but some had to be placed as well on the members of a society who could not perceive the harmful aims of the Zionist movement, or refused to take them into account, and went ahead and sold land to representatives of this movement. These same editorials pointed out a failure to raise popular consciousness regard-ing the gravity of this danger, and to organize Palestinian society to oppose it.

After World War I, the same themes recurred, and in time the frus-tration of those writing in the press became almost palpable. In this period, articles in many of the same newspapers we have followed before 1914 expressed frustration about the failure of the Palestinians to obtain a response from the British Mandatory administration, and the govern-ment in London to which this administration was responsible, but the problem in essence remained the same one: how to get a just hearing for what was by the early 1920s routinely described as "the Palestinian national cause."[23] Before 1914, the Palestinians had their own elected representatives in Istanbul who could raise their concerns in Parliament, albeit with little result. After 1918, in spite of repeated British promises to the Arabs about independence and representative government,[24] the Mandatory authorities prevented the creation of representative elected bodies in Palestine, for these would inevitably have reflected the will of the Arab majority and nullified the Balfour Declaration.

The Palestinians deeply resented what they saw as a form of discrimination against Palestine, among all the other Arab regions which came under Anglo-French control after the war. Thus, the nationalist Jerusalem newspaper *al-Sabah* wrote in 1921 that Palestine would have had few problems if it were not for the Balfour declaration. In the best case, Palestine would have been within the area of Arab independence and free Arab governments promised by Sir Henry McMahon to Sharif Husayn. In the worst case, if the Sykes-Picot accords had been implemented in Palestine, the country would have been under foreign control, but administered by its own people. By comparison, Iraq had an independent Arab government, a parliament, an Arab king, and had "a strong national life"; Syria, in spite of its bad situation imposed by the French, had national governments, and a parliament; Jordan had an Arab government with an Arab amir and internal independence. The article continued bitterly, "Why should Palestine have any less?," concluding that it was all because of Zionism, which was aiming for a privileged position and trying to take away Palestinian rights.[25]

In spite of this discrimination, the Palestinians nevertheless held national conferences, sent telegrams of protest, met British Ministers, such as Winston Churchill, who came to Palestine in April 1921, and in the fall of the same year sent a delegation to London to lay their concerns before the British government and people. All of this was to no avail in affecting the basic lines of British policy as regards Zionism, or in achieving Palestinian independence and self-determination. "The nation," a 1921 communiqué announcing the preparations for sending the Palestinian delegation to London stated, "desires the formation of a national government responsible to an elected parliamentary assembly which alone would have the authority to frame legislation and approve the formation of such a government."[26] Until 1948, and for as long as the British remained in Palestine and the country had an Arab majority, these unexceptionable wishes were to remain unfulfilled.

These failures to win concessions from the British were matched by failures in organizing Palestinian society, overcoming internal divisions, and stopping Arab land sales to the Zionist movement: thus in the 1920s the Jewish National Fund completed the purchase of the vast remaining Sursuq holdings in the Marj Ibn 'Amir, in transactions that dwarfed those at al-Shajara and al-Fula in the earlier part of the century (described in previous chapters), which were the source of such consternation at the time. Although the Palestinians were able to present a united front to their foes for many years after the war, the internal divisions among the elite eventually surfaced, ably exploited by the British, with their vast experience of dividing colonized societies in order to rule them more effectively, and by the Zionists, the workings of whose intelligence services in these early years have yet to be fully elucidated.[27] By the 1930s, the Palestinian leadership was polarized between a faction led by the British-appointed Mufti, Hajj Amin al-Husayni,[28] and another often aligned with the British and led by the former Mayor of Jerusalem, Raghib al-Nashashibi, which feuded bitterly with one another.[29]

To these divisions among the elite must be added another one: that between the elite itself and a growing current of discontent among younger Palestinians, among the landless urban poor who were flocking to the cities (especially Haifa and Jaffa), and among many in the countryside, saddled with debt to urban merchants and money-lenders.[30] This discontent was accentuated by economic distress in the early 1930s as the worldwide depression hit Palestine, and by the impact of rapidly mounting Jewish immigration as Nazi persecution drove thousands of Jews escaping from Europe to seek refuge in Palestine, at a time when most of the countries of the world shut their doors to them. In the year 1935 alone, at the height of this flood of refugees from Hitler's persecution, more than 60,000 Jewish immigrants arrived in Palestine, a number equal to the entire Jewish population of the country only twenty years earlier.

There was a swift reaction by the discontented and dispossessed elements in Palestinian society to the internecine divisions among the elite, and the hopeless ineffectiveness of its leadership of the national movement in the face of this mounting peril. The spark of armed revolt ignited by Shaykh 'Iz al-Din al-Qassam in the north of Palestine in late 1935—the first overt attempt at such a revolt directed against the British since the beginning of the Mandate, in contrast to more spontaneous outbreaks of violence directed against Jews in 1920 and 1929—was immediately stamped out by British troops, in a clash in which al-Qassam was killed. But the Shaykh had clearly touched a deep chord in the popular imagination, and was much more closely in tune with Palestinian sentiment than was the elite leadership. His death in battle was portrayed as a glorious "martyrdom," and was followed within a few months by the spontaneous outbreak of a nation-wide general strike in April 1936. In its wake, a three-year armed uprising erupted, in the course of which the British briefly lost control of much of the country, including cities like Jerusalem and Nablus, before a massive campaign of repression by tens of thousands of troops and numerous squadrons of aircraft in 1938–39 was able to restore "order."

In the end, the Arab revolt of 1936–39 was another massive failure for the Palestinians. It obtained no lasting concessions from the British, who in a 1939 White Paper promised limits on Jewish immigration, which proved impossible to implement in light of the revelation of the horrors of the Nazi Holocaust. The British promised as well that Palestine would obtain independence within ten years, yet another promise they failed to keep. The *yishuv* suffered during the years of the revolt, but nevertheless, benefiting from the Arab strikes and boycotts, implemented the principle of *avoda ivrit* [Hebrew labor] first put forward by the settlers of the second *aliya* in 1904, and fortified an exclusively Jewish "national" economy. It benefited as well from the significant assistance in armaments and military organization Britain provided in order to fight the common Arab enemy.

But from a Palestinian point of view, the worst effects of the failure of the revolt were on their own society: the Arab economy of Palestine was devastated by years of strikes, boycotts, and British reprisals, and the fighting forces suffered casualties—5,000 killed and 10,000 wounded—that were proportionately huge in an Arab population of about a million, and included the loss of hundreds of the bravest and most enterprising military cadres killed in battle or executed by the British. Finally, the traditional Palestinian leadership, which had been obliged by grassroots pressure to come together to form a joint national leadership, the Arab Higher Committee, at the outset of the general strike in 1936, was shattered by the end of the revolt, divided anew by differences over tactics, which were once again ably exploited by the British. Many individual leaders were exiled by the British in 1937, and others fled, some never to return to the country. The net result was that the Palestinians entered World War II in effect headless—without even the semblance of a unified leadership. In that condition they were to face their most fateful challenge in 1947–49.[31] The crippling defeat they had suffered in 1936–39 was among the main reasons they failed to overcome it.[32]

Thus the *nakba*, the "catastrophe," of 1947–49 was both the outcome and the conclusion of a series of failures, a series of defeats. The Palestinians, with a divided leadership, exceedingly limited finances, no centrally organized military forces, and no reliable allies, were facing a Zionist movement and a Jewish society in Palestine which, although small, was politically unified, had centralized institutions, and was exceedingly well led and extremely highly motivated—the horrors of the Holocaust had just been revealed, if any further spur to determined action to consummate the aims of Zionism were needed. As we have seen, the Zionist leadership had long since achieved territorial contiguity via land purchases and settlements which gave them holdings in the shape of an "N," running up the coastal strip, down the Marj Ibn 'Amir/Vale of Jezreel, and up the finger of eastern Galilee. They benefited as well from international backing—both the U.S. and USSR supported the partition of Palestine and immediately recognized the new state of Israel—and finally had understandings with the key Arab military power, Jordan, whose ruler's ambition was to control the Arab portions of Palestine that were not absorbed into Israel, and who also commanded the Iraqi forces sent to Palestine in 1948.

In view of this almost unbroken chronicle of failure on the part of the Palestinians, it was perhaps understandable that their enemies might assume that their rhetoric had been correct all along, and that there were indeed no Palestinians. In fact, it should have been understandable that in spite of the disparity in numbers in favor of the Palestinians, a larger economy (by 1948, the Jewish economy of Palestine was larger than the Arab one), greater firepower, superior organization, and considerable support from the great powers of the age would enable the new Israeli state to triumph over the poorly led and mainly rural, mainly illiterate Palestinian population of 1.4 million. Instead, the arrogance of victory convinced the winners not just that they were stronger, but that they had prevailed because their opponents had not had a truly "national" cause, or a unified identity. In other words, that they had not really existed!

The "disappearance" of the Palestinians was thus in some measure a function of their failures, at least in the perception of others, including, but not restricted to, their foes. This was not just an Israeli or Western perception. In the Arab world, voices could be heard saying that the Palestinians had sold their land,[33] or had not fought hard enough, or had left their homes too easily. And for some Arab regimes, these failures, although they confronted the entire Arab world with a militarily strong Israeli state in their midst, which had just decisively defeated their combined armies, also presented opportunities for aggrandizement. The Amirate of Transjordan was the first to benefit, winning the biggest prize on the Arab side as it absorbed the West Bank, including East Jerusalem, and becoming the Hashemite Kingdom of Jordan in the process. Others also benefited. Egypt gained control of the Gaza Strip, which, dubious prize though it might have been, was better than having either the Israelis or the Hashemites controlling the northeastern land gateway to Egypt. And Lebanon benefited, as Beirut became the uncontested transit port of the Eastern Mediterranean after its competitor, Haifa, lost this role because of the state of war between Israel and the Arab countries, and as oil pipelines which had run across Palestine were rerouted across Lebanon.

Several Arab states thus had a vested interest in Palestinian failure in some degree, although this was something which could not be admitted in public. For ever since the first decade of the century, when the press of Beirut, Damascus, and Cairo had first alerted their readers to the dangers to Palestine and the Arab world posed by the Zionist movement, public opinion in these and other centers of Arab political life was deeply sympathetic to the Palestinians, and suspicious of the Zionist movement, its Western friends, and those Arabs and Arab regimes that colluded with it. This sympathy put pressure on most newly independent Arab governments to act in support of the Palestinians at times when prudence might have dictated otherwise (this is a partial explanation for the entry of some Arab states into the 1948 war), but it also meant that the Palestine issue became a political football in the domestic politics of several Arab countries, and in inter-Arab politics.

Initially, and for many years after 1948, this meant that the Arab regimes exploited the Palestine issue at the expense of one another (Jordan was generally the target of such exploitation of the Palestine issue by other Arab regimes, notably those of Saudi Arabia and Egypt) and often at the expense of the Palestinians themselves. But once the latter had emerged from the "lost years" as an independent actor in Arab politics, this same reality meant that the Palestinians could turn the tables and use Arab popular sympathy to exploit the Palestine issue against the Arab regimes. They did this with some success for many years, starting in the mid-1960s, when the Palestinians contributed significantly to the outbreak of the 1967 war, and thereafter played Arab regimes off against one another over the Palestine issue.

III

We have explored the impact of a series of failures on those who dealt with the Palestinians: the Israelis, the West and the Arab states, and we have seen how these failures helped to justify the "disappearance" of the Palestinians, for a time at least. What of the impact of these failures on the Palestinians themselves?

On the Palestinian popular level the defeats, the dislocations, the dis-possession, the flight, and the expulsions ironically helped complete the process whose genesis we have traced in this book: these failures ultimately resulted in the universalization of a uniform Palestinian identity. To understand how and why this came about, it would be use-ful to recapitulate the stages of the emergence of Palestininan identity which have been chronicled in earlier chapters. In the first stage, before World War I, this identity was shared by a relatively restricted circle, largely composed of the urban, the literate, and the educated. They formed a new elite considerably wider than the old traditional notables, and including the new middle classes—the teachers, clerks, govern-ment officials and businessmen who proliferated in the last decades of Ottoman rule—but they were still a relatively restricted stratum, and among them as well as among the rural and illiterate majority of the population, the new sense of Palestinian identity competed and over-lapped with Ottomanism and Arabism, as well as older religious, local, and family loyalties.

In a second stage, the shocks of the first few years after World War I expanded this sense of Palestinian identity to include much wider seg-ments of the population, incorporating and winning over the entire political class. These shocks had also deepened the sense of a shared fate, making it a primary category of identity for many, if not most, Palestinians. The Mandate years, with their losing struggles with the Zionists and the British, only deepened this shared sense of identity, as a common set of "others" and a common sense of threat made increasing numbers of Palestinians perceive that they shared a common fate. These years also broadened the ranks of those exposed to the elements of this identity transmitted by the educational system and the press, as educa-tion continued to spread, such that by 1945, 45 percent of the Arab school-age population was in school, and literacy increased signifi-cantly.[34] But there remained differences in consciousness, education, and outlook in Palestinian society, as well as internecine conflicts rooted in the bitter internal struggles of the 1930s, and a gap between the urban and rural populations, between the well-to-do and the poor, and between the literate and the illiterate.

In the third and final stage, the events of 1948 and their aftermath obliterated many of these differences, erased many of these gaps, and decreased the importance of many pre-1948 conflicts. Urban and rural, hundreds of thousands of Palestinians found themselves in refugee camps, where their children all received an education, thanks to UNRWA

(something they had never been able to obtain from the British mandatory administration of Palestine), and where virtually universal literacy
among the young obtained within a generation. Equally important, 1948
proved both a great leveller, and a source of a universally shared experience, especially for that half of Palestinian society which had fled or been
expelled and had lost everything, and for those who were able to remain
in their homes, but were also traumatized by the events of 1948.

The turbulent and conflicting political currents that affected the
Palestinians immediately after the 1947–49 war completed this process.
For in spite of their dispersion and fragmentation among several new
successor states and forms of refugee status, what the Palestinians now
shared was far greater than what separated them; all had been dispossessed, none were masters of their own fate, all were at the mercy of cold,
distant, and hostile new authorities. If the Arab population of Palestine
had not been sure of their identity before 1948, the experience of
defeat, dispossession, and exile guaranteed that they knew what their
identity was very soon afterwards: they were Palestinians. The refugee
experience, the callous treatment by Israel and several of the Arab host
states, and the shared trauma of 1948, which all still had to come to
terms with, cemented and universalized a common identity as Palestinians which built on all the elements we have explored in these pages,
crowning it with this series of unforgettable shared experiences.

Palestinian identity is thus in some ways now similar to other
national identities in the Arab world and elsewhere. It has been determined in some respects by boundaries that are fairly recent, and yet has
based itself on elements of identity that go back in time far beyond the
origins of these modern boundaries. Some of these elements are local,
some religious, and some draw on other national narratives, and all
have been reshaped and reworked to fit a new narrative of identity.
Palestinian identity is different from most of these national identities
in several important respects, however. Like many other unfulfilled,
"unsuccessful" national identities, that of the Palestinians has been
fashioned without the benefit of the powerful machinery of the nation-
state to propagate it. Like the Kurds, like the Armenians, like the Jews
in Palestine before 1948, the Palestinians have asserted their identity
without the trappings of an independent state and against powerful
countervailing currents.

In the Palestinian case, repeated, crushing failure has been surmounted and survived, and in some sense has been incorporated into
the narrative of identity as triumph.[35] This brings up a characteristic of

the Palestinian experience that, while perhaps not unique—and that indeed may be shared with other long-"unsuccessful" national identities— has taken a specific form in the Palestinian case: the way in which Palestinian failure has been portrayed as triumph, or at least as heroic perseverence against impossible odds. Such a portrayal draws on the Palestinians' perception that throughout their modern history, they have faced a constellation of enemies so formidable as to be nearly insuperable. While drawing on undeniable verities—it is hard to imagine the British Empire abandoning Palestine under Arab pressure in the late 1930s, or the world supporting the Palestinians against the nascent Israeli state in the wake of the Holocaust—there can be little question that such a version of history conveniently absolves the Palestinians from the responsibility for their own fate. From this perspective, if their enemies were so numerous and powerful, it is hardly surprising that they were defeated.

This narrative of failure as triumph began during the Mandate, but reached its apogee in the years after 1948, when it was picked up and elaborated by the grassroots underground Palestinian nationalist organizations that would emerge and take over the PLO in the mid-1960s. The PLO was to give this narrative of events before 1948 its final shape, and to use it successfully as a tool in the mobilization of the Palestinian people. Ultimately, the more recent failures of the Palestinian people to achieve their aims under the leadership of the PLO came to be inscribed within the context of this same narrative, fitting seamlessly with the defeats of the 1930s, the 1940s, and the 1950s.

An example is the martyrdom of Shaykh 'Iz al-Din al-Qassam in 1935, an event that caused a great impact at the time, and would also later become an inspiration to all the underground organizations preaching the path of "armed struggle." His story came in later years to be narrated as a great event in sparking the struggle of the Palestinian people against their enemies, the British and the Zionists. As the tale was retold by Palestinian nationalists like Ghassan Kanafani in an influential article published in the PLO Research Center's magazine *Shu'un Filistiniyya* [Palestinian Affairs], and later widely disseminated in booklet form by the PFLP in Arabic and English,[36] or by activist-historians like 'Abdel-Wahhab Kayyali and Naji 'Alloush in influential works of theirs which went through numerous printings, al-Qassam had played a crucial role in winning the populace away from the elite-brokered politics of compromise with the British, and in showing them the "correct" path of popular armed struggle against the British and the Zionists.[37]

These same writers, and other less gifted ones, provided a similar version of the 1936–39 revolt, correctly perceiving it as a popular uprising that had taken the traditional elite by surprise, and in which the means chosen—the general strike, and later armed guerrilla action—were arrived at spontaneously. This same narrative stressed the heroic quality of the revolt, its successes in for a time bringing together the Palestinian people, and the fact that it had been "betrayed" by Arab governments and traditional Palestinian leaders beholden to the British. These narratives generally failed to mention the appalling losses suffered by the Palestinians during the course of the revolt, or to assess the uprising's slim possibilities of success from the very beginning, or to ask what the Palestinians might have done differently and more successfully in the same historical circumstances.

In treating the Palestinian aspect of the fighting of 1947–49, these accounts similarly stressed the heroism of the Palestinian peasant and urban fighters against heavy odds, highlighting the martyrdom in battle of charismatic leaders like 'Abd al-Qadir al-Husayni, and the self-interested machinations of the Arab regimes against the Palestinians, and downplaying the poor political calculations, and the disorganization, confusion, and leaderless chaos on the Palestinian side which contributed measurably to the debacle. What was at work in all these cases, of course, was a perfectly normal rewriting of history to fit the circumstances of the time it was written, providing a narrative appropriate for the 1960s, when the Palestinians were again being told by these same historian-activists, and by the PLO, to take their fate in their own hands and launch armed struggle against heavy odds.

Once the new movement had been launched, and tens of thousands of Palestinians had flocked to its ranks, the list of defeats narrated as triumphs against heavy odds increased. The narration of the "foundation myth" of the modern Palestinian commando movement, the battle of al-Karama on March 21, 1968, during which several brigades of Israeli troops crossed the Jordan River to attack Palestinian military bases in the abandoned town of al-Karama, and returned across the river after a hard day of fighting, was typical in this respect. Like all foundation myths, this one had a solid basis in fact: the Israeli army had apparently anticipated an easy time, as the commandos were expected to flee, in keeping with classical guerrilla doctrine when facing a superior regular force (and in keeping with Israeli expectations regarding the Arabs). They had not done so, and thereafter nothing had gone as the Israelis planned. The Fateh leadership had made a strategic decision to keep all of its limited forces in and around al-Karama, and to stand and fight; Jordanian artillery joined in the fray from the hills above when the unexpected resistance of the Palestinian commandos led to slow going for the Israeli forces, knocking out some tanks and armored personnel carriers; the Israelis suffered much heavier casualties than expected, and they were forced to leave behind several damaged vehicles, which were duly paraded through the streets of Amman to the cheering of jubilant multitudes.

These appearances notwithstanding, this was no Arab victory, at least not militarily: the Israelis had inflicted heavy casualties on the Palestinians, far heavier than they themselves had suffered, and had extricated their forces on the same day without losing any prisoners or leaving behind any bodies. It was politically significant, however, since inappropriate though the comparison was in fact, the Palestinians were able to contrast a situation where they had stood and fought, and at the end of the day were in control of the ground, with the inability of three regular Arab armies to do the same thing during the June war only a few months earlier.[38] The Palestinian commando organizations and the media sympathetic to them immediately picked up this theme, which found a ready response in an Arab world still reeling from the unexpected defeat of June 1967.

The name al-Karama, which as chance would have it means "dignity," became a symbol intensely exploited by Palestinian nationalist groups both to expand their ranks enormously with fresh recruits, and to put pressure on the Arab regimes to allow them greater freedom of action, and this relatively small battle soon helped make the PLO a force to reckon with in Arab politics. Like the commando actions the Palestinians carried out against Israel on other occasions, both before and after this battle, the results were far greater casualties for them than for their foes, and little change in the purely military balance of forces with the Israeli enemy.[39] Thus, the battle of al-Karama was a case of a failure against overwhelming odds brilliantly narrated as heroic triumph.

This portrayal of failure as triumph and defeat as victory was to become almost a stock in trade for the PLO. A case in point was the debacle in Jordan in September 1970, when the Palestinians were unable to discipline their own ranks, as a constituent group of the PLO, the PFLP, provoked the Hashemite regime beyond tolerance with a series of aircraft hijackings, and the Jordanian army finally reacted by routing the PLO in a crushing campaign which became known as Black September, ultimately expelling it from Jordan.[40] In the Palestinian narration of this devastating defeat, the heavy military odds against the PLO were typically mentioned prominently, but not the appalling Palestinian political mistakes between the battle of al-Karama in March 1968 and September of 1970, which squandered the massive public support the PLO had previously enjoyed in Jordan.[41]

Another case in point was the seemingly endless war in Lebanon, which the PLO allowed itself to be drawn into in 1975–76, an intense period of confused fighting that ended with the military intervention of Syria, a former ally, against the PLO and its Lebanese supporters. In this devastating phase of the conflict, three Palestinian refugee camps in the Beirut area, Tal al-Za'tar, Jisr al-Basha, and Dbayye, were overrun by Phalangist and allied militias backed indirectly by both Israel and Syria,[42] and their inhabitants subjected to massacre and expulsion.[43] This phase of the war was followed by a series of intense clashes over the next few years, many of them involving the PLO, marked by an Israeli incursion into the south of the country in 1978, and capped by Israel's massive invasion of Lebanon and its nine-week siege of the PLO in Beirut in the summer of 1982. The PLO, the Palestinian civilian population, and the Lebanese suffered extremely heavy casualties during the 1982 fighting, estimated at 19,000 killed and 30,000 wounded.[44]

The end result of this sequence of disasters and defeats was the American-brokered expulsion of the PLO to a number of even more distant places of exile, as its leadership, cadres, fighters, and institutions were forced to leave Beirut, where they had been established for well over a decade, and were scattered to Tunisia, Yemen, the Sudan, Syria, Iraq, and Libya. This defeat and its aftermath were particularly painful for Palestinians, as it evoked for many of them the exodus of 1948, and the more recent expulsion of the movement from Jordan. As in Jordan, one of the hardest things for the Palestinians to accept was that in Lebanon they had lost the support of the originally sympathetic local population, due largely to their own political mistakes.

When, at a meeting of the Palestine National Council (PNC) convened in Algiers in November 1982, a few months after the exodus from Beirut, this latest catastrophe was portrayed by some PLO leaders as yet another victory, yet another triumph, 'Isam Sirtawi, an iconoclastic middle-ranking leader of the movement who was to be assassinated in Portugal soon afterwards, rose to speak in exasperation. His voice dripping with sarcasm, he intoned: "Our defeat in Lebanon and our evacuation of Beirut has been described as a 'victory.' One more 'victory' like this one, and we will have the next meeting of the PNC in the Seychelles

Islands!" More substantively, one of the greatest Palestinian orators of his generation, and probably the most thoughtful, Shafiq al-Hout, the PLO representative in Lebanon, gave perhaps the most brilliant speech of his career at this meeting, denouncing those who would portray what had just happened in Lebanon as a victory, and accusing them of lying to the Palestinian people. His speech was received with thunderous applause by those present.[45]

For all its flaws in the eyes of al-Hout's audience, who had perhaps had enough of such costly "victories," the portrayal of failure as triumph seems nevertheless to have worked well for the PLO. Although this narrative obscured the role of poor leadership and bad decisionmaking in the years when the PLO led the national movement (which for PLO leaders was undoubtedly one of its great virtues), just as it did in describing the actions of the Palestinians during the 1930s and 1940s, it had the undeniable merit of making acceptable to the Palestinian people a story that involved the confrontation of daunting odds. A willingness to do so was obviously necessary for a few Palestinians to defy the will of virtually all the Arab regimes in the mid-1960s, and begin launching attacks on Israel; for a few of them to stand and fight the Israeli army in March 1968 at al-Karama; or for larger numbers of Palestinian fighters and militiamen to take on the Jordanian Army, the vaunted Arab Legion, in 1970; and to fight the Phalangist and allied Lebanese right-wing militias in 1975; the Syrian army in 1976; and the Israeli army in Lebanon in 1978 and 1982. Whether it was wise, or necessary, to do all these things was an entirely different matter, and one which this whole approach naturally did not address. But this Quixotic narrative put such actions into a perspective where they were acceptable, if not always entirely sensible.

More to the point, this narrative was one which enabled the Palestinians to make sense of a troubled history which involved enormous efforts against great odds simply for them to maintain their identity as a people. The PLO was not a government, and thus was without the authoritative means at the disposal of a national government for the propagation of an approved, official version of history to the entirety of its people—an educational system, control or at least influence over exclusive channels of the media, and the possibility of creating a network of museums, archaeological exhibits, national parks, and cultural manifestations to reinforce this version of history. It was nevertheless able to do some of these things with those Palestinian populations it was able to reach through its newspapers and periodicals, its publishing houses and research institutes, and especially its radio station *Sawt Filastin*, "The

Voice of Palestine," which was much listened to by Palestinians, for many of whom it soon took the place of Egypt's *Sawt al-'Arab*.

These and other media disseminated a version of the Palestinian experience meant both to engender a strong sense of group solidarity in the face of a formidable sequence of foes whom the Palestinians had to face, and to induce them to make the sacrifices necessary to further the national cause. That it was a self-serving retelling of Palestinian history, which in addition to highlighting the heroism of Palestinian fighters stressed the brave decisions made by PLO leaders, while downplaying all their errors of judgment, did not make it any less attractive to those who propagated it.

By the early 1980s, however, a corrosive counter-narrative had begun to emerge. This did not usually go so far as to ask why it was not possible to have victories which were real victories: most Palestinians saw their enemies, whether Israel, or the Arab regimes, or the American and other foreign governments which supported them, as collosi who could not easily be defeated. But it did question persistently whether better choices were not possible in some circumstances, and as 'Isam al-Sirtawi's sarcastic comment and the enthusiastic audience response to Shafiq al-Hout's speech to the PNC both indicate, many were ready to ask such questions. This willingness was a function of a disillusionment with the PLO leadership, particularly among Palestinians in the diaspora, which led to a Syrian-supported revolt in Fateh in 1983, and to a gradual decline in the loyalty the leadership in far-off Tunis was able to command. In these circumstances, the spontaneous outbreak of the *intifada*, the grassroots popular uprising in the occupied territories, in December 1987, which took the PLO leadership entirely by surprise, gave a much-needed boost to a Palestinian national movement that was clearly flagging. It also reestablished "the inside," Palestine itself, as the center of gravity of Palestinian politics, rather than "the outside," the Palestinian diaspora, where it had been located for so many decades.

The outbreak of the *intifada* also vindicated the strategy advocated since the late 1970s by Khalil al-Wazir (Abu Jihad), the so-called *Khiyar al-Urduni*, or "Jordanian Option." Reacting to the pointlessness of the PLO's involvement in the Lebanese quagmire, Abu Jihad had postulated that there was no future for the movement unless it reestablished itself inside the occupied territories. This could only be done, he argued, via Jordan, and to do so would require that the PLO improve its relationship with the Kingdom, which had been poor since Black September. Against much internal opposition, especially from within Fateh, the

PLO leadership managed to achieve a rapprochement with Jordan even before the defeat in Lebanon and, via the presence in Amman this made possible, was able to renew links with the West Bank and Gaza Strip.

This move betokened a realization by the PLO leadership that the future of the movement lay inside Palestine, rather than outside, but it was too little too late. The PLO was already sidetracked and ignored within the Arab world, its declining status indicated by the poor treatment it received at the Arab summit in Amman in November 1987. The precipitous decline of the Palestinian cause would have continued, had it not been for the spontaneous outbreak of the *intifada*, which galvanized the Palestinian people, impressed international public opinion, and, most importantly, convinced a sizeable number of Israelis that they could not indefinitely maintain the military occupation of the West Bank and Gaza Strip. All of these were prerequisites for the following phase, which began with the Madrid Peace Conference of October 1991. At that time a Palestinian delegation (albeit as part of a joint delegation with Jordan) sat down at a negotiating table with one from Israel for the first time in history. The meeting, while it changed nothing on the ground in Palestine, where Israel still held most of the cards, was of symbolic importance: the assertion of Palestinian national identity it betokened was undeniable.

IV

In 1993, Israel and the PLO signed a Declaration of Principles in Washington under the auspices of the U.S. government. As a result of this agreement and others that have followed it, Palestinian identity would appear to be firmly established today. PLO leaders like Yasser 'Arafat, once routinely reviled as "terrorists" by the western and Israeli media, have been honored guests in Israel and the United States, where they are recognized as legitimate representatives of an accepted entity, the Palestinian people. For an interim period of five years, the agreements signed with Israel have given a new Palestinian Authority dominated by the PLO control over the nearly 1 million Palestinian inhabitants of the Gaza Strip, but not over its Israeli settlements and the land annexed to them, nor of its Israeli army bases, roads, and borders, more than 30 percent of the Strip's territory in total. This authority gained control as well over most of the cities, towns, and villages in the West Bank, but not of the countryside, meaning that most of its territory remained under Israeli dominion.

Recognized by its most determined enemies, and at last able to establish itself on its national soil, the movement that has incarnated Palestinian identity for the past few decades appears at last to be responsible for a genuine achievement, rather than yet another disaster dressed up as a "victory." But there is an underside to this achievement. The Pales-. tinian Authority is not a national government, nor have self-determination, independence, and statehood yet been conceded by Israel in any of the agreements its government has signed, and it is not clear when, or whether, it will concede these things, or whether the Likud government that has emerged from the 1996 elections will honor the provisions of the interim accords already signed, let alone negotiate new ones determining the final status of all the matters at issue between the two sides. The jurisdiction and power of the Palestinian authority is moreover sharply circumscribed in many ways, not least of which is the fact that it does not yet have control over most of the territory of the West Bank and Gaza Strip after five years of negotiations which were supposed to end the Israeli occupation and give self-rule to the entire Palestinian population. Many other crucial issues have been deferred, some fear indefinitely.

The nightmare of many Palestinians is that Israel might freeze these unsatisfactory "interim arrangements," which would become the basis for the final status of the West Bank and Gaza Strip. They fear this because the iron logic behind the expansion during the last few years in the area and population of Israeli settlements, and with it the building of an extensive and costly network of strategic roads criss-crossing the West Bank and Gaza Strip, can only be that Israel will use the existence of both settlements and roads as a pretext to keep key parts of these areas under its permanent control. Given these far-reaching territorial dispositions, and the restricted jurisdiction over a fraction of the country Israel has conceded, they fear that even if an "independent" and "sovereign" Palestinian entity ultimately does emerge, it will involve only minor modifications in the size and status of the existing Palestinian islands in the Israeli-dominated sea of the West Bank and Gaza Strip. This misshapen and grotesque creation could then be baptized as a "Palestinian state": one with a flag, postage stamps, a marching band, ambassadors, and Presidential motorcades, but nothing resembling exclusive jurisdiction over most of the contiguous territory of the West Bank and Gaza Strip, nor anything recognizable in the real world as sovereignty.

These concerns, and the daily problems that have emerged since Oslo, are the basis for much dissatisfaction among Palestinians with the PLO leadership that negotiated these accords (although most polls still show that a majority of Palestinians support the agreements[46]), and for a strong undercurrent that argues the accords are deeply flawed, embodying too many vital concessions to the Israelis. Consequently, many Palestinians mutter that the same tired old PLO leaders who have portrayed their past failures as victories are trying to do the same thing again. But irrespective of the many flaws in the accords with Israel, and the bitter Palestinian critiques of them, a process with great import for issues of Palestinian identity has now begun. The most important feature of this entire process is that it is taking place inside Palestine, which has become the sole focus of Palestinian politics, thus completing a shift from outside to inside Palestine which started with the *intifada*.

As some exiles have returned, as PLO institutions have been integrated with local structures to constitute the new Palestinian Authority, and as Palestinian financiers and capitalists begin to invest their funds in the West Bank and Gaza Strip, it is clear that a recentering of Palestinian society is taking place, and with it a redefinition of identity in new circumstances. One unique circumstance is that although not sovereign or independent, and indeed although bound by myriad restrictions imposed by the agreements with the Israelis, the new Palestinian Authority has more power over more of its people in more of Palestine than any Palestinian agency has had in the twentieth century. With this power has come responsibility and accountability, which cannot be shirked or shunted off onto another actor. In these circumstances, although the Palestinian Authority can and undoubtedly will blame others for its failures, using the PLO's old scenario of Palestinians facing insuperable odds to explain away failures or describe them as triumphs, it is possible that for the first time this strategy will not work, and that the Palestinian leadership will be held accountable for its actions by its own people.

Regardless, Palestinian identity has come full circle. Once denied and scorned, its early history is being analyzed by mainstream Israeli social scientists,[47] and not just iconoclasts like the historian Yehoshua Porath, who began the process more than two decades ago.[48] Where American politicians once avoided having anything to do with anything Palestinian, an American President saw to it that the signing of the PLO-Israeli accord took place on the White House lawn in September 1993, and another in the White House in September 1995, although his administration had played virtually no positive role in either negotiation.[49] And after 1993, Israeli Labor Party leaders like the late Yitzhaq Rabin and Shimon Peres spoke freely about an independent Palestinian personality and a Palestinian people with a national cause—something that twenty-five years earlier Golda Meir could not bring herself to say. It remains to be seen whether their Likud successors will continue along this path, which is so antithetical to the traditions of their party.

In a sense a taboo has been broken, as part of a mutual process: just as at least some Israelis can finally bring themselves to recognize the existence of the Palestinian people, so the Palestinians can finally recognize that of the Israeli people. This ends a lengthy period of mutual denial, when both sides withheld recognition as if it were the ultimate weapon in a peculiar version of mutual deterrence. For just as the Zionists before 1948, and the Israelis and much western opinion after that, persisted in denying the Palestinians the legitimacy attached to an independent national identity, so did the Palestinians and the Arab world consistently deny that the Israelis were a people, or that Zionism could be considered as a legitimate national movement.[50]

With the abatement of perceptions of an existential threat to Israel, as peace treaties and diplomatic relations with the Arab countries slowly become the norm, and as realization of Israel's absolute strategic superiority over all its neighbors slowly overcomes Israelis' deeply ingrained perception of their country's vulnerability, it has become easier for some Israelis to accept the existence of the Palestinians, who are no longer seen as the spearhead of an implacable Arab campaign to destroy Israel— although other Israelis and some of their supporters still appear attached to this lurid vision. And for the Arabs, denial of Israel's existence—a particularly futile endeavor in any case given its ubiquitous intrusions into the lives of the Palestinians and in the Arab world over the past few decades—has both achieved one of its main aims with Israeli recognition of the Palestinians, and lost whatever tattered value it once had.

It would be a mistake to take the parallels too far, however, or to assume that the mutality is more than superficial. This is not a reconciliation between equals: it is a situation where dominance of one over the other prevails, and where after a century of conflict there is an unequivocal winner and a clear loser. Israel is an established nation-state, a regional nuclear superpower with one of the best armies and perhaps the best air force in the world, and has a strongly established sense of national identity which has been reinforced by its state structures and their parastate predecessors since well before the country achieved independence. It has a well-functioning political system, a large and thriving economy, and a firm, decades-old alliance with the greatest power on earth, not to speak of the unstinting support of wealthy, influential, and generous Jewish communities the world over. Moreover, Israel still has complete command—at least in terms of security—over every part of Palestine. In spite of all the agreements with the PLO, it has yet to concede ultimate security control over any part of the country.[51]

For Palestinians the contrast could not be greater: they have yet to achieve self-determination, independence, or statehood; they are only now painfully integrating their feeble parastate, which grew up in exile, into an administration with the limited powers the Israelis allow them; they have an economy in a shambles after three decades of occupation and several years of *intifada* (which probably had as devastating an impact on the Palestinian economy as did the 1936–39 revolt[52]); they control virtually no resources and have no real allies in the world. The Palestinians, of course, do have one asset in spite of everything: a powerful sense of national identity, which we have seen they were able to develop and maintain in spite of extraordinary vicissitudes.

Palestinian identity, however, is not now and never has been defined solely by the conflict with Zionism and Israel. It has many other aspects, which the Palestinians will have to resolve for themselves. One of them is that although it is clear to Palestinians what constitutes the identity of a Palestinian, hard though it may be to define, it is not so clear what are the dimensions of Palestine, this country the Palestinians come from and to which they relate their identity. In other words, as we asked at the outset, what are the limits of Palestine? Specifically, does it include the places on the map of the country now presumably irrevocably part of Israel, even though on the Palestinian "internal map" they will always be part of Palestine? Thus although Jaffa is today a rundown slum, a southern suburb of the Tel Aviv urban complex, with a poor, largely Arab population (and a small night life district much frequented by Israelis in old, renovated Arab homes), in the Palestinian imagination it is the place of origin of all those who still proudly call themselves Jaffans.

This issue, and others related to the prospect of a resolution of the conflict over Palestine raise a number of questions relating to essential issues of Palestinian identity, questions that may be with us for a long time. Mention of Jaffa, for example, raises a larger question: how will the Palestinians adapt to the final "amputation" of areas that have been integrated into Israel since 1948, but that they have always considered part of their country? For decades, during the "lost years" of the 1950s and 1960s, and then during the euphoric era when it seemed as if "liberation" were a possibility, these questions were never raised. Now they are coming up again, encouraged by the ability of some of the returning exiles to visit the parts of the country incorporated into Israel nearly three generations ago, and now nearly unrecognizable as Palestinian. Will this issue be harder to deal with for those Palestinians still in the refugee camps and with little to look forward to, or for those of the middle classes who have managed to integrate into society wherever they have ended up, but are still moved by nostalgia for Ramla or Lydd, or Jaffa or Haifa, which in many cases they have never seen?

More practical questions include that of how the Palestinians will find a substitute or substitutes for Haifa and Jaffa—as cultural, intellectual, and economic centers—and whether they will ever be able to function with Jerusalem as a political center. Today, in the patchwork of areas either still occupied by Israel, under control of the Palestinian Authority, or in some indeterminate intermediate status, there are in effect four main Palestinian urban centers: Gaza, largest city of the Gaza Strip and (temporary?) headquarters of the Palestinian Authority; the Ramallah/al-Bira conurbation, increasingly the most active economic center and a growing focus of intellectual life; Nablus, capital of the north of the West Bank; and Jerusalem, "the political capital" and now the largest Arab city in Palestine (albeit one with a huge Jewish majority today and under firm Israeli control), and the center of much cultural, intellectual, and economic activity.

Jerusalem is all of these things, but it is also a city cut off from its hinterland in the West Bank by Israeli closure measures in force for several years now, ostensibly for security reasons, but with obvious political implications for Israel's ultimate objective: the absorption of the entirety of the city into Israel. The answers to some of these questions as to the "recentering" of Palestinian national life can be determined only in light of the results of negotiations as yet uncompleted, such as those over Jerusalem, and the answers to others will presumably emerge "naturally" as urban growth, social change, and economic development take place.

There are several further questions emanating from those already posed. One is how will those parts of Palestine with clear Arab majorities and a considerable chance of achieving a large measure of self-rule (or even, perhaps, one day, full self-determination) such as most of the Gaza Strip, or the Nablus and Ramallah areas, relate to those either without such clear-cut majorities, such as Arab East Jerusalem, whose population now has a Jewish majority, or those like Hebron where even self-rule seems distant because of the presence of religious sites of importance to both sides to the conflict? The Arab population in all these areas is Palestinian, but while some are or will presumably soon be under Palestinian governance, others face the indefinite prospect of remaining under one form or another of Israeli control.

Where identity is concerned, the markers could go either way, or both ways, in such a situation: borders, security frontiers, control over antiquities, and road signs, for example, could indicate one set of things, while the educational system[53] or the identity cards people carry could indicate something else. These different sorts of markers of course indicate clear relations of dominance and subordination, and some of this extraordinary confusion is a function of the complex "interim" arrangements imposed because of Israel's insistence on not removing any of its West Bank and Gaza Strip settlements for several years at least, thus necessitating the bewildering patchwork arrangement that has been negotiated.

Some of it, however, is a function of the overlapping of Israelis with Palestinians and Palestinians with Israelis since 1967, as Israel has spread slowly into parts of the West Bank and Gaza Strip, while the Palestinian identity of the growing number of Palestinians left behind in Israel in 1948 has reemerged. And some of it is simply a function of the inextricable interweaving of the Israeli and Palestinian narratives which we stressed earlier, and visible at places like Jerusalem, and in Hebron, site of the Tomb of those like Abraham, Isaac, and Jacob, who are considered Patriarchs by both peoples.

This brings up the question of the nearly one million Palestinians who are also Israeli citizens, the descendants of the fewer than 200,000 who remained in 1948 and who today constitute more than 18 percent of Israel's population. How will they relate to their fellow-Palestinians in the West Bank and Gaza Strip once the final arrangements have been sorted out, and one lot are on one side of a final frontier and another on the other? One segment of Palestinians study Hebrew literature and Jewish history in school, carry Israeli passports and vote in Israeli elections; members of another are learning Arabic literature and Palestinian history, carry a bewildering array of travel documents or none at all, plus a new Palestinian passport whose value has yet to be tested, and voted in a Palestinian election. Yet both identify with the same national symbols (as is evidenced by the fact that a ceaseless stream of popular delegations of Palestinians from the Galilee and other Arab regions of Israel has poured into Gaza over the past two years to meet Yasser 'Arafat), and both groups regard themselves and each other as Palestinians.

Hard as all these questions are, harder ones still remain to be answered. Perhaps the most painful is that related to those Palestinians outside their homeland: not the privileged few PLO cadres, officials, and soldiers who have been able to return to Palestine with their families after decades of exile, nor the comfortable ones with foreign passports who can come and go freely, nor even the middle-class ones integrated into Jordan and most of whom have always been able at least to visit the West Bank. This question applies rather to those still in refugee camps (a distinct minority of Palestinians today, but an important one).[54] It was these Palestinians of the "outside" who first picked up the fallen banner of Palestinian nationalism after 1948, rebuilt the national movement, and then sustained it with their sacrifices. This question is most cruel, and most apt, when applied to those in Lebanon, who have suffered and sacrificed the most—perhaps 30,000 Palestinians have been killed in Lebanon since 1975 out of a population which never exceeded 400,000,[55] and is today down to about 300,000—and are unwanted by their host country. At the same time, as refugees who were originally from the Galilee, Jaffa and Haifa, they currently appear to stand little chance of returning to their homes, or even to other parts of Palestine, at least for the foreseeable future.

We have seen that for the approximately 700,000 Palestinians who became refugees in 1948, the idea of return became important very soon after they left their homes. The concept of a right of return was thus fostered by the early Palestinian organizations and later by the PLO as a central mobilizational slogan in response to this popular sentiment. This right rested on the language of General Assembly resolution 194 of December 11, 1948, which gave Palestinian refugees the option of return or compensation.[56] The PLO has since limited what was formerly postulated as an unrestricted "right of return" to this UN formula of return or compensation, but that still appears to be far beyond what the Palestinians are capable of achieving at this juncture of their history.[57] This issue has not yet been resolved between the Palestinians and Israelis—it is one of the so-called "final status issues," like Jerusalem, which was postponed until later[58]—and thus has not been entirely foreclosed. However, the adamant Israeli position on the issue of refugee return (which if unlimited has the potential to undo the effects of 100 years of successful Zionist efforts to change the demographic nature of Palestine), and the balance of forces between the two sides, do not promise a happy answer to this question for the 1948 refugees.

These are all questions without simple answers and indeed, like this one, some of them have a wide range of possible answers, none of which promises to be pleasant for the Palestinian people to absorb. The story of Palestinian identity would thus appear in sum to be one of both failure and success. It has been a failure in that in spite of all their sacrifices over so many generations, the Palestinian people have not so far achieved the self-determination and control over their own lives for which they have been striving for so long. Indeed, in light of the genesis of Palestinian identity we have just chronicled, in some respects the Palestinians have gone backwards since World War I, a time when this identity was not yet firmly established on a mass basis. From the perspective of today, the late Ottoman era, for all its many faults, in some ways looks almost like a golden age:[59] it was the last time the Palestinians had majority status throughout nearly the entirety of their own country, and the last time they had free, countrywide elections to a Parliament (albeit a multinational Ottoman parliament rather than a Palestinian national one), and had an almost completely free press able to challenge the authorities, as did the editors of *Filastin* in 1914.

This story has been a success in that a Palestinian identity has asserted itself and survived against all odds, and in spite of the many failures we have touched on. Dulles said in the 1950s that the Palestinians would disappear, and Golda Meir spoke in 1969 as if they had disappeared, going so far as to declare that they had never existed in the first place. But they have not disappeared, and even their most determined opponents seem to have begun to reconcile themselves to this uncomfortable fact. For these opponents, whether Israel, or some Arab states, or the great powers, the nonexistence of the Palestinians would have made things considerably easier at various stages of history. But inconvenient though their identity often has been for others, the Palestinians have remained stubbornly attached to it. This probably must be adjudged a success, although it is a small one.

The final question, an open-ended one like all the others, is whether this very limited success can be turned into the basis for building something lasting, something that will perhaps make possible a reversal of some of the failures of this past century, and finally allow the achievement of self-determination, statehood, and national independence the modern world has taught us is the "natural state" of peoples with an independent national identity like the Palestinians.

NOTES

Preface

1. This eventually resulted in the publication of Rashid Khalidi, *British Policy Towards Syria and Palestine, 1906–1914* (London: Ithaca Press, 1980).

2. Rashid Khalidi, *Under Siege: PLO Decisionmaking during the 1982 War* (New York: Columbia University Press, 1986).

3. The literature is so voluminous that it is possible to list only a few of the works I found most useful. These include Eric Hobsbawm, *Nations and Nationalism Since 1780: Programme, Myth, Reality.* (Cambridge: Cambridge University Press, 1990); Ernest Gellner, *Nations and Nationalism* (Ithaca: Cornell University Press, 1983); Eric Hobsbawm and Terence Ranger, eds., *The Invention of Tradition* (Cambridge: Cambridge University Press, 1983); Anthony D. Smith, *The Ethnic Origins of Nations* (Oxford: Oxford University Press, 1986) and his article "The Origins of Nations," *Ethnic and Religious Studies* 12, no. 3 (July 1989): 340–367; and Benedict Anderson, *Imagined Communities: Reflections on the Rise and Spread of Nationalism,* 2nd ed. (London: Verso, 1991).

4. The two approaches are well illustrated in Smith, "Origins," pp. 341 ff.

5. Gellner, *Nations and Nationalism,* pp. 1–7.

6. Hobsbawm, *Nations and Nationalism since 1780,* p. 10.

7. Gellner, *Nations and Nationalism,* pp. 48–9.

8. Eric Hobsbawm, "Introduction: Inventing Traditions," in Hobsbawm and Ranger, eds., *The Invention of* Tradition, 6.

9. Anderson, *Imagined Communities,* p. 9 and pp. 37 ff. See the interesting critique of Anderson in Partha Chatterjee, *Nationalist Thought in the Colonial World: A Derivative Discourse?* (London: Zed, 1986): 19–22.

10. Anthony D. Smith, *The Ethnic Revival in the Modern World* (Cambridge: Cambridge University Press, 1981): 63–86.

11. Smith, "Origins," p. 361.

12. Hobsbawm, *Nations and Nationalism*, p. 12.

13. The best introduction to their writings can be found in Ranajit Guha and Gayatri Spivak, eds. *Selected Subaltern Studies* (Oxford: Oxford University Press, 1988).

Chapter 1. Introduction

1. Israel annexed Arab East Jerusalem in 1967, while the treating the rest of the occupied West Bank as part of the so-called "administered territories." Israel imposed a physical separation of Jerusalem from the other occupied territories in March 1993. This "closure" has continued since then, notwithstanding either negotiations or agreements between the Palestinians and Israelis. Until 1993, Israel's annexation of the city had relatively little effect on the movement of Palestinians into or out of Jerusalem. The "closure," however, meant that West Bank residents needed a special pass to enter the city, which most of them could not obtain. Those who managed to do so had to wait in long lines of traffic to pass through army checkpoints on their way to work, schools, shopping, or prayer in Jerusalem.

2. At the height of the war in Lebanon from 1975 onwards, when checkpoints were set up at which kidnappings and killings on a sectarian or ethnic basis took place, those passing were asked at certain of these barriers to say the Arabic word for tomato: one pronunciation meant the speaker was Lebanese and could pass; another indicated that the speaker was Palestinian, and could be killed.

3. This existential situation is central to one of the most characteristic works of modern Palestinian literature, Ghassan Kanafani's prescient short novel *Rijal fil-shams* [Men in the Sun] (Beirut: n.p., 1963) in which a group of Palestinians without "proper" identity documents die inside an airless tanker truck while being smuggled into Kuwait.

4. Before 1988, all Jordanian passports were valid for five years. Previously, Palestinians were distinguishable from other Jordanians by a notation in their passports identifying them as having obtained Jordanian nationality by a special provision of the law (paragraph 3) used to grant residents of the West Bank Jordanian citizenship after the area was annexed to Jordan in 1950.

5. During a typical interrogation after a long wait at Cairo Airport, an Egyptian security officer, frustrated by my replies to his questions as to where I was from (I responded that I was Palestinian but was born in New York), was finally satisfied when I made it clear to him that my family had never lived in Egypt, that I had never been subject to Egyptian jurisdiction, and that I was therefore not one of "their" Palestinians. "What is your connection to Egypt?" he finally asked. "None," I answered. "Except a pan-Arab one [*Illa al-'alaqa al-qawmiyya*]," I added diplomatically after a brief pause, which brought a smile and the return of my U.S. passport with an entry stamp.

6. An example of a work that sometimes slips into this error, although it generally avoids it, is Baruch Kimmerling and Joel S. Migdal, *Palestinians: The Making of a People* (New York: The Free Press, 1993): "Had it not been for the pressures exerted on the Arabs of Palestine by the Zionist movement, the very concept of a Palestinian people would not have developed" (p. xvii). For my critique of the book, see my review in the

American Historical Review 99, no. 3 (June 1994): 947–948. The best work to date on the early Palestinian national movement is Muhammad Muslih, *The Origins of Palestinian Nationalism* (New York: Columbia University Press, 1988).

Chapter 2. Contrasting Narratives of Palestinian Identity

1. For a succinct statement of how a society's representations of time and space can affect the definition of of national identity, see Amnon Finkelstein, "Why Power? Why culture?," in R. D. Johnson, ed., *On Cultural Ground: Essays in International History* (Chicago: Imprint, 1994): 36–37. For a treatment that focuses on different treatments of space over time as part of the definition of the nation, see Smith, "The Origins," pp. 356–357.

2. In Stuart Hall, "Ethnicity: Identity and Difference," *Radical America*, 23 no. 4 (October–December 1989): 16.

3. Edward Said, *Orientalism*, 2nd ed. (New York: Vintage, 1994), pp. 331–332.

4. For more on this episode, see R. Khalidi, *Under Siege*, chapter 2; and "The Palestinians in Lebanon: The Repercussions of the Israeli Invasion," *Middle East Journal*, 38 no. 2 (Spring 1984): 255–266; and Rex Brynen, *Sanctuary and Survival: The PLO in Lebanon* (Boulder: Westview, 1990).

5. The Kurds and Armenians were candidates for self-determination during the negotiations over the post-war settlements, notably in the unratified 1920 treaty of Sèvres, but were ultimately abandoned to their fate by the European powers. Among the inhabitants of the Arab lands that fell under the League of Nations mandate system, only the Palestinians were never considered for self-determination by the powers. Unlike the mandates for Syria and Iraq, meant from the outset to prepare them to become "independent states," the Mandate for Palestine omitted any mention of independence or self-determination for the Palestinians, referring rather to the establishment of a "national home for the Jewish people" in Palestine. In the Balfour Declaration, which was incorporated into the text of the Mandate, the Palestinians (94 percent of the population at the time) were referred to as "existing non-Jewish communities in Palestine," whose civil and religious (but not political or national) rights were to be protected by the mandatory power.

6. Beshara Doumani, *Rediscovering Palestine: The Merchants and Peasants of Jabal Nablus, 1700–1900* (Berkeley: University of California Press, 1995), p. 245.

7. A typical example of the extensive modern popular literature in Arabic on the subject is the small volume on the battle in 1187 in which the Crusaders were decisively defeated by Saladin: Yusuf Sami al-Yusuf, *Hittin*, 2nd ed. (Acre: Dar al-Aswar, 1989).

8. Most scholarly literature on the Crusades, like the magisterial work of Sir Steven Runciman, *A History of the Crusades*, 3 vols. (Cambridge: Cambridge University Press, 1951–54), depends on Western sources rather than the voluminous Islamic and Eastern Christian sources. For the Arabic sources see Francesco Gabrieli, *Arab Historians of the Crusades* (London: Routledge, 1969); Amin Maalouf, *The Crusades Through Arab Eyes* (New York: Schocken, 1985); and Philip Hitti, *An Arab-Syrian Gentleman and Warrior in the Period of the Crusades* (Princeton: Princeton University Press, 1987). In the main, literature on the Crusades treat them as an extension of Western European history, albeit one taking place in an exotic locale.

9. Early Muslims also called the city "*Ilya*," derived from the Roman name, Aelia Capitolina, used before the Islamic period. Throughout this book, I will use the most

commonly accepted English names for Palestinian place-names, irrespective of their derivation: thus Jerusalem rather than *al-Quds*, and Hebron rather than *al-Khalil.*

10. Meron Benvenisti, *Conflicts and Contradictions* (New York: Villard, 1986), pp. 191–198, observes that under the Israeli map of the country, there lies another Arab map. His recent book, *Intimate Enemies: Jews and Arabs in a Shared Land* (Berkeley: University of California Press, 1995), examines these matters afresh. As deputy mayor of Jerusalem, Benvenisti played a part in Israeli settlement of Arab areas annexed to the newly expanded municipality after 1967; earlier, his father was one of the geographers assigned to give Hebrew names (some of them Hebrew versions of the original Arabic names) to localities throughout the country, a process accelerated after 1948, when more than 400 Arab villages were obliterated after their inhabitants had fled or been expelled. See the study compiled under the direction of Walid Khalidi, *All that Remains: The Palestinian Villages Occupied and Destroyed by Israel in 1948* (Washington: Institute for Palestine Studies, 1992).

11. Smith, "The Origins," pp. 356 ff., looks at how what he calls "educator-intellectuals" created a shared sense of attachment to a homeland via "historicizing natural features" and "naturalizing historical features" of a chosen area in order to obtain the same ends as Israeli geographers.

12. A striking attempt to do this is the slide show for visitors to the excavations along the Western Wall of the *Haram al-Sharif,* which are controlled jointly by the Israeli Ministry of Religion, the Israel Antiquities Authority and the Jerusalem municipality. This excavation involves subterranean tunnels driven through a substructure of arches constructed by Umayyad and Mameluke master-builders as foundations for several superb monuments of Islamic architecture at what is currently ground level, yet the slide show blots out everything but one segment of the city's history, linking the present to a "privileged" period 3,000 years ago. This process reached its logical extension in recent Israeli celebrations of the "3,000th anniversary" of Jerusalem, a city with a recorded past of more than 5,000 years. See Nadia Abu El-Hajj's outstanding dissertation, "Excavating the Land, Creating the Homeland: Archaeology, the State and the Making of History in Modern Jewish Nationalism," Duke University Department of Cultural Anthropology, 1995, notably chapter 3.

13. The most notable attempt to do this was the massive "Jerusalem 3000" celebration just referred to, organized by the Israeli government and the Jerusalem municipality in 1996, which highlighted King David's conquest of the city as marking its foundation, and ignored the preceding two millennia of the city's recorded history. For details, see K. J. Asali, "Jerusalem in History: Notes on the Origins of the City and its Tradition of Tolerance," *Arab Studies Quarterly* 16, no. 4 (Fall 1994): 37–45; and K. J. Asali, ed., *Jerusalem in History,* 2nd ed. (London: Kegan Paul, 1996).

14. The cover of the pamphlet reads: "*Tarjamat al-kurras al-mad'u muhamat 'an huquq Terra Sancta fil-maghara al-mad'uwa magharat al-halib al-ka'ina bil-qurb min Baytlahm. Mu'alafa wa muqaddama ila hukumat al-Quds al-Sharif min al-ab Rimigio Busayli, katib Terra Sancta, haziran sanat 1865. Tubi'a bi-Urshalim fi Dayr al-Ruhban al-Fransiscan.*" The pamphlet, which defends the rights of the Franciscan Terra Sancta order to a cave located in Bethlehem, is addressed to the Ottoman authorities.

15. The book is Shehadi and Nicola Khuri, *Khulasat tarikh kanisat urshalim al-urthoduksiyya* [A summary history of the orthodox church of Jerusalem] (Jerusalem: Matba'at Bayt al-Maqdis, 1925).

16. The editorial entitled "Jerusalem" in *The Times,* December 11, 1917, the day General Allenby entered Jerusalem, begins by stating that "The deliverance of

Jerusalem . . . must remain for all time a most memorable event in the history of Christendom"; describes the war itself as "a crusade for human liberties"; states that "the yoke of the Turk is broken for ever"; and discusses at length the history of the Crusades, indicating that a consciousness of this religious rivalry still remained alive. See Ronald Storrs, *Orientations* (London: Weidenfeld and Nicholson, 1945), the auto-biography of the man who was British military governor of the city from 1917 until 1920, for further evidence of this consciousness.

17. For analyses of this phenomenon, see Hassan Haddad and Donald Wagner, eds., *All in the Name of the Bible: Selected Essays on Israel and American Christian Fundamentalism* (Brattleboro: Amana, 1986).

18. Most later Islamic traditions—the text of the Qur'an (37:100–111) is not explicit—place the sacrifice at Mecca, although the Islamic commentators on the Qur'an state that Abraham was "in the fertile land of Syria and Palestine" at this time, according to the commentary on this passage in 'Abdullah Yusuf 'Ali, ed., *The Holy Qur'an: Text, Translation and Commentary* (Brentwood, MD: Amana, 1409/1989), p. 1149, n. 4096 [this is a reprint of the official Saudi translation of the Qur'an (Medina, 1405/1985)]. The only other divergence among the beliefs of adherents of the three monotheistic faiths is that the Muslim commentators unanimously consider Isma'il, Abraham's eldest son, to have been the intended victim, rather than Isaac. Although the relevant verses of the Qur'an are ambiguous in not mentioning Isma'il by name, the subsequent reference to Isaac and the clear implication that the intended victim was Abraham's eldest son bear out the traditional interpretation of these verses by the commentators as concerning Isma'il.

19. The mosque was first constructed some time between 636 and 670, and the dome was erected in 692 by the Umayyad caliph 'Abd al-Malik. See Rashid Khalidi, "The Future of Arab Jerusalem," *British Journal of Middle East Studies* 19, no. 2 (Fall 1992): 133–143, for more details on problems related to areas around the Haram al-Sharif.

20. Herod, who was imposed on Judea as a ruler by the Romans after the extinction of the Hasmonean dynasty, was "a Jew by religion" but not by origin. His father was Jewish, but his mother was a Nabatean princess from what is today Jordan. Culturally, Herod was thoroughly Roman. The words are those of the Israeli archaeologist Meir Ben Dov, *In the Shadow of the Temple: The Discovery of Ancient Jerusalem* (Jerusalem: Keter, 1985), p. 62.

21. This is true even in a relatively enlightened work such as that of Ben-Dov, *In The Shadow*. In it, he devotes 380 pages to a study of excavations around the southern end of the *Haram al-Sharif*, including his own discoveries of a series of massive and hitherto unknown seventh or eight century Umayyad buildings of great significance, without once mentioning the term *Haram al-Sharif*, the name used by Muslims for thirteen centuries for what he calls the Temple Mount.

22. The pretext later invoked for the shootings was that the Palestinians inside the *Haram* were throwing stones at Jewish worshippers at the Wailing Wall plaza below, an allegation that careful journalistic investigation later revealed was false. It is impossible to see the plaza from the *Haram*, given the high arcade that surrounds the latter, and the Palestinians were in fact throwing stones at Israeli security forces shooting at them from atop the *Haram*'s western wall and adjacent roofs. It has since been established that most Jewish worshippers were gone before stones thrown at the soldiers went over the arcade and into the plaza. See Michael Emery, "New Videotapes Reveal Israeli Cover-up" *The Village Voice*, November 13, 1990, pp. 25–29, and the reportage

by Mike Wallace on *60 Minutes*, December 2, 1990. For a detailed account based on testimonies of eyewitnesses, see Raja Shehadeh, *The Sealed Room* (London: Quartet, 1992), pp. 24–29.

23. For details, see R. Khalidi, "The Future." Moshe Gil writes in *A History of Palestine, 640–1099* (Cambridge: Cambridge University Press, 1992), pp. 646–650, of a Jewish synagogue during the early Muslim period which he locates in the vicinity of the Western Wall, but his pinpointing of its location seems singularly vague. He does state (p. 646) that in Jewish sources of that period, "we find that the Western Wall is mentioned almost not at all," while with regard to *Bab al-Rahme* (sometimes known as *Bawabat al-Rahme*, or Gates of Mercy) on the eastern side of the *Haram*, he notes (p. 643) that "the Jews of this period . . . used to visit the gate and pray alongside it, and write about it, mentioning its name (in the singular or the plural) in letters."

24. Gil, in *A History*, a revised version of his Hebrew-language work, *Eretz Israel during the First Muslim Period* (a more apt title than the English one, given the book's focus on the history of the Jewish community in Palestine) pp. 90 ff., states that the Muslims' veneration for Jerusalem began decades after they took the city, but fails to account for manifold indications of its sanctity to the earliest Muslims. These include the attention supposedly paid to Jerusalem and to the *Haram* by the caliph 'Umar, which Gil himself describes; the building of a large mosque on the site of the present *al-Aqsa* mosque, traditionally ascribed to 'Umar, but historically datable at least as far back as 670, when a large wooden structure was described in an account by a Christian pilgrim, Bishop Arculf; the sanctity attached to Jerusalem by the Prophet Muhammad in making it the first direction of prayer before Mecca was finally chosen; and the reference to *al-Masjid al-Aqsa* ("the farthest mosque") in the Qur'an. Gil argues that traditions relating this verse to Jerusalem are late ones, begging the question of how the earliest Muslims understood this verse, if not as referring to Jerusalem.

25. Ben Dov claims (*In the Shadow*, p. 286) that Muslim devotion to this site dates back only to the nineteenth century, and was a response to the growth of Jewish interest in the adjacent Wailing Wall. He refers to a fifteenth-sixteenth century work by the historian 'Abd al-Rahman b. Muhammdad al-'Ulaymi, known as Mujir al-Din, to show that Muslims earlier connected *al-Buraq* to *Bab al-Rahme* on the eastern side of the *Haram*. Mujir al-Din (d. 1521) does suggest this in *al-Uns al-jalil bi-tarikh al-Quds wal-Khalil* [The glorious history of Jerusalem and Hebron], 2 vols. (Amman: Maktabat al-Muhtasib, 1973), 2:28. But a much earlier source, *Ba'ith al-nufus ila ziyarat al-Quds al-mahrus* [Inspiration to souls to visit protected Jerusalem] (Khalidi Library MS), by Ibrahim b. Ishaq al-Ansari, known as Ibn Furkah (d. 1328), states (p. 26) that *al-Buraq* was tethered outside *Bab al-Nabi*, an old name for a gate that both Gil himself (*A History*, p. 645), and Mujir al-Din (*al-Uns al-jalil*, 2:31), identify with the very site along the southwestern wall of the *Haram* venerated by Muslims today! This dispute about the tethering place of an apocryphal winged horse shows that otherwise sober scholars risk getting carried away where religious claims in Jerusalem are concerned.

26. See R. Khalidi, "The Future" for more details on the destruction of *Haret al-Maghariba*.

27. Ben-Dov, *In the Shadow*, p. 378.

28. Two contrasting but complementary perspectives on the role of history and archaeology in the construction of Palestinian identity can be found in Meir Litvak, "A Palestinian Past: National Construction and Reconstruction," *History and Memory: Studies in the Representation of the Past* 6, no. 2 (Fall/Winter 1994): 24–56; and Albert

Glock, "Cultural Bias in the Archaeology of Palestine," *Journal of Palestine Studies* 24, no. 2 (Winter 1995): 48–59.

29. For details on how Christian and Muslim antiquities unearthed at this and other sites in the Old City of Jerusalem are treated, and the "privileging" of some, see Abu El-Hajj, "Excavating the Land," chapter 3. Another perspective on the significance of Jerusalem can be found in Jerome Murphy-O'Connor, *The Holy Land: An Archaeological Guide from Earliest Times to 1700*, 2nd ed. (Oxford: Oxford University Press, 1986), a work of erudition that occasionally betrays the author's preference for biblical antiquities over those of succeeding eras. Fr. Murphy-O'Connor sometimes goes beyond the mere expression of preferences, as with his occasional derogatory comments on structures associated with the Eastern churches, such as parts of the Holy Sepulcher (e.g., p. 49, where he describes the monument over Jesus' tomb as a "hideous kiosk"), or his description of Nablus: "the town has nothing to offer visitors, and the uncertain temper of the populace counsels speedy transit" (p. 309). Besides slighting the blameless inhabitants of Nablus, this judgment ignores such antiquities as the late Mameluke-era (fifteenth–sixteenth century) Qasr Touqan, an extensive palace-fortress in the heart of the old *qasaba* which was dynamited and partially destroyed by the Israeli military in reprisal for the killing of a soldier in 1989.

30. Smith, "The Origins," pp. 357–358, is particularly illuminating on "the uses of history" by "nationalist educator-intellectuals" to "direct the communal destiny by telling us who we are, whence we come and why we are unique."

31. Sa'id al-Husayni and Ruhi al-Khalidi were deputies for Jerusalem in the Ottoman Parliament elected in 1908, and put forward Palestinian and Arab concerns there, while remaining loyal to the Ottoman state; Najib Nassar and 'Isa al-'Isa were the most prominent newspaper editors of this period, whose papers, *al-Karmil* and *Filastin* were instrumental in shaping early Palestinian national consciousness and in stirring opposition to Zionism; Muhammad Hassan al-Budayri and 'Arif al-'Arif were the editors of a newspaper called *Suriyya al-Janubiyya* [Southern Syria], a pan-Arab journal of the post World War I era, and the main nationalist organ before its suppression by the British in 1920; Musa al-'Alami was a prominent lawyer, educator, and political figure, whose autobiography, *Palestine is my Country: The Story of Musa al-Alami* (London: Murray, 1969), shows how he looked at these different sources of identity.

32. On the way this process developed in these countries, see, *inter alia*, Israel Gershoni and James Jankowski, *Egypt, Islam and the Arabs: The Search for Egyptian Nationhood, 1900–1930* (New York: Oxford University Press, 1986), and *Redefining the Egyptian Nation, 1930–1945* (Cambridge: Cambridge University Press, 1995); Hanna Batatu, *The Old Social Classes and the Revolutionary Movements of Iraq* (Princeton: Princeton University Press, 1978); Philip Khoury, *Syria and the French Mandate: The Politics of Arab Nationalism, 1920–1945* (Princeton: Princeton University Press, 1987); and Kamal Salibi, *A House of Many Mansions: The History of Lebanon Reconsidered* (Berkeley: University of California Press, 1988).

33. An extreme, albeit typical, example of this view can be found in M. Curtis, J. Neyer, C. Waxman, and A. Pollack, eds., *The Palestinians: People, History, Politics* (New Brunswick: Transaction, 1975), p.4: "Palestinian Arab nationalism, stimulated by and reacting to the Jewish national liberation movement of Zionism, is even more recent. . . . Its chief impetus has come from opposition to Jewish settlement and to the State of Israel."

34. For more on the stimuli to Palestinian nationalism other than Zionism, in particular the disillusionment of many leading Palestinian Arabists with the incarnation

of Arab nationalism in Faysal's state in Syria in 1918–1920, and their reaction to the incipient nation-state nationalism of Syrians and others in Damascus during this period, see Muslih, *The Origins of Palestinian Nationalism.*

35. The best analysis of conflicting Lebanese national narratives is by Kamal Salibi, in his *A House of Many Mansions.* This is one of the most radical critiques extant of the national myths of any Arab country, and of some shared Arab national myths. See also Ahmad Beydoun's perceptive *al-Sira' 'ala tarikh Lubnan, aw al-hawiyya wal-zaman fi a'mal mu'arikhina al-mu'asirin* [The struggle over the history of Lebanon: Identity and time in the work of our modern historians] (Beirut: Lebanese University Press, 1989).

36. In *Palestine in Transformation, 1856–1882* (Washington, DC: Institute for Palestine Studies, 1993), Alexander Schölch shows convincingly how the idea of the Holy Land which had developed over centuries among Christians and Muslims helped to shape the modern concept of Palestine as a unit in the minds of its Arab inhabitants. We shall come back to this process in several different contexts, in the greatest detail in chapter 7, below.

37. The Ottomans in 1874 elevated the Jerusalem *sancak*, or district (including the area from the Jordan to the sea, and from a line north of Jaffa and Jerusalem to the region south of Beersheba, and encompassing Jerusalem, Jaffa, Gaza, Beersheba, Hebron, and Bethlehem) to the status of an independent administrative unit reporting directly to Istanbul. Earlier, Palestine was usually included as the separate *sancak*'s of Jerusalem, Nablus, and Acre in the *vilayet* [province] of Sidon, or in the *vilayet* of Syria. Under the Ottomans, Palestine was always administratively separate from the area east of the Jordan, which was governed directly from Damascus. The administrative boundaries of Ottoman Palestine were finally fixed in the 1880s, when the *sancak*s of Nablus and Acre were attached to the new *vilayet* of Beirut, an arrangement that remained stable until 1918.

38. Beshara Doumani, *Rediscovering Palestine,* is an excellent study of regional loyalty focusing on Jabal Nablus; he quotes a nineteenth century foreign observer as noting that its "inhabitants . . . are most proud of it, and think there is no place in the world equal to it" (p. 21). Doumani describes the Jabal Nablus region as a "social space" similar to Jabal al-Quds and Jabal al-Khalil, the regions centering on Jerusalem and Hebron respectively, noting how each differed from the other in significant respects.

39. This was the premise of the Johnston Plan, which American policymakers in the 1950s hoped would lead to the assimilation of the refugees into the surrounding countries: see Deborah J. Gerner, "Missed Opportunities and Roads not Taken: The Eisenhower Administration and the Palestinians," in *U.S. Policy on Palestine from Wilson to Clinton,* pp. 81–112 (Normal, IL: Association of Arab-American University Graduates, 1995). After a visit to the region, Secretary of State John Foster Dulles expressed the belief in a radio address to the nation on June 1, 1953 that most of the Palestinian refugees (described by him as "Arab refugees who fled from Palestine as Israel took over") should "be integrated into the lives of the neighboring Arab countries." *The Department of State Bulletin,* 27, no. 729 (June 15, 1953): 832.

40. On this matter many Zionist leaders and British officials were agreed in 1918, when Chaim Weizmann wrote that "The present state of affairs would necessarily tend towards the creation of an Arab Palestine, if there were an Arab people in Palestine," and William Ormsby-Gore (Assistant Secretary of the War Cabinet and later Colonial Secretary) stated that " . . . west of the Jordan the people were not Arabs, but only Arabic-speaking." Cited in Doreen Warriner, comp., *Palestine Papers, 1917–1922: Seeds of Conflict* (London: John Murray, 1972), pp. 32–33.

41. The details are recorded in Avi Shlaim *Collusion Across the Jordan* (New York: Columbia University Press, 1990), and Mary Wilson, *King Abdullah, Britain, and the Making of Jordan* (Cambridge: Cambridge University Press, 1988). Although the British in 1939 modified the unconditional support they had shown for Zionism for more than two decades, this change in policy was itself limited by Winston Churchill (as Prime Minister from 1940 to 1945), perhaps the most ardent Zionist in British public life, and by the fact that British hostility to Palestinian aspirations and leadership remained unabated.

42. Although much past writing on this subject has blurred this harsh reality, more recent research has borne it out: e.g. Anita Shapira, *Land and Power: The Zionist Recourse to Force, 1881–1948* (New York: Oxford University Press, 1992); Nur Masalha, *Expulsion of the Palestinians: The Concept of "Transfer" in Zionist Political Thought, 1882–1948* (Washington, DC: Institute for Palestine Studies, 1992); see also Zachary Lockman, *Comrades and Enemies: Arab and Jewish Workers in Palestine, 1906–1948* (Berkeley: University of California Press, 1996).

43. Neville Mandel, *Arab Reactions to Zionism 1882–1914* (Berkeley: University of California Press, 1986), is the best work on this early period. See also Rashid Khalidi, "The Role of the Press in the Early Arab Reaction to Zionism," *Peuples Méditerranéens/Mediterranean Peoples*, 20 (July–September 1982): 105–124, and chapter 6, below.

44. The entire text of the letter is quoted in Adel Manna', *A'lam Filastin fi awakhir al-'ahd al-'uthmani 1800–1918* [Notables of Palestine in the late Ottoman era] (Beirut: Institute for Palestine Studies, 1994), p. 190.

45. Iraq was far more afflicted by these problems than Syria, partly because the three Ottoman provinces, Basra, Baghdad, and Mosul, out of which the British had created Iraq, had little in common with one another, and their population was deeply divided on sectarian, ethnic, and other grounds—between Sunni and Shi'a, Arab and Kurd, urban and rural, settled and tribal populations. See Batatu, *Old Social Classes*. Syria suffered from some of these problems, but was a more homogenous society than Iraq, with a larger urban and settled population, a clear Sunni majority, less diversity among regions, and only two Ottoman provinces, Damascus and Aleppo, to be subsumed under the structure of a single state.

46. For the best account of how the Mandate systematically excluded Palestinians from senior positions of responsibility, see Bernard Wasserstein, *The British in Palestine: The Mandatory Government and the Arab-Jewish Conflict, 1917–1929*, 2nd ed. (Oxford: Blackwell, 1991), pp. 166–195.

47. The British tactic of reinforcing and manipulating traditional social structures in rural areas as a prop for their rule is examined by Ylana Miller, *Government and Society in Rural Palestine 1920–1948* (Austin: University of Texas Press, 1985). This policy was continued by Jordan in the West Bank from 1948 until 1967, and by Israel in Arab areas incorporated into Israel after 1948, and in the occupied West Bank after 1967. For an analysis that stresses the dichotomy between the coastal plain and the hill areas, see Baruch Kimmerling and Joel Migdal, *Palestinians: The Making of a People* (New York: Free Press, 1993). For a more sophisticated approach showing the interrelations between them in an earlier period, see Doumani, *Rediscovering Palestine*.

48. Population estimates are from Alfred Bonné, ed., *Statistical Handbook of Middle Eastern Countries*, 2nd ed. (Jerusalem: Economic Research Institute of the Jewish Agency for Palestine, 1945), pp. 3, 99.

49. For more on the coastal cities, see May Seikaly, *Haifa: Transformation of an Arab Palestinian Society, 1918–1939* (London: I. B. Tauris, 1995), and Lockman, *Comrades and Enemies*, as well as Kimmerling and Migdal, *Palestinians*.

50. Although the press was extremely active, and a number of political parties existed in Palestine in the 1930s, most of these parties were essentially vehicles for narrow family or individual interests, as were some of the newspapers. *Hizb al-Istiqlal al-'Arabi*, founded by 'Auni 'Abd al-Hadi, was probably the most developed example of a modern political party in Palestine. It is the subject of a University of Chicago Department of Near East Languages and Civilization dissertation in progress by L. Don Matthews, entitled "The Arab Istiqlal Party in Palestine, 1925–1934."

51. Ted Swedenburg, "The Role of the Palestinian Peasantry in the Great Revolt (1936–1939)," in E. Burke III and I. Lapidus, eds., *Islam, Politics and Social Movements*, pp. 169–203 (Berkeley: University of California Press, 1988). His book, *Memories of Revolt: The 1936–1939 Rebellion and the Palestinian National Past* (Minneapolis: University of Minnesota Press, 1955) is perhaps the best study of the revolt.

52. With the reestablishment of the Palestinian national movement in the West Bank and Gaza Strip after the PLO-Israel accords, it remains to be determined to what degree the development of effective modern institutions and structures that transcend these parochial divisions will make it possible to overcome the persistence of personal, family, regional and sectarian rivalries.

53. In *Imagined Communities*, p.6, Anderson defines a nation as "an imagined political community . . . imagined as both inherently limited and sovereign."

54. The article was published after the Ottoman Constitutional Revolution of July 1908, which liberated the press from the censorship of the old regime, making possible the freer expression of nationalist ideas.

55. *Le Réveil de la nation arabe* (Paris: n.p., 1905), predicted an inevitable collision between Zionism and Arabism in its opening paragraph. On 'Azuri, who was Lebanese by origin, see Mandel, *The Arabs and Zionism*, pp. 49–52.

56. Cited in n. 36. References to "the land of Palestine" are widespread in the Arabic-language press in Palestine and elsewhere before 1914. A typical example is a lengthy article on Zionism in the Beirut newspaper *al-Ittihad al-'Uthmani*, no. 559, July 19, 1910, p. 2, which warns against "Zionist colonization, in other words foreign seizure, of the land of Palestine."

57. These sites are mentioned repeatedly, e.g., in Mujir al-Din's fifteenth century *al-Uns al-jalil*, and in earlier works of this genre. They refer also to sites throughout Syria that are seen as having a certain sanctity, although a special place is reserved for Palestine, and Jerusalem in particular. Eleven sayings attributed to the Prophet Muhammad that have this same focus are recorded in the standard *hadith* compilations: Husni Adham Jarrar, *al-Hajj Amin al-Husayni* (Amman: Dar al-Dia', 1987), pp. 6–8.

58. For background, see Amnon Cohen, *Palestine in the Eighteenth Century* (Jerusalem: Hebrew University, 1985), and Fatma Müge Göçek, *East Encounters West: France and the Ottoman Empire in the Eighteenth Century* (New York: Oxford University Press, 1987).

59. This undated document in Arabic is located in the Khalidi Library in Jerusalem together with more than 300 documents that originate in the local Islamic court, the *mahkama shar'iyya*, from the seventeenth through the early twentieth centuries. During this time, members of the Khalidi family often held the senior local post in this court, as chief secretary and deputy to the *qadi*, who was appointed from Istanbul, and

generally served for only one year. For more on the Islamic religious hierarchy under the Ottomans, see Madeleine Zilfi, *The Politics of Piety: The Ottoman Ulema in the Post-Classical Age* (Minneapolis: Biblioteca Islamica, 1988), and R. C. Repp, *The Mufti of Istanbul: A Study in the Development of the Ottoman Learned Hierarchy* (London: Ithaca Press, 1986).

60. *Awwal [sic] al-qiblatayn wa thalith al-haramayn al-sharifayn.*

61. The assembled dignitaries expressed their displeasure that the Frenchman was entitled by the document he carried to receive treatment "like the Muslim Beys," including riding a horse and carrying weapons.

62. The wording could also mean "this region of Jerusalem," but either reading is possible, and there is an implication of sanctity in both cases. That this petition was not exceptional in its stress on the sanctity of Jerusalem is indicated by another more routine one in Ottoman Turkish, dating from later in the eighteenth century. In this undated petition, a large number of Jerusalem notables complain about the misbehavior of local military personnel in the city. The petition begins by stressing that Jerusalem is the "third of the holy places, its nobility protected until the day of Resurrection." The document, signed by the qadi of Jerusalem, Ma'nzade Muhammad, is also located in the Khalidi Library, Jerusalem.

63. Kamil J. Asali, "Jerusalem under the Ottomans 1516–1917 A.D.," in K.J. Asali, ed., *Jerusalem in History*, p. 219.

64. The two articles were in nos. 551 and 552, December 19 and 20, 1910. Two later articles deal with the sale, one of a series of sales by the wealthy Sursuq family of Beirut of property in the fertile and strategic Marj Ibn 'Amir (Jezreel Valley). For more on the al-Fula sale and its repercussions, see chapters 5 and 6 below.

65. Articles on the subject were widely reprinted in such papers as *Filastin* in Jaffa and *al-Karmil* in Haifa, as well as *al-Muqtabas* in Damascus and *Lisan al-Hal* in Beirut. In an article entitled "Majlis al-Mab'uthan: Jalsat 16 Ayyar," *Filastin*, May 27, 1911, pp. 1–2, carries lengthy citations from the texts of the Parliamentary speeches, having earlier carried summaries. The most extensive account of al-'Asali's speech, including his reference to Saladin, is "al-Isti'mar al-sihuyini fi majlis al-umma: Khitab rannan," [Zionist colonization in the Chamber of Deputies: A ringing speech] *al-Muqtabas*, no. 691, May 18, 1911, pp. 1–2.

66. This parliamentary debate will be discussed further in chapter 4 below.

67. For more on this election, see Rashid Khalidi, "The 1912 Election Campaign in the Cities of *Bilad al-Sham*," *International Journal of Middle East Studies* 16, no. 4 (November 1984): 461–474.

68. Zionism concerned al-Khalidi so greatly that he made an extensive study of the subject, about which he was completing a book when he died in 1913; it is described further in chapter 4, below.

69. The first use of the term "Palestinians" (*"filistiniyun"* in Arabic) which has been found is in the press of the 1908–1914 period; for examples see the final section of the following chapter.

70. Quotes are from *Filastin* and *al-Muqtabas*, cited in n. 65.

71. For a discussion of all of these problems, see Rashid Khalidi, "Arab Nationalism: Historical Problems in the Literature," *The American Historical Review* 95, no. 5 (December 1991): 1363–1364. Gil's *A History* illustrates the final ones mentioned perfectly: of its 840 pages, the last 350 are devoted almost exclusively to the history of the tiny Palestinian Jewish community, as are generous sections of the earlier parts of the book.

Chapter 3. Cultural Life and Identity in Late Ottoman Palestine:
The Place of Jerusalem

1. See Rashid Khalidi, "Ottomanism and Arabism in Syria Before 1914: A Reassessment," in R. Khalidi, L. Anderson, R. Simon, and M. Muslih, eds., *The Origins of Arab Nationalism*, pp. 55–57 (New York: Columbia University Press, 1991), for more on the contrast between the cities of the littoral and the interior in greater Syria. See n. 5, below, for the possibility that Nablus may have been bigger than Jerusalem in the mid-nineteenth century. On the problems of urban demographic analysis in Palestine during this period, see Justin McCarthy, *The Population of Palestine: Population Statistics of the Late Ottoman Period and the Mandate* (New York: Columbia University Press, 1990), pp. 15–16, and Yehoshua Ben Arieh, "The Population of the Large Towns in Palestine during the first Eighty Years of the Nineteenth Century, According to Western Sources," in M. Ma'oz, ed., *Studies on Palestine during the Ottoman Period*, pp. 49–69 (Jerusalem: The Magnes Press, 1975), especially the table on p.68.

2. For more on the growth of the coastal cities, especially Jaffa and Haifa, see Ruth Kark, "The Rise and Decline of Coastal Towns in Palestine," in G. Gilbar, ed., *Ottoman Palestine 1800–1914: Studies in Economic and Social History*, pp. 69–90 (Leiden: Brill, 1990), as well as Seikaly, *Haifa*, Lockman, *Comrades and Enemies*, and Kimmerling and Migdal, *Palestinians*. See also Mahmud Yazbak, *al-Nuzum al-idariyya wal-buna al-ijtima'iyya fi Haifa fi awakhir al-'ahd al-'uthmani* [Administrative arrangements and social structure in Haifa at the end of the Ottoman era] (Nazareth: al-Nahda Press, 1994).

3. McCarthy, *The Population of Palestine*, p. 163.

4. Kimmerling and Migdal, *Palestinians*, correctly stress the importance of Jaffa and Nablus, but in doing so slight Jerusalem and Haifa: for a more detailed critique of their approach, see my review of their book in *The American Historical Review* 99, no. 3 (June 1994): 947–948.

5. Doumani, *Rediscovering Palestine*, p. 1. He also suggests (p. 25) that in 1850 Nablus was "possibly the largest city in Palestine," on the basis of figures cited in his "The Political Economy of Population Counts in Ottoman Palestine: Nablus, circa 1850," *International Journal of Middle East Studies* 26, no. 1 (February 1994): 1–17.

6. Two works that treat this process in detail and with exceptional acuity are Schölch, *Palestine in Transformation*, for the period 1856–1882, and Haim Gerber, *Ottoman Rule in Jerusalem, 1890–1914*, Unterschungen, Islamkundliche vol. 101 (Berlin: Klaus Schwarz, 1985).

7. For what remains the best analysis of the position of the provincial Arab notables before these changes took place, see the seminal article by Albert Hourani which first proposed the concept of "the notables," "Ottoman Reform and the Politics of the Notables" in W. Polk and R. Chambers, eds., *The Beginnings of Modernization in the Middle East: The Nineteenth Century*, pp. 41–68 (Chicago: University of Chicago Press, 1968).

8. The expansion of the state educational system is examined in a Ph.D. dissertation by Ben Fortna, entitled "Ottoman State Schools During the Reign of Abdul Hamit, 1876–1908," Department of Near Eastern Languages and Literature, University of Chicago, 1997.

9. Published beginning in 1876, the *Mecelle* (*Majallat al-ahkam al-'adliyya* in Arabic) was applied in the new state *Nizamiye* courts, while the shari'a courts continued to use the traditional sources of Islamic jurisprudence.

10. For illustrations of this autonomy in several major Arab centers in the eighteenth century see Abdul-Karim Rafeq, *The Province of Damascus 1723–1783* (Beirut: Khayat, 1970); Percy Kemp, *Territoires d'Islam: Le monde vu de Mossoul au xvii siècle* (Paris: Sindbad, 1982); Abraham Marcus, *The Middle East on the Eve of Modernity: Aleppo in the Eighteenth Century* (New York: Columbia University Press, 1989); and Daniel Crecelius, *The Roots of Modern Egypt: A Study of the Regimes of 'Ali Bey al-Kabir and Muhammad Bey Abu al-Dhahab* (Minneapolis: Biblioteca Islamica, 1981).

11. See Zilfi, *The Politics of Piety.* Among those who reached such high levels was the Jerusalemite Musa Effendi al-Khalidi, who was *Kadiasker* of Anatolia in 1832, and whose daughter, Khadija, bequeathed the sum with which the Khalidi Library, *al-Maktaba al-Khalidiyya*, was established at the turn of the twentieth century by her grandson, al-Hajj Raghib al-Khalidi. See also Haim Gerber, *State, Society and Law in Islam: Ottoman Law in Comparative Perspective* (Albany: State University of New York Press, 1994), chapter 2, "The Making of Ottoman Law: The Rise of the *Kadi* and the *Shari'a* court," pp. 58–78.

12. The original document, located in the Khalidi Library, Jerusalem, is dated 27 Rajab 1213 = 5 January 1799.

13. *Diwan Labid al-'Amiri, riwayat al-Tusi* [title in German: *Der Diwan des Lebid*] (Vienna: Carl Gerold, for the Imperial Academy of Science, 1880), pp. 148–149.

14. See David Dean Commins, *Islamic Reform: Politics and Social Change in Late Ottoman Syria* (New York: Oxford University Press, 1990), p.91.

15. Of the 255 manuscripts of the al-Aqsa Library that have been catalogued and bear a date of copying, 39 were copied in the nineteenth and early twentieth centuries, the majority of them after 1850. This can be deduced from the two-volume work edited by Khadr Ibrahim Salama, Director of the Library, entitled *Fihras makhtutat maktabat al-Masjid al-Aqsa* [Index of manuscripts in the al-Aqsa Library], vol. 1 (Jerusalem: Awqaf Administration, 1980); vol. 2 (Amman: al-Majma' al-Maliki li-Buhuth al-Hadara al-Islamiyya, 1983).

16. This is clear from the two-volume catalogue compiled by Khudr Ibrahim Salama, *Fihris makhtutat al-Maktaba al-Budayriyya* [Index of manuscripts in the al-Budayriyya Library] (Jerusalem: Awqaf Administration, 1987).

17. A much-delayed annotated catalogue of the Library's manuscript holdings is scheduled to be completed in 1997, and published soon thereafter. See L. Conrad and B. Kellner-Heinkele, "Ottoman Resources in the Khalidi Library in Jerusalem," in A. Singer and A. Cohen, eds., *Scripta Hierosolymitana*, 30, *Aspects of Ottoman History*, pp. 280–293 (Jerusalem: Magnes Press, 1994).

18. The ongoing cataloging of printed books in this library should be completed in 1997 as well.

19. This was a one-volume edition of *al-Muqaddima*, without the remaining volumes of the author's *Kitab al-'Ibar.* There are older Arabic- and Turkish-language printed books in the library in other fields.

20. These include five sets of the standard 7-volume 1284/1867 Bulaq edition of Ibn Khaldun's *Kitab al-'Ibar* in its entirety, including the *Muqaddima*; three sets of the 1283/1866 Bulaq edition of al-Kutubi's *Fawat al-Wafayat*; two of the 1284/1867 Cairo edition of al-Muhibbi's *Khulasat al-Athar*; four of the 1286/1869 Istanbul edition of Abu al-Fida's *Tarikh*; three of the 1291/1874 Bulaq edition of al-Muradi's *Silk al-Durar*; two copies of the 1297/1879 Cairo edition of al-Jabarti's *'Aja'ib al-Athar*; four of the 1299/1881 Bulaq edition of Ibn Khallikan's *Wafayat al-A'yan*; and four of the 1303/1885 Cairo edition of Ibn al-Athir's *al-Kamil fil-Tarikh*.

21. In 1918, Massignon visited the library and donated an inscribed copy of his 1913 edition of al-Hallaj's *Kitab al-Tawasin*. The visitors' book of the library contains the names of numerous ulama' and Western scholars, and is an indication of the role it played in the intellectual life of the city, particularly in the first decades after its establishment.

22. The best work treating the *salafi* movement in a specific context is Commins, *Islamic Reform.*

23. On al-Jaza'iri, see Joseph Escovitz, " 'He was the Muhammad 'Abdu of Syria': A Study of Tahir al-Jaza'iri and his Influence," *International Journal of Middle East Studies* 18, no. 3 (August 1986): 293–310.

24. Fourteen volumes of his influential periodical, *al-Manar*, are also among the Library's holdings.

25. The work by 'Abdu, one of many in the library, is his report on the reform of the shari'a courts in Egypt, with an introduction by Rashid Rida: *Taqrir fadilat Mufti al-Diyar al-Misriyya, al-Ustadh al-Shaykh Muhammad 'Abdu fi islah al-mahakim al-shar'iyya* [Report of his Excellency the Mufti of Egypt, al-Ustadh al-Shaykh Muhammad 'Abdu regarding reform of the religious courts] (Cairo: al-Manar, 1317/1900).

26. The photo is inscribed on the verso by al-Afghani (who signs himself "Jamal al-Din al-Asadabadi") with the words: "Tidhkar ila alif al-haq wa halif al-sidq wa 'ashiq al-'adl, mab'uth al-Quds al-Sharif sahib al-sa'ada Yusuf Diya' Basha al- Qudsi al-Khalidi" [A momento to the supporter of right, ally of uprightness and lover of justice, Deputy of Jerusalem, His Excellency Yusuf Diya' Paşa al-Qudsi al-Khalidi].

27. The Library has three copies of one book, which originally belonged to different members of the family, *Kitab al-husun al-hamidiyya li-muhafazat al-'aqa'id al-islamiyya* [Praiseworthy virtues of preserving Islamic beliefs] (Tripoli: Muhammad Kamil al-Buhayri, n.d.). Multiple copies also exist of al-Jisr's *Kitab al-risala al-hamidiyya fi haqiqat al-diyana al-islamiyya wa haqqiyyat al-shari'a al-muhammadiyya* [Praiseworthy essay on the truth of the Islamic religion and the verity of Muhammadan law] (Beirut: Hassan al-Qaraq, 1305/1890). The frequent utilization of the term "*hamidiyya*" in the titles of these and other works is a reference to Sultan 'Abd al-Hamid, and constitutes an obvious attempt by the authors to obtain the favor of the autocratic, mercurial, and vain Sultan.

28. (Paris: Firmin-Didot, 1884). This volume was dedicated to Yusuf Diya' al-Khalidi in Istanbul in 1888 by a former student with the inscription "Resurgat Arabia!" The other works by Le Bon in the library are: *Ruh al-Akvam*, a Turkish translation by Abdullah Cevdet of *Les Lois psychologiques de l'evolution des peuples* (Cairo: Matba'at al-Ijtihad, 1908); *Ruh al-ijtima'*, a translation by Ahmad Fathi Zahglul Paşa of *La Psychologie des Foules* (Cairo: Matba'at al-Rahmaniyya, 1909); *Sir tatawwur al-umam*, a translation by Ahmad Fathi Zaghlul Paşa of *Les Lois psychologiques de l'évolution des peuples* (Cairo: Matba'at al-Rahmaniyya, 1909); *Muqadimmat al-Hadarat al-uwla*, a translation by Muhammad Sadiq Rustum of the introduction to *Les premieres civilisations* (Cairo: al-Matba'a al-Salafiyya, 1341/1922); and *Ruh al-tarbiyya*, a translation by Taha Husayn of *Psychologie de l'Education* (Cairo: Dar al-Hilal, 1925).

29. One example was the Palestine Educational Company, established in Jerusalem in 1910 (with a branch later established in Jaffa) by Wadi' Sa'id. By 1930 this had become the largest Arab bookseller in Palestine: see their half-page advertisement in Luke and Keith-Roach, eds., *The Handbook of Palestine and Trans-Jordan*, 2nd ed. (London: Macmillan, 1930), ads, p. 24.

30. The term *qutr* means region, country, or land. In current parlance, influenced by Arab nationalist denigrations of the existing Arab nation-states, "region" would usually be the most accurate rendering of the word (e.g. *"al-qutr al-suri,"* literally "the Syrian region," meaning the state of Syria). In rendering the idiom of 1912, however, the word "country" is more appropriate.

31. *"Ila ahl al-'ilm wal-adab"* [To people of learning and culture], *al-Munadi*, no. 17, May 28, 1912, p.1.

32. *"A'lan bi-ta'sis maktaba 'umumiyya fil-Quds al-sharif,"* [Announcement of the founding of a public library in Jerusalem," n.d. [1899–1900], document located in Khalidi Library. al-Hajj Raghib al-Khalidi is the author of a two-part series entitled "al-Kulliyat al-islamiyya," *Filastin*, nos. 52 and 53, July 19 and 22, 1911, p. 1, which examines Islamic educational institutions, and then focuses on the poor state of Islamic schools in Jerusalem, which he ascribes to their being run by "ignorant fools" [*"al-juhula al-aghbiya'* "].

33. The first dependable literacy figures for Palestine date from the mandate period: among Muslims, literacy was 25% among males and 3% among females; among Christians, 72% and 44% respectively. Needless to say, the literacy rates among the Jewish population were much higher: 93% and 73% respectively: E. Mills, *Census of Palestine*, 2 vols. (London: HMSO, 1932) 2:110; see also Said Himadeh, *The Economic Organization of Palestine* (Beirut: American University of Beirut, 1938), p. 36.

34. For a discussion of these processes, see Rashid Khalidi, "Society and Ideology in Late Ottoman Syria: Class, Education, Profession and Confession," in J. Spagnolo, ed., *Problems of the Middle East in Historical Perspective: Essays in Honour of Albert Hourani*, pp. 119–132 (Reading: Ithaca Press, 1992).

35. For figures on tourists and pilgrims visiting Jerusalem at the end of the Ottoman era see Marwan Buheiry, "British Consular Reports and the Economic Evolution of Palestine: The Mutasarrifiya of Quds al-Sharif 1885–1914," paper presented to the Third International Conference on the History of Bilad al-Sham, Amman, April, 1980. The published version of this study ["The Agricultural Exports of Southern Palestine, 1885–1914," *Journal of Palestine Studies* 10, no. 4 (Summer, 1981): 61–81], omits the statistics on pilgrimage and tourism.

36. Throughout bilad al-Sham, these included institutions such as *al-Madrasa al-Wataniyya* established in Beirut by Butrus al-Bustani in 1868, the schools set up in Beirut by *Jam'iyyat al-Maqasid al-Khayriyya al-Islamiyya* [Islamic Association of Charitable Intentions] established in 1878, *al-Madrasa al-Hamidiyya*, set up in Tripoli in 1895, the famous Maktab 'Anbar in Damascus, and many others. Some were short-lived, and others like Maktab 'Anbar came under state control, but there was a constant proliferation of such schools during the last half century of Ottoman rule in the Arab provinces. They included as well such schools as the Mar Mitri secondary school set up by the Greek Orthodox Patriarchate of Jerusalem to train teachers and prepare students for seminary training as priests: "Mudhakkirat kahin al-Quds: al-Khuri Niqula al-Khuri, Bir Zayt 1885-Bayrut 1954," *Dirasat 'Arabiyya* 30, nos. 5–6 (1994): 62–76.

37. These figures are from *Salnameh Vilayet Suriyye 1288*, Damascus, 1288/1871, pp. 149–150, which does not break down the non-Muslim schools or students. This volume is nevertheless an exceedingly valuable source on Palestine and other parts of Syria for this period, containing much more data than do most other provincial *Salnames*. The Jerusalem *sancak* soon thereafter ceased to be a part of the Damascus

vilayet, and after 1874 became an autonomous *sancak*, but since it was not a *vilayet*, did not issue a provincial *Salname*.

38. Shimon Landman, *Ahya' a'yan al-Quds kharij aswariha fil-qarn al-tasi' 'ashr* [Quarters of the notables of Jerusalem outside its walls in the nineteenth century] (Tel Aviv: Dar al-Nashr al-'Arabi, 1984), pp. 93–95.

39. A.L. Tibawi, *Arab Education in Mandatory Palestine: A Study of Three Decades of British Administration* (London: Luzac, 1956), pp. 20, 270.

40. Anon., [As'ad Daghir] *Thawrat al-'arab* [Revolt of the Arabs] (Cairo, n.p., 1916), p. 133.

41. Tibawi, *Arab Education*, p. 271. Ottoman and Mandatory educational statistics are hard to compare, among other reasons, because under the Ottoman system the school age population was counted as those from seven to eleven years of age, while under the Mandate, it was those from five to fourteen.

42. On this institution see Martin Strohmeier, "*Al-Kulliyya al-Salahiyya*, a late Ottoman University in Jerusalem," unpublished article, courtesy of the author.

43. The situation continued into the early British Mandate period: according to Raqiyya al-Khalidi, who started school at the end of the Ottoman period, there were never enough places in the government or private schools for girls in Jerusalem. She herself attended both types of school in this period (interview, Jerusalem, October 7, 1993). An article in the Jerusalem paper *al-Munadi* paints a fascinating picture of the condition of the educational system in Palestine at this time, calling for the implementation of the Ottoman Constitution's promise of free universal primary education: "*al-Ta'lim al-ijbari*" [Compulsory education], *al-Munadi*, no. 19, November 6, 1912, pp. 1–2.

44. *Burnamij Madrasat Rawdat al-Ma'arif* [Syllabus of the Garden of Education School] (Jerusalem: Matba'at al-Nadi, 1331/1912).

45. For example, the schools mentioned in n. 36, about whose influence on their students much has been written: see R. Khalidi, "Society and Ideology."

46. Tibawi, *Arab Education*, p. 59.

47. Muhammad al-Shanti, "*Hadith 'an 'adliyyat al-Quds wa-ma'arifuha bayna mutasarrif al-Quds wa mudir ma'arifuha wa mudir al-Iqdam*" [Discussion on judicial and educational institutions in Jerusalem between the Governor of Jerusalem and its director of education and the director of *al-Iqdam*], *al-Iqdam*, no. 15, May 4, 1914, pp. 1–2. al-Shanti also visited six new government schools, in Jerusalem, Lydd, Ramallah, Hebron, Nablus, and Bir al-Sabi', and found that they were of high quality, and used Arabic as the first language of instruction.

48. Ibid. A leader of the Arabist *Hizb al-Lamarkaziyya* in Cairo, al-Shanti returned to Palestine upon the outbreak of the war, and was among the Arab nationalist leaders hanged by the Ottoman authorities in 1916.

49. 'Ajaj Nuwayhid, *Rijal min Filastin, ma bayna bidayat al-Qarn hatta 'am 1948* [Men from Palestine, between the beginning of the century and the year 1948] (Beirut, Manshurat Filastin al-Muhtalla, 1981), pp. 57–60.

50. *Yawmiyyat Khalil al-Sakakini: Katha ana ya dunya* [Diaries of Khalil al-Sakakini: I am thus oh world] (Jerusalem: al-Matba'a al-Tijariyya, 1955), pp. 51–52.

51. There is a long article on the school, "*al-Madrasa al-Dusturiyya al-Wataniyya fil-Quds*," in *Filastin*, no. 65, September 2, 1911, pp. 3–4, signed by its four founders.

52. A. L. Tibawi, *British Interests in Palestine 1800–1901* (Oxford: Oxford University Press, 1961), pp. 260–261.

53. Jam'iyat al-Tabshir al-Kanisiyya (C.M.S.), *al-Madrasa al-Kulliya al-Inkliziyya fil-Quds* [The English college school in Jerusalem] (Jerusalem: CMS, 1904), p. 2. For details on the lengthy feud between the Bishop and the CMS which led to the founding of St. George's School, see Tibawi, *British Interests*, pp. 237 ff.

54. Miller, *Government and Society*, pp. 98 ff.

55. "*al-Ta'lim al-ijbari*" [Compulsory education], *al-Munadi*, no. 19, November 6, 1912, pp. 1–2.

56. al-Shanti's article, cited in n. 47 above, is one example of such awareness.

57. For an example of the sacrifices parents were willing to make, see Khuri, "*Mudhakkirat*," pp. 63–66

58. For details, see Rashid Khalidi, "The Press as a Source for Modern Arab Political History," *Arab Studies Quarterly* 3, no. 1 (Winter, 1981): 22–42. The standard source on the press is Philippe de Tarazi, *Tarikh al-sihafa al-'arabiyya* [History of the Arab press], 4 vols. (Beirut: al-Matba'a al-Adabiyya and al-Matba'a al-Amarkiyya, 1913–1933). See also Ami Ayalon, *The Press in the Arab Middle East: A History* (New York: Oxford University Press, 1995).

59. Tarazi, *Tarikh*, 4: 66–68, 138–141, lists only three newspapers and periodicals founded in all of Palestine before the 1908 revolution, whereas 32 were established between then and the outbreak of World War I

60. This refers notably to comments made by some participants at a 1986 Columbia University conference on early Arab nationalism, recorded in R. Khalidi, et al., eds., *The Origins of Arab Nationalism*, p. ix.

61. Ya'qub Yehoshua, *Tarikh al-sihafa al-'arabiyya fi Filastin fil-'ahd al-'uthmani (1909–1918)* [The history of the Arab press in Palestine in the Ottoman era, 1908–1918] (Jerusalem: Matba'at al-Ma'arif, 1974), p. 17 estimates that most Palestinian newspapers in the Ottoman era printed only several hundred copies, with some of them reaching 2,000 during the Mandate period. He does, however, note (p. 44) that *al-Quds*, the most widely read Jerusalem paper, printed nearly 1,500 copies before 1914, some of which were sent abroad to immigrants to North and South America.

62. The Khalidi Library has seven years of *al-Jawa'ib*; eight years of *al-Jinan*; twenty-six years of *al-Muqtataf*; eight years of *al-Hilal*; fourteen years of *al-Manar*; and six years of *al-Muqtabas*. All are bound, and are additional to a large number of incomplete volumes of these and other periodicals.

63. The al-Aqsa Library holdings of *al-Muqtataf* are continuous from vols. 5–57; *al-Hilal* from 1–31; *al-Manar* from 1–22; and of the shorter-lived *al-Muqtabas* from 2–7.

64. Ruhi Bey al-Khalidi was a contributor, under the pseudonym "al-Maqdisi," to *al-Hilal* and a number of other periodicals and newspapers, while he was Ottoman Consul-General in Bordeaux. In 1902–1903, for example he published a series of studies of Victor Hugo and European and Arab literature in *al-Hilal*. See chapter 4 for more on his writings.

65. "*A'lan bi-ta'sis maktaba 'umumiyya fil-Quds al-sharif*," cited in n. 32, above. It is clear from the visitors' book of the Library that all manner of local and foreign scholars, and many ordinary people, availed themselves of its facilities, particularly in its first few decades of operation.

66. al-Buhayri's press was *Matba'at al-Balagha*, where among other things he printed collections of articles from his newspaper

67. In Jerusalem owners of printing presses who also published newspapers besides Hanania included Bandali Mushahwar, publisher of *al-Insaf*; Iliya Zakka, pub-

lisher of *al-Nafir* (he later moved it and his press to Haifa); and Shaykh 'Ali Rimawi, publisher of *al-Najah*; and in Jaffa 'Isa and Yusuf al-'Isa, publishers of *Filastin*.

68. *Suriyya al-Janubiyya* began publication in 1919, and lasted for less than one year; after it was closed by the British authorities, *al-Sabah* was founded in 1921. The same press may have been used to publish a paper in the Ottoman period, but the evidence is unclear.

69. Hanania complained about the small size of the Jerusalem publishing market: in an editorial in the first issue of his paper he noted that even though the Arabic-language presses in Jerusalem were few in number "they still do not find enough work": *al-Quds*, no. 1, September 18, 1908, p. 1.

70. *al-Quds*, no. 364, Setpember 30, 1913, p. 1. Hanania went on to ask: "How is an editor to make a living" in such a situation?

71. *al-Quds al-Sharif/Quds Şerif*, which was printed in Arabic and Turkish on opposite sides of the page, was first published from 1902–1907, and then resumed publication in 1913. *al-Quds* was founded in 1908 and continued publishing for the rest of the Ottoman period. *al-Najah* was founded in 1908, but did not last long. *al-Nafir*, founded in Alexandria in 1904 by Ibrahim Zakka, was moved in 1908 to Jerusalem where his cousin Iliya Zakka took it over, and then moved again to Haifa in 1913. *al-Munadi*, founded in 1912, published until the outbreak of the war, as did *al-Dustur*, founded in 1910 by Khalil al-Sakakini, and then taken over in 1913 by Jamil al-Khalidi. *Bayt al-Maqdis*, founded in 1908, seems to have appeared irregularly thereafter, only to reappear after the war, together with the papers mentioned in n. 68 above. For more details, see Tarazi, *Tarikh al-sihafa al-'arabiyya*, as well as Yusuf Khuri, comp., *al-Sihafa al-'arabiyya fi Filastin* [The Arab press in Palestine] (Beirut, Institute for Palestine Studies, 1976); and Yehoshua, *Tarikh al-sihafa al-'arabiyya fi Filastin*.

72. For details, see n. 61, above.

73. "*Mawt al-adab fi Filastin*" [The death of culture in Palestine], *al-Munadi*, no. 16, May 21, 1912, pp. 1–2. Examination of *al-Himara* reveals why it may have sold more copies than *al-Munadi*: it was printed attractively, was well-written, and included amusing cartoons. See e.g., the satirical articles ridiculing critics of the May 1911 anti-Zionist parliamentary speeches of Ruhi al-Khalidi and Shukri al-'Asali (both entitled "*Muhawara*," "Conversation"): *al-Himara*, nos. 31 and 32, June 2 and 9, 1911, p. 2.

74. What will ultimately be required is research into reading habits in the Arab world in this and other periods, along the lines of Robert Darnton's essay "First Steps Towards a History of Reading," pp. 154–187 in his *The Kiss of Lamourette: Reflections in Cultural History* (New York: Norton, 1990).

75. *Filastin*, no. 241–244, September 29, 1913, p. 1.

76. See, e.g. the editorial "*al-Ta'lim al-ijbari*" [Compulsory education], *al-Munadi*, no. 19, November 6, 1912, pp. 1–2, cited in n. 55, above.

77. Yehoshua, *Tarikh al-sihafa al-'arabiyya fi Filastin*, p. 52, who notes (pp. 53–54) that Zakka was "close to the Jews," that most of his subscribers and advertisers were Jewish, and that *al-Nafir* was described as "the hired newspaper" by *al-Munadi*, and was involved in polemics with other Palestinian papers, including *al-Quds*, *Filastin*, *al-Munadi*, and *al-Jarab al-Kurdi*.

78. "*Fi'ata al-sihyuniyya*" [The two factions of Zionism], *Filastin*, no. 84–287, November 8, 1913, p. 1.

79. Yehoshua, *Tarikh al-sihafa al-'arabiyya fi Filastin*, p. 55, n.1. This statement appeared on the masthead only with issue no. 1–48, following a brief closure of the paper. An editorial in the paper explicitly stated "you will not see in it an article which

does not concern the Palestinians or goes beyond the conditions of their country": *al-Munadi*, no. 12, April 14, 1912, p. 1.

80. Cited in notes 31 and 73 above.

81. Yehoshua, *Tarikh al-sihafa al-'arabiyya fi Filastin*, p. 54.

82. "*Aham arkan al-najah: aw al-tijara wal-sina'a wal-zira'a fi rubu' Filastin*" [The most important pillars of success: or commerce, industry and agriculture in the corners of Palestine], *al-Quds*, no. 96, October 13, 1909.

83. Muhammad al-Shanti, "*Ahadith mudir al-Iqdam ma' a'yan al-Quds,*" [*al-Iqdam*'s director converses with the notables of Jerusalem], *al-Iqdam*, no. 15, April 5, 1914, p.2.

84. One article, "*Ihtijaj ahali al-Quds*" [Protest by the people of Jerusalem], *al-Quds*, no. 268, October 17, 1911, describes a petition against the Italian attack on Libya signed by various religious dignitaries (muftis, bishops, rabbis), and by the Mayor and members of the Municipal Council as "the elected bodies of the Palestinian population"; another, "*Kitab maftuh ila mutasarrif al-liwa*" [Open letter to the governor of the province], *al-Munadi*, no. 6, March 12, 1912, attacks members of the Municipal Council as "enemies of the country"; finally, a report entitled "*Laqad faza al-itti-hadiyun*" [The Unionists have won], *al-Munadi*, no. 14, May 7, 1912, reports that the three deputies elected in 1912 for Jerusalem *sancak* were the choice of "all the land of Palestine" (*kul al-bilad al-Filistiniyya*).

85. The memoirs of Muhammad 'Izzat Darwaza, *Khamsa wa tis'una 'aman fil-hayat: Mudhakirat wa-tasjilat* [95 years of life: memoirs and records], eds., A. Jarbawi and H. Shakhshir, vol. 1 (Jerusalem: Arab Thought Forum, 1993), pp. 187 ff. give a lively account of the interplay of local organizations in Nablus, such as *Jam'iyyat al-Shaykh 'Abbas*, and Empire-wide parties like the Committee of Union and Progress [CUP].

86. Documents in the Khalidi Library show the continuing importance of the family as a social unit, as a focus for loyalty, and as a framework for a variety of activities. A letter from the founder of the Library, al-Hajj Raghib al-Khalidi, to Ruhi Bey al-Khalidi, dated 16 Ramadan 1316/1898, asking for assistance in restarting the library project that Ruhi had originally begun, is replete with references to the family and concludes: "In this way, we can preserve the name of the al-Khalidi family, as long as learning is alive, and the waqf is preserved, and write in its history."

87. McCarthy, *The Population of Palestine*, pp. 23–24.

88. This is an extrapolation from the figures given in the table in ibid., p. 158, showing the urban populations in 1922. McCarthy notes, p. 15, that "The population of the cities and towns of Ottoman Palestine is particularly difficult to estimate." Much has been made of Jerusalem supposedly having a Jewish majority before 1914, but the Ottoman sources indicate no such thing, and the non-Ottoman sources are dubious at best: for, as McCarthy points out, how could anyone but the state have had any systematic way of counting population? After the 1922 census, these problems disappeared, as within the gerrymandered municipal boundaries drawn up by the British Mandatory authorities so as to include every Jewish population concentration in the general vicinity, however many miles distant, and to exclude numerous nearby Arab population centers such as Silwan, immediately under the walls of the Old City, Jerusalem clearly came to have a Jewish majority.

89. The Khalidi Library contains a number of elementary Hebrew-language books, most of them belonging to Yusuf Diya' Pasha and his nephew Ruhi Bey al-Khalidi, who briefly attended an Alliance school in Jerusalem, as did his fellow deputy in the 1908 Parliament, Sa'id al-Husayni. See the following chapters for more details on all three.

90. Some clearly foresaw the struggle to come. Among the first was Najib 'Azuri, who set down this prediction in his *Réveil de la Nation Arabe* (Paris: n.p., 1904). We have seen others who looked with foreboding to the growth of the Zionist enterprise in Palestine, including the journalists Najib Nassar and 'Isa al-'Isa, and the deputies Ruhi al-Khalidi and Sa'id al-Husayni, who will be further discussed in the following three chapters. Among early Zionist writers, Ahad Ha'am [Asher Ginsberg] was among the most perceptive in foreseeing conflict between the two peoples, as early as 1891: Walter Laqueur, *A History of Zionism* (New York: Schocken, 1972), pp. 210–211.

91. Gerber, *Ottoman Rule*, pp. 145–159, provides case studies from the records of the state (*nizami*) courts in Jaffa in 1887, showing that they had taken over many of the functions of the *shari'a* courts.

92. For a good example of state encouragement of popular religion during the Hamidian period, in this case in the Nablus area, see Darwaza, *Khamsa wa tis'una 'aman*, pp. 104–112.

93. Schölch, *Palestine in Transformation*, pp. 244–249. The al-Husaynis were traditionally among the main participants in the annual *Nabi Musa* festival, which brought religious and popular processions to Jerusalem from many parts of the country, and thereafter to the *Nabi Musa* shrine on the road to Jericho for several days of celebrations in honor of the prophet Moses.

94. On changes in the occupational structure of the country, see Gerber, *Ottoman Rule*, pp. 69–74.

95. *Catalogue of the Syrian Protestant College, Beirut, Syria, 1912–1913* (Beirut, The College Press, 1913), p. 13.

Chapter 4. Ottoman Notables in Jerusalem: Competing and Conflicting Loyalties

1. See R. Khalidi, "Arab Nationalism."

2. Muhammad Farid, *Tarikh al-dawla al-'aliyya al-'uthmaniyya* [History of the Ottoman state] (Beirut: n.p., 1981). An earlier Beirut edition (Dar al-Jil, 1977) is simply a reprint of the original 1912 edition, without any preface or commentary. A relatively recent work of history follows the same lines: 'Abd al-'Aziz Muhammad al-Shinawi, *al-Dawla al-'uthmaniyya: Dawla islamiyya muftari 'alayha* [The Ottoman Empire: A maligned Islamic state], 4 vols. (Cairo: Matba'at Jami'at al-Qahira, 1980–1986).

3. Wajih Kawtharani, *Bilad al-sham, al-sukkan, al-iqtisad wal-siyasa al-faransiyya fi matla' al-qarn al-'ishrin: Qira'a fil-watha'iq* [*Bilad al-Sham*, population, economy and French policy at the outset of the twentieth century: A reading of the documents] (Beirut: Ma'had al-Inma', 1980). Along the same lines, see Muhammad al-Khayr 'Abd al-Qadir, *Nakbat al-umma al-'arabiyya bi-suqut al-khilafa: Dirasa lil-qadiyya al-'arabiyya fi khamsin 'aman, 1875–1925* [The disaster of the Arab nation through the fall of the caliphate: A study of the Arab cause over 50 years, 1875–1925] (Cairo: Maktabat Wahba, 1985). It may be significant that a wave of such publications appeared soon after the Islamic revolution in Iran.

4. For a balanced recent assessment of this topic, see 'Abd al-Jalil al-Tamimi, "Importance de l'heritage arabo-turque et son impact sur les relations arabo-turques," in his *Etudes sur l'Histoire Arabo-Ottomane, 1453–1918/Dirasat fil-tarikh al-'arabi al-'uthmani*, pp. 9–19 (Zeghouan: CEROMDI, 1994).

5. This is the main argument of R. Khalidi, "Ottomanism and Arabism."

6. For the situation before these changes in the eighteenth century see the works cited in chapter 3, n. 10, above. On career patterns, see Joseph Szyliowicz, "Changes in the Recruitment Patterns and Career-lines of Ottoman Provincial Administrators during the Nineteenth Century," in Ma'oz, ed., *Studies on Palestine*, pp. 249–283.

7. The disturbances during the years of Egyptian control, 1831–39, which first upset local power balances in Palestine, are dealt with in the Ph.D. dissertation of Judith Mendelsohn Rood, "Sacred Law in the Holy City: A Study in the Theory and Practice of Government in Jerusalem Under Ottoman and Khedival Rule," Department of History, University of Chicago, 1993, as well as in Doumani, *Rediscovering Palestine.*

8. On the destruction of these rural power-bases, see Schölch, *Palestine in Transformation*, especially the chapter "The Disempowerment of the Local Lords," pp. 197–240; and the less incisive account of Donna Robinson Divine, *Politics and Society in Ottoman Palestine* (Boulder: Lynne Rienner, 1994), in the chapter "Restoration and Early Reforms, 1840–1875," pp. 77–106. On the way the process proceeded in the Nablus region, see Doumani, *Rediscovering Palestine*, pp. 39–53; 233–236.

9. This process is well explained in Butros Abu Manneh, "Jerusalem in the Tanzimat Period: The New Ottoman Administration and the Notables," *Die Welt des Islams* 30 (1990): 1–44; and Schölch, *Palestine in Transformation*, pp. 241–292. For Nablus, see the exposition of this process in Doumani, *Rediscovering Palestine*, pp. 48–53; 230–232; 236–243.

10. The title *ra'is al-kuttab* is frequently rendered using the Turkish term *başkatib*, which is often the preferred one, even in many documents and sources in Arabic.

11. A brief biography of Muhammad 'Ali al-Khalidi can be found in Manna', *A'lam Filastin*, pp. 145–146.

12. For an excellent account of how these courts functioned, and the value of their records as sources, see Bishara B. Doumani, "Palestinian Islamic Court Records: A Source for Socioeconomic History," *MESA Bulletin* 19, no. 2 (December 1985): 155–172.

13. The qadi of Jerusalem also had authority over the courts in other parts of Palestine, including Nablus, Acre, Haifa, and Hebron, whose judges he appointed, and where the Jerusalem *na'ib* had great influence: for an important 1807 case in the Nablus shari'a court involving Muhammad 'Ali al-Khalidi, who at that time held the post of *na'ib* of the Jerusalem court, see Doumani, *Rediscovering Palestine*, pp. 205–206.

14. See Zilfi, *The Politics of Piety*, n. 56, p. 79. The post of qadi of Jerusalem was one of 17 great judgeships in major political or religious centers of the Empire for which competition was intense in the Ottoman system, as there were always more candidates than posts; hence the institution of annual tenure by the late seventeenth century.

15. Muhammad San'allah, whose grandfather had been qadi of Jerusalem (which by the eighteenth century would have been a very unusual appointment for a native of Jerusalem), came from a long line of religious scholars, three of whom had held the position of Hanafi *Qadi al-qudat* in Mameluke Egypt in the ninth/fifteenth century. The history of the al-Khalidi family is summarized in Nasir al-Din al-Asad, *Ruhi al-Khalidi* (Cairo: Ma'had al-Buhuth wal-Dirasat al-'arabiyya, 1970), pp. 25–30. See also Kamal Salibi, "Listes chronologiques des grands cadis de l'Egypte sous les Mamelouks," *Revue des Etudes Islamiques* 25 (1957): 104–107, where the original family name of "al-Dayri" is used.

16. These are part of a collection of documents in the possession of the al-Khalidi family which are to be placed in the renovated Khalidi Library in Jerusalem once they have been catalogued and organized. Forty-six of these documents are described in Donald P. Little and A. Uner Turgay, "Documents from the Ottoman Period in the Khalidi Library in Jerusalem," *Die Welt des Islams* 20, nos. 1–2 (1980): 44–72.

17. Several Jerusalem families have such collections, notably the al-Husaynis, whose papers were used by 'Adil Manna' to compile *A'lam Filastin*. See Butrus Abu Manneh, "The Husaynis: The Rise of a Notable Family in 18th Century Palestine," in David Kushner, ed., *Palestine in the Late Ottoman Period: Political Social and Economic Transformation*, pp. 93–108 (Jerusalem: Yad Izhak Ben-Zvi, 1986). Members of the al-Husayni family occupied the post of Hanafi mufti of Jerusalem from the early eighteenth century, as is shown in the 1701 petition referred to in chapter 2 which lists Muhammad b. 'Abd al-Rahim al-Husayni as mufti of Jerusalem. The degree of continuity of Jerusalem families is remarkable: the signatories on this document include members of the Dajani, al-Imam, al-'Alami, al-'Asayli, al-Khatib, Abu al-Sa'ud, Rayyes and other present-day Jerusalem families. The al-Husaynis, like the al-Khalidis, apparently held high religious posts under the Mamelukes: Mujir al-Din, *al Uns al-jalil*, 2, pp. 220, 226, 233, refers to several of them, but Abu Manneh points out (p. 107, n.7) that "there were other families in Jerusalem that carried the family name 'Husayni,' and who might have been distant relatives of this family."

18. Written on good quality paper, and rolled up with summaries of their contents visible on the outside, the documents were generally in good condition, even though nearly all of them were more than 100 years old, and over fifty were more than 200 years old. Indeed the few twentieth-century documents, on inferior paper, were generally in the worst condition.

19. The best overview is provided by Schölch, *Palestine in Transformation*, pp. 197–240.

20. In keeping with standard Ottoman practice for holders of the post of qadi (but not local ones such as that of *başkatib*), he held these posts elsewhere than his native Jerusalem.

21. For details of Yasin's career, see Manna', *A'lam Filastin*, pp. 154–155.

22. The treatment of Yusuf Diya' al-Khalidi in this chapter draws on Alexander Schölch, "Ein palastinischer Reprasentant der Tanzimat Periode," *Der Islam* 57 (1980) 316 ff. [translated as the chapter "A Palestinian Reformer: Yusuf al-Khalidi," in *Palestine in Transformation*, pp. 241–252]; Abu Manneh, "Jerusalem in the Tanzimat Period," pp. 40–43; Manna', *A'lam Filastin*, pp. 156–161; as well as his uncatalogued papers, located in the Khalidi Library, including an eight-page autobiographical sketch covering the period until 1875.

23. He is described on the cover page of a work he published in Vienna in 1880 as "Jusuf Dija-ad-Din Al-Chalidi, Professor an der K.K. Orientalischen Akademie in Wien."

24. This 319 pp. work is entitled *al-Hadiyya al-hamidiyya fil-lugha al-kurdiyya* [The Hamidian gift in the Kurdish language] (Istanbul: Martabey Matba'asi, 1310/1892). It grew in part out of Yusuf Diya's service as *qa'immaqam* in a Kurdish district in Bitlis province during the late 1880s, one of several minor posts to which he was assigned after falling foul of the Sultan a decade earlier. The work includes a 30-page analysis of the Kurdish language, 233 pages of definitions of words in Kurdish, followed by 39 pages of examples of poetry and prose in Kurdish, concluding with 13 pages of endorsements by various religious and literary luminaries in Istanbul, including the Sultan's favorite, Shaykh Abu al-Huda al-Sayyadi.

25. Notably Schölch, Abu Manneh and Manna', cited in n. 22, above.

26. For more on Sa'id and Ahmad Rasim al-Husayni, see Manna', *A'lam Filastin*, pp. 91, 109–110. Sa'id al-Husayni has a large collection of papers belonging to his grandfather (who bore the same name), which are illuminating regarding aspects of his career.

27. According to Raqiyya al-Khalidi (interview, Jerusalem, September 23, 1995), Yusuf Diya's three sisters, her great-aunts Amina, Hafiza, and Zaynab, were not educated; only toward the end of the century did females in the family begin to receive modern educations: interview, Wahida al-Khalidi, Beirut, December 12, 1977. See also 'Anbara Salam al-Khalidi, *Jawla fil-dhikrayat bayna Lubnan wa Filastin* [Journey of memories between Lebanon and Palestine]. Beirut: al-Nahar, 1978.

28. See e.g. the contemptuous description of him by the German Consul in Jerusalem, cited in Schölch, *Palestine in Transformation*, p. 250.

29. These details are taken from the autobiographical sketch mentioned in n.22, above. In his own writings and his correspondence with his nephew Ruhi, Yusuf Diya' often refers to the importance of Western learning. See, e.g., the conclusion to his edition of the poetry of Labid ibn Rabi'a, *Diwan Labid*, pp. 147–151. See also Schölch, *Palestine in Transformation*, pp. 242–243.

30. With the exception of Yasin, little else is known about the careers of the brothers of Yusuf Diya', beyond the fact that they became 'ulama and held the post of *ra'is al-kuttab* in Jerusalem at different times. It is also known that Raghib, grandfather of the founder of the Khalidi Library, died young. Yasin was close to his younger brother Yusuf Diya', as is clear from their correspondence preserved by the family: a dozen letters between them survive solely for the years 1317/1900 and 1318/1901, the latter being the year of Yasin's death.

31. Yusuf Diya's textbooks from Malta and other language texts with his name in them can be found in the Khalidi Library. Having met him briefly in Vienna, Charles Doughty reported the German Orientalist Alfred von Kremer's comment that he "was a litterate [sic] Moslem, a school-teacher . . . in Jerusalem, who had some smattering of European languages": *Travels in Arabia Deserta*, 2 vols. (Cambridge: Cambridge University Press, 1888), 2:419. However, the American Consul-General in Istanbul reported in 1877 that he "spoke English and French very well," and a later Consul-General described him as "speaking English with fluency and much accuracy": Robert Devereux, *The First Ottoman Constitutional Period* (Baltimore: Johns Hopkins University Press, 1963), p. 267, n. 40). He taught in German at the Imperial-Royal Oriental Academy in Vienna in the 1870s and 1880s.

32. The exact title was Head of the Municipal Council, which had been established in 1863, well ahead of other Ottoman cities, which obtained similar forms of municipal government only as a result of the 1864 and 1871 Provincial Laws: see Carter Findlay, "The Evolution of the System of Provincial Administration as Viewed from the Center," in Kushner, ed., *Palestine in the Late Ottoman Period*, pp. 3–29. The details of his efforts to establish this school are described differently in a manuscript autobiography "Mudhakkirat al-Hajj Raghib al-Khalidi" [Memoirs of al-Hajj Raghib al-Khalidi], n.d. p. 31, copy in possession of author.

33. Schölch, *Palestine in Transformation*, pp. 243–244, Manna', *A'lam Filastin*, pp. 156–157, and Yusuf Diya's autobiographical sketch describe some of his activities as mayor, which also emerge from letters and publications on water supply, road-building and archaeology among his correspondence (including an 1870 letter from Maj. Gen. Henry James R.E. of the British War Office regarding an effort by Yusuf Diya' to

improve the Jerusalem water supply). His activism did not earn Yusuf Diya' unanimous praise: Schölch (p. 249, n. 752) reports the hostile attitude of French diplomats in Jerusalem toward him, accompanied by the accusation that he was "pro-German," perhaps occasioned by his firm stand against French consular moves in support of their religious interests in Jerusalem, or his good relations with the British.

34. The words are those of Yusuf Diya', in his autobiographical sketch.

35. Copies of a lengthy exchange of telegrams (in French) with the Foreign Ministry and the Ottoman Embassy in St. Petersburg protesting his sudden removal and requesting reimbursement for expenses incurred in Poti are located in the Khalidi Library. There is also a droll eleven-page manuscript account in French of the circumstances of Yusuf Diya's replacement by his predecessor in Poti, a man he describes as "l'ambitiuex ignorant et renommé illetré, Hassan-Agha." This document, in the form of a letter dated Poti, November 5, 1874, reads as if it were prepared for publication (Yusuf Diya' talks of himself in the third person).

36. The Russian passport issued to him to allow him to leave the country, dated December 10, 1874, is to be found among his papers in the Khalidi Library

37. For details on the Ottoman electoral system, see Hasan Kayali, "Elections and the Electoral Process in the Ottoman Empire, 1876–1919," *International Journal of Middle East Studies* 27, no. 3 (August 1995): 265–286.

38. Devereux, *The First Ottoman Constitutional Period*, p. 267, n. 40.

39. See ibid., pp. 148, 156, 166–167, 241–242, 247–288. See also Abu Manneh, "Jerusalem," pp. 41–42.

40. Devereux, *First Ottoman Constitutional Period*, p. 156.

41. This was Mahmud Cellaledin Pasa, who was one of the Sultan's ministers at this time, in his memoirs *Mir'at-i hakikat*, 3 vols. (Istanbul: Matbaa-i Osmaniye, 1326–1327), 3:61, cited in ibid., pp. 247–248.

42. See Abu Manneh, "Jerusalem in the Tanzimat Period,," pp. 40–43; Schölch, *Palestine in Transformation*, pp. 247–249; and David Kushner, "The Ottoman Governors of Palestine," *Middle Eastern Studies* 23, no. 3 (July 1987): 283.

43. *Diwan Labid*.

44. The Consul General was Eugene Schuyler, in a letter dated May 13, 1877, cited in Devereaux, *First Ottoman Constitutional Period*, p. 267.

45. This is clear both from correspondence from several such individuals, including Alfred von Kremer (some of it in Arabic but most in European languages), and from books by Ernest Renan, Robert Bosworth-Smith, Charles Clermont-Ganneau and other leading European Orientalists of the day inscribed with warm dedications to Yusuf Diya' found among his personal library, and now in the Khalidi Library in Jerusalem.

46. For a sense of the atmosphere at court during the Sultan's lengthy reign, see the fictional but highly plausible account in Michel de Grèce, *Le Dernier Sultan* (Paris: Olivier Orban, 1991), which purports to tell his story from 'Abd al-Hamid's own perspective, and is based at least in part on the memoirs of the Sultan's daughter and the author's compilation of the recollections of two of his grandsons.

47. In view of the acidic satirical poetry Yusuf Diya' wrote, the sharpness of his tongue, and his profound dislike of 'Abd al-Hamid, the lines addressed to the Sultan in the introduction of *Diwan Labid* (p. 1) can be read only as a thinly veiled parody (though 'Abd al-Hamid's censors must have taken them at face value): "Renewer of the structure of the Ottoman state, raiser of the pavilions of security and charity, spreader of the paths of justice with mercy and compassion on the horizons, worthy holder of the throne of the sultanate, protector of the people, benefactor of knowl-

edge, possessor of all benefactions, *khalifa* of God on earth, prince of the faithful, victor of his age, absolute crown of sultans of the world, spreader of the shari'a to the horizons, his highness, our lord and master, the sultan, son of the sultan, son of the sultan, father of victories and conquests, the conquering sultan 'Abd al-Hamid II" [there follow seven more equally fulsome lines]. The endorsement by the Sultan's confidant, Shaykh Abu al-Huda al-Sayyadi, mentioned earlier, must have help secure publication of this work.

48. *Salname-i devlet-i aliyye-i osmaniyye* [Ottoman state yearbook] (Istanbul: Matba'at Amira, 1307/1890), p. 55. Later yearbooks (1309/1892 and 1314/1896) list similar diplomatic assignments which appear to have been purely nominal.

49. Another Arab official, the Lebanese Najib 'Azuri, was sentenced to death in absentia on such charges: see Manna', *A'lam Filastin*, pp. 258–259.

50. We can follow Yusuf Diya's movements for the last decade of his life from the 83 surviving letters he wrote his nephew Ruhi between 1897 and 1906. He appears to have first been allowed to leave Istanbul and travel to Jerusalem briefly in December 1900 (when his brother Yasin was ill), and then for longer periods in several succeeding years. Few of Ruhi's letters to him survive.

51. Manna', *A'lam Filastin*, p. 159. For the personal dedication to Yusuf Diya' on a photograph of al-Afghani located in the Khalidi Library, see chapter 3 above, n.26. For more on al-Afghani's exile in Istanbul, see Homa Nategh, "Mirza Aqa Khan, Sayyed Jamal al-din et Malkom Khan à Istanbul (1860–1897)," Th. Zarcone and F. Zarinebaf, eds., *Les Iraniens d'Istanbul*, pp. 45–60 (Paris, Teheran, Istanbul: Institut Francais de Recherches en Iran and Institut Francais d'Etudes Anatoliennes, 1993).

52. He received the knight's cross of the Order of Franz-Joseph on the occasion of the Austrian emperor's visit to Jerusalem while he was mayor in 1869: Schölch, *Palestine in Transformation*, p. 249.

53. In spite of being prevented from publishing, he continued to write, as is evident from the manuscripts in various stages of completion among his papers, now located in the Khalidi Library. The longest is a 76-page manuscript analyzing the Bible, entitled "Risalat mumahakat al-ta'wil fi munaqadat al-injil" [Disputes in interpretation regarding the contradictions of the Bible], dated Istanbul 1281 [1864] on the title page and 1296 [1878–79] on the final page. This closely reasoned treatise seems to have been started when its author was a student in Istanbul, and completed while he was in exile in Vienna fifteen years later. Other manuscripts include a 10-page poem entitled "*al-'Arsh wal-haykal*" [The throne and the temple], dated 1295 [1878].

54. Yusuf Diya' sent six letters to Ruhi from July to September 1899 from the Russian hospital in Istanbul, where he was receiving treatment. Letters he sent from Palestine in the following few years also mention ill health.

55. The letter is quoted in Manna', *A'lam Filastin*, p. 160. Herzl's response is reprinted in Walid Khalidi, ed., *From Haven to Conquest* (Beirut: Institute for Palestine Studies, 1971), pp. 91–93. See also Mandel, *The Arabs and Zionism*, pp. 47–48.

56. The articles are mentioned in Manna', *A'lam Filastin*, p. 157.

57. Bentwich often sent him his writings: one, "The Progress of Zionism," *The Fortnightly Review* (December 1898), carried the inscription "With H. B.'s greetings in Zion"; another, *Palestine and Her Critics*, a 1900 pamphlet, enclosed a card engraved "With Mr. Herbert Bentwich's Compliments."

58. The amusing and varied forms of greeting used by the older man in his letters to the younger bespeak strong feelings of affection and solicitude.

59. Yusuf Diya' and Ruhi's father Yasin also devoted much of their correspondence (12 letters between them have survived) to discussing means of advancing Ruhi's career, as did Yasin in the 16 existing letters to his son. It is clear from the entire collection that advancement in the Ottoman bureaucracy was quite difficult without reliance on such influential relatives.

60. A passage by a European contemporary observer describing Yusuf Diya' is cited in Manna', *A'lam Filastin*, p. 159.

61. This incident is described in Ruhi al-Khalidi, *Asbab al-inqilab al-'uthmani wa turkiyya al-fatat* [The causes for the Ottoman revolution and the Young Turks] (Cairo: al-Manar Press, 1326/1908), p. 99, which does not give the name of the individual who berated Ghanem. A marginal note by Ahmad Badawi al-Khalidi dated 1327 reveals that the anonymous deputy was Yusuf Diya'. The remark is characteristic of the man.

62. For a balanced assessment of education under 'Abd al-Hamid, see A. L. Tibawi, *A Modern History of Syria, including Lebanon and Palestine* (London: MacMillan, 1969), pp. 194–96.

63. This emerges from the data provided in Rafiq Tamimi and Muhammad Bahjat, 2 vols. *Wilayat Bayrut* [The province of Beirut] (Beirut: al-Iqbal Press, 1335–36/1917), 2:151–53. Tamimi was born in Nablus and educated in Istanbul and France, while Bahjat, from Aleppo, was educated in law in Istanbul; both were government officials (for details, see Doumani, *Rediscovering Palestine*, p. 292, n. 42). Their comprehensive survey of government and society in the province of Beirut, based on a detailed field study, is one of the best pre-1918 sources on the region. For more on education in this province see Martin Strohmeier, "Muslim Education in the Vilayet of Beirut, 1880–1918," in C. E. Farah, ed., *Decision-making and Change in the Ottoman Empire*, pp. 215–241 (Kirkville, MO: Thomas Jefferson University Press, 1993).

64. He won prizes for coming in first in Turkish, French, and Arabic grammar, as well as religious sciences, and came in second in his class in English translation and mathematics, winning a prize for good conduct as well. The prizes (mainly works of literature and moral uplift in French) and many of his school-books, are preserved at the Khalidi Library

65. He received the highest grades in 10 of 22 subject areas, including *kalam*, *tafsir* and *hadith*, land law, criminal law, legal procedure, and military law. The original of his diploma and the texts he used at the *Mülkiye* are also preserved at the Khalidi Library.

66. Ruhi's older brother, Thurayya, also received both a traditional and a modern education at the instigation of their father, and became a commissioner of antiquities in Palestine during the late Ottoman period, supervising foreign excavations: interview with Raqiyya al-Khalidi (Thurayya's daughter), Jerusalem, October 8, 1993. His books and papers are also preserved in the Khalidi Library.

67. This sketch appeared in the Jaffa periodical *al-Asma'i* 1, no. 7 (December 1, 1908): 152–160. For more on Ruhi, see al-Asad, *Ruhi al-Khalidi*; Khairieh Kasmieh, "Ruhi al-Khalidi 1864–1913: A Symbol of the Cultural Movement in Palestine toward the end of Ottoman Rule," in T. Philipp, ed., *The Syrian Land in the 18th and 19th Century*, pp. 123–146 (Stuttgart: Fritz Steiner, 1992); and Manna', *A'lam Filastin*, pp. 137–141.

68. The two dozen or so books dating from this youthful period of Ruhi's life are mainly inexpensive editions of legal works such as *Tafsil li-tawdih al-qawa'id al-fiqhiyya wal-usuliyya fi awwal majallat al-ahkam al-'adliyya* [Clarification of the rules of

jurisprudence in the legal code],(Istanbul: n.p. 1299/1881); a book on inheritance in the shari'a, Shaykh Yusuf al-Asir, *Sharh ra'id al-fara'id* (Beirut: n.p., 1290/1873); collections of poetry like Butrus Karami, ed., *al- Muwashahat al-andalusiyya* (Beirut: n.p., 1864); and *Nukhab diwan Ibrahim b. Sahl al-Isra'ili al-Andalusi al-Ashbili*, n.p., n.d.; and books like *Kanz lughat*, a Turkish-Persian dictionary by Faris al-Khuri (Beirut: n.p., 1876).

69. The *ijaza* (or diploma) is dated 1314AH/1897. There are a number of letters extant in the Khalidi Library between Ruhi al-Khalidi and al-Husayni, testifying to the former's continued interest in religious topics long after he had completed his education. For details on al-Imam, whose grandmother was a member of the al-Khalidi family, see Manna', *A'lam Filastin*, p. 47.

70. The incident is described in the autobiographical article cited earlier, with the author's intimation that he was not fully worthy of this honor, which may have been conferred on him out of the desire of the *Shaykh al-Islam*, 'Üryanizade Ahmet Esad Efendi, to favor Ruhi's uncle, a *'alim* of distinction, whom Ruhi was accompanying.

71. Among the books in Hebrew from this period in the Khalidi Library are Arabic- Hebrew, Russian-Hebrew, and French-Hebrew dictionaries, as well as a number of Hebrew language text books, some of which belonged to Ruhi al-Khalidi, and some apparently to his uncle, Yusuf Diya.'

72. For more on the *salafi* trend, see Commins, *Islamic Reform*, and Escovitz, " 'He was the Muhammad 'Abdu of Syria,' " pp. 293–310. There are at least three copies of al-Jisr's book *al-Risala al-hamidiyya* (Beirut: n.p., 1305/1887) in the Khalidi Library, originally owned by different members of the family.

73. He apparently got into trouble with the authorities immediately after finishing at the *Mülkiye*, where his diploma shows he had received the highest grades in the category "Good Conduct," which would have been unlikely had he been suspected of involvement in forbidden political activities at that time.

74. There is reference to the story about al-Afghani in the autobiographical note published in *al-Asma'i*, and elsewhere.

75. Attestation by Derenbourg, dated Paris, October 23, 1897, appended to *ijaza* from Shaykh Yusuf al-Sadiq al-Imam al-Husayni.

76. Ruhi al-Khalidi, *Risala fi sur'at intishar al-din al-islami fi aqsam al-'alam* [Essay on the speed of the spread of the Islamic religion in the regions of the world] (Tripoli: al-Balagha Press, 1897), [67 pp.].

77. One of the skeptics was the chair of the session, Ruhi's professor Hartwig Derenbourg, who said "Even if the speaker exaggerated in estimating the number of Muslims as one fifth of the human race, we believe that the Muslims number more than 200 million." Ibid., p. 65.

78. Ibid.

79. In addition to those mentioned in n.76 and n.80 below, his published works include the following books and monographs: *Tarikh 'ilm al-adab 'ind al-ifranj wal-'arab wa Victor Hugo* [The history of literature among the Arabs, the Franks and Victor Hugo] (Cairo: Dar al-Hilal, 1904), [272 pp.], a book that was in print in an edition published in Damascus until recently; *al-Inqilab al-'uthmani* [The Ottoman revolution] (Cairo: Dar al-Hilal, 1909), [171 pp.]; *al-Muqaddima fil-mas'ala al-sharqiyya munthu nash'atiha al-uwla ila al-rub' al-thani min al-qarn al-thamin 'ashr* [An introduction to the Eastern Question from its inception until the second quarter of the 18th century] (Jerusalem: Dar al-Aytam, n.d.), [printed posthumously ca. 1920 by his brother, Thurayya; 81 pp.]; *al-Kimiya 'ind al-'arab* [Chemistry under the Arabs] (Cairo: Dar al-

Ma'arif, 1953), [printed posthumously; 85 pp.]. Many of them were initially published in serial form in periodicals such as *al-Hilal*, *al-Muqtabas*, and *Tarablus al-Sham*.

80. *al-Habs fil-tuhma wal-imtihan 'ala talab al-iqrar wa-izhar al-mal* [Imprisonment on accusation and the test for a request for a decision and revelation of wealth] (Jerusalem [?]: n.p., 1321/1903), [86 pp.].

81. There are Masonic books and pamphlets in the Khalidi Library in English, French, and Arabic, several belonging to Ruhi al-Khalidi (which indicate he was a member of the Grand Orient of France and possibly another order in Cairo), as well as a number of French- and Arabic-language anti-Masonic tracts authored by Jesuits.

82. "Osmanli Ittihad ve Terakki Cemiyeti 1327 senasi siyasi programi" [Political program of the Ottoman Committee of Union and Progress] (Istanbul, Tanin, 1327/1909). The rarity of this 16-page pamphlet was pointed out to me by Şükrü Hanioglu, an expert on the CUP.

83. *al-Hadiyya al-hamidiyya*, pp. 2–3.

84. *al-Asma'i*, pp. 152–157.

85. *al-Muqaddima fil-mas'ala al-sharqiyya*, pp. b-j [ba-jim].

86. The debate was widely published in the Arabic press, in some cases verbatim; see e.g., *Filastin*, no. 37, May 14 [*sic*], 1911, pp. 1–2; *al-Karmil*, no. 145, May 19, 1911, p. 1; *al-Muqtabas*, no. 691, May 18, 1911, pp. 1–2; *Lisan al-Hal*, no. 6649, May 18, 1911, p. 1. See also Mandel, *The Arabs and Zionism*, pp. 112–116. The first two papers, as well as European and Zionist press reports cited by Mandel, state that al-Khalidi opened the debate; *Lisan al-Hal* describes al-'Asali as speaking first, while *al-Muqtabas*, which al-'Asali wrote for and later edited, provides only a long report on his speech by Haqqi al-'Azm. The following account draws on all these sources. In Ruhi's own folder of press clippings and other materials on Zionism, located in the Khalidi Library, he preserved the text of his speech as printed in *Filastin*, as well as what appear to be drafts of the speech.

87. *Lisan al-Hal*, no. 6649, May 18, 1911.

88. Ruhi al-Khalidi lived in France from 1893 until 1908, and was therefore exposed to the Dreyfus affair from its inception to its conclusion. His library included numerous books analyzing anti-Semitism, including Zola's famous tract on the affair, *Humanité-Verité-Justice: L'Affaire Dreyfus. Lettre à la Jeunesse par Emile Zola* (Paris: Eugene Fasquelle, 1897).

89. *Lisan al-Hal*, no. 6649, May 18, 1911.

90. Ibid. See also *Filastin*, no. 37, May 14, 1911, p. 2.

91. *al-Muqtabas*, no. 691, May 18, 1911, pp. 1–2. The al-Fula sale is discussed in detail in chapter 5, and some of its repercussions in the press in chapter 6.

92. While Shukri al-'Asali was a spellbinding orator according to a number of sources (see R. Khalidi, "The 1912 Election Campaign," p. 467), Ruhi al-Khalidi apparently did not inherit his uncle's talent for public speaking: Manna', *A 'lam Filastin*, p. 140.

93. The Khalidi Library contains Hebrew-language textbooks which belonged to both men, as well as a few other books in Hebrew, and a large collection of Judaica, books on Biblical archaeology, and numerous editions of the history of Josephus in several languages.

94. *Filastin*, no. 37, May 14, 1911, p. 1.

95. This is certainly the impression given by the comments of other non-Arab deputies during the debate, although the perhaps overenthusiastic reports by *Filastin* and *al-Muqtabas*, cited above, stress how well the speeches were received. Mandel, *The*

Arabs and Zionism, pp. 115–116, suggests some of the reasons why the issue of Zionism did not attract the attention of most non-Arab deputies at this time.

96. This work, still in manuscript, is analyzed by Walid Khalidi in an article entitled *"Kitab al-sionism, aw al-mas'ala al-sihyuniyya li-Muhammad Ruhi al-Khalidi, al-mutawafi sanat 1913"* [The book "Zionism or the Zionist Question," by Muhammad Ruhi al-Khalidi, died 1913], in Hisham Nashabeh, ed. *Studia Palaestina: Studies in honour of Constantine K. Zurayk/ Dirasat filistiniyya: majmu'at abhath wudi'at takriman lil-duktur Qustantin Zurayq*, pp. 37–81 (Beirut: Institute for Palestine Studies, 1988).

97. Ibid., p. 43.

98. Ibid.

99. Nassar's 65-page work is entitled *al-Sihyuniyya: tarikhuha, gharaduha, ahamiyatuha* [Zionism: its history, aims and importance] (Haifa: al-Karmil Press, 1911), and bears the notation that it is "summarized from the *Encyclopedia Judaica*," although it contains a brief introduction, a conclusion and several pages of commentary by Nassar.

100. Ruhi al-Khalidi, *"Kitab al-sionism, aw al-mas'ala al-sihyuniyya"* [Zionism or the Zionist question], undated manuscript, copy in possession of author, pp. 111–112.

101. W. Khalidi, *"Kitab al-sionism,"* p. 78.

102. Ibid., p. 81.

103. Most sources indicate that he died of typhoid, which must have struck rapidly, as he was only ill for two or three days. His niece, Raqiyya al-Khalidi, whose father Thurayya collected Ruhi's effects in Istanbul and brought them back to Jerusalem, recalled (interview, Jerusalem, June 28, 1992) that her father told her that in Istanbul Ruhi al-Khalidi's colleagues claimed he had been poisoned, presumably by government agents. There is no evidence for this assertion, and it is possible that when she heard this story in later years (she was a small child in 1913), her uncle Ruhi had been turned into a posthumous Arabist martyr to Turkish persecution by Jerusalem society. It is also possible that such rumours were circulating in Istanbul, but were untrue.

104. See *Filastin*, May 18, 1911, pp. 1–2, and Mandel, *The Arabs and Zionism*, pp. 112–116.

105. Schölch, *Palestine in Transformation*, p. 246.

106. Yusuf Diya' al-Khalidi, ed., *Diwan Labid*, p. 148

107. See Şükrü Hanioglu, "The Young Turks and the Arabs before the Revolution of 1908," in R. Khalidi et. al., eds., *The Origins of Arab Nationalism*, pp. 31–49 for early evidence of these tendencies, which were often perceived in exaggerated form by many Arabs in this period.

108. His private correspondence shows Ruhi al-Khalidi to have been deeply moved by the privations and humiliations imposed on his uncle by the Sultan.

109. For more on the CUP, see Feroz Ahmed, *The Young Turks: The Committee of Union and Progress in Power, 1908–1914* (Oxford: Oxford University Press, 1969); and Erik Jan Zürcher, *The Unionist Factor: The Role of the Committee of Union and Progress in the Turkish National Movement, 1905–1926* (Leiden: Brill, 1984).

110. Examples can be found in the al-Khalidi and al-Husayni families: religious education continued to be the standard for at least one more generation among the offspring of Yusuf Diya's brothers, after which, around the turn of twentieth century, secular, professional education became the norm. Similarly, while one branch of the al-Husayni family held the post of Hanafi mufti of Jerusalem until the 1930s, we have seen that younger members of other branches of the family like Sa'id al-Husayni acquired modern educations and obtained leading government positions such as Mayor of Jerusalem and parliamentary deputy.

111. See Abu Manneh, "Jerusalem in the Tanzimat Period," pp. 40 ff. for details.

112. For more details see R. Khalidi, "The 1912 Election Campaign."

113. In his autobiographical sketch for *al-Asma'i*, p. 157.

114. Cited in n.99 above.

115. al-Asad's biography of Ruhi is subtitled *Ra'id al-bahth al-tarikhi al-filastini*, [Pioneer of Palestinian historiography].

116. The phrase is again that of Benedict Anderson, from the title of his book, *Imagined Communities*.

Chapter 5. Elements of Identity I: Peasant Resistance to Zionist Settlement

1. Beyond these overt forms of disruption due to bombing, closures, and so forth, the functioning of these institutions was also affected and their priorities distorted by the demands imposed on them by the nearly constant crises that affected the Palestinian people from the late 1960s through the mid-1990s.

2. Among the exceptions in the generation which grew to maturity before 1948 are 'Arif al-'Arif, *al-Nakba: Nakbat Bayt al-Maqdis wal-firdaws al-mafqud, 1947–1952* [The catastrophe: The catastrophe of Jerusalem and the lost paradise, 1947–52], 6 vols. (Sidon: al-Maktaba al-'Asriyya, 1956–58); Ihsan al-Nimr, *Tarikh Jabal Nablus wal-Balqa'* [History of the Nablus region], 4 vols. (Nablus: Jam'iyyat 'Ummal al-Matabi' al-Ta'awuniyya, 1976 [originally published published 1936–1961]); and works by 'Abd al-Latif Tibawi, Muhammad 'Izzat Darwaza, and Walid Khalidi, several of which have already been cited. For general background see Tarif Khalidi, "Palestinian Historiography: 1900–1948," *Journal of Palestine Studies*, 10, no. 3 (Spring 1981): 59–76; and Beshara B. Doumani, "Rediscovering Ottoman Palestine: Writing Palestinians into History," *Journal of Palestine Studies*, 21, no. 2 (Winter 1992): 5–28. Works by a younger generation of Palestinian scholars include Musa Budeiri, *The Palestinian Communist Party, 1919–1948* (London: Ithaca, 1979); 'Abd al-Wahhab Kayyali, *Tarikh Filastin al-Hadith*, 4th ed. (Beirut: Arab Institute for Research and Publishing, 1978; translated as *Palestine: A Modern History*, London: Croom Helm, 1978); Philip Mattar, *Mufti of Jerusalem: Al-Hajj Amin al-Husayni and the Palestinian National Movement* (New York: Columbia University Press, 1988); Muslih, *Origins of Palestinian Nationalism*; Emile Sahliyeh, *The PLO after the Lebanon War* (Boulder: Westview, 1986); Elias Sanbar, *Palestine 1948: L'expulsion* (Paris: Livres de la Revue d'Etudes Palestiniennes, 1984); and Doumani's *Rediscovering Palestine*.

3. Yehoshua Ben Arieh, *Jerusalem in the 19th Century: The Old City* (Jerusalem and New York: Yad Izhak Ben Zvi Institute and St. Martin's Press, 1984). See my review of this book in *Middle East Studies Association Bulletin*, 21, no.1 (Spring 1987): 25–26.

4. Isaiah Fiedman, *The Question of Palestine 1914–1918*, subtitled *A Study of British-Jewish-Arab Relations* (London: Routledge and Kegan Paul, 1973).

5. Porath's *The Emergence of the Palestinian-Arab National Movement, 1919–1929* (London: Frank Cass, 1973), and *The Palestinian Arab National Movement 1929–1939: From Riots to Rebellion* (London: Frank Cass, 1977); and Lesch's *Arab Politics in Palestine, 1917–1939* (Ithaca: Cornell University Press, 1979) are the standard works on the subject.

6. Neville Mandel, *The Arabs and Zionism before World War I* (Berkeley: University of California Press, 1976).

7. The best discussion of this bias in favor of elites and against the subaltern, can be found in Guha and Spivak, eds. *Selected Subaltern Studies*, especially the foreword by Edward Said (pp. v-x) and the introductory sections and the first essay by Guha, pp. 35–86.

8. See, e.g. his "Crop-Sharing Economics in Mandatory Palestine," part 1, *Middle Eastern Studies* 11, no. 1 (January 1975): 3–23; part 2, 11, no. 2 (April 1975): 188–203; "Production and Trade in an Islamic Context: Sharika Contracts in the Transitional Economy of Northern Samaria, 1853–1943," part 1, *International Journal of Middle East Studies* 6, no. 2 (April 1975): 185–209; part 2, 6, no. 3 (July 1975): 308–324; and "The Land-Equalizing *musha'* Village: A Reassessment," in Gilbar, ed., *Ottoman Palestine*, pp. 91–129.

9. Ylana Miller, *Government and Society in Rural Palestine, 1920-1948* (Austin: University of Texas Press, 1985). Other examples of scholarship using archival and other sources to investigate issues at this level are several of the studies in Roger Owen, ed. *Studies in the Economic and Social History of Palestine in the Nineteenth and Twentieth Centuries* (London: Macmillan, 1982); Schölch, *Palestine in Transformation*, and Gershon Shafir, *Land, Labor and the Origins of the Israeli-Palestinian Conflict, 1882–1914* (Cambridge: Cambridge University Press, 1989). Using primarily Zionist sources, Anita Shapira has shed light on some of the same issues from a different perspective in her *Land and Power*, although these sources lead her into making mistaken statements such as (p. x): "the association of Palestine and Palestinian with the Arab population of the country now living outside Israel did not develop until after the establishment of the state."

10. The controversy over *From Time Immemorial* (New York: Harper and Row, 1984), which was lavishly praised by Barbara Tuchman, Saul Bellow, Elie Wiesel, Arthur Goldberg, Theodore White, and other luminaries, finally reached the columns of the *New York Times* in late 1985. The lapses in the research for it were first documented by Norman Finkelstein and William Farrell, in reviews published in *In These Times* on September 11, 1984, and the *Journal of Palestine Studies* 14, no. 1 (Fall 1984): 126–134, respectively. In a devastating review by Israeli historian Yehoshua Porath, entitled "Mrs. Peter's Palestine," in the *New York Review of Books*, January 16, 1986, pp. 36–39, the book was finally shown to be in large part a work of plagiarism, and utterly worthless as scholarship. This conclusion is further documented in Finkelstein's "Disinformation and the Palestine Question: The Not-So-Strange Case of Joan Peters's *From Time Immemorial*, in Said and Hitchens, eds., *Blaming the Victims*, pp. 33–69.

11. Arieh Avneri, *The Claim of Dispossession: Jewish Land Settlement and the Arabs 1878–1948* (New Brunswick, NJ: Transaction Books, 1984).

12. These demographic issues are carefully addressed by Porath, in the review mentioned in note 10 above; by Alexander Schölch, "The Demographic Development of Palestine, 1850–1882," *International Journal of Middle East Studies* 17 no. 4 (November 1985): 485–505; and most thoroughly in McCarthy, *The Population of Palestine.*

13. Edward Said, "Permission to Narrate," *Journal of Palestine Studies* 13, no. 3 (Spring 1984): 27–48.

14. A thorough treatment of the theme of the absence of the Palestinians from Zionist discourse, an absence of long-standing, can be found in Shapira, *Land and Power*, pp. 40–82.

15. Mandel, *The Arabs and Zionism*, pp. xvii-xviii, summarizes this perspective well: "the conventional view is that all was well between Arab and Jew in Palestine before

1914. . . . Among the Arabs there was, at most, only rudimentary opposition to Jewish settlement in Palestine and only a vague awareness of Zionist aims."

16. The debates over the issue of Zionism in the pre-war Arab press are dealt with in Mandel, *The Arabs and Zionism*, and chapters 4–6 of R. Khalidi, *British Policy*. Well over 600 articles on Zionism were published in Cairo, Beirut, Damascus, Haifa, Jaffa, and Jerusalem newspapers from 1909 until 1914, as is discussed in detail in chapter 6, below

17. Mandel, *The Arabs and Zionism* is the most thorough. Others include Kayyali, *Palestine: A Modern History*, and the introductory section of Naji 'Allush, *al-Muqawama al-'arabiyya fi Filastin, 1917–1948* [The Arab resistance in Palestine, 1917–1948] (Beirut: Palestine Research Center, 1967).

18. For more on this development, see R. Khalidi et al., eds., *The Origins of Arab Nationalism*.

19. The literature on the impact of early Jewish immigration to Palestine is vast. Among the most stimulating recent studies are Shafir, *Land, Labor, and the Origins*, and Shapira, *Land and Power*.

20. The figures are taken from McCarthy, *Population of Palestine*, p. 23.

21. Roger Owen, *The Middle East in the World Economy, 1800–1914* (London: Methuen, 1981); Charles Issawi, *An Economic History of the Middle East and Northern Africa* (New York: Columbia University Press, 1982); and *The Fertile Crescent, 1800–1914: A Documentary History*, (New York: Oxford University Press, 1988). Two studies illustrating these changes in different regions are Leila Fawaz, *Merchants and Migrants in Nineteenth-Century Beirut* (Cambridge: Harvard University Press), 1983 and Doumani, *Rediscovering Palestine*.

22. This code is the subject of a 1995 University of Chicago History Department doctoral dissertation by Denise Jorgens, "A Study of the Ottoman Land Code and Khedive Sa'id's Land Law of 1858," which compares the Ottoman and Egyptian land laws of the same years, and shows that they produced fewer changes in land ownership patterns than was formerly believed to be the case. Much recent research is coming to the same conclusion.

23. See chapter 9, "Land Problems and Land Registration," in Gerber, *Ottoman Rule in Jerusalem*, pp. 199–222 for a careful treatment of villages in the hilly Jerusalem area on the basis of an examination of Ottoman records.

24. The best analysis of *musha'* in the regions of Palestine where it predominated is in Firestone, "The Land-Equalizing *musha'* Village."

25. This process is described in A. Granott, *The Land System in Palestine: History and Structure* (London: Eyre and Spottiswoode, 1952), pp. 72–77. As Managing Director of the Jewish National Fund, Granott was perhaps the foremost expert on Zionist land purchase, having been deeply involved in such transactions throughout the Mandate. See also Doreen Warriner, *Land Reform and Development in the Middle East: A Study of Egypt, Syria, and Iraq*, 2nd ed. (London: Oxford University Press, 1962), pp. 60–70, and the articles of Y. Firestone, cited in note 8.

26. Hisham Sharabi, *Arab Intellectuals and the West: The Formative Years, 1875–1914* (Baltimore: Johns Hopkins Press, 1970), p. 3; Mandel, *The Arabs and Zionism*, p. xvii.

27. On forms taken by peasant resistance in different contexts, see James C. Scott, *Weapons of the Weak: Everyday Forms of Peasant Resistance* (New Haven: Yale University Press, 1985).

28. McCarthy, *Population of Palestine*, table, p. 10. See also Doumani, "The Political Economy of Population Counts," pp. 1–17 for more on the politics of Ottoman enumerations of the population in the nineteenth century.

29. McCarthy, *Population of Palestine*, pp. 17–24 for an analysis of where the figure of 85,000 came from, and why it is wrong. It was formerly the commonly accepted figure: see Mandel, *The Arabs and Zionism*, p. xxiv, and Porath, *Emergence*, p. 17, for example. Since, Mandel notes, "as many as one in every two immigrants may have departed again," and since Ottoman figures probably did not count some immigrants who retained European nationalities rather than become Ottoman subjects, figures on Jewish population before the 1920s are problematic. McCarthy makes the obvious point (p. 5) that "the only ones who can properly evaluate population numbers are those who count the population. For the Ottoman Empire, it has been shown that no population statistics but those of the Ottoman government provide usable demographic data."

30. A good map can be found in Mandel, *The Arabs and Zionism*, p. xv.

31. See Buheiry, "Agricultural Exports," Table 2, p. 59. Schölch, *Palestine in Transformation*, pp. 80–92. For the 1923–24 figures, see *Survey of Palestine*, 2 vols. (Jerusalem: Government of Palestine, 1946), Table 2, 1:337.

32. Buheiry, "Agricultural Exports," p. 92.

33. Roger Owen, *The Middle East in the World Economy* (London: Methuen, 1981), p. 265. The dunum in Palestine was equivalent to a hectare during the Mandate, and to just under a hectare before World War I. About four *dunums* equal an acre.

34. For more on the impact of this law, see Granott, *The Land System in Palestine*, Doumani, "Rediscovering Ottoman Palestine," pp. 11–12, and especially Peter Sluglett and Marion Farouk-Sluglett, "The Application of the 1858 Land Code in Greater Syria: Some Observations," in Tarif Khalidi, ed., *Land Tenure and Social Transformation in the Middle East* (Beirut: American University Press, 1984), pp. 409–424.

35. See the suggestive comments in this regard on the concluding pages of Doumani's book, *Rediscovering Palestine*, pp. 244–245.

36. See Shafir, *Land, Labor and the Origins*, pp. 43–44.

37. For demography in general, consult McCarthy, *The Population of Palestine*. For patterns of land settlement, see Schölch, *Palestine in Transformation*, pp. 35–43, 110–117. The number of newly established villages was small: while a few were established in the Jezreel Valley, Table 14, p. 39 in Schölch shows the number of villages in Galilee declining from the 1870s to the 1880s, although total population and the size of most individual villages had grown considerably.

38. *Little Common Ground: Arab Agriculture and Jewish Settlement in Palestine, 1920–1948* (Pittsburgh: University of Pittsburgh Press, 1991), p. 259. Although it deals with the mandatory period, this is an excellent treatment of the overall impact of Jewish land purchase and settlement on the rural Arab society and economy.

39. For details, see Mandel, *The Arabs and Zionism*, pp. 35–37, and Shafir, *Land, Labor and the Origins*, pp. 200–201.

40. Mandel, *The Arabs and Zionism*, p. 36; Shafir, *Land, Labor and the Origins*, p. 200.

41. Mandel, *The Arabs and Zionism*, p. 36.

42. Ibid., pp. 37–38; there are a few additional details in Shafir, *Land, Labor and the Origins*, p. 201.

43. Mandel, *The Arabs and Zionism*, pp. 30–31. For the changes resulting from the second *aliya* see Alex Bein, *The Return to the Soil: A History of Jewish Settlement in Israel* (Jerusalem: Youth and Hechalutz Department of the Zionist Organization, 1952), pp. 36 ff. See also Shapira, *Land and Power*, pp. 53–82, and Shafir, *Land, Labor and the Origins*, pp. 45–90.

44. Shapira, *Land and Power*, pp. 40–42.

45. *Kol Kitve Ahad Ha-Am*, p. 23. Summing up this period, Mandel writes (*The Arabs and Zionism*, p. 31): "Most members of the New Yishuv were genuinely taken aback to find Palestine inhabited by so many Arabs." A few committed Zionist visitors to Palestine were able to ignore this reality, however: Shapira, *Land and Power*, p. 45 describes how Menachem Ussishkin came to the opposite conclusions after a visit to the country.

46. Arthur Ruppin, "The Arab Population in Israel," *Arakhim*, 3, 1971, p. 10. The original quote is from 1930, but these views were current much earlier, as can be seen from an influential lecture entitled "A Hidden Question," published in *Hashiloah* 15 (1907): 193 ff., in which a contemporary of Ahad Ha-Am, Yitzhak Epstein, described how the lands of the villagers of Ras al-Zawiyya and Metulla were bought out from under them when they were sold by absentee landlords in 1882 and 1896, and the settlements of Rosh Pinna and Metullah were founded on these sites.

47. This account is drawn in part from an article by Chaim Kalvarisky in *Jewish-Arab Affairs* (Jerusalem), 1931, pp. 11–14, reprinted in part in Neville Barbour, *Palestine: Star or Crescent?* (New York: Odyssey Press, 1947), pp. 133–134. The details on land ownership are taken from a table on p. 111 of the manuscript by Ruhi al-Khalidi, "*al-Sionism*," cited in chapter 4. See also Bein, *The Return to the Soil*, p. 31. For the background to this incident, and later clashes over the same land, see Mandel, *The Arabs and Zionism*, pp. 22–23, 67–70

48. Mandel, *The Arabs and Zionism*, p. 22.

49. Barbour, *Palestine*, p. 134.

50. Details drawn from the table in Ruhi al-Khalidi, "*al-Sionism*," p. 111; and Bein, *The Return to the Soil*, p. 31.

51. Mandel, *The Arabs and Zionism*, p. 67.

52. For more on the awakening of Arab feeling in the Ottoman Empire at this time see R. Khalidi, *British Policy*, chapter 4; "Arab Nationalism in Syria: The Formative Years," in W. Haddad and W. Ochsenwald, eds., *Nationalism in a Non-National State: The Dissolution of the Ottoman Empire* (Columbus: Ohio University Press, 1977), pp. 207–237; and "Ottomanism and Arabism," pp. 50–69.

53. The fact that he was a Druze, which was irrelevant in this context, is commented on by Mandel (*The Arabs and Zionism*, p. 23) who says that Arslan, "although a Druze, supported the Arab nationalist cause." He appears to share the peculiar notion, propagated by some Israeli Orientalists affiliated with their country's political, military, and intelligence establishment (presumably for divide-and-rule purposes), that the Druze are not Arabs.

54. Barbour, *Palestine*, p. 134.

55. This topic is dealt with in detail in the next chapter.

56. Mandel, *The Arabs and Zionism*, p. 67.

57. Shafir, *Land, Labor and the Origins*, p. 138, and Shapira, *Land and Power*, p. 70. For more on Ha-Shomer, see Bein, *The Return*, pp. 44, 77.

58. Shapira, *Land and Power*, p. 71–72, states that members of *Ha-Shomer* took both the bedouin and the Cossack as models to emulate. Yigal Allon, *The Making of Israel's Army* (London: Valentine, Mitchell, 1970), has a 1909 photo of *Ha-Shomer* guards in Galilee facing p. 20; there is another 1909 photo of twenty-three members of the group facing p. 86, in Ze'ev Schiff, *A History of the Israeli Army, 1874 to the Present*, 2nd ed. (New York: Macmillan, 1985), and yet another of four of them, including the founder of the organization, at Kfar Tavor on the dust jacket of Shafir, *Land, Labor*

and the Origins. It is clear from these photos that many members of the group cultivated the "desperado" look.

59. *The Arabs and Zionism,* p. 67.

60. Allon, *The Making of Israel's Army,* p. 4.

61. Schiff, *A History of the Israeli Army,* pp. 1–3.

62. See 'Abd al-Qadir Yasin, *Kifah al-sha'b al-filastini qabl al-'am 1948* [The struggle
of the Palestinian people before the year 1948] (Beirut: PLO Research Center, 1975,
pp. 5–26), 'Allush, *al-Muqawama,* pp. 28–30, and Kayyali, *Palestine,* pp. 40–41 for
examples of how early acts of armed peasant resistance are seen as precursors of others to follow, and for the way in which a narrative of the continuity of armed Palestinian resistance to Zionism is constructed.

63. One of those killed near al-Shajara in 1909, Radi al-Saffuri, is described in JCA
documents cited by Mandel, *The Arabs and Zionism,* p. 68, as "a well-known robber."
We know nothing else about him, or the others involved in these incidents. For a later
period, al-Arif, in *al-Nakba,* vol. 6, is able to list the names, dates, and places of death
of 1,953 Palestinians (out of a total he puts at 13,000) who died as "martyrs" in the
war of 1947–49. On the subject of "robbers" and "bandits," see E. J. Hobsbawm,
Bandits (London: Weidenfeld and Nicholson, 1969).

64. Granott, *The Land System,* pp. 80–81. The 1883 figure was obtained by Laurence
Oliphant from Alfred Sursuq himself, who complained that it cost him $50,000 to
transport his crops to Haifa and Acre for export: *Haifa: or Life in Modern Palestine*
(Edinburgh: Wm. Blackwood, 1887), pp. 42, 60.

65. The JNF was founded in 1901 by a decision of the Zionist Congress, and in 1907
opened its first office in Jaffa, under the direction of Ruppin. Its local agency, The
Palestine Land Development Corporation, created in 1909, was meant to centralize
and coordinate Jewish land purchase in Palestine, and was successful in this endeavor:
according to Barbara Smith, *The Roots of Separation in Palestine: British Economic Policy,
1920–1929* (Syracuse: Syracuse University Press, 1995), p. 89, "it is estimated that
about 70% of all land acquired by Jews in Palestine was bought through the PLDC."

66. Mandel, *The Arabs and Zionism,* p. 103.

67. *al-Muqtabas,* nos. 551 and 552, December 19, 1910, p. 1, and December 20,
1910, p. 1.

68. *al-Ittihad al-'Uthmani,* no. 735, February 18, 1911, p. 1. For a discussion of al-
'Asali's newspaper articles, see chapter 6, especially note 65.

69. Shafir, *Land, Labor and the Origins,* p. 139.

70. Bein, *The Return,* p. 78. Bein places the "natural resentment of the former cultivators" third in a list of reasons for their attacks, which is headed by their desire "to
steal," and their dislike of "the intrusion of Jews into what was a purely Arab neighborhood." The idea that in the eyes of the *fellahin* it was their land which was being
stolen is of course not mentioned. In this account, as in so much else written about
the earliest clashes between Jews and Arabs in Palestine from the perspective of the
settlers, there is near-blindness to the full weight of this resentment, with the results
often contemptuously written off as "Arab marauding."

71. Ibid. Mandel, *The Arabs and Zionism,* pp. 216–217, cites the same incident as
one of numerous clashes which "reflected peasant resentment" between 1909
and 1913, in which a total of eleven Jewish settlers were killed and others injured,
while Shafir, *Land, Labor and the Origins,* p. 141 notes that Jewish critics argued that
Ha-Shomer "members behaved aggressively and rashly in using firearms" in the
Merhavia incident.

72. Mandel, *The Arabs and Zionism*, pp. 112, 106–7, covers the al-Fula affair, and on pp. 112 ff. assesses al-'Asali's impact in the Ottoman Parliament.

73. *al-Ittihad al-'Uthmani*, no. 737, February 21, 1911, p. 2.

74. *al-Muqtabas*, no. 740, July 29, 1911, p. 2, and no. 748, August 7, 1911, p. 2.

75. *al-Karmil*, no. 153, June 23, 1911, p. 3.

76. *al-Karmil*, no. 151, June 9, 1911, p. 3.

77. *al-Ittihad al- 'Uthmani*, no. 737, February 21, 1911, p. 2.

78. See e.g., *al-Karmil*, no. 171, August 25, 1911, p. 1 editorial; *al-Muqtabas*, no. 767, August 29, 1911, p. 3; no. 771, September 3, 1911, p. 2; no. 782, September 16, 1911, p. 2; no. 784, September 18, 1911, p. 2; *al-Haqiqa*, no. 373, August 24, 1911, p. 1 editorial; *al-Ahram*, no. 10167, August 21, 1911, p. 1; no. 10172, August 25, 1911, p. 1.

79. Kenneth Stein, *The Land Question in Palestine, 1917–1939* (Chapel Hill: University of North Carolina Press, 1984), pp. 226–227 gives a table drawn from the Central Zionist Archives listing a total of 1.39 million dunums of registered Jewish land purchases in Palestine to 1945. Granott's table *(The Land System,* p. 277, table 32) thus represents about 50 per cent of this total.

80. Ibid.

81. Ruhi al-Khalidi, "*al-Sionism,*" p. 111. The table listing Jewish settlements and the sellers of the land involved is partly based on lists published in *Le Jeune Turc,* May 18, 1911, p. 1, and March 24, 1911, p. 1, but includes many additions, especially regarding vendors of land, which are not in these lists and can be seen from his notebooks (located in the Khalidi Library, Jerusalem) to be the results of Ruhi al-Khalidi's own research.

82. For a more detailed critique of the book, see my review of it, the author's response, and my rejoinder in *The Journal of Palestine Studies* 17, no. 1 (Autumn 1987): 146–149; and 17, no. 4 (Summer 1988): 252–256.

83. Stein, *The Land Question*, p. 218.

84. Ibid., p. 59.

85. *Land, Labor and the Origins*, pp. 43–44.

86. Stein, *The Land Question*, p. 226.

87. W. Khalidi, "*Kitab al-Sionism,*" p. 80.

88. Mandel, *The Arabs and Zionism*, p. 70, quotes a local JCA official as describing Nassar as "one of the principal outside instigators" of the incidents at al-Shajara. We have no way of knowing whether Nassar played such a role, or simply became involved out of sympathy with the peasants concerned.

89. The importance of al-Qassam is underlined in works such as those by 'Allush and Kayyali cited in note 17, above, and Ghassan Kanafani, "Thawrat 1936–1939 fi Filastin: Khalfiyya, tafasil wa tahlil" [The 1936–1939 revolution in Palestine: Background, details and analysis], *Shu'un Filistiniyya* 6 (January 1972): 45–77. The writings of 'Allush, Kayyali, and Kanafani, who were all active in Palestinian nationalist politics (the latter two until their assassinations in 1980 and 1972 respectively), played a major part in shaping modern perceptions of this period. The struggle over the meaning of al-Qassam's life and actions continues: there is an extensive current literature on him, stressing his Islamic roots, e.g. Samih Hammuda, *al-Wa'i wal-thawra: Dirasa fi hayat wa jihad al-Shaykh 'Iz al-Din al-Qassam* (Amman: Dar al-Sharq, 1986).

90. S. Abdullah Schleifer, "The Life and Thought of 'Izz-id-Din al-Qassam," *The Islamic Quarterly* 22, no. 2 (1979): 61–81. See also his " 'Izz al-Din al-Qassam: Preacher and *Mujahid,*" in E. Burke III, ed., *Struggle and Survival in the Modern Middle East*, pp. 164–178 (Berkeley: University of California Press, 1993).

91. Ibid., p. 70.

92. For contemporary documentation of al-Qassam's importance, see Akram Zu'aytir, *Al-haraka al-wataniyya al-filistiniyya 1935–1939: Yawmiyyat Akram Zu'aytir* [The Palestinian national movement 1935–1939: The diaries of Akram Zu'aytir] (Beirut, Institute for Palestine Studies, 1980), pp. 27 ff; and *Watha'iq al-haraka al-wataniyya al-filistiniyya 1918–1939: Min awraq Akram Zu'aytir* [Documents of the Palestinian national movement 1918–1939: From the papers of Akram Zu'aytir] (Beirut: Institute for Palestine Studies, 1979), pp. 397–401.

93. A good work on the decisive, later stage in this process is Smith, *The Roots of Separation.*

94. E.g., Uzi Benziman, *Sharon: An Israeli Caesar* (New York: Adama, 1985), p. 2: "At first, the conflict took the form of criminal assaults on Jews and Jewish property by Arab marauders"; and Allon, *The Making of Israel's Army*, p. 11, who writes of the first Jewish settlers practicing "self-defense against robbery, theft, marauding, murder and rape. These for the most part were non-political in nature." In the words of Walter Laqueur, in *A History of Zionism*, pp. 247–248, "Even the most sophisticated Zionist ideologists were usually inclined to deny that the Arabs had been able to develop a national consciousness. Arab attacks were described as mere acts of theft and murder carried out by criminal elements among the Arab population or by a mob incited by agitators devoid of moral scruples." For a penetrating analysis of the logic of this elite and/or colonial discourse directed against the rural lower classes, see Ranajit Guha, "The Prose of Counter-Insurgency," in Guha and Spivak, eds., *Selected Subaltern Studies*, pp. 45–86.

Chapter 6. Elements of Identity II: The Debate on Zionism in the Arabic Press

1. On the "Syrians" (the term used for all those originating in *bilad al-Sham*) in Egypt, see Thomas Philipp, *The Syrians in Egypt 1725–1975* (Stuttgart: Franz Steiner Verlag, 1985), and Mas'ud Daher, *al-Hijra al-lubnaniyya ila Misr fil-qarnayn al-tasi' 'ashar wal-'ashrin* [Lebanese emigration to Egypt in the eighteenth and nineteenth centuries] (Beirut: Lebanese University, 1986).

2. For more on this point, see R. Khalidi, "The Press as a Source."

3. See A. L. Tibawi, *British Interests in Palestine, 1800–1901: A Study of Religious and Educational Enterprise* (Oxford: Oxford University Press, 1961).

4. The results of an earlier survey, covering a smaller number of papers, were published in 1982 in R. Khalidi, "The Role of the Press." These results have since been updated with additional data based on a number of newspapers that were not available at the time of the original survey.

5. These figures are taken from the map on p. xv of N. Mandel, *The Arabs and Zionism.* This data, however, differs significantly from that given in some sources, e.g., Bein, *The Return to the Soil*, pp. 555–572, who gives a total of 33 settlements before 1914, and later foundation dates for many of those listed by Mandel.

6. 'Isa and Yusuf al-'Isa were cousins, not brothers as is stated by a number of authors, including Ayalon, *The Press in the Arab Middle East*, p. 230 (he has the relationship correct on pp. 66 and 96, however). The articles published in *Filastin* on literary topics are listed in Qustandi Shomali, *Fihras al-nusus al-adabiyya fi jaridat Filastin 1911–1967* [An index of literary texts in the newspaper *Filastin*, 1911–1967] (Jerusalem: Arab Studies Society, 1990).

7. For more on al-'Uraisi and *al-Mufid*, see R. Khalidi, "The Press as a Source."

8. See Samir Seikaly, "Damascene Intellectual Life in the Opening Years of the Twentieth Century: Muhammad Kurd 'Ali and *al-Muqtabas*," in Marwan Buheiry, ed., *Intellectual Life in the Arab East, 1890–1939*, pp. 125–153 (Beirut: American University of Beirut, 1981).

9. These papers were available for the following number of years: *al-Karmil*, 4; *Filastin*, 3; *al-Mufid*, 3; *al-Muqtabas*, 6 with gaps; *al-Muqattam* and *al-Ahram*, 7; *Lisan al-Hal*, 7; *al-Ittihad al-'Uthmani*, 7; *al-Haqiqa*, 4; and *al-Iqbal*, 4.

10. These twelve include the Palestinian publications *al-Nafa'is al-'Asriyya*, *al-Quds*, and *al-Munadi*, and *al-Iqdam*, published in Cairo by a Palestinian, Muhammad al Shanti, all of which were mentioned in chapter 3.

11. Tarazi, *Tarikh al-sihafa al-'arabiyya*, 4, pp. 224, 194, 70.

12. Although Malul is mentioned in different capacities in Mandel's text, it is only in the "Note on Sources" on p. 237 that he is referred to as author of the press reports on which Mandel largely based his book. See Porath, *The Emergence*, p. 30, for another reference to Malul.

13. For a very uncomplimentary view of Nassar, claiming that he had originally acted as an agent for land sales to the JCA, see Yehoshua, *Tarikh al-sihafa al-'arabiyya fi Filastin*, pp. 136–142, much of which is based on articles by Nisim Malul and others in the pre-1914 Hebrew press. For a more positive appraisal of Nassar, see Qustandi Shomali, "Nagib Nassar: L'intransigéant, 1873–1948," *Revue d'Etudes Palestiniennes* 54 (1995): 80–90.

14. The booklet was published in Haifa at Nassar's own *al-Karmil* press in 1911. The series ran in *al-Karmil* beginning with issue no. 133, March 31, 1911, and ending with no. 149, June 2, 1911.

15. *al-Karmil*, no. 149, June 2, 1911.

16. "*al-Mu'tamar al-sihyuni*" [The Zionist Congress], *al-Karmil*, no. 358, August 15, 1913.

17. See, e.g., the editorial "*al-Qadiyya al-'arabiyya*" [The Arab Question] in *al-Karmil*, no. 297, January 10, 1913, See also R. Khalidi, "The Press as a Source," for more details on the connections between Arab nationalism and anti-Zionism.

18. Mandel, *The Arabs and Zionism*, wrongly claims (e.g. on p. 130) that *al-Karmil* was pro-CUP throughout the period.

19. See, e.g., the article on *al-Madrasa al-Dusturiyya*, cited in chapter 3, n. 51, and the two-part series on Islamic education in Palestine by al-Hajj Raghib al-Khalidi, in *Filastin*, nos. 52 and 53, July 19 and 22, 1911, both p. 1.

20. During the newspaper's first year of publication a column devoted to this subject appeared in virtually every issue, usually under the rubric "*Shu'un urthuduksiyya*" [Orthodox affairs].

21. See, e.g., the touching multi-part series entitled "*Rasa'il fallah*" [Letters of a fallah], published in serial form in the paper in October 1911.

22. E.g., "*al-Waraqa al-hamra*," [The red card—referring to the document issued by the Ottoman authorities and allowing three months' residence to pilgrims], *Filastin*, no. 69, September 16, 1911, p. 1; and "*Istimlak al-ajanib*" [Possession by foreigners], *Filastin*, no. 70, September 20, 1911, p.1.

23. Sulayman Musa, *al-Haraka al-'arabiyya* (Beirut: al-Nahar, 1970), p. 103. The full name of the organization, probably the most important of the pre-World War I Arabist groupings, was *al-Jam'iyya al-'arabiyya al-fatat* [The Young Arab Society].

24. There was a wave of articles on al-Asfar in the press at this time, e.g.: "*Mashru'*
al-Asfar" [The al-Asfar plan], *al-Karmil*, no. 117, January 17, 1911, p. 1; "*Mashru' al-*
Asfar wal-yahud" [The al-Asfar plan and the Jews] *al-Karmil*, no. 122, February 7,
1911; Taha al-Mudawwar, "*al-Mashru' al-jadid, la mashru' al-Asfar*" [The new project,
not the al-Asfar project] *al-Ra'i al-'Am*, August 19, 1911, p. 1; Haqqi al-'Azm, "*Iqtirah*
fi mashru' Najib Bey al-Asfar al-jadid" [A proposal regarding the new project of Najib
Bey al-Asfar] *al-Ra'i al-'Am* September 16, 1911, p. 1; Muhammad Mahmud Habbal,
"*Mashru' al-Asfar, huwa al khatar al-akbar 'ala al-dawla wal-umma*" [The al-Asfar project
is the greatest danger to the nation and the state], *al-Islah*, no. 72–1468, August 2,
1913, pp. 1–2.

25. Articles by Nassar were printed in *al-Mufid* in nos. 608, May 5, 1911; 1383,
September 23, 1913; and 1425, November 16, 1913. Articles from *al-Mufid* were
reprinted in *al-Karmil* in nos. 122, February 7, 1911; and 334, May 20, 1913.

26. See, e.g., articles by Shukri al-'Asali in nos. 619, February 18, 1911 and 620,
February 19, 1911, of *al-Mufid* which are discussed below.

27. *al-Mufid*, no. 1153, December 18, 1912, p. 3.

28. See the French dispatches cited in R. Khalidi, *British Policy*, p. 328, note 149;
and p. 365, note 65. Ayalon, in *The Press in the Arab Middle East*, p. 66 calls *al-Muqtabas*
one of the two "most important . . . opposition papers" in the Arab provinces.

29. *al-Muqtabas*, nos. 551, December 19, 1910; 552, December 20, 1910; 562,
January 1, 1911; 574, January 15, 1911; 891, January 30, 1912; 1404, February 3, 1914,
the latter four written by Najib Nassar.

30. *al-Muqtabas*, no. 562, January 1, 1911.

31. *al-Muqtabas*, no. 574, January 15, 1911.

32. *al-Muqtabas*, no. 568, January 7, 1911.

33. *al-Muqtabas*, no. 1268, August 13, 1913.

34. Circulation figures for this period are hard to obtain and unreliable. We have
already given some for the Palestinian press in chapter 3. These for *al-Ahram* and *al-*
Muqattam are from an article by al-'Uraisi written from Paris: *al-Mufid* no. 912,
February 19, 1912, in which he also gives the circulation of *al-Mu'ayyad* as 14,000 and
that of *al-Jarida* as 2,000. Ayalon, *The Press in the Arab East*, p. 58, gives somewhat lower
circulation figures for the leading Egyptian papers in this period. A dispatch to the
Zionist Executive from the Zionist Office in Jaffa, cited in Mandel, *The Arabs and*
Zionism, pp. 125–126, gives the circulation of the Beirut newspapers *Lisan al-Hal* and
al-Nasir as 10,000–12,000 and 6,000–8,000 copies respectively.

35. According to Mandel, *The Arabs and Zionism*, p. 149, n. 2, this was the pseudonym of Robert Ghazl, an Egyptian Jew. Five articles or letters by him appeared in *al-*
Ahram and three in *al-Muqattam*. A number of other pro-Zionist articles in the two
papers are signed with what appear to be other pseudonyms, perhaps used by Ghazl
or Malul. Malul himself wrote 12 articles for *al-Muqattam* and three for *al-Ahram*
under his own name, and six more for the former and one more for the latter under
the name Nisim Ben Sahl.

36. al-'Azm, the President of the *Hizb al-Lamarkaziyya al-Idariyya al-'Uthmaniyya* (the
Ottoman Administrative Decentralization Party based in Egypt), and a major figure
in the pre-war Arabist movement, wrote four articles for *al-Muqattam* (in nos. 6679,
March 17, 1911; 7616, April 14, 1914; 7654, May 29, 1914; and 7655, May 30, 1914),
and one for *al-Ahram* (no. 10027, March 8, 1911). Arslan wrote two, in nos. 6929,
January 15, 1912; and 6939, January 26, 1912. The former is discussed briefly below.

37. *al-Muqattam*, no. 6929, January 15, 1912.

38. *al-Muqattam*, no. 7626, April 27, 1914.

39. *al-Muqattam*, no. 7630, May 1, 1914.

40. *al-Muqattam*, nos. 7648, May 22, 1914; and 7655, May 30, 1914.

41. *al-Ahram*, no. 9339, December 3, 1908.

42. *al-Ahram*, no. 9345, December 11, 1908.

43. *al-Ahram*, no. 9517, July 7, 1909.

44. Ayalon, *The Press in the Arab World*, pp. 67–68 says *Lisan al-Hal* was the most popular Lebanese newspaper in the pre-war period, and sold 3,500 copies daily in 1914. See different figures in n. 34, above.

45. Mandel, *The Arabs and Zionism*, p. 130. In his otherwise extremely balanced book, *The Press in the Arab World*, Ayalon also focuses inordinately on the differences between newspapers edited by Muslims and Christians in Palestine, Lebanon, Syria, and Egypt in this period. While some such differences certainly existed and had some importance, they were often not as great as he makes them out to be.

46. Ibid.

47. See R. Khalidi, "The Press as a Source" for more on al-'Uraisi's attitude toward Europe, and his handling of sectarian issues. Mandel's sweeping comments about Muslim editors in Beirut and Damascus must be surprising to anyone who has carefully read the press of the period, which is remarkable for its relative lack of sectarian prejudice. See, e.g., the numerous articles by Christians such as Rafiq Rizq Sallum in *al-Mufid*.

48. Issues from seven years of *al-Barq* were examined, but they were not complete. *al-Hawadith* and *al-Sha'b* were available for three years each, but also were incomplete.

49. *al-Sha'b*, no. 187, December 29, 1910. This article, signed by 'Izzat al-Jundi, is the second of a two-part series criticizing the possible sale of state lands in Palestine to Zionist interests, but the preceding issue of the paper is unavailable.

50. *al-Sha'b*, no. 195, February 14, 1911.

51. *al-Sha'b*, no. 197, February 18, 1911.

52. *Lisan al-Hal*, no. 6581, March 10, 1911.

53. *Lisan al-Hal*, no. 6733, September 9, 1911.

54. *Lisan al-Hal*, no. 7535, May 1, 1914.

55. Mandel, *The Arabs and* Zionism, pp. 129–133, especially p. 133.

56. Yehoshua, *Tarikh al-sihafa al-'arabiyya fi Filastin*, notes on p. 55 that "we consider *al-Munadi* the first Arabic Islamic newspaper published in the country." At least 16 major papers had appeared before *al-Munadi* was published in Jerusalem by Sa'id Jarallah in 1912.

57. The only other exception in Palestine was the unimportant Jaffa paper *al-Akhbar*. See chapter 3, above, note 77, for more on how pro-Zionist papers were subsidized.

58. Ayalon, *The Press in the Arab Middle East*, p. 71, citing Amin Sa'id, *al-Thawra al-'arabiyya al-kubra*, [The Great Arab Revolt], 2 vols. (Cairo: Dar al-'Ilm lil-Malayin, 1934), 1:58–92.

59. *al-Ittihad al-'Uthmani*, nos. 679, December 10, 1911; 724, February 6, 1911; 1548, November 8, 1913; and 1550, November 14, 1913 (the latter article is reprinted from *Filastin*).

60. *al-Mufid*, nos. 608, February 5, 1911; 1383, September 23, 1913; and 1425, November 16, 1913; *al-Haqiqa*, no. 370, August 14, 1911.

61. *al-Ittihad al-'Uthmani*, no. 679, December 10, 1910.

62. *al-Ittihad al-'Uthmani*, no. 724, February 6, 1911; and *al-Mufid*, no. 608, February 5, 1911.

63. For more on al-'Asali, see pp. 223–243 of R. Khalidi, *British Policy*. See also Mandel, *The Arabs and Zionism*.

64. Cited in ibid., p. 84. al-Zahrawi was also hanged by the Ottoman authorities in 1916.

65. *al-Muqtabas*, nos. 542, December 5, 1910; 752, August 11, 1911; 753, August 2, 1911; and 756, August 15, 1911; *al-Karmil*, nos. 118, January 20, 1911; 126, February 24, 1911; and 168, August 15, 1911; *al-Mufid*, nos. 619 and 620, February 18 and 19, 1911; *al-Haqiqa*, nos. 321 and 322, February 20 and 23, 1911; *al-Ittihad al-'Uthmani*, nos. 689, December 28, 1910; and 735, February 18, 1911; *al-Iqbal*, no. 376, November 19, 1910.

66. The article appeared in no. 735 of *al-Ittihad al-'Uthmani* and in two parts in *al-Mufid* and *al-Haqiqa*, all cited in n. 65 above.

67. The Vali's reply is printed in *al-Ittihad al-'Uthmani*, no. 737, February 21, 1911. Most Beirut papers carried the same letter by Nur al-Din Bey.

68. For more details see R. Khalidi, *British Policy*, pp. 223–224, and chapters 4 and 5, above.

69. *al-Haqiqa*, nos. 275, August 29, 1910; 283, September 26, 1910; 287, October 17, 1910; 295, November 14, 1910; and 298, November 24, 1910.

70. See, e.g., the pro-Zionist article in *al-Ittihad al-'Uthmani* (the first and only one of its kind in this paper) no. 1422, June 10, 1913, by Rizq Allah Arqash, a leader of the Beirut Reform Society and delegate to the First Arab Congress in Paris.

71. Mandel, *The Arabs and Zionism*, p. 162.

72. *al-Ittihad al-'Uthmani*, no. 1550, November 14, 1913.

73. *al-Ittihad al-'Uthmani*, no. 1558, November 24, 1913.

74. Three such exceptions were mentioned in the previous chapters: Najib Nassar was accused by the Zionists of organizing the peasants to resist the JCA's purchases at al-Shajara; Shukri al-'Asali tried to prevent the transfer of the al-Fula lands to the JCA while *qa'immaqam* of Nazareth in 1910; and Amir Amin Arslan, while *qa'immaqam* of Tiberias in 1901, supported the resistance of the local peasants to JCA land purchase in that region.

75. Anderson, *Imagined Communities*.

76. *al-Karmil*, nos. 30 and 31, July 10 and 17, 1909 (the paper was a weekly for the first year of publication). The articles are reprinted from *al-Muqattam*, nos. 6152, June 10, 1909 and 6155, June 13, 1909.

Chapter 7. The Formation of Palestinian Identity: The Critical Years, 1917–1923

1. Such polemics, which have long been a feature of American and Israeli public discourse on the question of Palestine, generally affirm the nonexistence, or the illegitimacy, or the recent provenance, of a separate Palestinian identity. They are epitomized by Joan Peters' *From Time Immemorial*, referred to in chapter 5 above, n. 10.

2. These works include Porath, *The Emergence*; Kayyali, *Palestine: A Modern History*; Lesch, *Arab Politics in Palestine*; Muslih, *The Origins of Palestinian Nationalism*; and Kimmerling and Migdal, *Palestinians*.

3. These models retain their seductive power notwithstanding attempts to modify them: for one such attempt, see Peter Sahlins, *Boundaries: The Making of France and Spain in the Pyrenees* (Berkeley: University of California Press, 1989). Most of the stan-

dard works on nationalism, from Hans Kohn [*A History of Nationalism in the East* (New York: Harcourt, Brace, 1929) and *The Idea of Nationalism* (New York: Collier, 1967)] through Ernest Gellner [*Nations and Nationalism*], Benedict Anderson [*Imagined Communities*], and Eric Hobsbawm [*Nations and Nationalism Since 1780*], have taken European models as the basis of their analysis, even while noting that they are often inapplicable to non-European cases. On this subject see Chatterjee, *Nationalist Thought and the Colonial World.*

4. This sort of multifocal identity, or even the paler and more tame "ethnic diversity," which is sometimes held up as an ideal in the United States, would be unthinkable in a European country with a unitary national myth like France, where citizens, whatever their color, religion, or origin are French—or at least so the myth goes. French citizens of North African and other immigrant origins frequently find that the reality bears little relation to this myth.

5. Perhaps the only intellectual to reflect on the implications of the collision of the Palestinians with the potent Jewish/Israeli narrative is Edward Said, in *The Question of Palestine* (New York: Vintage, 1979), and elsewhere.

6. This intertwining is reflected even in the way information is organized and presented in the catalogues and on the shelves of major libraries, where books on Palestine and Palestinian history are to be found intermingled with others on Israel, Zionism, and Jewish history.

7. Hall, "Ethnicity: Identity and Difference," p. 16.

8. To see how much has changed in this regard, it is necessary only to note how much more coolly Zionism is treated in most works on Jewish history produced before the period from the rise of Hitler until 1967, when this synthesis was established and became hegemonic, under the impact of the Nazi Holocaust, the establishment of Israel, and Israel's triumph in the 1967 war. In this context, see the ongoing work of University of Chicago historian Peter Novick on the historiography of the Holocaust—the only part of which published so far is "Holocaust Memorials in America," in James Young, ed., *The Art of Memory: Holocaust Memorials in History* (New York: Prestell, with the Jewish Museum, 1994, pp. 157–163—as well as Tom Segev, *The Seventh Million: The Israelis and the Holocaust* (New York: Hill and Wang, 1993).

9. One of the first disparaging comments on the legitimacy of Palestinian aspirations came from none other than British Foreign Secretary Arthur J. Balfour, author of the Balfour Declaration. In a Foreign Office memo dated August 11, 1919, cited in J. C. Hurewitz, ed., *The Middle East and North Africa in World Politics*, 2 vols. (New Haven: Yale University Press, 1979) 2:189, he stated: "Zionism, be it right or wrong, good or bad, is rooted in age-long traditions, in present needs, in future hopes, of far greater import than the desires and prejudices of the 700,000 Arabs who now inhabit that ancient land." For Balfour, the Zionists had traditions, needs, and hopes; the Arabs of Palestine (who "*now*"—i.e. recently—inhabited the country) only desires and prejudices.

10. *The Sunday Times* (London), June 15, 1969, p. 12. This was only one instance of the success of Israeli leaders like Meir, Abba Eban, Shimon Peres, and Yitzhaq Rabin in shaping U.S. public opinion. Although leaders of Likud like Menachem Begin and Yitzhaq Shamir did not have the same broad success, they won acceptance for many of their extreme ideas among key segments of American elite opinion. In trying to obtain support from the American Jewish community and the U.S. Congress for its policies of rapprochement with the Palestinians, the recently defeated Labor government struggled with the consequences of the past propaganda successes of both Likud and earlier Labor governments.

11. For an early example of the terms in which this debate was framed, see Marwan Buheiry, "Bulus Nujaym and the Grand Liban Ideal 1908–1919," in Buheiry, ed., *Intellectual Life in the Arab East,* pp. 62–83. Salibi, *A House of Many Mansions,* is the best survey of the struggle over the historiography of Lebanon. See as well Beydoun, *al-Sira' 'ala tarikh Lubnan.*

12. Fateh (a reverse acronym for *"Harakat al-tahrir al-watani al-filastini"* —the Palestinian National Liberation Movement), which held its first conference in Kuwait in 1959, grew out of a number of small Gaza- and Egypt-based student and commando groups formed in the wake of the 1948 war. Similarly, the PFLP, founded in 1968, grew out of the Movement of Arab Nationalists which came into being at the American University of Beirut, also in the wake of the 1948 war. For more on this generation of Palestinian nationalists, see Helena Cobban, *The Palestinian Liberation Organization* (Cambridge: Cambridge University Press, 1984); Abu Iyyad with Eric Rouleau, *My Home My Land: A Narrative of the Palestinian Struggle* (New York: Times Books, 1984); Alain Gresh, *The PLO: The Struggle Within* (London: Zed, 1988); Walid Kazziha, *Revolutionary Transformation in the Arab World* (New York: St. Martin's, 1975); and Laurie Brand, *The Palestinians in the Arab World* (New York: Columbia University Press, 1988).

13. Among the manifestations of this outlook are a tendency to look anachronistically at eighteenth-century leaders such as Zahir al-'Umar as the forbears of Palestinian nationalism, and a predeliction for seeing in peoples such as the Cananites, Jebusites, Amorites, and Philistines the lineal ancestors of the modern Palestinians.

14. The reference, once again, is to Benedict Anderson's *Imagined Communities.* Anderson's stress on the crucial role of what he calls "print capitalism" in the genesis and growth of nationalism seems particularly apt in the Palestinian case.

15. *Palestine in Transformation,* pp. 9–17.

16. This echoes a traditional Hebrew term used to describe the country, *ha-eretz ha-mikdash.* Given the brief adoption of Jerusalem as a direction of prayer by the early Muslims, and other important Jewish influences on early Islam, there is very possibly a connection.

17. See Kamil al-'Asali, *Makhtutat Fada'il Bayt al-Maqdis* [Manuscripts on the "Merits of Jerusalem"] (Amman: Dar al-Bashir, 1984), for an extensive listing and analysis of medieval Muslim works of this genre.

18. Kamil al-'Asali, *Mawsim al-Nabi Musa fi Filastin: Tarikh al-mawsim wal-maqam* [The Nabi Musa Festival in Palestine: The history of the festival and the shrine], Amman: Dar al-Karmil, 1990; Schölch, *Palestine in Transformation,* p. 16; Porath, *The Emergence,* pp. 1–9. See also Muhammad 'Izzat Darwaza's memoir, *Khamsa wa tis'una 'aman,* 1:92–95, for an account of his participation in the Nabi Musa rites together with others from Nablus in his youth.

19. Schölch, *Palestine in Transformation,* pp. 12–15; Abu Manneh, "Jerusalem in the Tanzimat Period"; and "The Rise of the Sanjak of Jerusalem in the Late 19th Century," in Ben Dor, ed., *The Palestinians and the Middle East Conflict* pp. 21–32 (Ramat Gan: Turtle Dove, 1978). See also 'Abd al-'Aziz Muhammad 'Awad, "Mutasarrifiyyat al-Quds, 1874–1914," [The district of Jerusalem] in *al-Mu'tamar al-Duwali al-Thalith li-Tarikh Bilad al-Sham: Filastin* [Third international conference on the history of *bilad al-Sham:* Palestine], 3 vols. (Amman: Jordanian University/Yarmuk University, 1983), 1:204–223.

20. 'Azuri's article, originally published in the Turkish paper *Sabah,* was reprinted in Arabic in *Thamarat al-Funun,* September 23, 1908, p. 7. It is interesting that a copy

of the article was among papers which Ruhi al-Khalidi was carrying with him to Istanbul from Marseilles in 1908 after he was elected as deputy from Jerusalem: Ruhi al-Khalidi papers, Khalidi Library, Jerusalem.

21. Schölch, *Palestine in Transformation*, p. 15.

22. Porath, *The Emergence*, pp. 8–9.

23. The rivalries of the European powers over Palestine in the century before 1914 have not received the treatment they deserve. Works on the subject include Tibawi, *British Interests in Palestine*; R. Khalidi, *British Policy*; Norman Rose, ed., *From Palmerston to Balfour: Collected Essays of Mayir Vereté* (London: Cass, 1992); Jacques Thobie, *Intérets et imperialisme français dans l'Empire ottoman, 1895–1914* (Paris: Sorbonne, 1977); and Isaiah Friedman, *Germany, Turkey, and Zionism, 1897–1918* (Oxford: Clarendon, 1977).

24. Undated [1701] document located in Khalidi Library, cited in chapter 2 above, n. 59.

25. These include older works such as the *fada'il* literature, e.g., Muhammad Ibn Ahmad al-Maqdisi [1306–1344], *Fada'il al-Sham* [The merits of Syria] (Tanta: Dar al-Sahaba, 1988) which focused on Jerusalem, and Mujir al-Din's *al-Uns al-Jalil*; and more recent ones like Ihsan al-Nimr's *Tarikh Jabal Nablus*; 'Arif al-'Arif's *al-Mufassal fi tarikh al-Quds* [A detailed history of Jerusalem], 2nd ed. (Jerusalem: Dar al-Andalus, 1961); and Mustafa Murad al-Dabbagh's multivolume *Biladuna Filastin* [Our country, Palestine], 10 vols. (Beirut: Dar al-Tali'a, 1965–1976).

26. On pride in the village, see Ted Swedenburg, "The Role of the Palestinian Peasantry in the Great Revolt (1936–1939)," in E. Burke III and I. M. Lapidus, eds., *Islam, Politics and Social Movements*, pp. 169–203 (Berkeley: University of California, 1988), and Doumani, *Rediscovering Palestine*, pp. 27–29; and Michael Gilsenan, *Lords of the Lebanese Marches: Violence and Narrative in an Arab Society* (Berkeley: University of California Press, 1996).

27. A recent joke shows the persistence of local loyalties, and how they can still be imagined as transcending broader bonds: the scene is a Jerusalem street, where two Arab Jerusalemites (nowadays outnumbered by Israelis and "newcomers" from Hebron) witness a fight between a Hebronite and an Israeli. When the first asks why the other does not intervene, he answers: "Why should I? It is a fight between settlers." The continuing strength of these loyalties can also be seen from the vitality of associations for inhabitants of the towns of Ramallah, Beitunia, al-Birah, and Deir Dibwan (to name only four) among Palestinians all over the United States.

28. Rosemary Sayigh, *Palestinians: From Peasants to Revolutionaries* (London: Zed, 1979), is the best analysis of this phenomenon. See also her more recent book, *Too Many Enemies: The Palestinian Experience in Lebanon* (London: Zed, 1994).

29. *Filastin* special issue (described on the masthead as closed by order of the Ministry of the Interior, an order which this issue, disguised as a one-page broadsheet "open letter to subscribers," was presumably defying), 7 Nisan 1330/May 1914 [rest of date erased on only copy extant], p. 1. For details of this affair, see R. Khalidi, *British Policy*, pp. 356–357. While *umma* can also mean "community," the more common meaning of nation is clearly meant here since the same article speaks of "*al-umma al-'arabiyya*"—which can only mean the Arab nation—in another section cited below.

30. Ibid. A French consular official, commenting on this incident, remarked that it indicated widespread opposition to Zionism among the urban population of Palestine.

31. *Filastin*, special issue, 7 Nisan 1330/May 1914, p. 1.

32. Ibid.

33. For more on the struggle of Arabic-speaking Greek Orthodox in Syria and Palestine to free their church from the control of its Greek hierarchy and to Arabize it, see Derek Hopwood, *Russian Interests in Syria and Palestine, 1800–1901* (Oxford: Oxford University Press, 1966).

34. The speech is reported as having been delivered "at the end of the Second World War" in 'Ajaj Nuwayhid, *Rijal min Filastin ma bayna bidayat al-qarn hatta 'am 1948* [Men from Palestine from the beginning of the century until 1948] (Amman: Filastin al-Muhtalla, 1981), p. 30.

35. See R. Khalidi, "Arab Nationalism."

36. They perceived this "Turkification" largely after the fact in the years after World War I (although the term was used in the pre-War Arabic press). The rewriting of Arab history in the interwar years to fit this new version of events is a fascinating story that has yet to find its historian.

37. How Arabism supplanted Ottomanism as an ideology is best treated in C. Ernest Dawn's seminal *From Ottomanism to Arabism: Essays on the Origins of Arab Nationalism* (Urbana: University of Illinois Press, 1973). See also R. Khalidi et al., eds. *The Origins of Arab Nationalism*, especially R. Khalidi, "Ottomanism and Arabism" as a corrective to some of Dawn's views.

38. Khalil al-Sakakini, *Filastin ba'd al-harb al-kubra* [Palestine after the great war] (Jerusalem: Bayt al-Maqdis Press, 1925), p. 9. This 56-page pamphlet is a collection of articles originally published in the Cairo newspaper *al-Siyasa* in 1923.

39. The total number of Palestinians executed for nationalist activities during the war is not known. Bayan Nuwayhid al-Hut, *al-Qiyadat wal-mu'assasat al-siyasiyya fi Filastin, 1917–1948* [Political leaderships and institutions in Palestine, 1917–1948] (Beirut: Institute for Palestine Studies, 1981), pp. 46–52, discusses the cases of nine leading Palestinian personalities executed by the Ottoman authorities or who died in prison. In addition, hundreds of others were exiled to Anatolia with their families during the war on similar charges.

40. McCarthy, *The Population of Palestine*, pp. 25–27.

41. For an assessment of the impact of all these factors, see R. Khalidi, "The Arab Experience in the First World War," in H. Cecil and P. Liddle, eds., *Facing Armageddon: The First World War Experienced* (London: Routledge, in press).

42. See R. Khalidi, *British Policy*, especially the final two chapters, for more on pre-war concerns about the occupation of Syria and Palestine by the European powers.

43. al-Hut, *al-Qiyadat wal-mu'assasat*, pp. 77–78, notes that although the text of the Balfour Declaration was not officially published in Palestine until 1920, within a few days of its issuance on November 2, 1917, the Egyptian press had published details of it and of the jubilant reactions to it in the Egyptian Jewish community. These provoked a strong reaction among Palestinians when the news reached them soon afterwards.

44. Laqueur, *A History of Zionism*, p. 145, notes that David Wolffsohn, the President of the Zionist movement following Herzl, from 1905 until World War I, backed off from the idea of a Jewish state expounded by Herzl, as well as from the idea of an internationally guaranteed status in Palestine for Zionism, which Laqueur describes as "tactical changes, shifts in emphasis rather than in the basic attitude of the movement."

45. The conclusions of the conference are summarized in Parliamentary Command papers, Cmd. 5957, "Correspondence between Sir Henry McMahon and the Sharif Husain of Mecca, July 1915–March 1916," (London: His Majesty's Stationary Office, 1939). The background to the three British engagements is analyzed in R. Khalidi, *British Policy*. See also George Antonius, *The Arab Awakening* (London: Hamish

Hamilton, 1938), a classic statement of the Arab case, as well as Elie Kedourie, *In the Anglo-Arab Labyrinth* (London: Weidenfeld & Nicolson, 1977) for one approach to the dispute, and A. L. Tibawi, *Anglo-Arab Relations and the Question of Palestine, 1914–1921* (London: Luzac, 1977), for another.

46. See Jacob Burckhardt, *Judgements on History and Historians*, tr. Harry Zohn (Boston: Beacon, 1958), pp. 221 ff. See also Erik Erikson, *A Way of Looking at Things: Selected Papers from 1930 to 1980*, S. Schlier, ed. (New York: Norton, 1987), pp. 675–684, for reflections on the psycho-social roots of identity.

47. The rapidity with which fundamental and lasting shifts in attitudes took place among Palestinians and Lebanese in Beirut under conditions of extreme stress from 1973 until 1983 bears out the observation that attitudes can change substantially and swiftly in times of crisis: most Palestinians in Lebanon completely changed their views and came to accept the idea of a Palestinian state alongside Israel during this period, while the attitudes of most Lebanese toward the Palestinians worsened dramatically during the same time: see R. Khalidi, *Under Siege*, ch. 1; "The Palestinians in Lebanon: The Social Repercussions of the Israeli Invasion," *Middle East Journal* 38, no. 2 (Spring 1984): 255–266; and "The Palestinian Dilemma: PLO Policy after Lebanon," *Journal of Palestine Studies* 15, no. 1 (Autumn 1985), pp. 88–103; and Sayigh, *Palestinians: From Peasants to Revolutionaries*; and *Too Many Enemies*.

48. Akram Zu'aytar, ed., *Watha'iq al-haraka al-wataniyya al-filistiniyya* [Papers of the Palestinian national movement] (Beirut: Institute for Palestine Studies, 1979), includes a total of 36 documents reflecting Palestinian political positions in 1918, 1919, and 1920, with more than 50 each from 1921 and 1922. There are considerably fewer from the years immediately following, a period of relative political quiescence.

49. For examples of British prejudices, see Smith, *The Roots of Separatism*, p. 53 who notes the attitudes toward the Arabs of Sir Herbert Samuel, the first High Commissioner, Balfour, and other British officials. The memoirs of Samuel's son, Edwin, who served in Palestine for most of the mandate period, reveal his lack of knowledge of Arabic, or of Palestinian society: Edwin Samuel, *A Lifetime in Jerusalem: The Memoirs of the Second Viscount Samuel* (London: Valentine, Mitchell, 1970. See also Edward Keith-Roach, *Pasha of Jerusalem: Memoirs of a District Commissioner Under the British Mandate* (London: Radcliffe Press, 1994.

50. Ronald Storrs, *Orientations* (London: Ivor Nicholson and Watson, 1937), pp. 336–338. Storrs was the first British Military Governor of Jerusalem.

51. Papers from the files of *Suriyya al-Janubiyya* and *al-Sabah* in the possession of Dr. Musa Budayri, Jerusalem. For the Ottoman and British press laws, see Khuri, ed., *al-Sihafa al-'arabiyya fi Filastin*, pp. 147–225.

52. After the war, his cousin Yusuf, who had founded *Filastin* with him, remained in Damascus where he established the newspaper *Alif Ba*.

53. *Filastin*, no. 1–328, March 19, 1921, "Hadith qadim wa bayan jadid" ["An old story and a new statement"], p. 1.

54. Khuri, ed., *al-Sihafa al-'arabiyya fi Filastin*, pp. 14–15. Zakka appears to have benefited from subventions from the Zionist Organization once again after the war: Yehoshua, *Tarikh al-sihafa al-'arabiyya fi Filastin*, p. 52.

55. Only a few issues of the paper exist, some in the Khalidi Library in Jerusalem, and others in the possession of Dr. Musa Budayri. *Suriyya al-Janubiyya*, as well as *al-Sabah*, first published in 1921 by Muhammad Hassan al-Budayri's cousin, Muhammad Kamil al-Budayri, was printed in a small set of rooms belonging to the al-Budayri family immediately adjacent to the Haram al-Sharif which is now the site of *al-Maktaba al-*

Budayriyya. Suriyya al-Janubiyya is described by Bernard Wasserstein in *The British in Palestine*, p. 60, as "the nationalist newspaper."

56. R. Khalidi, "The Press as a Source."

57. See Muslih, *The Origins of Palestinian Nationalism*, p. 168, who notes that al-Budayri, al-'Arif and Hajj Amin al-Husayni, who wrote frequently for the paper, were leading members of *al-Nadi al-'Arabi.*

58. *Suriyya al-Janubiyya*, no. 11, November 11, 1919, "Suriyya al-janubiyya" [Southern Syria: this is the title of the article], p. 6. See also Wasserstein, *The British in Palestine*, pp. 180–82, who incorrectly ascribes to al-'Arif alone all the credit for producing the paper.

59. See Malcolm B. Russell, *The First Modern Arab State: Syria Under Faysal, 1918–1920* (Minneapolis: Biblioteca Islamica, 1985), for the best account of the new Syrian state. The introductory chapters of Philip Khoury's magisterial *Syria and the French Mandate: The Politics of Arab Nationalism, 1920–1945* (Princeton: Princeton University Press, 1987), is the most judicious exposition of the tangled diplomacy of the end of Faysal's state.

60. For the somewhat different attitudes of some Syrians, and especially some Damascenes, to the new state, see the dissertation of James Gelvin, "Popular Mobilization and the Foundations of Mass Politics in Syria, 1918–1920," Harvard University, History and Middle Eastern Studies, 1992; Russell, *The First Modern Arab State*; and Muslih, *The Origins of Palestinian Nationalism.*

61. Among the Palestinians who served Faysal and his government were 'Auni 'Abd al-Hadi, 'Isa al-'Isa, and Muhammad 'Izzat Darwaza. See *Dhikra Istiqlal Suriyya* [A commemoration of the independence of Syria] (Damascus: n.p., 1920).

62. See R. Khalidi, *British Policy*, and R. Khalidi et al., eds, *The Origins of Arab Nationalism*, for details of these pre-war evolutions.

63. Until the 1940s many Lebanese, particularly Sunnis, refused to accept the legitimacy of Lebanon as an entity, preferring to consider the country only as the Syrian coastal region. This attitude was expressed in a series of "Conferences of the Coast" (a name implying a refusal to accept that these regions were part of Lebanon), held in the 1920s and into the 1930s. See Salibi, *A House of Many Mansions, pp.* 167ff.

64. Report dated August 5, 1920 in the Central Zionist Archives, cited in Porath, *The Emergence*, p. 107.

65. "al-Anba' al-mulafaqa" ["Concocted news"], *Suriyya al-Janubiyya*, no. 8, October 2, 1919, p. 1.

66. "Illa natadhakar Filastin?" ["Shall we not remember Palestine?"], ibid., pp. 3–4.

67. "Zubdat al-akhbar" ["The best—literally 'the butter'—of the news"], *Suriyya al-Janubiyya*, no. 11, November 11, 1919, p. 5.

68. "Hawla al-mas'ala al-sihyuniyya" ["Regarding the Zionist issue"], *Suriyya al-Janubiyya*, no. 16, November 27, 1919, p. 4.

69. Samuels' speech is Cited in Wasserstein, *The British in Palestine*, p. 76. Porath, *The Emergence*, p. 319, n. 17 suggests regarding the strong Arab reaction to this speech that "perhaps Samuel had not precisely said what was later attributed to him," and was misunderstood by the Arabs. As the quotation from the speech cited by Wasserstein shows, however, Samuel said exactly what the Arabs thought he had: that Zionism aimed for a Jewish majority and, eventually, complete control of the country.

70. The only other important newspapers to publish in Palestine while *Suriyya al-Janubiyya* appeared were Bulus Shahada's *Mir'at al-Sharq*, published in Jerusalem starting in September 1919 (this became the organ of the anti-Husayni faction in the

early 1920s, and a nationalist organ later on, when Ahmad Shuqayri and Akram Zu'aytir wrote for it), and *al-Nafir* and *al-Karmil,* reopened in Haifa in September 1919 and February 1920 respectively. A few other papers established at this time rapidly folded, or had little circulation or influence. As mentioned earlier, *Filastin* did not resume publication until March 1921.

71. "Hidhar, Hidhar!," *Suriyya al-Janubiyya,* no. 22, December 23, 1919, p. 2.

72. "Hawla al-mas'ala al-sihyuniyya" ["Regarding the Zionist issue": this had become a regular column in the paper by this time], *Suriyya al-Janubiyya,* no. 48, March 26, 1920, p. 3. This and the preceding article cited reffered obliquely to Amir Faysal's agreement of January 1919 with Chaim Weizmann, which was fiercely criticized in Palestine when it became known.

73. See Russell, *The First Modern Arab State,* pp. 124–125; Muslih, *The Origins of Palestinian Nationalism,* pp. 117–125, and 146–151; and Porath, *The Emergence,* pp. 102–103.

74. For the calculations of Syrian politicians and the responses of Palestinian officials and activists in Syria at the time, see Muslih, *The Origins of Palestinian Nationalism,* pp. 151–154.

75. "Wa la tay'asu min ruh Allah" ["And do not despair of the spirit of God"], *Suriyya al-Janubiyya,* no. 11, November 11, 1919, p. 3.

76. *Suriyya al-Janubiyya,* no. 32, January 23, 1920, p. 2. The rhetorical devices used, while reminiscent of romantic nineteenth-century European nationalism, are steeped in Arabic and Islamic imagery and terminology. Such overheated prose has remained a staple of Palestinian political rhetoric down to the present day, in the speeches of politicians like Ahmad Shuqayri (who in the 1920s was a journalist for this paper's rival, *Mir'at al-Sharq*), and later was the first head of the Palestine Liberation Organization, and his successor, Yasser Arafat.

77. See Lesch, *Arab Politics in Palestine,* pp. 84–88, Muslih, *The Origins of Palestinian Nationalism,* pp. 158–163, and Porath, *The Emergence,* pp. 32–34, for the significance of these societies. Muslih and Porath report claims that some British officials encouraged their establishment, presumably as a counterweight to the Zionist movement.

78. *Suriyya al-Janubiyya,* no. 48, March 26, 1920, *"Taqrir min Ghazza"* [Report from Gaza], p. 2. The word *wataniyya,* which can mean either nationalism or patriotism, is derived from *watan,* meaning homeland. The article in question reported on the strong local reaction to what were described as attempts by Jewish merchants, with the connivance of the British authorities, to purchase large quantities of livestock and other food products in Gaza, and the effect of this in driving up local prices.

79. *Suriyya al-Janubiyya,* no. 48, March 26, 1920, p. 1.

80. *al-Sabah,* no. 1, October 21, 1921. This paper was published by Muhammad Hassan al-Budayri's cousin Muhammad Kamil Budayri in the same offices and with the same political line as *Suriyya al-Janubiyya.* This terminology soon became routine: on p. 228, Sabri Sharif 'Abd al-Hadi's geography text *Jughrafiyyat Suriyya wa Filastin al-Tabi'iyya* [The natural geography of Syria and Palestine] (Cairo: al-Maktaba al-Ahliyya, 1923), discussed at the end of this chapter, noted in its description of Palestine that Jerusalem is "the capital of the country."

81. *Mir'at al-Sharq,* no. 1, September 17, 1919, p.1.

82. Wasserstein, *The British in Palestine,* p. 59; he also notes (p. 150) that the paper's editor, Bulus Shahada, for a time received a subvention from Zionist funds.

83. These documents, collected by Dr. Musa Budayri, are cited in n. 51, above.

84. Each devotes a chapter to this subject: Muslih, *The Origins of Palestinian Nationalism*, pp. 131–154; Porath, *The Emergence*, pp. 70–122. In his chapter, Porath occasionally uses the press as a source, although far more frequently relying on Zionist, British and other Arab sources.

85. For the texts of these declarations, see Hurewitz, *The Middle East and North Africa*, 2:110–112.

86. The most influential of these counselors was T. E. Lawrence, who was rarely separated from Faysal when he was in London or Paris. His well known self-loathing regarding this period seems to have been related to his (undoubtedly correct) belief that he was deceiving the Arabs as to British intentions. Passages throughout Lawrence's *Seven Pillars of Wisdom* appear to confirm this.

87. al-Hut, *al-Qiyadat wal-mu'assasat*, pp. 63–65.

88. There is a controversy over whether the British or the Arab army entered Damascus first. It is clear from the most recent and apparently most careful examination of the evidence, by Eliezer Tauber, in *The Arab Movements in World War I* (London: Cass, 1993), pp. 231–238, that Australian and Arab forces entered the city from different directions on the morning of the same day, October 1, 1918, with the Australians perhaps an hour earlier. Thereafter in Damascus, Amir Faysal was recognized by the British as the commander of the Arab army and therefore the senior allied military commander in Occupied Enemy Territory Administration [East], rather than in any overtly political capacity. His appointees, first Shukri al-Ayyubi and then General 'Ali Rida al-Rikabi, were confirmed by Allenby as Chief Administrators of OETA-East.

89. Storrs, *Orientations*, pp. 353–354. Wasserstein, *The British in Palestine*, points out (p. 42, n. 34) that initially Hebrew was not recognized as an official language by the military administration, but that by the end of 1919 this ruling had been overturned.

90. The speeches of Zionist leaders abroad, reported for decades in the Arabic press, had long aroused anti-Zionist sentiment in Palestine and elsewhere in the Arab world, as we saw in chapter 6, above. After the war, speeches such as that of Sir Herbert Samuel, mentioned above and in n. 69, provoked a fierce reaction. But it was the speeches and actions of Zionist leaders and officials in Palestine that provoked the greatest response from Palestinians. The Arabic press of the period is replete with lurid reports of the alleged misdeeds and the provocative statements of leading Zionists in Palestine.

91. For Syria, see James Gelvin, "The Other Arab Nationalism: Syrian/Arab/Populism in Its Historical and International Contexts," in I. Gershoni and J. Jankowski, eds., *Rethinking Nationalism in the Arab World* (New York: Columbia University Press, forthcoming) and for Iraq the article by Mahmud Haddad in R. Khalidi et al., eds., *The Origins of Arab Nationalism*, pp. 120–150.

92. [Title illegible] *al-Sabah*, no. 1, October 21, 1921, p. 1.

93. "Sanatuna al-khamisa" ["Our fifth year"], *Filastin*, no 1–367, March 19, 1921, p. 1.

94. A brilliant satirical illustration of this reality, and of the cruel contrast between it and the high-flown rhetoric of Arabism is Duraid Lahham's film " *'Ala al-Hudud.*"

95. Wasserstein, *The British in Palestine*, p. 134.

96. These figures are derived from tables on pp. 270–271 of A. L. Tibawi, *Arab Education* (those for school-age population and government school enrollment are for 1947–48; the last available figures for private schools are for 1945–46—it is likely that by 1947–48 more children were enrolled in private schools, and that the actual percentage was therefore a bit higher). See Miller, *Government and Society in Mandatory*

Palestine, pp. 90–118, for an excellent account of the spread of education in rural areas, generally at the instigation of the rural population, and of the frustration of the rural pupulation at the obstacles placed in their way by the British.

97. Miller, *Government and Society in Mandatory Palestine,* p. 98, citing the Palestine Government Department of Education *Annual Report, 1945–46.*

98. Wasserstein, *The British in Palestine,* p. 179.

99. For the nationalist critique of the teaching of history see Tibawi, *Arab Education,* pp. 88–89.

100. Cited in n. 80, above. The book was used widely in Palestinian schools.

Chapter 8. The "Disappearance" and Reemergence of Palestinian Identity

1. This is the origin of the title of the seminal work by Qustantin Zurayq, *Ma'na al-Nakba* [The meaning of the catastrophe] published in Beirut immediately after the 1948 war, and translated as *The Meaning of the Disaster* by R. Bayley Winder (Beirut: Khayat, 1956). Zurayq, a Princeton-trained historian who served at different times in his career as a Syrian Minister, Acting President of the American University of Beirut, President of the Syrian University, and Chairman of the Board of Trustees of the Institute for Palestine Studies, was one of the leading exponents of Arabism from the 1930s onwards.

2. The PLO was founded in 1964 by the Arab League in response to pressures Arab states felt from burgeoning independent Palestinian organizations and from Palestinian popular sentiment, and was meant to contain and control these pressures. Although it was thus initially not an independent actor, the Arab states quickly lost control of it, as it was refashioned by these organizations into the primary vehicle of Palestinian nationalism, a process which was completed by 1968.

3. Shlaim, *Collusion Across the Jordan* is the best source on this aspect of the 1948 war. See also Wilson, *King Abdullah.*

4. The standard work on the subject is now Benny Morris, *The Birth of the Palestinian Refugee Problem 1947–1949* (Cambridge: Cambridge University Press, 1987). Based on Israeli sources, this work has put to rest some of the most tenacious fabrications regarding the Palestinian refugee problem. See also Morris's *1948 and After,* rev. ed. (Oxford: Oxford University Press, 1994). For problems with some of the conclusions Morris draws from the evidence he presents, however, see Norman G. Finkelstein, *Image and Reality of the Israel-Palestine Conflict* (London: Verso, 1995), pp. 51–87.

5. Nationality was another matter: in Israel this is not automatically associated with citizenship, but rather with religion. On the question of nationality and citizenship in Israel, see Baruch Kimmerling, "Between the Primordial and the Civil Definition of the Collective Identity: *Eretz Israel* or the State of Israel?," in E. Cohen, M. Lissak, U. Almagor, eds., *Comparative Social Dynamics,* pp. 262–283 (Boulder: Westview, 1985).

6. This entire process is chronicled in Morris, *The Birth of the Palestinian Refugee Problem,* in W. Khalidi, ed. *All That Remains,* and in Tom Segev, *1949: The First Israelis* (New York: Free Press, 1986).

7. The best works on this period are Cobban, *The Palestinian Liberation Organization,* Kazziha, *Revolutionary Transformation,* Gresh, *The PLO,* and Brand, *Palestinians in the Arab World.* Also extremely revealing is the memoir of one of the founders of Fateh, Abu Iyyad, *My Home, My Land.*

8. A photo of 'Arafat, clean-shaven and in double-breasted suit and tie, present-ing a petition to Egyptian President Nagib together with other student leaders, can be found in Alan Hart, *Arafat: Terrorist or Peacemaker* (London: Sidgwick & Jackson, 1984) following p. 224.

9. These names were usually not invented: Khalaf's eldest son is named Iyyad, whence the name traditional in Arab society of Abu (father of) Iyyad; al-Wazir's eldest son is Jihad, and so forth. 'Arafat, known as Abu 'Ammar, who was unmarried at the time, was an exception to this rule.

10. A few of them were absorbed by the Jordanian political establishment, where they had no more independent political power than any other Jordanian politician, but instead, with the exception of a few brief periods, became instruments of the regime of King Abdullah and his grandson, King Husayn.

11. Rosemary Sayigh, *Palestinians: From Peasants to Revolutionaries* (London: Zed, 1979), pp. 168–179, notes how the deference to age which is a normal feature of tra-ditional Arab society dissolved in the refugee camps in Lebanon in the wake of the 1948 war, as the younger generation saw their elders as ineffective, and held them responsible for the disasters that had befallen the Palestinians. The process Sayigh describes in the camps in Lebanon was at work within Palestinian society at large.

12. *The Sunday Times* (London), June 15, 1969, p. 12.

13. One of the great ironies of Egypt's taking on the mantle of pan-Arab leader-ship in this period was the fact that Egypt was relatively late to subscribe to the tenets of Arabism, having espoused a separate Egyptian nationalism for many decades pre-viously: see Gershoni and Jankowski, *Egypt, Islam and the Arabs*, and *Redefining the Egyptian Nation*. See also the section of Nasir's *Philosophy of the Revolution*, reprinted in *Nasser Speaks: Basic Documents* (London: Morssett, 1972), pp. 44–55, where he explains how he came to understand before and during the 1948 war that Arabism was a cru-cial element in Egypt's future.

14. Over time indeed, use of the term *qawmiyya*, nationalism, which we have seen used to describe Palestinian patriotism in 1914, was restricted in many parts of the Eastern Arab world to Arab nationalism: from this pan-Arab perspective, regional and nation-state nationalisms were accorded the lesser term, *wataniyya*, patriotism, or even the pejorative *iqlimiyya*, regionalism.

15. Kazziha, *Revolutionary Transformation*, is the best book on this movement's early years.

16. This idea of return, with its implied corollary that Palestine was a lost paradise, could be found in forms other than the overtly political, such as the subtitle of 'Arif al-'Arif's 6-volume history, *al-Nakba*: "The catastrophe of Jerusalem and the lost par-adise." Doumani has a perceptive discussion of this theme of a lost paradise in the his-torical writings of Ihsan al-Nimr and al-'Arif in "Rediscovering Ottoman Palestine," pp. 14–17.

17. Abu Iyyad, *My Home, My Land*, pp. 20–28, gives an excellent account of these conflicts with the Egyptian authorities, as do the sections of Cobban, *The Palestinian Liberation Organization*, pp. 21–35, and Hart, *Arafat*, pp. 98–120, which are drawn from their interviews with Abu Jihad, Abu Iyyad, 'Arafat, and other founders of Fateh. For more on this period, see Avi Shlaim, "Conflicting Approaches to Israel's Relations with the Arabs: Ben Gurion and Sharett, 1953–1956," *Middle East Journal* 37, no. 2 (Spring 1983): 180–201.

18. A scene is reported by Robert Stephens in *Nasser: A Political Biography* (New York: Simon and Schuster, 1971), p. 173, of a Downing Street dinner given by Eden

for Nuri al-Sa'id, Prime Minister and long-time strongman of Iraq, and no friend of 'Abd al-Nasir's, at which the normally urbane Eden launched into a violent tirade on the subject of the Egyptian leader, shocking those present. Nutting also describes the enraged response of Eden to a Foreign Office memo which called for isolating 'Abd al-Nasir: "But what's all this nonsense about isolating Nasser or 'neutralising' him, as you call it? I want him destroyed, can't you understand? I want him removed . . . And I don't give a damn if there's anarchy and chaos in Egypt." Cited in Anthony Nutting, *No End of a Lesson: The Story of Suez* (London: Potter, 1967), pp. 31–35

19. The examples of this genre of argumentation are legion, and can still be found in advertisements in the back pages of periodicals like *The Nation* and *Harper's*: a semi-scholarly work like Curtis, Neyer, Waxman, and Pollack, eds., *The Palestinians*, is replete with examples of it.

20. A developing scholarly literature has begun to explore these early initiatives, notably the work of Wilson, *King Abdullah*; Shlaim, *Collusion across the Jordan*; Itamar Rabinovich, *The Road Not Taken: Early Arab-Israeli Negotiations* (Oxford: Oxford University Press, 1991); Benny Morris, *Israel's Border Wars, 1949–1956: Arab Infiltration, Israeli Retaliation, and the Countdown to the Suez War* (Oxford: Oxford University Press, 1993); Ilan Pappé, *Britain and the Arab-Israeli Conflict, 1948–51* (London: Macmillan, 1988); and *The Making of the Arab-Israeli Conflict, 1947–1951*, rev. ed. (London: I. B. Tauris, 1994). One of the first books to break the iron consensus that the Arabs never wanted peace with Israel was Simha Flapan, *The Birth of Israel: Myths and Realities* (New York: Free Press, 1987).

21. The early work of Yehoshaphat Harkabi, a former Chief of Israeli Military Intelligence, especially his influential books, *Arab Attitudes to Israel* (New York: Hart, 1972); and *Arab Strategies and Israel's Response* (New York: Free Press, 1977), formed the basis for many of these more lurid interpretations by others, less knowledgeable than he. Ironically, Harkabi ended his career as one of Israel's most outspoken doves.

22. *Filastin*, 7 Nisan 1330, 1-page broad-sheet "Open Letter to Subscribers."

23. *Filastin*, April 12, 1921, "Ila qawmi" [To my nation], p. 1 editorial signed by Yusuf al-'Isa, and either reprinted from his Damascus newspaper *Alif Ba'*, or written specially for *Filastin*.

24. Beyond the Husayn-McMahon correspondence, the British and French issued a declaration in November 1918 in which they promised the peoples of the Arab world "complete liberation and the establishment of popular governments which will draw their power from the free choice of the citizens" and encouraged "the establishment of popular governments in Syria and Iraq, which the allies have already liberated. . . ." Text of communique distributed by Muslim-Christian Association in Jerusalem, by order of the British Military Governor in Jerusalem, November 7, 1918: uncatalogued papers, Khalidi Library.

25. *al-Sabah*, no. 15, November 29, 1921, "Hal hadha huwa al-waqi'?" ["Is this the situation?"], p. 1, signed " 'A" ['Arif al-'Arif?].

26. "*Bayan min al-wafd al-'arabi al-filastini lil-umma al-karima*" [Communique from the Palestinian Arab delegation to the nation], dated July 8, 1921 and signed by the head of the delegation, Musa Kazim al-Husayni: Budayri papers.

27. Lockman, *Comrades and Enemies*, pp. 220–222, provides much illuminating material on Reuven Shilo'ah, who organized the Israeli intelligence services. In addition to establishing the networks dedicated to spying on the Arab countries in the

1930s, he was also a labor organizer among Palestinian Arabs. The center for Middle Eastern studies at Tel Aviv University was originally named for him.

28. Hajj Amin, whose brother and three generations of his family before him had held the post of Hanafi Mufti of Jerusalem, was appointed to the post by Sir Herbert Samuel ahead of other apparently more qualified, and older, candidates in a gamble that this young radical, only recently pardoned for his nationalist activities, would serve British interests by maintaining calm in return for his elevation to the post. Despite constant Zionist complaints about him, it could be argued that the gamble paid off for the British for a decade and a half, until the mid-1930s, when the Mufti could no longer contain popular passions. For the best treatment of the subject, see Mattar, *Mufti of Jerusalem.*

29. A biography of al-Nashashibi, by the journalist Nasser Eddin Nashashibi, *Jerusalem's Other Voice: Ragheb Nashashibi and Moderation in Palestinian Politics, 1920–1948* (Exeter: Ithaca Press, 1990), must be used with care, but includes much primary material.

30. The rural operations of some of these merchants and money-lenders in the late nineteenth century are outlined in Doumani, *Rediscovering Palestine.*

31. A useful perspective on these inter-elite conflicts is provided by Issa Khalaf, *Arab Factionalism and Social Disintegration, 1939–1948* (Albany: State University of New York Press, 1991).

32. See Haim Levenberg, *The Military Preparations of the Arab Community of Palestine, 1945–48* (London: Cass, 1993), for a generally accurate but somewhat confused account of the background to the Palestinian defeats of 1947–48.

33. Many of these voices were, ironically, to be found in Lebanon, where the absentee landlords who had sold the most land resided.

34. Based on tables in Appendix C of Tibawi, *Arab Education*, pp. 270–271.

35. The word that perhaps best sums up this sense in which failure has been surmounted and survived, which in itself is a sort of victory, is *sumud*, commonly translated as "steadfastness," but encompassing all the meanings just suggested. The word was ubiquitous in Palestinian narrations both of the various stages of the fighting in Lebanon from the late 1960s until 1982, and of resistance to the occupation in the West Bank and Gaza Strip from 1967 until the *intifada* began in 1987. This approach constrasts with that of Ranajit Guha, who states in *Selected Subaltern Studies* (p. 43), that the "historic failure of the nation to come into its own . . . constitutes the central problematic of the historiography of colonial India."

36. Ghassan Kanafani, *Thawrat 1936 fi Filastin: Khalfiyyat wa tafasil wa tahlil* (Beirut: Popular Front for the Liberation of Palestine, 1974).

37. Kayyali, *Palestine: A Modern History*; 'Allush, *al-Muqawama al-'arabiyya.*

38. All substantial works on the PLO give this important episode a full treatment: Cobban, *The Palestinian Liberation Organization*, Gresh, *The PLO*, and Abu Iyyad, *My Home My Land*, are among the best.

39. See the forthcoming book by Yezid Sayigh, *Armed Struggle and the Search for State: The Palestinian National Movement, 1949–1993* (Oxford: Oxford University Press, 1997), which deals with this subject.

40. On the 1970 fighting in Jordan, see John Cooley, *Green March, Black September: The Story of the Palestinian Arabs* (London: Cass, 1973).

41. The PFLP engaged in vigorous self-criticism of its behavior at an internal conference soon afterwards, forswearing further airplane hijackings, but it eventually

emerged that some in the PFLP leadership were turning a blind eye to the continuation of such operations, provoking a major split in the group in 1972.

42. The notorious episode when the Arab League mediator in Lebanon, Hassan Sabri al-Kholi, arrived at the Phalangist headquarters to halt the massacre at Tal al-Za'tar in August 1976, only to find there two Syrian liaison officers, Col. 'Ali al-Madani and Col. 'Ali al-Kholi, and two Israeli liaison officers, widely reported in the Lebanese press at the time, was confirmed in an Israeli Knesset debate six years later when Defense Minister Ariel Sharon defended himself against charges of Israeli complicity in the Sabra and Shatila massacres by citing a similar Israeli role in the Tal al-Za'tar massacre under a Labor government: *The Jerusalem Post*, October 15, 1982.

43. On this phase of the Lebanese conflict, see W. Khalidi, *Conflict and Violence in Lebanon* (Cambridge: Harvard University Press, 1979).

44. See R. Khalidi, *Under Siege*, p. 200, n.5, for details of casualties.

45. Tape of Shafiq al-Hout speech, November 1982.

46. A series of regular polls of a sample of more than 1,000 by the Nablus-based Center for Palestine Research and Studies have shown consistent majority support, ranging from 50% to 70%, for the interim agreements negotiated with Israel by the PLO, and for the PLO leadership. The September 1995 results show 70.6% of respondents supporting "continuation of the current peace negotiations between the PLO and Israel," while 53.7% supported 'Arafat as a candidate for President of the Palestinian Authority: "Results of Public Opinion Poll #19, The West Bank Bank and the Gaza Strip, August/September, 1995," (Nablus: Center for Palestine Research and Studies, 1995). A poll with 2,770 respondents on election day, January 20, 1996, found that 50.3% supported the Oslo accords and 16.5% opposed them, while 57.4% supported Fateh: "Palestinian Elections: Election Day Survey, 20, January, 1996" (Nablus: Center for Palestine Research and Studies, 1996).

47. Baruch Kimmerling and Joel Migdal, *The Palestinians* is a case in point.

48. Porath's *The Emergence of the Palestinian-Arab National Movement, 1919–1929,* and *The Palestinian Arab National Movement 1929–1939* (published in 1973 and 1977 respectively) remain the standard works on the period, and were pioneering efforts in terms of historical discourse inside Israel about the Palestinians.

49. Indeed, the inept American diplomatic initiatives during the last two rounds of the bilateral Israeli-Palestinian negotiations in Washington in May and June of 1993 were among the factors that brought the PLO leadership to intensify their secret direct contacts with Israel in Oslo and elsewhere, and to abandon Washington as a negotiating venue and the United States as a mediator.

50. For Palestinians this was because they could not but see Zionism as a European colonial-settler movement which claimed their country, and therefore as necessarily illegitimate, both in terms of its origins and its aims.

51. This is the case notwithstanding the entry of more than 20,000 PLO soldiers into Palestine under the guise of policemen, with the full agreement of Israel.

52. This comparison has been explored in Kenneth Stein, *The Intifadah and the 1936–1939 Uprising: A Comparison of the Palestinian Arab Communities* (Atlanta: Carter Center Occasional Papers, 1, March 1990).

53. This is currently the situation in Jerusalem, where since early in the occupation, the Israeli authorities permitted the Jordanian curriculum to remain in force, in spite of their annexation of the Arab eastern part of the city, and where today Arab children in private schools study with textbooks bearing the Palestinian flag and issued by the Palestinian Authority's educational department in Ramallah.

54. Contrary to an impression assiduously cultivated by Israel and its supporters, most Palestinian refugees were not "kept in the camps by the Arab governments." While this happened in the Gaza Strip from 1948 until 1967, refugees in Jordan and Syria (the overwhelming majority of refugees outside Palestine) were never restricted as to their movement within the country, while the former had full citizenship rights, and the latter had all rights of citizenship except voting in national elections and carrying the national passport. Over time, the majority of refugees in both countries have moved out of the camps: according to UNRWA figures, in 1993 only 22% of registered refugees in Jordan, and 28% in Syria still lived in camps: *Palestinian Refugees: Their Problem and Future* (Washington, D.C.: Center for Policy Analysis on Palestine, 1994), pp. 29–30. The same process occurred in Lebanon after the PLO took control of the camps in 1968, but has been reversed since 1982: in 1993, 52% of registered refugees in Lebanon lived in camps.

55. There are neither accurate figures on the Palestinian population of Lebanon, nor reliable data on casualties among them, but the best estimates are summed up in R. Khalidi, "The Palestinians in Lebanon," pp. 255–257.

56. Article 11 of the resolution qualifies the possibility of return by saying that the returning refugees must be willing "to live at peace with their neighbours," and mandates compensation "for loss of or damage to property" even for those who choose to return: George J. Tomeh, ed., *United Nations Resolutions in Palestine and the Arab-Israeli Conflict*, 3 vols. (Washington, D.C.: Institute for Palestine Studies, 1975) 1:15–17.

57. See R. Khalidi, "Observations on the Palestinian Right of Return," *Journal of Palestine Studies* 21, no. 2 (Winter 1992): 29–40; and "The Palestinian Refugee Question: Toward a Solution," in *Palestinian Refugees: Their Problem and Future. A Special Report* (Washington, D.C.: Center for Policy Analysis on Palestine, October 1994), pp. 21–27.

58. This does not apply to Palestinians who became refugees in 1967. Officially described under the rubric "displaced persons," their fate was supposed to be settled as part of the "interim" negotiations, and in principle most of them should be allowed to return to the West Bank, although the modalities have not yet been fully agreed upon, and it is not clear when, or if, they will be.

59. This indeed is exactly what Ihsan al-Nimr claims it was in his *Tarikh Jabal Nablus*, 1: 139, cited in Doumani, "Rediscovering Ottoman Palestine," p. 14.

BIBLIOGRAPHY

I. PRIMARY SOURCES

A. *Interviews*

al-Khalidi, Wahida. Beirut, December 12, 1979.
al-Khalidi, Raqiyya. Jerusalem, June 28, 1992; October 8, 1993; September 23, 1995.

B. *Unpublished Sources*

1. IN THE KHALIDI LIBRARY, JERUSALEM

Ba'ith al-nufus ila ziyarat al-Quds al-mahrus [Inspiration to souls to visit protected Jerusalem] (Khalidi Library MS), by Ibrahim b. Ishaq al-Ansari, known as Ibn Furkah (d. 1328).

Letter from 'Abdallah Faydallah [governor of Gaza], to the Qadi, Mufti, notables and military commanders of Jerusalem, warning of approach of a French army, dated Rajab 27, 1213/January 5, 1799.

Petition to Sultan Mustafa II from notables of Jerusalem [n.d.: 1701].

al-Khalidi, Raghib. *A'lan bi-ta'sis maktaba 'umumiyya fil-Quds al-sharif,* [Announcement of the founding of a public library in Jerusalem], n.d. [1899–1900].

——. *Mudhakkirat al-Hajj Raghib al-Khalidi* [Memoirs of al-Hajj Raghib al-Khalidi], n.d. 31 pp.

——. Letter to Ruhi al-Khalidi, 16 Ramadan 1316/1898.

al-Khalidi, Ruhi. School prizes from Beirut *Sultaniye* school, 1887.

——. Diploma from *Mekteb-i Mülkiye*, 1311M/1893.

——. *Ijaza* from al-Hajj Yusuf al-Sadiq al-Imam al-Husayni, Shafi'i Mufti in Jerusalem, certifying completion of religious training, 11 Jumada al-awwal, 1314/October 19, 1896.

——. Folder of press clippings, published materials on Zionism.

al-Khalidi, Yasin. Sixteen letters to Ruhi al-Khalidi 1897–1900.

——. Twelve letters to Yusuf Diya' al-Khalidi 1898–1900

al-Khalidi, Yusuf Diya'. *al-'Arsh wal-haykal* [The throne and the temple], 10-page poem in manuscript dated 1295 [1878].

——. *Risalat mumahakat al-ta'wil fi munaqadat al-injil* [Disputes of interpretation regarding the contradictions of the Bible], 76-page manuscript dated Istanbul 1281 [1864] on the title page and 1296 [1878–79] on the final page.

——. Autobiography of Yusuf Diya' al-Khalidi, covering 1842–1875, from autograph original preserved by Shaykh 'Ali al-Laythi, 8 pp., Vienna, 10 Muharram 1292/February 17, 1875.

——. Seven letters to Ruhi al-Khalidi from Istanbul, July–September 1899.

——. Copies of telegrams (in French) to the Foreign Ministry and the Ottoman Embassy in St. Petersburg, November 1874.

——. Letter (recipient unclear), 11 pp., dated Poti, November 5, 1874.

——. Letter from Maj. Gen. Henry James, Royal Engineers, the War Office, London, respecting supply of water to Jerusalem, June 23, 1870.

——. Letter from Conrad Schick, respecting excavations in Jerusalem, Jerusalem, July 2, 1870.

——. Russian travel document in name of Yusuf Diya' al-Khalidi, December 10, 1874.

——. Photograph of Jamal al-Din al-Asadabadi (al-Afghani), inscribed *verso* to Yusuf Diya' al-Khalidi.

Anglo-French declaration distributed by Muslim-Christian Association in Jerusalem, by order of the British Military Governor in Jerusalem, November 7, 1918.

2. OTHER

Bayan min al-wafd al-'arabi al-filastini lil-umma al-karima [Communique from the Palestinian Arab delegation to the nation], signed by the head of the delegation, Musa Kazim al-Husayni, July 8, 1921: Budayri papers.

al-Hout Shafiq. Speech to Palestine National Congress, Algiers, November, 1982, tape recording.

al-Husayni, Sa'id. Private papers, in possession of Sa'id al-Husayni, Jerusalem.

Storrs, Sir Ronald. Two letters to Mustafa al-Budayri, both dated August 16, 1921; letter from Storrs to Muhammad Kamil al-Budayri, dated August 22, 1921, from the files of the newspapers *Suriyya al-Janubiyya* and *al-Sabah*: Budayri papers.

"Palestinian Elections: Election Day Survey, 20 January 1996." Nablus: Center for Palestine Research and Studies, 1996.

"Results of Public Opinion Poll #19, The West Bank Bank and the Gaza Strip, August/September, 1995," Nablus: Center for Palestine Research and Studies, 1995.

C. Dissertations

Abu El-Hajj, Nadia. "Excavating the Land, Creating the Homeland: Archaeology, the State and the Making of History in Modern Jewish Nationalism." Duke University, Department of Cultural Anthropology, 1995.

Fortna, Ben. "Ottoman State Schools During the Reign of Abdul Hamit, 1876–1908." University of Chicago, Department of Near Eastern Languages and Literatures, 1997.

Gelvin, James L. "Popular Mobilization and the Foundations of Mass Politics in Syria, 1918–1920." Harvard University, Departments of History and Middle Eastern Studies, 1992.

Jorgens, Denise. "A Study of the Ottoman Land Code and Khedive Sa'id's Land Law of 1858." University of Chicago, Department of History, 1995.

Matthews, L. Don. "The Arab Istiqlal Party in Palestine, 1925–1934." University of Chicago, Department of Near East Languages and Civilizations, 1997.

Rood, Judith Mendelsohn. "Sacred Law in the Holy City: A Study in the Theory and Practice of Government in Jerusalem under Ottoman and Khedival Rule." University of Chicago, Department of History, 1994.

D. Published Sources

1. NEWSPAPERS AND PERIODICALS CONSULTED

al-Ahram, Cairo.
al-Asma'i, Jaffa.
al-Barq, Tripoli.
Bayt al-Maqdis, Jerusalem.
The Department of State Bulletin, Washington, D.C.
al-Dustur, Jerusalem.
Filastin, Jaffa.
al-Haqiqa, Beirut.
al-Hawadith, Tripoli.
al-Hilal, Cairo.
al-Himara al-Qahira, Haifa.
al-Iqbal, Beirut.
al-Iqdam, Cairo.
al-Islah, Beirut.
al-Ittihad al-'Uthmani, Beirut.
al-Jarida, Cairo.
al-Jawa'ib, Istanbul.
The Jerusalem Post, Jerusalem.
al-Jinan, Beirut.
al-Karmil, Haifa.
Lisan al-Hal, Beirut.
al-Manar, Cairo.
Mir'at al-Sharq, Jerusalem.
al-Mu'ayyad, Cairo.

al-Mufid, Beirut.
al-Munadi, Jerusalem.
al-Muqtabas, Beirut.
al-Muqtataf, Cairo.
al-Nafa'is al-'Asriyya, Jerusalem.
al-Nafir, Alexandria, Jerusalem, Haifa.
al-Najah, Jerusalem.
al-Nasir, Beirut.
al-Ra'i al-'Am, Cairo.
al-Quds, Jerusalem.
al-Sabah, Istanbul.
al-Sabah, Jerusalem.
al-Sha'b, Aleppo.
The Sunday Times, London.
Suriyya al-Janubiyya, Jerusalem.
The Times, London.
Tarablus al-Sham, Tripoli.

2. BOOKS AND PAMPHLETS

'Abd al-Hadi, Sabri Sharif. *Jughrafiyyat Suriyya wa Filastin al-Tabi'iyya* [The natural geography of Syria and Palestine]. Cairo: al-Maktaba al-Ahliyya, 1923.

'Abd al-Nasser, Gamal. *Philosophy of the Revolution,* reprinted in *Nasser Speaks: Basic Documents.* London: Morssett, 1972.

'Abdu, Muhammad. *Taqrir fadilat Mufti al-Diyar al-Misriyya, al-Ustadh al-Shaykh Muhammad 'Abdu fi islah al-mahakim al-shar'iyya* [Report of his Excellency the Mufti of Egypt, al-Ustadh al-Shaykh Muhammad 'Abdu regarding reform of the religious courts]. Cairo: al-Manar, 1317/1900.

Abu Iyyad [Salah Khalaf] with Eric Rouleau. *My Home My Land.* New York: Times Books, 1984.

Alami, Musa, with Geoffrey Furlonge. *Palestine Is My Country: The Story of Musa al-Alami.* London: John Murray, 1969.

Anon., [As'ad Daghir]. *Thawrat al-'arab* [Revolt of the Arabs]. Cairo, n.p., 1916.

al-Asir, Shaykh Yusuf, *Sharh ra'id al-fara'id* [Exposition of the rule of religious duty]. Beirut: n.p., 1290/1873.

Azoury, Négib [Najib 'Azuri]. *Le Reveil de la nation arabe.* Paris: n.p., 1905.

Bentwich, Norman. *Palestine and Her Critics.* London: n.p., 1900.

——. "The Progress of Zionism." *The Fortnightly Review* (December 1898): 928–943.

Burnamij Madrasat Rawdat al-Ma'arif [Syllabus of the Garden of Education School]. Jerusalem: Matba'at al-Nadi, 1331/1912.

Busayli, Rimigio. *Tarjamat al-kurras al-mad'u muhamat 'an huquq Terra Sancta fil-maghara al-mad'uawa magharat al-halib al-ka'ina bil-qurb min Baytlahm* [Defence of the rights of Terra Sancta in the cave called the Cave of Milk near Bethlehem]. Jerusalem: Franciscan Monastery, 1965.

Catalogue of the Syrian Protestant College, Beirut, Syria, 1912–1913. Beirut, The College Press, 1913.

Cellaledin, Mahmud Pasa. *Mir'at-i hakikat* [Mirror of reality] 3. vols. Istanbul: Matbaa-i Osmaniye, 1326–27.

Darwaza, Muhammad 'Izzat. *Khamsa wa tis'una 'aman fil-hayat: Mudhakirat wa-tasjilat* [95 years of life: memoirs and records], eds., A. Jarbawi and H. Shakhshir, vol. 1. Jerusalem: Arab Thought Forum, 1993.

Dhikra Istiqlal Suriyya [A commemoration of the independence of Syria]. Damascus: n.p., 1920.

Doughty, Charles. *Travels in Arabia Deserta*, 2 vols. Cambridge: Cambridge University Press, 1888.

Great Britain. *Parliamentary Command Papers*, Cmd. 5957. "Correspondence between Sir Henry McMahon and the Sharif Husain of Mecca, July 1915–March 1916." London: HMSO, 1939.

Jam'iyat al-Tabshir al-Kanisiyya. *al-Madrasa al-Kulliya al-Inkliziyya fil-Quds* [The English college school in Jerusalem]. Jerusalem: Christian Missionary Society, 1904.

al-Jisr, Husayn. *Kitab al-husun al-hamidiyya li-muhafazat al-'aqa'id al-islamiyya* [Praiseworthy virtues of preserving Islamic beliefs]. Tripoli: Muhammad Kamil al-Buhayri, n.d.

——. *Kitab al-risala al-hamidiyya fi haqiqat al-diyana al-islamiyya wa haqqiyyat al-shari'a al-muhammadiyya* [Praiseworthy essay on the truth of the Islamic religion and the verity of Muhammadan law]. Beirut: Hassan al-Qaraq, 1305/1890.

Karami, Butrus, ed. *al-Muwashahat al-andalusiyya* [Andalusian poetry]. Beirut: n.p., 1864.

Keith-Roach, Edward. *Pasha of Jerusalem: Memoirs of a District Commissioner Under the British Mandate*. London: Radcliffe Press, 1994.

al-Khalidi, 'Anbara Salam. *Jawla fil dhikrayat bayna Lubnan wa Filastin* [Journey of memories between Lebanon and Palestine]. Beirut: al-Nehar, 1978.

al-Khalidi, Ruhi. *Asbab al-inqilab al-'uthmani wa turkiyya al-fatat* [The causes of the Ottoman revolution and the Young Turks]. Cairo: al-Manar Press, 1326/1908.

——. *al-Habs fil-tuhma wal-imtihan 'ala talab al-iqrar wa-izhar al-mal* [Imprisonment on accusation and the test for a request for a decision and revelation of wealth]. Jerusalem [?]: n.p., 1321/1903.

——. *al-kimiya 'ind al-'arab* [Chemistry under the Arabs]. Cairo: Dar al-Ma'arif, 1953.

——. *al-Muqaddima fil-mas'ala al-sharqiyya muntha nash'atiha al-uwla ila al-rub' al-thani min al-qarn al-thamin 'ashr* [An introduction to the Eastern Question from its inception until the second quarter of the 18th century]. Jerusalem: Dar al-Aytam, n.d., [1920].

——. *Risala fi sur'at intishar al-din al-islami fi aqsam al-'alam* [Essay on the speed of the spread of the Islamic religion in the regions of the world]. Tripoli: al-Balagha Press, 1897.

——. *Tarikh 'ilm al-adab 'ind al-ifranj wal-'arab wa Victor Hugo* [The history of literature among the Arabs, the Franj and Victor Hugo]. Cairo: Dar al-Hilal, 1904.

al-Khalidi, Yusuf Diya' al-Din, ed. *Diwan Labid al-'Amiri, riwayat al-Tusi* [title in German: *Der Diwan des Lebid*]. Vienna: Carl Gerold, for the Imperial Academy of Science, 1880.

——. *al-Hadiyya al-hamidiyya fil-lugha al-kurdiyya* [The Hamidian gift in the Kurdish language]. Istanbul: Martabey Matba'asi, 1310/1892.

Faris al-Khuri. *Kanz lughat* [Turkish-Persian dictionary]. Beirut: n.p., 1876.

Le Bon, Gustave. *La Civilisation des Arabes*. Paris: Firmin-Didot, 1884.

——. *Les premières civilisations*. [Arabic translation by Muhammad Sadiq Rustum, *Muqadimmat al-Hadarat al-uwla*]. Cairo: al-Matba'a al-Salafiyya, 1341/1922.

———. *Les Lois psychologiques de l'évolution des peuples* [Turkish translation by Abdullah Jevdet, *Ruh al-Akvam*]. Cairo: Matba'at al-Ijtihad, 1908. [Arabic translation by Ahmad Fathi Zaghlul Pasha *Sir tatawwur al-umam*]. Cairo: Matba'at al-Rahmaniyya, 1909.

———. *La Psychologie de l'Education* [Arabic translation by Taha Husayn, *Ruh al-tarbiyya*]. Cairo: Dar al-Hilal, 1925.

———. *La Psychologie des Foules* [Arabic translation by Ahmad Fathi Zahglul Pasha, *Ruh al-ijtima'*]. Cairo: Matba'at al-Rahmaniyya, 1909.

al-Maqdisi, Muhammad Ibn Ahmad [1306–1344]. *Fada'il al-Sham* [The merits of Syria]. Tanta: Dar al-Sahaba, 1988.

Nassar, Najib. *al-Sihyuniyya: tarikhuha, gharaduha, ahamiyatuha* [Zionism: Its history, aims and importance]. Haifa: al-Karmil Press, 1911.

Nukhab diwan Ibrahim b. Sahl al-Isra'ili al-Andalusi al-Ashbili [Selections from the poetry of Ibrahim Ibn Sahl al-Isra'ili al-Andalusi al-Ashbili]. N.p., n.d.

Nutting, Anthony. *No End of a Lesson: The Story of Suez.* London: Potter, 1967.

Osmanli Ittihad ve Terakki Cemiyeti 1327 senasi siyasi programi [Political program of the Ottoman Committee of Union and Progress]. Istanbul: Tanin, 1327/1909.

al-Sakakini, Khalil. *Filastin ba'd al-harb al-kubra* [Palestine after the great war]. Jerusalem: Bayt al-Maqdis Press, 1925.

———. *Yawmiyyat Khalil al-Sakakini: Katha ana ya dunya* [Diaries of Khalil al-Sakakini: I am thus oh world]. Jerusalem: al-Matba'a al-Tijariyya, 1955.

Salname-i devlet-i aliyye-i osmaniyye, 1307. [Ottoman state yearbook]. Istanbul: Matba'at Amira, 1307/1890.

———, *1309.* Istanbul: Matba'at Amira, 1309/1892.

———, *1314.* Istanbul: Matba'at Amira, 1314/1896.

Salname Vilayet Suriyye 1288 [Yearbook of the Province of Syria]. Damascus: n.p, 1288/1871

Samuel, Edwin. *A Lifetime in Jerusalem: The Memoirs of the Second Viscount Samuel.* London: Valentine, Mitchell, 1970.

Storrs, Ronald. *Orientations.* London: Weidenfeld and Nicholson, 1945.

Tafsil li-tawdih al-qawa'id al-fiqhiyya wal-usuliyya fi awwal majallat al-ahkam al-'adliyya [Details clarifying the basic legal rules in the compendium of legal judgements]. Istanbul: n.p. 1299/1881.

Tamimi, Rafiq and Muhammad Bahjat. 2 vols. *Wilayat Bayrut* [The province of Beirut]. Beirut: al-Iqbal Press, 1335–36/1917.

de Tarazi, Philippe. *Tarikh al-sihafa al-'arabiyya* [History of the Arab press], 4 vols. Beirut: al-Matba'a al-Adabiyya and al-Matba'a al-Amarkiyya, 1913–1933.

Tomeh, George J., ed. *United Nations Resolutions in Palestine and the Arab-Israeli Conflict,* 3 vols. Washington, D.C.: Institute for Palestine Studies, 1975.

al-'Ulaymi, 'Abd al-Rahman b. Muhammdad, [Mujir al-Din, d. 1521]. *al-Uns al-jalil bi-tarikh al-Quds wal-Khalil* [The glorious history of Jerusalem and Hebron], 2 vols. Amman: Maktabat al-Muhtasib, 1973.

Zola, Emile. *Humanité-Verité-Justice: L'Affaire Dreyfus. Lettre à la Jeunesse par Emile Zola.* Paris: Eugene Fasquelle, 1897.

Zu'aytir, Akram. *Al-haraka al-wataniyya al-filistiniyya 1935–1939: Yawmiyyat Akram Zu'aytir* [The Palestinian national movement 1935–1939: The diaries of Akram Zu'aytir]. Beirut, Institute for Palestine Studies, 1980.

——— *Watha'iq al-haraka al-wataniyya al-filistiniyya 1918–1939: Min awraq Akram Zu'aytir*

[Documents of the Palestinian national movement 1918–1939: From the papers of Akram Zu'aytir]. Beirut: Institute for Palestine Studies, 1979.

II. BOOKS AND MONOGRAPHS

'Abd al-Qadir, Muhammad al-Khayr. *Nakbat al-umma al-'arabiyya bi-suqut al-khilafa: Dirasa lil-qadiyya al-'arabiyya fi khamsin 'aman, 1875–1925* [The disaster of the Arab nation through the fall of the caliphate: A study of the Arab cause over 50 years, 1875–1925]. Cairo: Maktabat Wahba, 1985.

'Ali, 'Abdullah Yusuf, ed. *The Holy Qur'an: Text, Translation and Commentary.* Brentwood, MD: Amana, 1409/1989.

'Allush, Naji. *al-Muqawama al-'arabiyya fi Filastin, 1917–1948* [The Arab resistance in Palestine, 1917–1948]. Beirut: Palestine Research Center, 1967.

Ahmed, Feroz. *The Young Turks: The Committee of Union and Progress in Power, 1908–1914.* Oxford: Oxford University Press, 1969.

Allon, Yigal. *The Making of Israel's Army.* London: Valentine, Mitchell, 1970.

Anderson, Benedict. *Imagined Communities: Reflections on the Rise and Spread of Nationalism.* 2nd ed. London: Verso, 1991.

Antonius, George. *The Arab Awakening.* London: Hamish Hamilton, 1938.

al-'Arif, 'Arif. *al-Nakba: Nakbat Bayt al-Maqdis wal-firdaws al-mafqud, 1947–1952* [The catastrophe: The catastrophe of Jerusalem and the lost paradise, 1947–52], 6 vols. Sidon: al-Maktaba al-'Asriyya, 1956–58.

al-Asad, Nasir al-Din. *Ruhi al-Khalidi: Ra'id al-bahth al-tarikhi al-filastini* [Ruhi al-Khalidi: Pioneer of Palestinian historiography]. Cairo: Ma'had al-Buhuth wal-Dirasat al-'Arabiyya, 1970.

al-'Asali, Kamil. *Makhtutat Fada'il Bayt al-Maqdis* [Mansuscripts on the "Merits of Jerusalem"] Amman: Dar al-Bashir, 1984.

——. *Mawsim al-Nabi Musa fi Filastin: Tarikh al-mawsim wal-maqam* [The Nabi Musa Festival in Palestine: The history of the festival and the shrine]. Amman: np, 1990.

——, ed. *Jerusalem in History.* 2nd ed., London: Kegan Paul 1996.

Avneri, Arieh. *The Claim of Dispossession: Jewish Land Settlement and the Arabs 1878–1948.* New Brunswick, NJ: Transaction Books, 1984.

Ayalon, Ami. *The Press in the Arab Middle East: A History.* New York: Oxford University Press, 1995.

Barbour, Neville. *Palestine: Star or Crescent?.* New York: Odyssey Press, 1947.

Batatu, Hanna. *The Old Social Classes and the Revolutionary Movements of Iraq.* Princeton: Princeton University Press, 1978.

Bein, Alex. *The Return to the Soil: A History of Jewish Settlement in Israel.* Jerusalem: Youth and Hechalutz Department of the Zionist Organization, 1952,

Ben Arieh, Yehoshua. *Jerusalem in the 19th Century: The Old City.* Jerusalem and New York: Yad Izhak Ben Zvi Institute and St. Martin's Press, 1984.

Ben-Dov, Meir. *In the Shadow of the Temple: The Discovery of Ancient Jerusalem.* Jerusalem: Keter, 1985.

Benvenisti, Meron. *Conflicts and Contradictions.* New York: Villard, 1986.

——. *Intimate Enemies: Jews and Arabs in a Shared Land:* Berkeley: University of California Press, 1995.

Benziman, Uzi. *Sharon: An Israeli Caesar.* New York: Adama, 1985.

Beydoun, Ahmad Beydoun. *al-Sira' 'ala tarikh Lubnan, aw al-hawiyya wal-zaman fi a'mal mu'arikhina al-mu'asirin* [The struggle over the history of Lebanon: Identity and time in the work of our modern historians]. Beirut: Lebanese University Press, 1989.

Bonné, Alfred, ed. *Statistical Handbook of Middle Eastern Countries,* 2nd ed. Jerusalem: Economic Research Institute of the Jewish Agency for Palestine, 1945.

Brand, Laurie. *The Palestinians in the Arab World.* New York: Columbia University Press, 1988.

Brynen, Rex. *Sanctuary and Survival: The PLO in Lebanon.* Boulder: Westview, 1990.

Budeiri, Musa. *The Palestinian Communist Party, 1919–1948.* London: Ithaca, 1979.

Buheiry, Marwan ed., *Intellectual Life in the Arab East, 1890–1939.* Beirut: American University of Beirut, 1981.

Burckhardt, Jacob. *Judgements on History and Historians.* Tr. Harry Zohn. Boston: Beacon, 1958.

Burke, Edmund III and I. Lapidus, eds. *Islam, Politics and Social Movements.* Berkeley: University of California Press, 1988.

Chatterjee, Partha. *Nationalist Thought and the Colonial World: A Derivative Discourse?* London: Zed, 1986.

Cobban, Helena. *The Palestinian Liberation Organization.* Cambridge: Cambridge University Press, 1984.

Cohen, Amnon. *Palestine in the Eighteenth Century.* Jerusalem: Hebrew University, 1985.

Commins, David Dean. *Islamic Reform: Politics and Social Change in Late Ottoman Syria.* New York: Oxford University Press, 1990.

Cooley, John. *Green March, Black September: The Story of the Palestinian Arabs.* London: Cass, 1973.

Crecelius, Daniel. *The Roots of Modern Egypt: A Study of the Regimes of 'Ali Bey al-Kabir and Muhammad Bey Abu al-Dhahab.* Minneapolis: Biblioteca Islamica, 1981.

Curtis, M., J. Neyer, C. Waxman and A. Pollack, eds. *The Palestinians: People, History, Politics.* New Brunswick: Transaction, 1975.

al-Dabbagh, Mustafa Murad. *Biladuna Filastin* [Our country, Palestine]. 10 vols. Beirut: Dar al-Tali'a, 1965–1976.

Daher, Mas'ud. *al-Hijra al-lubnaniyya ila Misr fil-qarnayn al-tasi' 'ashar wal-'ashrin.* [The Lebanese emigration to Egypt in the nineteenth and twentieth centuries] Beirut: Lebanese University, 1986.

Darnton, Robert. *The Kiss of Lamourette: Reflections in Cultural History.* New York: Norton, 1990.

Dawn, C. Ernest. *From Ottomanism to Arabism: Essays on the Origins of Arab Nationalism.* Urbana: University of Illinois Press, 1973.

Devereux, Robert. *The First Ottoman Constitutional Period.* Baltimore: Johns Hopkins University Press, 1963.

Divine, Donna Robinson. *Politics and Society in Ottoman Palestine.* Boulder: Lynne Rienner, 1994.

Doumani, Beshara. *Rediscovering Palestine: The Merchants and Peasants of Jabal Nablus, 1700–1900.* Berkeley: University of California Press, 1995.

Elpeleg, Zvi. *The Grand Mufti: Haj Amin al-Hussaini, Founder of the Palestinian National Movement.* London: Frank Cass, 1993.

Erikson, Erik. *A Way of Looking at Things: Selected Papers from 1930 to 1980,* S. Schlier, ed. New York: Norton, 1987.

Farah, C. E., ed. *Decision-making and Change in the Ottoman Empire.* Kirkville, MO: Thomas Jefferson University Press, 1993.

Farid, Muhammad. *Tarikh al-dawla al-'aliyya al-'uthmaniyya* [History of the Ottoman state]. Beirut: n.p., 1981.

Fawaz, Leila. *Merchants and Migrants in Nineteenth-Century Beirut.* Cambridge: Harvard University Press, 1983.

Finkelstein, Norman G. *Image and Reality of the Israel-Palestine Conflict.* London: Verso, 1995.

Flapan, Simha. *The Birth of Israel: Myths and Realities.* New York: Free Press, 1987.

Friedman, Isiah. *Germany, Turkey, and Zionism, 1897–1918.* Oxford: Clarendon, 1977.

Friedman, Isaiah. *The Question of Palestine 1914–1918: A Study of British-Jewish-Arab Relations.* London: Routledge and Kegan Paul, 1973.

Gabrieli, Francesco Gabrieli. *Arab Historians of the Crusades.* London: Routledge, 1969.

Gellner, Ernest. *Nations and Nationalism.* Ithaca: Cornell University Press, 1983

Gerber, Haim. *Ottoman Rule in Jerusalem, 1890–1914,* Islamkundliche Unterschungen, vol. 101. Berlin: Klaus Schwarz, 1985.

——. *State, Society and Law in Islam: Ottoman Law in Comparative Perspective.* Albany: State University of New York Press, 1994.

Gershoni, Israel and James Jankowski, *Egypt, Islam and the Arabs: The Search for Egyptian Nationhood, 1900–1930.* New York: Oxford University Press, 1986.

——. *Redefining the Egyptian Nation, 1930–1945.* Cambridge: Cambridge University Press, 1995.

Gil, Moshe. *A History of Palestine, 640–1099.* Cambridge: Cambridge University Press, 1992. First published in Hebrew as *Eretz Israel During the First Muslim Period.*

Gilbar, G., ed. *Ottoman Palestine 1800–1914: Studies in Economic and Social History.* Leiden: Brill, 1990.

Gillis, John R., ed. *Commemorations: The Politics of National Identity.* Princeton: Princeton University Press, 1994.

Gilsenan, Michael. *Lords of the Lebanese Marches: Violence and Narrative in an Arab Society.* Berkeley: University of California Press, 1966.

Göçek, Fatma Müge. *East Encounters West: France and the Ottoman Empire in the Eighteenth Century.* New York: Oxford University Press, 1987.

Granott, A. *The Land System in Palestine: History and Structure,* London: Eyre and Spottiswoode, 1952

de Grèce, Michel. *Le Dernier Sultan.* Paris: Olivier Orban, 1991.

Gresh, Alain. *The PLO: The Struggle Within.* New York, 1988

Guha, Ranajit, and Gayatri Spivak, eds. *Selected Subaltern Studies.* Oxford: Oxford University Press, 1988.

Haddad, Hassan and Donald Wagner, eds. *All in the Name of the Bible: Selected Essays on Israel and American Christian Fundamentalism.* Brattleboro: Amana, 1986.

Haddad, W. and W. Ochsenwald, eds. *Nationalism in a Non-National State: The Dissolution of the Ottoman Empire.* Columbus: Ohio University Press, 1977.

Hammuda, Samih. *al-Wa'i wal-thawra: Dirasa fi hayat wa jihad al-Shaykh 'Iz al-Din al-Qassam.* Amman: Dar al-Sharq, 1986.

Harkabi, Yehoshaphat. *Arab Attitudes to Israel.* New York: Hart, 1972.

——. *Arab Strategies and Israel's Response.* New York: Free Press, 1977.

Alan Hart. *Arafat: Terrorist or Peacemaker.* London: Sidgwick & Jackson, 1984.

Himadeh, Said. *The Economic Organization of Palestine.* Beirut: American University of Beirut, 1938.

Hitti, Philip. *An Arab-Syrian Gentleman and Warrior in the Period of the Crusades.* Princeton: Princeton University Press, 1987.

Hobsbawm, Eric. *Bandits.* London: Weidenfeld and Nicholson, 1969.

——. *Nations and Nationalism Since 1780: Programme, Myth, Reality.* Cambridge: Cambridge University Press, 1990.

—— and Terence Ranger, eds. *The Invention of Tradition.* Cambridge: Cambridge University Press, 1983.

Hopwood, Derek. *Russian Interests in Syria and Palestine, 1800–1901.* Oxford: Oxford University Press, 1966.

Hurewitz, J.C., ed. *The Middle East and North Africa in World Politics.* New Haven: Yale University Press, 1979, vol. 2, p. 189.

al-Hut, Bayan Nuwayhid. *al-Qiyadat wal-mu'assasat al-siyasiyya fi Filastin, 1917–1948* [Political leaderships and institutions in Palestine, 1917–1948]. Beirut: Institute for Palestine Studies, 1981.

Issawi, Charles. *An Economic History of the Middle East and Northern Africa.* New York: Columbia University Press, 1982

——. *The Fertile Crescent, 1800–1914: A Documentary History.* New York: Oxford University Press, 1988.

Jarrar, Husni Adham. *al-Hajj Amin al-Husayni.* Amman: Dar al-Dia', 1987.

Kamen, Charles S. *Little Common Ground: Arab Agriculture and Jewish Settlement in Palestine, 1920–1948.* Pittsburgh: University of Pittsburgh Press, 1991.

Kanafani, Ghassan. *Thawrat 1936 fi Filastin: Khalfiyyat wa tafasil wa tahlil* [The 1936 Revolt in Palestine: Background, details and analysis]. Beirut: Popular Front for the Liberation of Palestine, 1974).

Kawtharani, Wajih. *Bilad al-sham, al-sukkan, al-iqtisad wal-siyasa al-faransiyya fi matla' al-qarn al-'ishrin: Qira'a fil-watha'iq* [*Bilad al-Sham*, population, economy and French policy at the outset of the twentieth century: A reading of the documents]. Beirut: Ma'had al-Inma', 1980.

Kayyali, 'Abd al-Wahhab. *Tarikh Filastin al-Hadith*, 4th ed. Beirut: Arab Institute for Research and Publishing, 1978. (English translation: *Palestine: A Modern History.* London: Croom Helm, 1978.)

Kazziha, Walid. *Revolutionary Transformation in the Arab World.* New York: St. Martin's, 1975.

Kedourie, Elie. *In the Anglo-Arab Labyrinth.* London: Weidenfeld & Nicolson, 1977.

Kemp, Percy. *Territoires d'Islam: Le monde vu de Mossoul au xvii siecle.* Paris: Sindbad, 1982.

Khalaf, Issa. *Arab Factionalism and Social Disintegration, 1939–1948.* Albany: State University of New York Press, 1991.

Khalidi, Rashid. *British Policy towards Syria and Palestine 1906–1914: A Study of the Antecedents of the Hussein-McMahon Correspondence, the Sykes-Picot Agreement and the Balfour Declaration.* London: Ithaca Press, 1980

——. *Under Siege: PLO Decision-making During the 1982 War.* New York: Columbia University Press, 1986.

——, L. Anderson, R. Simon and M. Muslih, eds., *The Origins of Arab Nationalism.* New York: Columbia University Press, 1991.

Khalidi, Tarif ed. *Land Tenure and Social Transformation in the Middle East.* Beirut: American University Press, 1984.

Khalidi, Walid. *All that Remains: The Palestinian Villages Occupied and Destroyed by Israel in 1948.* Washington: Institute for Palestine Studies, 1992.

——. *Conflict and Violence in Lebanon*. Cambridge: Harvard University Press, 1979.

——, ed. *From Haven to Conquest*. Beirut: Institute for Palestine Studies, 1971.

Khoury, Philip. *Syria and the French Mandate: The Politics of Arab Nationalism, 1920–1945*. Princeton: Princeton University Press, 1987.

Khuri, Shehadi and Nicola. *Khulasat tarikh kanisat urshalim al-urthoduksiyya* [A summary history of the orthodox church of Jerusalem]. Jerusalem: Matba'at Bayt al-Maqdis, 1925.

Khuri, Yusuf, comp., *al-Sihafa al-'arabiyya fi Filastin* [The Arab press in Palestine]. Beirut, Institute for Palestine Studies, 1976.

Kimmerling, Baruch and Joel Migdal. *Palestinians: The Making of a People*. New York: Free Press, 1993.

Kohn, Hans. *A History of Nationalism in the East*. New York: Harcourt, Brace, 1929.

——. *The Idea of Nationalism*. New York: Collier, 1967.

Kushner, David, ed. *Palestine in the Late Ottoman Period: Political Social and Economic Transformation*. Jerusalem: Yad Izhak Ben-Zvi, 1986.

Landman, Shimon. *Ahya' a'yan al-Quds kharij aswariha fil-qarn al-tasi' 'ashr* [Quarters of the notables of Jerusalem outside its walls in the 19th century]. Tel Aviv: Dar al-Nashr al-'Arabi, 1984.

Laqueur, Walter. *A History of Zionism*. New York: Schocken, 1972.

Layne, Linda H. *Home and Homeland: The Dialogics of Tribal and National Identities in Jordan*. Princeton: Princeton University Press, 1994.

Lesch, Anne M. *Arab Politics in Palestine, 1917–1939*. Ithaca: Cornell University Press, 1979.

Levenberg, Haim. *The Military Preparations of the Arab Community of Palestine, 1945–48*. London: Frank Cass, 1993.

Lockman, Zachary. *Comrades and Enemies: Arab and Jewish Workers in Palestine, 1906–1948*. Berkeley: University of California Press, 1996.

Ma'oz, Moshe, ed. *Studies on Palestine During the Ottoman Period*. Jerusalem: The Magnes Press, 1975.

Maalouf, Amin. *The Crusades Through Arab Eyes*. New York: Schocken, 1985.

Mandel, Neville. *The Arabs and Zionism before World War I*. Berkeley: University of California Press, 1976.

Manna', Adel. *A'lam Filastin fi awakhir al-'ahd al-'uthmani 1800–1918* [Notables of Palestine in the late Ottoman era], rev. ed. Beirut: Institute for Palestine Studies, 1994.

Marcus, Abraham. *The Middle East on the Eve of Modernity: Aleppo in the Eighteenth Century*. New York: Columbia University Press, 1989.

Masalha, Nur. *Expulsion of the Palestinians: The Concept of "Transfer" in Zionist Political Thought, 1882–1948*. Washington, D.C.: Institute for Palestine Studies, 1992.

Mattar, Philip. *Mufti of Jerusalem: Al-Hajj Amin al-Husayni and the Palestinian National Movement*. New York: Columbia University Press, 1988.

McCarthy, Justin. *The Population of Palestine: Population Statistics of the Late Ottoman Period and the Mandate*. New York: Columbia University Press, 1990.

Miller, Ylana. *Government and Society in Rural Palestine 1920–1948*. Austin: University of Texas Press, 1985.

Mills, E. *Census of Palestine*. 2 vols. London: HMSO, 1932.

Morris, Benny. *The Birth of the Palestinian Refugee Problem 1947–1949*. Cambridge: Cambridge University Press, 1987.

——. *Israel's Border Wars, 1949–1956: Arab Infiltration, Israeli Retaliation, and the Countdown to the Suez War*. Oxford: Oxford University Press, 1993.

——. *1948 and After: Israel and the Palestinians*. Oxford: Oxford University Press, 1990.

Murphy-O'Connor, Jerome. *The Holy Land: An Archaeological Guide from Earliest Times to 1700*, 2nd ed. Oxford: Oxford University Press, 1986.

Musa, Sulayman. *al-Haraka al-'Arabiyya* [The Arab movement]. Beirut: al-Nahar, 1970.

Muslih, Muhammad Muslih, *The Origins of Palestinian Nationalism*. New York: Columbia University Press, 1990.

Nashabeh, Hisham, ed. *Studia Palaestina: Studies in honour of Constantine K. Zurayk/ Dirasat filistiniyya: majmu'at abhath wudi'at takriman lil-duktur Qustantin Zurayq*. Beirut: Institute for Palestine Studies, 1988.

Nashashibi, Nasser Eddin. *Jerusalem's Other Voice: Ragheb Nashashibi and Moderation in Palestinian Politics, 1920–1948*. Exeter: Ithaca Press, 1990.

al-Nimr, Ihsan. *Tarikh jabal Nablus wal-Balqa'* [History of the Nablus region], 4 vols., Nablus: Jam'iyyat 'Ummal-Matabi' al-Ta'awuniyya, 1976 [orig. publ. 1936–1961].

Nuwayhid, 'Ajaj. *Rijal min Filastin, ma bayna bidayat al-Qarn hatta 'am 1948* [Men from Palestine, between the beginning of the century and the year 1948]. Beirut: Manshurat Filastin al-Muhtalla, 1981.

Oliphant, Laurence. *Haifa: or Life in Modern Palestine*. Edinburgh: Wm. Blackwood, 1887.

Owen, Roger, ed. *Studies in the Economic and Social History of Palestine in the Nineteenth and Twentieth Centuries*. London: Macmillan, 1982.

——. *The Middle East in the World Economy, 1800–1914*. London: Methuen, 1981.

Palestinian Refugees: Their Problem and Future. Washington, D.C.: Center for Policy Analysis on Palestine, 1994.

Pappé, Ilan. *Britain and the Arab-Israeli Conflict, 1948–51*. London: Macmillan, 1988.

——. *The Making of the Arab-Israeli Conflict, 1947–1951*, rev. ed. London: I. B. Tauris, 1994.

Peters, Joan. *From Time Immemorial*. New York: Harper and Row, 1984.

Philipp, T., ed. *The Syrian Land in the 18th and 19th Century*. Stuttgart: Fritz Steiner, 1992.

——. *The Syrians in Egypt 1725–1975*. Stuttgart: Franz Steiner Verlag, 1985.

Polk, William and Richard Chambers, eds. *The Beginnings of Modernization in the Middle East: The Nineteenth Century*. Chicago: University of Chicago Press, 1968.

Porath, Yehoshuah. *The Emergence of the Palestinian-Arab National Movement, 1919–1929*. London: Frank Cass, 1973.

——. *The Palestinian Arab National Movement 1929–1939*. London: Frank Cass, 1977.

Rabinovich, Itamar. *Roads Not Taken: Early Arab-Israeli Negotiations*. Oxford: Oxford University Press, 1991.

Rafeq, Abdul-Karim. *The Province of Damascus 1723–1783*. Beirut: Khayat, 1970.

Repp, R. C. *The Müfti of Istanbul: A Study in the Development of the Ottoman Learned Hierarchy*. London: Ithaca Press, 1986.

Rose, Norman, ed. *From Palmerston to Balfour: Collected Essays of Mayir Vereté*. London: Frank Cass, 1992.

Russell, Malcolm B. *The First Modern Arab State: Syria Under Faysal, 1918–1920* (Minneapolis: Biblioteca Islamica, 1985.

Runciman, Sir Steven. *A History of the Crusades*, 3 vols. Cambridge: Cambridge University Press, 1951–54.

Sahliyeh, Emile. *The PLO after the Lebanon War*. Boulder: Westview, 1986.

Sa'id, Amin. *al-Thawra al-'arabiyya al-kubra,* [The Great Arab Revolt], 2 vols. Cairo: Dar al-'Ilm lil-Malayin, 1934.

Said, Edward. *Orientalism.* 2nd ed. New York: Vintage, 1994.

———. *The Question of Palestine.* New York: Vintage, 1979.

———.and Hitchens, Christopher, eds. *Blaming the Victims: Spurious Scholarship and the Palestinian Question.* New York: Verso, 1988.

Sahlins, Peter. *Boundaries: The Making of France and Spain in the Pyrenees.* Berkeley: University of California Press, 1989.

Salama, Khadr Ibrahim, ed. *Fihras makhtutat maktabat al-Masjid al-Aqsa* [Index of manuscripts in the al-Aqsa Library]; vol. 1. Jerusalem: Awqaf Administration, 1980; vol. 2. Amman: al-Majma' al-Maliki li-Buhuth al-Hadara al-Islamiyya, 1983.

———, comp. *Fihris makhtutat al-Maktaba al-Budayriyya* [Index of manuscripts in the al-Budayriyya Library]. Jerusalem: Awqaf Administration, 1987.

Salibi, Kamal. *A House of Many Mansions: The History of Lebanon Reconsidered.* Berkeley: University of California Press, 1988.

Sanbar, Elias. *Palestine 1948: L'expulsion.* Paris: Livres de la Revue d'Etudes Palestiniennes, 1984

Sayigh, Rosemary. *Palestinians: From Peasants to Revolutionaries.* London: Zed, 1979,

———. *Too Many Enemies: The Palestinian Experience in Lebanon.* London: Zed, 1994.

Sayigh, Yezid. *Armed Struggle and the Search for State: The Palestinian National Movement., 1949–1993.* Oxford: Oxford University Press, 1997.

Schiff, Ze'ev. *A History of the Israeli Army, 1874 to the Present,* 2nd ed. New York, Macmillan, 1985,

Schölch, Alexander. *Palestine in Transformation, 1856–1882.* Washington, D.C.: Institute for Palestine Studies, 1993.

Scott, James C. *Weapons of the Weak: Everyday Forms of Peasant Resistance.* New Haven: Yale University Press, 1985.

Segev, Tom. *1949: The First Israelis.* New York: Free Press, 198?.

———. *The Seventh Million: The Israelis and the Holocaust.* New York: Hill and Wang, 1993.

Seikaly, May. *Haifa: Transformation of an Arab Palestinian Society, 1918–1939.* London: I. B. Tauris, 1995.

Shafir, Gershon. *Land, Labor, and the Origins of the Israeli-Palestinian Conflict, 1882–1914.* Cambridge: Cambridge University Press, 1989.

Shapira, Anita. *Land and Power: The Zionist Recourse to Force, 1881–1948.* New York: Oxford University Press, 1992.

Sharabi, Hisham. *Arab Intellectuals and the West: The Formative Years, 1875–1914.* Baltimore: Johns Hopkins Press, 1970.

Shehadeh, Raja. *The Sealed Room.* London: Quartet, 1992.

al-Shinawi, 'Abd al-'Aziz Muhammad. *al-Dawla al-'uthmaniyya: Dawla islamiyya muftari 'alayha* [The Ottoman Empire: A maligned Islamic state], 4 vols. Cairo: Matba'at Jami'at al-Qahira, 1980–1986.

Shlaim, Avi. *Collusion Across the Jordan.* New York: Columbia University Press, 1990.

Shomali, Qustandi Shomali. *Fihras al-nusus al-adabiyya fi jaridat Filastin 1911–1967* [An index of literary texts in the newspaper *Filastin,* 1911–1967]. Jerusalem: Arab Studies Society, 1990.

Singer, A. and A. Cohen, eds., *Scripta Hierosolymitana,* 30, *Aspects of Ottoman History.* Jerusalem: Magnes Press, 1994.

Smith, Anthony D. *The Ethnic Origins of Nations.* Oxford: Oxford University Press, 1986.

———. *The Ethnic Revival in the Modern World.* Cambridge: Cambridge University Press, 1981.

Smith, Barbara. *The Roots of Separation in Palestine: British Economic Policy, 1920–1929.* Syracuse: Syracuse University Press, 1995.

Spagnolo, J., ed. *Problems of the Middle East in Historical Perspective: Essays in Honour of Albert Hourani.* Reading: Ithaca Press, 1992.

Stein, Kenneth. *The Intifadah and the 1936–1939 Uprising: A Comparison of the Palestinian Arab Communities.* Atlanta: Carter Center Occasional Papers, 1, March 1990.

———. *The Land Question in Palestine, 1917–1939.* Chapel Hill: University of North Carolina Press, 1984

Stephens, Robert. *Nasser: A Political Biograpahy.* New York: Simon and Schuster, 1971.

Suleiman, Michael. *U.S. Policy on Palestine from Wilson to Clinton.* Normal, IL: Association of Arab-American University Graduates, 1995.

al-Tamimi, 'Abd al-Jalil. *Etudes sur l'Histoire Arabo-Ottomane, 1453–1918/Dirasat fil-tarikh al-'arabi al-'uthmani.* Zeghouan: CEROMDI, 1994.

Tauber, Eliezer. *The Arab Movements in World War I.* London: Frank Cass, 1993.

Thobie, Jacques. *Intérets et imperialisme français dans l'Empire ottoman, 1895–1914.* Paris: Sorbonne, 1977.

Tibawi, A.L. *Anglo-Arab Relations and the Question of Palestine, 1914–1921.* London: Luzac, 1977.

———. *Arab Education in Mandatory Palestine: A Study of Three Decades of British Administration.* London: Luzac, 1956.

———. *British Interests in Palestine 1800–1901.* Oxford: Oxford University Press, 1961.

———. *A Modern History of Syria, including Lebanon and Palestine.* London: MacMillan, 1969.

Warriner, Doreen. *Land Reform and Development in the Middle East: A Study of Egypt, Syria and Iraq,* 2nd ed. London: Oxford University Press, 1962.

———, comp. *Palestine Papers, 1917–1922: Seeds of Conflict.* London: John Murray, 1972.

Wasserstein, Bernard. *The British in Palestine: The Mandatory Government and the Arab-Jewish Conflict, 1917–1929.* 2nd ed. Oxford: Basil Blackwell, 1991.

Wilson, Mary. *King Abdullah, Britain and the Making of Jordan.* Cambridge: Cambridge University Press, 1988.

Yasin, 'Abd al-Qadir. *Kifah al-sha'b al-filastini qabl al-'am 1948* [The struggle of the Palestinian people before the year 1948]. Beirut: PLO Research Center, 1975.

Yazbak, Mahmud. *al-Nuzum al-idariyya wal-buna al-ijtima'iyya fi Haifa fi awakhir al-'ahd al-'uthmani* [Administrative arrangements and social structure in Haifa at the end of the Ottoman era]. Nazareth: al-Nahda Press, 1994.

Yehoshua, Ya'qub. *Tarikh al-sihafa al-'arabiyya fi Filastin fil-'ahd al-uthmani (1909–1918)* [The history of the Arab press in Palestine in the Ottoman era, 1908–1918]. Jerusalem: Matba'at al-Ma'arif, 1974.

Zarcone, Theodore and Fariba Zarinebaf, eds. *Les Iraniens d'Istanbul.* Paris, Teheran, Istanbul: Institut Français de Recherches en Iran and Institut Francais d'etudes Anatoliennes, 1993.

Zilfi, Madeleine. *The Politics of Piety: The Ottoman Ulema in the Post-Classical Age.* Minneapolis: Biblioteca Islamica, 1988.

Zurayq, Qustantin. *Ma'na al-Nakba* [The meaning of the catastrophe]. Beirut: Dar al'Ilm Lil-Malayin, 1948; translated as *The Meaning of the Disaster* by R. Bayley Winder. Beirut: Khayat, 1956.

Zürcher, Erik Jan. *The Unionist Factor: The Role of the Committee of Union and Progress in the Turkish National Movement, 1905–1926*. Leiden: Brill, 1984.

III. ARTICLES

Abu Manneh, Butrus. "The Husaynis: The Rise of a Notable Family in 18th Century Palestine." In D. Kushner, ed., *Palestine in the Late Ottoman Period: Political Social and Economic Transformation*, pp. 93–108. Jerusalem: Yad Izhak Ben-Zvi, 1986.

Abu Manneh, Butros. "Jerusalem in the Tanzimat Period: The New Ottoman Administration and the Notables." *Die Welt des Islams* 30 (1990): 1–44.

———. "The Rise of the Sanjak of Jerusalem in the Late 19th Century." In G. Ben Dor, ed. *The Palestinians and the Middle East Conflict*, pp. 21–32. Ramat Gan: Turtle Dove, 1978.

Asali, K. J. "Jerusalem in History: Notes on the Origins of the City and its Tradition of Tolerance." *Arab Studies Quarterly* 16 (Fall 1994): 37–45.

———. "Jerusalem Under the Ottomans 1516–1831 A.D." In K. Asali, ed., *Jerusalem in History*, pp. 200–227. New York: Olive Branch, 1990.

'Awad, 'Abd al-'Aziz Muhammad. "Mutasarrifiyyat al-Quds, 1874–1914." In *al-Mu'tamar al-Duwali al-Thalith li-Tarikh Bilad al-Sham: Filastin* [Third international conference on the history of *bilad al-Sham*: Palestine], 1: 204–223. Amman: Jordanian University/Yarmuk University, 1983.

Ben Arieh, Yehoshua. "The Population of the Large Towns in Palestine During the First Eighty Years of the Nineteenth Century, According to Western Sources." In M. Ma'oz, ed., *Studies on Palestine During the Ottoman Period*, pp. 49–69. Jerusalem: The Magnes Press, 1975.

Buheiry, Marwan. "The Agricultural Exports of Southern Palestine, 1885–1914." *Journal of Palestine Studies* 10 (Summer 1981): 61–81.

———. "Bulus Nujaym and the Grand Liban Ideal 1908–1919." in M. Buheiry, ed., *Intellectual Life in the Arab East, 1890–1939*, pp. 62–83. Beirut: American University of Beirut, 1981.

Conrad, L. and B. Kellner-Heinkele. "Ottoman Resources in the Khalidi Library in Jerusalem." In A. Singer and A. Cohen, eds. *Scripta Hierosolymitana*. Vol. 30, *Aspects of Ottoman History*, pp. 280–293. Jerusalem: Magnes Press, 1994.

Darnton, Robert. "First Steps Towards a History of Reading." In R. Darnton, ed., *The Kiss of Lamourette: Reflections in Cultural History* pp. 154–187. New York: Norton, 1990.

Doumani, Bishara. "Palestinian Islamic Court Records: A Source for Socioeconomic History." *MESA Bulletin* 19 (December 1985): 155–172.

———. "The Political Economy of Population Counts in Ottoman Palestine: Nablus, circa 1850." *International Journal of Middle East Studies* 26 (February 1994): 1–17.

———. "Rediscovering Ottoman Palestine: Writing Palestinians into History." *Journal of Palestine Studies* 21 (Winter 1992): 5–28.

Emery, Michael. "New Videotapes Reveal Israeli Cover-up." *The Village Voice*, November 13, 1990, pp. 25–29.

Epstein, Yitzhaq. "A Hidden Question." *Hashiloah* 15 (1907): 193–98 .

Escovitz, Joseph. " 'He Was the Muhammad 'Abdu of Syria': A Study of Tahir al-Jaza'iri and His Influence." *International Journal of Middle East Studies* 18 (August 1986): 293–310.

Findlay, Carter. "The Evolution of the System of Provincial Administration as Viewed from the Center." In D. Kushner, ed., *Palestine in the Late Ottoman Period: Political Social and Economic Transformation*, pp. 93–108. Jerusalem: Yad Izhak Ben-Zvi, 1986.

Finkelstein, Amnon. "Why Culture? Why Power?" In R. D. Johnson, ed., *On Cultural Ground: Essays in International History*, pp. 23–46. Chicago: Imprint, 1994.

Finkelstein, Norman. "Disinformation and the Palestine Question: The Not-So-Strange Case of Joan Peters's *From Time Immemorial*." In E. Said and C. Hitchens, eds., *Blaming the Victims*, pp. 33–69. New York: Verso, 1988.

Firestone, Ya'kov. "Crop-Sharing Economics in Mandatory Palestine." Part 1, *Middle Eastern Studies* 11 (January 1975): 3–23; part 2, 11 (April 1975): 188–203.

——. "The Land-Equalizing *musha'* Village: A Reassessment." In G. Gilbar, ed., *Ottoman Palestine 1800–1914: Studies in Economic and Social History*, pp. 69–90. Leiden: Brill, 1990.

——. "Production and Trade in an Islamic Context: Sharika Contracts in the Transitional Economy of Northern Samaria, 1853–1943." Part 1, *International Journal of Middle East Studies* 6 (April 1975): 185–209; part 2, 6 (July 1975): 308–324.

Gelvin, James. "The Other Nationalism: Syrian/Arab/Populism in Its Historical and International Contexts." In I. Gershami and J. Jankowsi, eds., *Rethinking Arab Nationalism in the Arab World*: New York: Columbia University Press, forthcoming.

Gerner, Deborah J. "Missed Opportunities and Roads Not Taken: The Eisenhower Administration and the Palestinians." In M. Suleiman, ed., *U.S. Policy on Palestine from Wilson to Clinton*, pp. 81–112. Normal, IL: Association of Arab-American University Graduates, 1995.

Glock, Albert. "Cultural Bias in the Archaeology of Palestine." *Journal of Palestine Studies* 24 (Winter 1995): 48–59.

Guha, Ranajit. "The Prose of Counter-Insurgency." In R. Guha and G. Spivak, eds. *Selected Subaltern Studies*. Oxford: Oxford University Press, 1988.

Haddad, Mahmud. "Iraq Before World War I: A Case of Anti-European Arab Ottomanism." In R. Khalidi et. al., eds., *The Origins of Arab Nationalism*, pp. 120–150. Columbia University Press, 1991.

Hall, Stuart. "Ethnicity: Identity and Difference." *Radical America* 23 (October-December 1989): 14–20.

Hanioglu, Şükrü. "The Young Turks and the Arabs before the Revolution of 1908." In R. Khalidi et. al., eds., *The Origins of Arab Nationalism*, pp. 31–49. New York: Columbia University Press, 1991.

Hourani, Albert. "Ottoman Reform and the Politics of the Notables." In W. Polk and R. Chambers, eds., *The Beginnings of Modernization in the Middle East: The Nineteenth Century*, pp. 41–68. Chicago: University of Chicago Press, 1968.

Kalvarisky, Chaim. *Jewish-Arab Affairs* (1931): 11–14.

Kanafani, Ghassan. "Thawrat 1936–1939 fi Filastin: Khalfiyya, tafasil wa tahlil" [The 1936–1939 revolution in Palestine: Background, details and analysis]. *Shu'un Filistiniyya* 6 (January 1972): 45–77.

Kark, Ruth. "The Rise and Decline of Coastal Towns in Palestine." In G. Gilbar, ed., *Ottoman Palestine 1800–1914: Studies in Economic and Social History*, pp. 69–90. Leiden: Brill, 1990.

Kasmieh, Khairieh. "Ruhi al-Khalidi 1864–1913: A Symbol of the Cultural Movement in Palestine Towards the End of Ottoman Rule." In T. Philipp, ed., *The Syrian Land in the 18th and 19th Century*, pp. 123–146. Stuttgart: Fritz Steiner, 1992.

Kayali, Hasan. "Elections and the Electoral Process in the Ottoman Empire, 1876–1919." *International Journal of Middle East Studies* 27 (August 1995): 265–286.

Khalidi, Rashid. "The Arab Experience in the First World War." In H. Cecil and P. Liddle, eds., *Facing Armageddon: The Great War Experienced.* London: Pen and Sword Books, 1996.

——. "Arab Nationalism: Historical Problems in the Literature." *The American Historical Review* 95 (December 1991): 1363–4.

——. "Arab Nationalism in Syria: The Formative Years." In W. Haddad and W. Ochsenwald, eds., *Nationalism in a Non-National State: The Dissolution of the Ottoman Empire*, pp. 207–237. Columbus: Ohio University Press, 1977.

——. "The Future of Arab Jerusalem." *British Journal of Middle East Studies* 19 (Fall 1992): 133–143.

——. "Observations on the Palestinian Right of Return." *Journal of Palestine Studies* 21 (Winter 1992): 29–40.

——. "Ottomanism and Arabism in Syria Before 1914: A Reassessment." In R. Khalidi et al. eds., *The Origins of Arab Nationalism*, pp. 55–57. New York: Columbia University Press, 1991.

——. "The Palestinian Dilemma: PLO Policy after Lebanon." *Journal of Palestine Studies* 15 (Autumn 1985): 88–103.

——. "The Palestinians in Lebanon: The Repercussions of the Israeli Invasion." *Middle East Journal* 38 (Spring 1984): 255–266.

——. "The Palestinian Refugee Question: Toward a Solution." In *Palestinian Refugees: Their Problem and Future. A Special Report*, pp. 21–27. Washington, D.C.: Center for Policy Analysis on Palestine, October 1994,

——. "The Press as a Source for Modern Arab Political History." *Arab Studies Quarterly* 3 (Winter, 1981): 22–42.

——. "The Role of the Press in the Early Arab Reaction to Zionism." *Peuples Mediterraneens/Mediterranean Peoples* 20 (July–September 1982): 105–124.

——. "Society, and Ideology in Late Ottoman Syria: Class, Education, Profession and Confession." In J. Spagnolo, ed., *Problems of the Middle East in Historical Perspective: Essays in Honour of Albert Hourani*, pp. 119–132. Reading: Ithaca Press, 1992.

——. "The 1912 Election Campaign in the Cities of *Bilad al-Sham.*" *International Journal of Middle East Studies* 16 (November 1984): 461–474.

Khalidi, Tarif. "Palestinian Historiography: 1900–1948." *Journal of Palestine Studies* 10 (Spring 1981): 59–76.

Khalidi, Walid. *"Kitab al-sionism, aw al-mas'ala al-sihyuniyya li-Muhammad Ruhi al-Khalidi, al-mutawafi sanat 1913"* [The book "Zionism or the Zionist Question," by Muhammad Ruhi al-Khalidi, d. 1913]. In Hisham Nashabeh, ed., *Studia Palaestina: Studies in honour of Constantine K. Zurayk/ Dirasat filistiniyya: majmu'at abhath wudi'at takriman lil-duktur Qustantin Zurayq*, pp. 37–81. Beirut: Institute for Palestine Studies, 1988.

al-Khuri, Niqula. "Mudhakkirat kahin al-Quds: al-Khuri Niqula al-Khuri, Bir Zayt 1885-Bayrut 1954." *Dirasat 'Arabiyya* 30 (1994): 62–76.

Kimmerling, Baruch. "Between the Primordial and the Civil Definition of the Collective Identity: *Eretz Israel* or the State of Israel?" In E. Cohen, M. Lissak, U. Almagor, eds., *Comparative Social Dynamics*, pp. 262–283. Boulder: Westview, 1985.

——. "Process of Formation of Palestinian Collective Identities: The Ottoman and Colonial Periods." *Comparative Studies in Society and History*, forthcoming.

Kushner, David. "Ali Ekrem Bey, Governor of Jerusalem, 1906–1908." *International Journal of Middle East Studies* 28 (August 1996): 349–362.

——. "The Haifa-Damascus Railway: The British Phase, 1890–1902." In C. Farah, ed., *Decision-Making and Change in the Ottoman Empire*, pp. 193–213. Kirksville, MO: Thomas Jefferson University Press, 1993.

——. "The Ottoman Governors of Palestine." *Middle Eastern Studies* 23 (July 1987): 274–290.

Little, Donald P. and A. Uner Turgay. "Documents from the Ottoman Period in the Khalidi Library in Jerusalem." *Die Welt des Islams* 20 (1980): 44–72.

Litvak, Meir. "A Palestinian Past: National Construction and Reconstruction." *History and Memory: Studies in the Representation of the Past* 6 (Fall/Winter 1994): 24–56

Nategh, Homa. "Mirza Aqa Khan, Sayyed Jamal al-din et Malkom Khan a Istanbul (1860–1897." In. Th. Zarcone and F. Zarinebaf, eds., *Les Iraniens d'Istanbul*, pp. 45–60. Paris, Teheran, Istanbul: Institut Français de Recherches en Iran and Institut Français d'etudes Anatoliennes, 1993).

Novick, Peter. "Holocaust Memorials in America." In J. Young, ed., *The Art of Memory: Holocaust Memorials in History*, pp. 157–163. New York: Prestel, with the Jewish Museum, 1994.

Ruppin, Arthur. "The Arab Population in Israel." *Arakhim* 3 (1971): 10–6.

Said, Edward. "Permission to Narrate." *Journal of Palestine Studies* 13 Spring 1984): 27–48.

Salibi, Kamal. "Listes chronologiques des grands cadis de l'Egypte sous les Mamelouks." *Revue des Etudes Islamiques* 25 (1957): 104–107.

Schleifer, S. Abdullah. " 'Izz al-Din al-Qassam: Preacher and *Mujahid.*" In E. Burke III, ed., *Struggle and Survival in the Modern Middle East*, pp. 164–178. Berkeley: University of California Press, 1993.

——. "The Life and Thought of 'Izz-id-Din al-Qassam." *The Islamic Quarterly* 22 (1979): 61–81.

Schölch, Alexander. "The Demographic Development of Palestine, 1850–1882." *International Journal of Middle East Studies* 17 (1985): 485–505.

——. "Ein palastinischer Reprasentant der Tanzimat Periode." *Der Islam* 57 (1980): 316ff.

Seikaly, Samir. "Damascene Intellectual Life in the Opening Years of the 20th Century: Muhammad Kurd 'Ali and *al-Muqtabas.*" In M. Buheiry, ed., *Intellectual Life in the Arab East, 1890–1939*, pp. 125–153. Beirut: American University of Beirut, 1981.

Shlaim, Avi. "Conflicting Approaches to Israel's Relations with the Arabs: Ben Gurion and Sharett, 1953–1956." *Middle East Journal* 37 (Spring 1983): 180–201.

Shomali, Qustandi. "Nagib Nassar: L'intransigéant, 1873–1948." *Revue d'Etudes Palestiniennes* 54 (1995): 80–90.

Sluglett, Peter and Marion Farouk-Sluglett. "The Application of the 1858 Land Code in Greater Syria: Some Observations." In T. Khalidi, ed., *Land Tenure and Social Transformation in the Middle East*, pp. 409–424. Beirut: American University Press, 1984.

Smith, Anthony D. "The Origins of Nations." *Ethnic and Religious Studies* 12 (July 1989): 340–367.

Strohmeier, Martin. "al-Kulliyya al-Salahiyya, a Late Ottoman University in Jerusalem." In R. Hillenbrand and S. Auld, eds., *Ottoman Jerusalem*, forthcoming.

——. "Muslim Education in the Vilayet of Beirut, 1880–1918." in C. Farah, ed., *Decision-making and Change in the Ottoman Empire*, pp. 215–241. Kirksville, MO: Thomas Jefferson University Press, 1993.

Swedenberg, Ted. "The Role of the Palestinian Peasantry in the Great Revolt (1936–1939)." In E. Burke III and I. Lapidus, eds., *Islam, Politics and Social Movements*, pp. 169–203. Berkeley: University of California Press, 1988.

Szyliowicz, Joseph. "Changes in the Recruitment Patterns and Career-lines of Ottoman Provincial Administrators During the Nineteenth Century." In M. Ma'oz, ed., *Studies on Palestine During the Ottoman Period*, pp. 249–283. Jerusalem: The Magnes Press, 1975.

al-Tamimi, 'Abd al-Jalil. "L'Importance de l'heritage arabo-turque et son impact sur les relations arabo-turques." In 'A. Tamimi, ed., *Etudes sur l'Histoire Arabo-Ottomane, 1453–1918/Dirasat fil-tarikh al-'arabi al-'uthmani*, pp. 9–19. Zeghouan: CEROMDI, 1994.

INDEX